Selena Gomez

Topic relevant selected content from the highest rated wiki entries, typeset, printed and shipped.

Combine the advantages of up-to-date and in-depth knowledge with the convenience of printed books.

A portion of the proceeds of each book will be donated to the Wikimedia Foundation to support their mission: to empower and engage people around the world to collect and develop educational content under a free license or in the public domain, and to disseminate it effectively and globally.

The content within this book was generated collaboratively by volunteers. Please be advised that nothing found here has necessarily been reviewed by people with the expertise required to provide you with complete, accurate or reliable information. Some information in this book maybe misleading or simply wrong. The publisher does not guarantee the validity of the information found here. If you need specific advice (for example, medical, legal, financial, or risk management) please seek a professional who is licensed or knowledgeable in that area.

Sources, licenses and contributors of the articles and images are listed in the section entitled "References". Parts of the books may be licensed under the GNU Free Documentation License. A copy of this license is included in the section entitled "GNU Free Documentation License"

All used third-party trademarks belong to their respective owners.

Contents

Articles

References

OCT - 2011

Article Licenses

Selena Gomez

Selena Gomez	
 Selena Gomez attending "The 6th Annual Hollywood Style Awards" in Beverly Hills, California on October 10, 2009.	
Background information	
Birth name	Selena Marie Gomez
Born	July 22, 1992 Grand Prairie, Texas, United States
Genres	Dance-pop, pop rock
Occupations	Actress, singer, songwriter
Instruments	Vocals
Years active	2002–present
Labels	Hollywood (2008–present)
Associated acts	Selena Gomez & the Scene, Forever the Sickest Kids, Demi Lovato, Drew Seeley
Website	Official website [1]

Selena Marie Gomez (born July 22, 1992)[2] is an American actress, singer-songwriter, and UNICEF Goodwill Ambassador; best known for her portrayal of Alex Russo on the Emmy Award winning Disney Channel Original Series *Wizards of Waverly Place*. She has starred in the television movies *Another Cinderella Story* and *Princess Protection Program*. In 2010, Gomez made her theatrical film debut as Beatrice "Beezus" Quimby in *Ramona and Beezus*. She is also the lead singer for the pop rock band Selena Gomez & the Scene.

Before Disney, she had one of the kid roles on *Barney & Friends*. In 2008, she signed a record deal with Hollywood Records and contributed to the *Tinker Bell*, *Another Cinderella Story* and *Wizards of Waverly Place* soundtracks.

Early life

Gomez was born in Grand Prairie, Texas[2] to Ricardo Gomez and former stage actress Mandy Teefey (née Cornett).[3] [4] Her father is Mexican American and her mother is of half Italian descent.[5] [6] Her birth parents divorced when she was five years old, and she was raised as an only child by her working mother.[3] [7] In 2006, Mandy remarried Brian Teefey.[8] She is named after Tejano singer Selena.[9] In a 2009 interview with *People*, Gomez mentioned that she developed an early interest in acting from watching her mother prepare for and act in theater productions.[7] She earned a high school diploma through homeschooling in May 2010.[10]

Career

Acting career

Gomez on the studio set of *Wizards of Waverly Place* before filming an episode for the show's first season in April, 2007

Gomez began her acting career at age seven, playing Gianna on *Barney & Friends*. She said that she learned "everything" about how to act while on the show. Season 7 of Barney & Friends, when Selena Gomez was on the show, was held up for some time. Because of this, the episodes featuring Gomez did not air until she was in 5th grade. This resulted in some mild controversy/confusion as to whether she was on Barney in the 5th grade or the 1st grade.[11] She later had minor roles in *Spy Kids 3-D: Game Over* and the TV film *Walker, Texas Ranger: Trial By Fire*. In 2004, Gomez was discovered by the Disney Channel in a nation wide scouting.[12] Gomez appeared as a guest star on *The Suite Life of Zack & Cody* and had a guest appearance – that later turned into a recurring role – on *Hannah Montana* from season's two to three. In early 2007 Gomez was cast in the Disney Channel series *Wizards of Waverly Place* as one of the three main characters, Alex Russo.

In 2008, Gomez appeared in *Another Cinderella Story*, the direct-to-DVD sequel to the 2004 Hilary Duff film, opposite Drew Seeley. She also had a minor voiceover role as one the Mayor's ninety-six daughters in *Horton Hears a Who!* which released in March of that year. In April, Lacey Rose, of *Forbes* ranked Gomez as being fifth on their "Eight Hot Kid Stars To Watch" list; and Rose described Gomez as having been "a multitalented teen".[13] In June, 2009, Gomez appeared in the made-for-television Disney Channel movie, *Princess Protection Program* with her then best friend Demi Lovato.[14] On August 28, one month after appearing in *Princess Protection Program*, Gomez appeared in *Wizards of Waverly Place: The Movie*, a made-for-television film based on the show.[15]

In 2009, Gomez did a guest appearance as herself in one episode, of Lovato's *Disney Channel* television show *Sonny With a Chance*, entitled "Battle of The Network Stars". Gomez, along with two cast members of *Wizards of Waverly Place* appeared in a television three-way cross-over episode with *Hannah Montana* and *The Suite Life on Deck*, entitled *Wizards on Deck with Hannah Montana*. In February 2009, Gomez signed on to star as one of the two female leads in *Ramona and Beezus*, a film adaption of the children's novel series by Beverly Cleary.[16] [17] In March, 2010, Variety reported that Gomez was set to star as one of the three lead roles in *Monte Carlo*.[18]

Selena on location in Paris, France filming *Monte Carlo* in June 2010

Solo music career

In 2008, Gomez recorded a cover of "Cruella de Vil" -which included a music video for – for the compilation album *DisneyMania 6*. Gomez recorded three songs for the *Another Cinderella Story* soundtrack, which Gomez appears in. Gomez also recorded "Fly to Your Heart" for the 2008 animated film *Tinker Bell*. In July 2008 – before Gomez' sixteenth birthday, she signed a recording deal with Hollywood Records, a music label owned by *Disney*.[19] In 2009, Gomez recorded "One and the Same" for *Princess Protection Program* as a duet with Lovato – they both appear in the film.[20] Gomez recorded four songs, one of which was a cover, for the *Wizards of Waverly Place* soundtrack, only one single (Magic) from the album was released. In May, of the same year, Gomez was featured – with Forever the Sickest Kids, on a duet version of the non-album song "Whoa Oh!".[21]

Selena Gomez & the Scene

Formed in 2009, Selena Gomez & the Scene (aka Selena & The Scene) is a teen pop band which consists of Selena Gomez on vocals, Ethan Roberts on guitar, Joey Clement on bass, Greg Garman on drums and Dane Forrest on keyboards. *Kiss & Tell* is the band's debut studio album and was released on September 29, 2009 by Hollywood Records. On March 5, 2010, the album was certified Gold by RIAA.[22] The album's single, "Naturally", was certified Platinum by the RIAA on July 15, 2010.[22] The band's second album *A Year Without Rain* was released on September 17, 2010. The record debuted on the Billboard 200 at number 4, selling 66,000 copies.

Other work

Philanthropy

Gomez was involved in the UR Votes Count campaign which helped encourage teenagers to learn more about 2008 Presidential candidates (Barack Obama and John McCain).[23] In October 2008, Gomez participated in St. Jude's Children's Hospital "Runway For Life" benefit.[24] Gomez is a spokesperson for Borden Milk; she is featured in the campaign's print and television ads.[25] She is the ambassador of DoSomething.org after being involved with the charity Island Dog, which help dogs in Puerto Rico.[26] She got involved while filming *Wizards of Waverly Place: The Movie* in Puerto Rico.[27] Gomez is a spokesperson for State Farm Insurance, and is featured in their TV commercials; which air on the Disney Channel, to raise awareness of being a safe driver.[28] Gomez is also involved with the charity RAISE Hope For Congo, the charity helps raise awareness about the violence against Congolese women, in the Congo.[29]

In October 2008, Gomez was named UNICEF's spokesperson for the Trick-or-Treat for UNICEF campaign, which encouraged children to raise money on Halloween to help children around the world.[30] She said that she was "extremely excited" to "encourage other kids to make a difference in the world."[30]

In August 2009, a 17-year-old Gomez became the youngest UNICEF ambassador ever, passing fellow songstress Hayley Westenra, who had been 18. In her first official field mission, Gomez traveled to Ghana on September 4, 2009 for a week to witness first-hand the stark conditions of vulnerable children that lack vital necessities including clean water, nourishment, education and healthcare.[31] [32] Gomez explained during a interview with Associated Press that she wanted to use her star power to bring awareness to Ghana: "That's why I feel very honored to have a voice that kids listen to and take into consideration [...] I had people on my tour asking me where IS Ghana, and they Googled it […] and because I went there, they now know where Ghana is. So it's pretty incredible."[32] [33] Gomez said of her role as ambassador that: "Every day 25,000 children die from preventable causes. I stand with UNICEF in the belief that we can change that number from 25,000 to zero. I know we can achieve this because every moment, UNICEF is on the ground providing children with the lifesaving assistance needed to ensure zero becomes a reality."[31]

Gomez was named spokesperson for UNICEF's 2009 Trick-or-Treat campaign, for the second year in a row.[34] Gomez, who raised over $700,000 for the charity in 2008, stated that she hopes to be able to raise 1 million dollars in 2009.[32] Gomez participated in a celebrity auction[35] and hosted a live web cast series on Facebook in support of the Trick-or-Treat for UNICEF campaign.[36] Gomez will return as the UNICEF spokesperson for the 60th anniversary of Trick-or-Treat for UNICEF campaign in 2010.[37]

Gomez is involved in Disney's Friends for Change, an organization which promotes "environmentally-friendly behavior", and appears in its public service announcements to raise awareness for the cause on the Disney Channel.[38] Gomez, Demi Lovato, Miley Cyrus, and the Jonas Brothers recorded "Send It On", a charity single which serves as the theme song for Disney's Friends for Change in 2009. The song debuted on the Hot 100 at number twenty.[39] [40] Disney's Friends For Change will direct all of its proceeds from "Send it On" to environmental charities to the Disney Worldwide Conservation Fund.[39] On October 6, 2009, Gomez made a surprise visit to a Los Angeles elementary school as part of the "A Day Made Better" program that was sponsored by OfficeMax.[41] During her visit, Gomez gave the school an award, and gave them $1,000 worth of school supplies. Gomez spent the day with the students and talked about the importance of giving back to the community.[41] [42]

Entrepreneurship

Gomez on the set of her music video for "Tell Me Something I Don't Know" in July 2008

Gomez was part of Sears back-to-school fashion ad campaign.[43] As part of the campaign Gomez was featured in the television commercials. In August 2009, Gomez also hosted the "Sears Arrive Air Band Casting Call" – to select five people for the first-ever "Sears Air Band", which performed at the 2009 MTV Video Music Awards.[44]

In October 2008, Gomez launched her own production company, July Moon Productions, and partnered with XYZ Films to create star vehicles for Gomez. As part of the agreement Gomez will have the opportunity to be able option articles, hire writers and create talent packages to shop to studios.[45] [46] Also, as part of the deal, "XYZ Films will allow Gomez to star in and produce at least two films.[41] *Variety* reported that: "In August, XYZ [Films] inked a similar deal with Time Inc. and management-production company the Collective to finance the development of the print media giant's content for the bigscreen [...] As part of the July Moon-XYZ deal, [Selena] Gomez will have the ability to cherry-pick projects from the vast Time Inc. library, which includes Time, Sports Illustrated, Fortune and Life."[46]

In October, 2009, Gomez announced her plan to launch her own fashion line, called "Dream Out Loud by Selena Gomez", which is set to launch in fall 2010.[47] [48] The clothing line will consist of and feature bohemian dresses, floral tops, jeans, skirts, jackets, scarves and hats, all made from recycled or eco-friendly materials.[49] [50] Gomez said that the line will reflect her own personal style[51] and described the clothing as being "pretty, feminine, and bohemian," and: "With my line, I really want to give the customer options on how they can put their own looks together [...] I want the pieces that can be easy to dress up or down, and the fabrics being eco-friendly and organic is super important [...] Also, the tags will all have some of my inspirational quotes on them. I'm just looking to send a good message."[47] [50] Gomez, who has no background in fashion, teamed up with designers Tony Melillo and Sandra Campos, both who have worked with big-name fashion houses.[48] Gomez said of the partnering: "When I met Tony and Sandra, I was instantly comfortable with them and now they are just like family to me [...] They are so creative and I love how I can just call them up whenever and talk to them about everything, even if it's just about changing a button [...] They've been so cool about everything."[47] [48] [49] [50] The brand will be manufactured by, Melillo and Campos teamed with New York-based Adjmi Apparel and formed by Adjmi CH Brands LLC; which is the holding company for the brand.[52]

Personal life

Gomez began wearing a purity ring when she was 12 years old.[53] She is the owner of five rescue dogs and describes herself as a "huge animal lover".[54] After Gomez and Lovato, whom she first met at the *Barney & Friends* auditions, posted a video blog on YouTube in March 2008, Miley Cyrus and her friend Mandy Jiroux uploaded a parody of that video, which caught the interest of entertainment media. Reports included the theory that Gomez and Lovato might replace Cyrus.[55] Gomez clarified there was no feud,[56] saying: "I'm not interested in being anybody but myself, and I'm not here to replace anyone. I think that she's a wonderful performer, and of course it's a compliment. But I would like to take a different route."[57] In answering a question on Hispanic heritage, to stationary provider Scholastic's news service for kids and teens, Gomez said: "My family does have Quinceañeras, and we go to the communion church. We do everything that's Catholic, but we don't really have anything traditional except go to the park and have barbeques on Sundays after church."[58]

Filmography

Feature films			
Year	Film	Role	Notes
2003	*Spy Kids 3-D: Game Over*	Waterpark Girl	Minor Role
2008	*Horton Hears a Who!*	Helga	Voiceover
2009	*Arthur and the Vengeance of Maltazard*	Princess Selenia	Voice (replaced Madonna)
2010	*Ramona and Beezus*[59]	Beatrice "Beezus" Quimby	Main role
2011	*Monte Carlo*[60]	Grace	

Films made for television			
Year	Title	Role	Notes
2005	*Walker, Texas Ranger: Trial by Fire*	Julie	
2006	*Brain Zapped*	Emily Grace Garcia	
2009	*Princess Protection Program*	Carter Mason	Disney Channel Original Movie; Main role
	Wizards of Waverly Place: The Movie	Alex Russo	

Direct-to-video release			
Year	Title	Role	Notes
2008	*Another Cinderella Story*	Mary Santiago	Main Role

Television			
Year	Title	Role	Notes
2002–2003	*Barney & Friends*	Gianna	Recurring Role That Season
2007–present	*Wizards of Waverly Place*	Alex Russo	Main Role

Television guest appearances			
Year	Title	Role	Notes
2006	*The Suite Life of Zack & Cody*	Gwen	"A Midsummer's Nightmare" (Season 2, episode 22)

2007–2008	*Hannah Montana*	Mikayla	"I Want You to Want Me... to Go to Florida" (Season 2, episode 13)
			"That's What Friends Are For?" (Season 2, episode 18)
			"(We're So Sorry) Uncle Earl" (Season 2, episode 22) (uncredited)
2009	*Sonny With a Chance*	Herself	"Battle of the Networks' Stars" (Season 1, episode 13)
	The Suite Life on Deck	Alex Russo	"Double-Crossed" (Season 1, episode 21)

Music video			
Year	**Title**	**Artist**	**Notes**
2008	"Burnin' Up"	Jonas Brothers	Played Nick Jonas' love interest

Discography

Singles

Year	Song	Chart positions		Album
		US	**CAN**	
2008	"Tell Me Something I Don't Know"	58	—	*Another Cinderella Story*
2009	"Magic" (Originally by Pilot)	61	86	*Wizards of Waverly Place*
As a featured artist				
2009	"Whoa Oh!" (with Forever The Sickest Kids)	—	—	Non-album single
	"One and the Same" (with Demi Lovato)	82	—	*Disney Channel Playlist*
	"Send It On" (with Demi Lovato, Jonas Brothers, and Miley Cyrus)	20	—	Non-album song

Soundtracks

Year	Song	Album
2006	"Brain Zapped"	*Brain Zapped*
2008	"Cruella de Vil"	*DisneyMania 6*
	"Tell Me Something I Don't Know"	*Another Cinderella Story*
	"New Classic" (featuring Drew Seeley)	
	"Bang a Drum"	
	"New Classic" (Live) (featuring Drew Seeley)	
	"Fly to Your Heart"	*Tinker Bell*
2009	"One and the Same" (with Demi Lovato)	*Disney Channel Playlist*
	"Everything Is Not What It Seems"	*Wizards of Waverly Place*
	"Disappear"	
	"Magical"	
	"Magic"	
2010	"Trust in Me" (From Disney's The Jungle Book)	*DisneyMania 7*
	"Live Like There's No Tomorrow" (as Selena Gomez & the Scene)	*Ramona and Beezus OST & A Year Without Rain*
	"Shake It Up" (as Selena Gomez & the Scene)	*Shake It Up Theme Song*

Music videos

Year	Title
2008	"Cruella de Vil"
	"Tell Me Something I Don't Know"
	"Fly To Your Heart"
2009	"One and the Same" (with Demi Lovato)
	"Magic"
	"Send It On" (with Miley Cyrus, Demi Lovato, and Jonas Brothers)

Awards and nominations

Year	Award	Category	Work	Outcome

2008	Alma Award[61]	Outstanding Female Performance in a Comedy Television Series	*Wizards of Waverly Place*	Nominated
	Imagen Awards[62]	Best Actress – Television		
2009	NAACP Image Awards[63]	Outstanding Performance in a Youth/Children's Program – Series or Special		
	Nickelodeon Kids' Choice Awards[64]	Favorite TV Actress		Won
	Young Artist Award[65]	Best Performance in a TV Movie, Miniseries, or Special – Leading Young Actress	*Another Cinderella Story*	
		Best Performance in a TV Series – Leading Young Actress	*Wizards of Waverly Place*	Nominated
		Best Performance in a Voice-over Role	*Horton Hears a Who!*	
	Teen Choice Awards[66]	"Choice Summer- Celebrity Dancer"	*Another Cinderella Story*	Won
		"Choice Summer – TV Star-Female"	*Princess Protection Program*	
		"Choice Other Stuff – Red Carpet Icon: Female"	Herself	
	Imagen Awards[67]	Best Actress – Television	*Wizards of Waverly Place*	Nominated
	Alma Award[68]	Special Achievement Comedy - Television - Actress		Won
	Nickelodeon Australian Kids' Choice Awards[69]	Fave International TV Star		Nominated
2010	Gracie Award[70]	Outstanding Female Rising Star in a Comedy Series		Won
	NAACP Image Awards[71]	Outstanding Performance in a Youth/Children's Program – Series or Special		Nominated
	Nickelodeon Kids' Choice Awards[72]	Favorite TV Actress		Won
	Young Artist Award[73]	Best Performance in a TV Movie, Miniseries, or Special – Leading Young Actress	*Princess Protection Program*	Nominated
	BET Awards[74]	YoungStars Award	*Wizards of Waverly Place*	
	American Latino Awards[75]	Favorite American Latino Actor		Pending
	Teen Choice Awards[76]	Choice TV Actress: Comedy		Won
		Choice Red Carpet Fashion Icon: Female	Herself	
		Choice Summer: Movie Star- Female	*Ramona and Beezus*	Nominated
	Imagen Awards[77]	Best Actress - Television	*Wizards of Waverly Place: The Movie*	
	Nickelodeon Australian Kids' Choice Awards[78]	Fave TV Star	*Wizards of Waverly Place*	Won

References

[1] http://www.selenagomez.com

[2] "Celebrity Central – Selena Gomez: Snapshot" (http://www.people.com/people/selena_gomez). People Magazine. . Retrieved 2009-01-30. "Birth Date July 22, 1992 Birth Place Grand Prairie, Texas"

[3] Chuck Barney (February 7, 2008). Selena Gomez could be next Disney 'it' girl (http://findarticles.com/p/articles/mi_qn4176/is_20080207/ai_n21415751). *Oakland Tribune*. Retrieved 2008-08-01.

[4] Lauren Waterman (May 2009). Selena Gomez: spell bound (http://www.teenvogue.com/industry/coverlook/2009/05/teen-vogue-cover-girl-selena-gomez_090511) *Teen Vogue*. Retrieved 2009-05-11.

[5] Selena Gomez and Jake T. Austin on being latin (http://www.showbizcafe.com/en/interviews/exclusive-selena-gomez-on-being-latin/1247)

[6] Lee Hernández (March 22, 2008). Teen star Selena Gómez looks beyond Disney (http://www.nydailynews.com/latino/2008/03/22/2008-03-22_teen_star_selena_gmez_looks_beyond_disne.html). *NY Daily News*. Retrieved 2008-08-01.

[7] "All About Selena Gomez" (http://www.people.com/people/archive/article/0,,20287091,00.html). *People.com*. 2009-08-22. . Retrieved 2009-11-05.

[8] Michelle Tan (2008-05). "Is Selena Gomez... the Next Miley Cyrus?" (http://www.people.com/people/archive/article/0,,20203953,00.html). *People.com*. . Retrieved 2009-11-05.

[9] "Selena Gomez's Famous Name" (http://www.eonline.com/videos/v31013_Selena_Gomez__Famous_Name.html). *E!Online.com*. 2008-08-22. . Retrieved 2009-11-05.

[10] Selena Gomez Graduates High School – On Screen & Off l Access Hollywood - Celebrity News, Photos & Videos (http://www.accesshollywood.com/selena-gomez-graduates-high-school-on-screen-and-off_article_32234). Access Hollywood (2010-05-12). Retrieved on 2010-11-17.

[11] Selena Gomez. "Selena Gomez Biography" (http://www.people.com/people/selena_gomez/biography). *People.com*. . Retrieved 2009-08-06.

[12] "Disney Star Selena Gomez and General Growth Properties Give Teens a Voice in the 2008 Presidential Campaign" (http://www.smartbrief.com/news/aaaa/industryBW-detail.jsp?id=488E0DB0-5D3F-4DDB-A818-D7FFF639F61F). SmartBrief.com. 2008-08-04. . Retrieved 2008-11-02.

[13] "In Pictures: Eight Hot Kid Stars To Watch" (http://www.forbes.com/2008/04/09/entertainment-disney-lovato-biz-media-cx_lr_0409kidstars_slide_4.html?thisSpeed=15000). *Forbes.com*. 2002-05-22. . Retrieved 2009-08-06.

[14] "The Princess Diary" (http://www.people.com/people/archive/article/0,,20287116,00.html). *People.com*. 2009-07-22. . Retrieved 2009-11-04.

[15] "Wizards of Waverly Place Movie" (http://www.disneychannelmedianet.com/DNR/2009/doc/WOWP_MoviePremiere.doc). Disney Channel. . Retrieved 2009-07-12.

[16] Vena, Jocelyn (2009-02-06). "Selena Gomez To Star In 'Ramona and Beezus' Movie" (http://www.mtv.com/movies/news/articles/1604489/story.jhtml). *MTV.com*. . Retrieved 2009-10-21.

[17] Kilday, Gregg (2009-02-05). "Young actresses cast for 'Beezus and Ramona'" (http://www.reuters.com/article/filmNews/idUSTRE51515A20090206). *Reuters.com*. . Retrieved 2009-10-21.

[18] Pamela McClintock (2010-03-03). "Fox, New Regency head to 'Monte Carlo'" (http://www.variety.com/article/VR1118016027.html?categoryId=13&cs=1). *Variety*. . Retrieved 2010-03-11.

[19] Marc Malkin (July 22, 2008). Selena Gomez's Supersweet 16 (http://www.eonline.com/uberblog/b3322_selena_gomezs_supersweet_16.html). E! Online. Retrieved 2009-07-07.

[20] "Behind the Scenes!" (http://www.people.com/people/archive/article/0,,20287110,00.html). *People.com*. 2009-07-22. . Retrieved 2009-11-04.

[21] "Forever the Sickest Kids at Absolute Punk" (http://www.absolutepunk.net/showthread.php?t=305685). *Absolute Punk*. . Retrieved 2009-10-27.

[22] RIAA – GOLD & PLATINUM (http://www.riaa.com/goldandplatinumdata.php?resultpage=1&table=SEARCH_RESULTS&action=&title=&artist=selena gomez &format=&debutLP=&category=&sex=&releaseDate=&requestNo=&type=&level=&label=&company=&certificationDate=&awardDescription=&catalogNo=&aSex=&rec_id=&charField=&gold=&platinum=&multiPlat=&level2=&certDate=&album=&id=&after=on&before=on&startMonth=1&endMonth=8&startYear=1958&endYear=2010&sort=Artist&perPage=25)

[23] Dagostino, Mark (2008-10-27). "Selena Gomez: 'I'll be 30 Before I Get My License!'" (http://www.people.com/people/article/0,,20235767,00.html). *People.com*. . Retrieved 2009-08-06.

[24] "Stars Hit The Catwalk For St. Judes" (http://www.looktothestars.org/news/1382-stars-hit-the-catwalk-for-st-judes). Looktothestars.org. 2008-10-14. . Retrieved 2009-08-06.

[25] "Selena Gomez Borden Milk Ad" (http://www.sugarslam.com/selena-gomez-borden-milk-ad/). Sugarslam.com. 2009-05-26. . Retrieved 2009-08-06.

[26] "Selena Gomez Cares For Dogs In Puerto Rico" (http://popdirt.com/selena-gomez-cares-for-dogs-in-puerto-rico/72217/). popdirt.com. 2009-03-08. . Retrieved 2009-08-06.

[27] NBC Official Site (2009-06). "Late Night with Jimmy Fallon − Video Blogs − Tonight's Guest: Selena Gomez − Jimmy Fallon's Video Blog" (http://www.latenightwithjimmyfallon.com/blogs/2009/06/tonights-guest-selena-gomez/). *LateNightWithJimmyFallon.* . Retrieved 2009-08-05.

[28] Oh, Eunice (2009-02-03). "FIRST LOOK: Selena Gomez's Cell-Free Safety Pitch − Good Deeds, Selena Gomez" (http://www.people.com/people/article/0,,20256299,00.html). *People.com.* . Retrieved 2009-08-06.

[29] "Celebrities Raise Hope For Congo" (http://www.looktothestars.org/news/2789-celebrities-raise-hope-for-congo). Looktothestars.org. 2009-07-10. . Retrieved 2009-08-06.

[30] "Selena Gomez Trick-Or-Treats For UNICEF" (http://www.looktothestars.org/news/1350-selena-gomez-trick-or-treats-for-unicef). Looktothestars.org. 2008-10-09. . Retrieved 2009-08-06.

[31] "Teen Sensation Selena Gomez Appointed UNICEF Ambassador" (http://www.reuters.com/article/pressRelease/idUS178135+03-Sep-2009+PRN20090903). *Reuters.com.* 2009-09-03. . Retrieved 2009-10-22.

[32] "Selena Gomez: Trip to Africa was 'life-changing'" (http://www.google.com/hostednews/ap/article/ALeqM5gXQVPHT2lU525QpACXyin-pm1sjAD9B37HM81). *GoogleNews.com.* Associated Press. 2009-10-02. . Retrieved 2009-10-25.

[33] "Selena Gomez: Trip to Africa Was 'Life-Changing'" (http://www.youtube.com/watch?v=dFwJxxPzSpg&feature=player_embedded). *Youtube.com: Associated Press.* Associated Press. 2009-10-02. . Retrieved 2009-10-25.

[34] "Trick-or-Treat for UNICEF Spokesperson Selena Gomez :: Trick-or-Treat for UNICEF:: Youth Action :: U.S. Fund for UNICEF − UNICEF USA" (http://youth.unicefusa.org/trickortreat/selena-gomez.html). *Youth.UnicefUsa.org.* 2009. . Retrieved October 5, 2009.

[35] "Meet Selena Gomez at the Concert of Your Choice" (http://www.charitybuzz.com/catalog_items/100611). *CharityBuzz.com.* . Retrieved 2009-10-21.

[36] UNICEF (2009-10-08). "UNICEF Ambassador Selena Gomez named spokesperson for Trick-or-Treat for UNICEF campaign" (http://www.stamfordplus.com/stm/information/nws1/publish/News_1/UNICEF-Ambassador-Selena-Gomez-named-spokesperson-for-Trick-or-Treat-for-UNICEF-campaign6260.shtml). *StamFordPlus.com.* . Retrieved 2009-10-26.

[37] "Trick-or-Treat for UNICEF celebrates 60 years of America's youth making a difference throughout the world" (http://www.unicefusa.org/news/releases/trick-or-treat-for-unicef-long-lead-release.html). 2009-05-26. . Retrieved 2010-05-30.

[38] "Friends For Change: Disney Groups" (http://disney.go.com/disneygroups/friendsforchange/#/disneygroups/friendsforchange/). *Disney.go.com.* . Retrieved 2009-10-21.

[39] Disney Channel (August 6, 2009). ""SEND IT ON," AN ANTHEM BY THE WORLD'S BIGGEST TEEN STARS, MILEY CYRUS, JONAS BROTHERS, SELENA GOMEZ AND DEMI LOVATO, FOR DISNEY'S "FRIENDS FOR CHANGE: PROJECT GREEN," WILL DEBUT ON RADIO DISNEY, DISNEY CHANNEL, DISNEY.COM AND iTUNES" (http://www.disneychannelmedianet.com/DNR/2009/doc/Send_It_On_Disneys_Friends_for_Change _081909.doc) (DOC). Press release. . Retrieved August 20, 2009.

[40] "Send It On (feat. Demi Lovato, Jonas Brothers, Miley Cyrus & Selena Gomez) − Single" (http://itunes.apple.com/WebObjects/MZStore.woa/wa/viewAlbum?id=325770503&s=143441). *iTunes Store.* Apple Inc.. August 11, 2009. . Retrieved August 20, 2009.

[41] "Selena Gomez to Star in 'What Boys Want'" (http://www.parade.com/celebrity/hollywood-wire/2009/10/20/selena-gomez-to-star-in-what-boys-want.html). *Parade.* 2009-10-20. . Retrieved 2009-10-21.

[42] FOX 411 Editor (2009-10-07). "Selena Gomez Helps Give Back To Her Community" (http://entertainment.blogs.foxnews.com/2009/10/07/selena-gomez-helps-gives-back-to-her-community/). *FOXNews.com.* . Retrieved 2009-10-25.

[43] "Sears Arrive Lounge − The Hottest Guys & Girls Fashion with Selena Gomez" (http://www.arrivelounge.com/). *ArriveLounge.* . Retrieved 2009-10-20.

[44] Bee-Syuan Chang (2009-07-31). "Selena Gomez and Sears Team Up For Back To School Style" (http://www.stylelist.com/blog/2009/07/31/selena-gomez-and-sears-team-up-for-back-to-school-style/). *Stylist.com.* . Retrieved 2009-10-21.

[45] Joyce Eng (2008-10-30). "*Wizards* ' Selena Gomez Conjures Own Production Company (http://www.tvguide.com/News/Selena-Gomez-Forms-35034.aspx)"]. *TVGuide.com.* . Retrieved 2009-10-21.

[46] Tatianna Siegel (2008-10-29). "Selena Gomez forms production co." (http://www.variety.com/article/VR1117994893.html?categoryid=13&cs=1). *Variety.* . Retrieved 2009-10-21.

[47] Lauren Joskowitz (2009-10-15). "Selena Gomez Introduces 'Dream Out Loud,' Her Own Line Of Eco-Friendly, Bohemian Clothes" (http://hollywoodcrush.mtv.com/2009/10/15/selena-gomez-introduces-dream-out-loud-her-own-line-of-eco-friendly-bohemian-clothes/). *MYV.com.* . Retrieved 2009-10-22.

[48] Ella Ngo (2009-10-15). "Seelna Gomez Gets Her Own Fashion Line" (http://www.eonline.com/uberblog/b149093_selena_gomez_gets_her_own_fashion_line.html). *E!Online.com.* . Retrieved 2009-10-22.

[49] "Selena Gomez to Launch Clothing Line" (http://www.transworldnews.com/NewsStory.aspx?id=130338&cat=2). *TransWorldNews.com.* 2009-10-15. . Retrieved 2009-10-22.

[50] April MacIntyre (2009-10-15). "Selena Gomez launches fashion line in fall 2010" (http://www.monstersandcritics.com/lifestyle/fashion/news/article_1507339.php/Selena-Gomez-launches-fashion-line-in-fall-2010). *MonsterandCritics.com.* . Retrieved 2009-10-22.

[51] Emily H (2009-10-15). "Selena Gomez: From Wizard to Fashionista?!" (http://www.examiner.com/x-5019-San-Diego-Celebrity-Headlines-Examiner~y2009m10d15-Selena-Gomez-From-Wizard-to-Fashionista). *Examiner.com.* . Retrieved 2009-10-22.

[52] Julee Kaplan (2009-10-15). "Disney Star Selena Gomez Launching Fashion Brand" (http://www.wwd.com/markets-news/as-a-designer-selena-gomez-has-big-dreams-2343323). *WWD.com.* . Retrieved 2009-10-25.

[53] "Purity for Selena Gomez A Personal Promise to God, Not A Trend" (http://www.theinsider.com/news/
      986018_Purity_for_Selena_Gomez_A_Personal_Promise_to_God_Not_A_Trend). *The Insider.* . Retrieved 2009-08-06.

[54] "BFFs Selena Gomez & Demi Lovato Show Off Their Furry Best Pals" (http://www.peoplepets.com/news/celebrities/
      bffs-selena-gomez-demi-lovato-show-off-their-furry-best-pals/1). *PeoplePets.com.* 2009-06-18. . Retrieved 2009-08-06.

[55] "Miley Cyrus Sorry for Mocking Selena Gomez in YouTube Video" (http://www.foxnews.com/story/0,2933,392042,00.html).
      FoxNews.com. 2008-07-28. . Retrieved 2008-08-01.

[56] "Disney Star Selena Gomez: I'm Not Feuding With Miley" (http://www.people.com/people/article/0,,20207513,00.html). *People.com.*
      2008-06-18. . Retrieved 2009-10-21.

[57] Jocelyn Vena (2008-08-01). "Selena Gomez Makes It Clear: There's No Beef With Miley Cyrus" (http://www.mtv.com/news/articles/
      1591988/20080801/gomez__selena.jhtml). *MTV.com.* . Retrieved 2009-10-21.

[58] "Star Spotlight: Selena Gomez" (http://www2.scholastic.com/browse/article.jsp?id=3750390). Scholastic. September 26, 2008. .
      Retrieved June 20, 2010.

[59] "Selena Gomez, Joey King Are Beezus and Ramona" (http://artistdirect.com/nad/news/article/0,,4968744,00.html). Artistdirect.com. .
      Retrieved 2009-08-06.

[60] http://www.imdb.com/title/tt1067774/

[61] "Alma Awards 2008" (http://web.archive.org/web/20080730002201/www.almaawards.com/2008-nominees.html). *AlmaAward.com.*
      2008. . Retrieved 2009-10-20.

[62] "Hbo'S Rodrigo Garcia, Ugly Betty'S Tony Plana And Writer Ligiah Villalobos Of La Misma Luna To Receive Top Honors" (http://www.
      imagen.org/awards/2008/nominees). *Imagen.org.* . Retrieved 2009-08-06.

[63] "The 40th NAACP Image Awards" (http://www.naacpimageawards.net/40/win_tv.php). *Naacpimageawards.net.* . Retrieved
      2009-08-06.

[64] "Nickelodeon Kids' Choice Awards 2009 Press Kit" (http://www.nickkcapress.com/2009KCA/). *Nickkcapress.com.* 2009-03-30. .
      Retrieved 2009-08-06.

[65] "30th Annual Young Artist Awards" (http://www.youngartistawards.org/noms30.html). *YoungArtistAwards.org.* 2009-06-21. . Retrieved
      2009-10-20.

[66] "Teen Choice Awards 2009: The Winners" (http://www.myfoxla.com/dpp/story/Teen_Choice_2009_Winners_20090809).
      teenchoiceawards.com/. . Retrieved 2009-08-10.

[67] "Nominees for 24th Annual Imagen Awards Announced" (http://www.imagen.org/awards/2009/nominees). *Imagen.org.* 2009. .
      Retrieved 2009-12-21.

[68] "2009 ALMA Award Nominees & * Winners" (http://www.chiff.com/pop-culture/alma-awards.htm). *Alma Award.* . Retrieved
      2009-09-19.

[69] David Knox (2009-09-20). "2009 Kid's Choice Awards: Nominees: TV Tonight" (http://www.tvtonight.com.au/2009/09/
      2009-kids-choice-awards-nominees.html). *TVTonight.au.com.* . Retrieved 2009-10-20.

[70] "2010 Gracie Awards® Winners" (http://thegracies.org/2010-grace-awards.php). *Gracie Allen Award.* . Retrieved 2010-02-25.

[71] "The 41st NAACP Image Awards" (http://www.naacpimageawards.net/41/nominees-and-voting/nominees/). *Naacpimageawards.net.* .
      Retrieved 2010-01-06.

[72] "2010 Nickelodeon Kids' Choice Awards" (http://www.chiff.com/pop-culture/kids-choice-awards.htm). *Nickkcapress.com.* 2010-02-14.
      . Retrieved 2010-02-14.

[73] "31st Annual Young Artist Award" (http://www.youngartistawards.org/noms31.html). *youngartistawards.org/.* . Retrieved 2010-02-22.

[74] "YOUNGSTARS AWARD" (http://betawards.bet.com/nominees/category/youngstars-award). *Bet.com.* 2010-06-27. . Retrieved
      2010-06-27.

[75] "Welcome to the 4th Annual American Latino TV Awards" (http://www.americanlatino.tv/awards). *americanlatino.tv.* 2010. . Retrieved
      2010-06-05.

[76] "2010 Teen Choice Awards Winners List" (http://www.mtv.com/news/articles/1645401/20100809/story.jhtml).
      TeenChoiceAwards.com. . Retrieved 2010-06-15.

[77] "Winners of 25th Annual Imagen Awards Announced Honoring Latinos in Entertainment, includes Multiple Wins for the Brothers Bratt"
      (http://www.imagen.org/awards/2010/winners). *imaged.org.* 2010-08-16. . Retrieved 2010-08-17.

[78] "Australian Nickelodeon Kids' Choice Awards 2010 Winners" (http://www.cambio.com/more/news/
      australian-nickelodeon-kids-choice-awards-2010-winners). http://www.cambio.com/. 2010-10-10. . Retrieved 2010-10-09.

External links

- Official website (http://http://www.selenagomez.com/)
- Selena Gomez (http://www.tv.com/person/350805/summary.html) at TV.com
- Selena Gomez (http://www.imdb.com/name/nm1411125/) at the Internet Movie Database

Alex Russo

Wizards of Waverly Place character	
First appearance	"Crazy 10-Minutes Sale"
Created by	Todd J. Greenwald
Portrayed by	Selena Gomez
Nickname(s)	Alex (by Everyone) Lexie (by her maternal grandmother) Brown eyes (by Mason) Little Meatball (by Mason)
Gender	Female
Occupation	Waitress (at the Waverly Sub Station) 9th grader (season 1) 10th grader (season 2) 11th grader(season 3) 12th grader(season 4)
Family	Jerry Russo (father), Theresa Russo (mother), Justin Russo (older brother), Max Russo (younger brother), Megan Brooke Russo (paternal aunt), Kelbo Russo (paternal uncle), Magdelena Larkin (maternal grandmother) Ernesto Larkin (maternal uncle), Duke Russo (paternal grandfather), Rose Russo (paternal grandmother)

Alexandra Margarita "Alex" Russo[1] is the main protagonist of the Disney Channel sitcom *Wizards of Waverly Place*, portrayed by Selena Gomez.[2] As the middle child and only Russo daughter, she is sly, outgoing, and sometimes rude to her family and friends. Alex usually underachieves when it comes to regular high school. She is good at heart though. She often gets into trouble because of her constant schemes (usually involving magic).

Alex is smart but not hardworking. Her brother Justin hates this because he himself is a hard worker and he can't bear the feeling that even though his sister doesn't work hard, she gets everything. Alex became a full wizard in "Wizards of Waverly Place: The Movie".

In 2008, AOL named her the twentieth greatest witch in television history.[3] Selena Gomez, who portrays Alex, is one of the only two cast members to appear in every single episode of the series to date; the only other cast member to appear in all episodes that have aired so far is David Henrie, who portrays Justin Russo.

Personality

Her mother describes her as "A beautiful girl who is full of mischief" in the episode "Alex's Brother Maximan". Fights towards Justin are frequent, because she secretly wants to be like him but doesn't know what to do about it. In the season three episode *"Alex's Logo"*, while she is under a truth spell, it is revealed that the reason that Alex acts mean is simply because she wants to be liked and actually fears being hated. She also is seen many times eating sliced pickles, suggesting that maybe they're her other favorite food besides biscuits and loose corn. But in the end she makes everything work out.

Alex claims everyone takes her advice as she knows a lot about fashion, relationships, girls, and guys, but above all she can be very sneaky and tricky[4] to the extent that she's even willing to admit that she's usually up to no good, and feels uncomfortable when others say the opposite. Her best friend since childhood is Harper Finkle (Jennifer Stone), who often tries to keep her out of trouble. In the episode *"Third Wheel"*, Alex says to Harper that she is like her sister. Her temporary best friend at Wizard School is Hugh Normous (Josh Sussman), as she said in one episode, that he was "the worst best friend ever". Though she continues to torment her older brother Justin, the two seem to have a close bond that neither seem to have with any other character on the show. Her enemy since kindergarten is Gigi Hollingsworth (Skyler Samuels), ever since Gigi spilled juice on Alex's blanket and told everybody that Alex had an "accident" during nap time in their kindergarten years which but Alex still hasn't got over it.[2]

Alex often uses magic to solve her problems, which frequently ends up giving her even more problems than she began with. Her tendency to use magic without permission is often caused by her lack of work-ethic and respect for the rules she deems unnecessary. Alex hardly ever considers the consequences of magic and is often unprepared when the situation goes haywire, which requires the help of her more sensible brother Justin when she finds she can't fix them by herself, often grudgingly accepting his offer to work together. Alex has not advanced as far as Justin (or even Max, as shown in *"Night at the Lazerama"*), but she is very skilled at "Make-'em-Ups", when a wizard can make up their own emergency spell. It is revealed in *"Doll House"* that Alex didn't know about magic when she was five.

Riley (Brian Kubach) had been Alex's crush for most of the first season, and to impress him, she calls herself his good luck charm and manipulates Justin without him figuring out to magically win his — and Riley's, as she was always quick to emphasize — baseball game, though when Justin stops once their father makes him realize what Alex has been doing, Alex has to use magic herself by the bleachers in order to be Riley's date, cleverly managing to win the game for Riley even with Jerry and Justin's attempts to foil her magic, further showing how skilled she can be at magic by the way she countered Justin's magic so easily and discreetly at the baseball game where humans who didn't know about magic were, despite Justin's and Jerry's knowledge of magic, when it clashes with her understanding of it — however small her amount of understanding of it may be at the start.[5] She had also got Riley jealous by enchanting a mannequin to come alive and date her—after he breaks up with her—in the episode "*Alex's Spring Fling*".[6]

She is a Daddy's Girl and according to her father, Jerry (David DeLuise), she uses her puppy dog eyes to get out of trouble. She can't tell when her dad's being overprotective, she just thinks he's being crazy and doesn't make the situation better by saying she's growing up. In *"You Can't Always Get What You Carpet"*, however, she tells her dad she will always be his little girl. She isn't fazed very much — if not at all — when he's overprotective and still does whatever it is he doesn't want her to do. For example in *"Alex's Brother Maximan"*, Jerry hears Alex tell her mom that her boyfriend, Dean (Daniel Samonas), wants to kiss her, and he says "Kissing? Who are you kissing?" and begins to freak out. Later in the episode, she does kiss Dean, but when her dad questions it, she tries to change the subject by saying something about him being proud of his children.[7]

Alex is often depicted as a slacker, somewhat more so with regular high school than in wizardry and witchcraft school. If Alex does not want to do anything that is school-related, she will make an excuse or scheme about why she does not want to do it, and how unnecessary she finds it or will just simply not do it. She will often rebel against mandatory assignments with glee and has displayed little, if any, ambition, freely admitting that she always arrives in school during third period and never cares.[8] She has been shown to be sent to the principal's office so often that she and Mr. Laritate have a regular routine down, even pouring each other coffee and giving each other donuts,[9] and even has a pillow, a hammock, and a CD player containing rain forest sounds stashed in Mr. Laritate's office whenever she gets detention.[10] She has even resorted to trying extreme measures in order to get out of a school project despite the cost being much greater, once going as far as attempting to injure herself on purpose by jumping off the stage after she is named as Harper's replacement as Tinker Bell in the school production of *Peter Pan* (this after she already auditioned to be Harper's understudy, thinking that she would not have to do anything in the play), when Harper accidentally falls off the stage during rehearsal. Art is her favorite school subject and is pretty much the only class she takes seriously, and excels greatly at, being the best in her class and even being the co-art teacher.[11] [12]

After her parents complain how she never has never been in any school clubs, she lied and said she was in reading club and tried to steal the award from Justin's room and scratch out his name and put hers. Justin, however, is fed up with her always getting past his defenses to keep her out of his room and stealing his stuff, so he created Frankie (Franken Girl) to guard his room, but Alex still managed to shut down Frankie when she figures out that Frankie's brain worked like a computer, and when Justin made Frankie immune to shutting down like a computer and cast a spell to make her think of Alex as her best friend — much to Alex's disdain — and Alex was then forced to put up with her before noticing that Frankie fit a lot of her best friend requirements, and became fast friends with Frankie. Justin then put a spell on Frankie to like cheerleading and she wanted Alex to be on the squad with her. In *"Monster Hunter"*, Alex gets jealous of Justin when he moves forward in wizard training so she creates a spell song where she can remember the spells she learn, hoping to catch up with him.

Alex and Justin act as foils, as the two are near-polar opposites in terms of personality; Justin is responsible, kind, unselfish, sensible, and hard working, fair in judgment, though not very witty with his words nor outgoing, mostly like that just because he secretly competes to be the best at magic since he loves it but is easily insecure at witnessing Alex and her great magical feats accomplished so effortlessly by her. Alex is lazy, carefree, witty, funny, sarcastic, stubborn, and biased when it comes to herself or her loved ones against other people, magical or not, not very good at expressing herself in terms of emotions and frustration-causing desires on her part like wanting to be like Justin, cunning, mischievous, and a complete natural at magic despite not being as serious as Justin when discussed or performed, his performance full of constant measuring and intense concentration, while hers laid-back and careless. Their similarities though, are surprisingly many, despite how rarely they show themselves, as they are very strong during the moments they do shine through.

Positive qualities

Despite her frequent unkindness and pranks, Alex is far from heartless and has numerous instances of generosity, loyalty, and compassion. She deeply cares for Harper, going so far as to reveal her secret to her in *"Harper Knows"* out of guilt for lying. She also loves Justin dearly despite their constant antagonism, most notably shown in "Moving On", where she went out of her way to help Justin move on from Juliet. Alex can also feel remorse and guilt for her actions and has apologized and taken responsibility for them, and often goes out of her way to set things right whenever her disregard for the consequences directly affect her friends and/or family. Though these instances are rare, Alex does occasionally use magic unselfishly or with good intentions, such as in *"Taxi Dance"*, where she repairs Cab 804 to allow herself and her family to continue to cherish the memories of her birth. Additionally, in *"The Good, the Bad, and the Alex"*, she apparently joins forces with Stevie, a fellow wizard, and starts a revolution to end the wizard competition, but this is revealed to be a ruse; just as Stevie is about to succeed, Alex transforms her into a rock-like substance and shatters her. Alex is also very much like her aunt Megan, as both love art and hate hard work. In fact, Max said that Megan is just like Alex's twin only older in *"Retest"*, though the key difference between the two, according to Justin, is that Alex is capable of apologizing for her actions, something that Megan never learned to do. She also has a strong sense of justice, and frequently scolds anyone who is being unfair or cruel, going far to the point of stand against her own parents in the first part of "*Wizard vs Vampire*" when they berates Justin for dating Juliet. Alex also hates "fake" people; in "Alex Does Good", when she is forced to join the Happy Helper's Club, Alex is openly disgusted that the club members only do mundane everyday tasks for people rather than actual good deeds, and are only doing so for rewards. She even goes so far as to refuse to accept a ribbon to protest their behavior, but immediately accepts it when she discovers that she faces suspension. In Season 3, Alex is rarely the source of magical problems anymore, instead often being the one to solve them, though she still has a bad reputation and is always the first to blame when magic causes a situation to go haywire.

In *Wizards of Waverly Place: The Movie*, Alex says that Justin was everything that she ever wanted to be and she was jealous of how smart he was and how kind he is, while Justin responds in kind saying how he is jealous of how everything comes easy to her, especially magic, which is why he strives so hard to be perfect.

In *Alex tells the World*, Alex, along with Justin, are found guility for exposing magic to the human world. Professer Crumbs revealed that the "government" was actually a Wizard Test, and they failed. Since Alex told the "world" and Justin told the "government" about the wizards, their punishment is a drop from Level 3 to Level 1 for Wizards Studies, putting Max in the lead. Alex subsequently decided to become a mortal in order to be with Mason, her boyfriend. Unfortunately, it's turned out that, since she is now mortal, their relationship is against the wizard law, due to the fact that werewolves always devour their (mortal) girlfriends, and they have no choice but to break up.

Alex's love interests

- **Brad Sherwood** (Shane Lyons, season 1) – seen in "Potion Commotion"; Alex tries to get Brad to like her with a love potion, but she accidentally drinks both halves of the potion and falls in love with herself. Later, Brad came over to her house and gave her chocolates, on the same night of Justin's interview for the World School Summit. She soon found out that Brad only came over just to sabotage Justin's interview. Alex then broke up with him, even though they were never going out.

- **Riley** (Brian Kubach, season 1) – long term; first seen in "I Almost Drowned in a Chocolate Fountain", where he and Alex went on a so-called 'date'. In "The Supernatural", Alex got Riley to believe that she was his good luck charm in baseball, and charmed the ball so his team would win each time. They broke up in "Alex's Spring Fling" (List of WOWP episodes), but Alex made Riley jealous by dating mannequin she brought to life, and they got back together. Apparently they broke-up, because Riley was never to be been seen again in season 2. And Alex dates Dean Moriarty in season 2.

- **Manny Quin** (Matt Smith, season 1) – A male mannequin that Alex used magic on to come to life, and briefly dated to make Riley jealous in "Alex's Spring Fling".

- **Dean Moriarty** (Daniel Samonas, season 2) – long term; first seen in "Smarty Pants", last seen in "Wizards vs. Vampires: Dream Date". Dean discovered Alex liked him in "Graphic Novel", and admitted he liked her in "Racing". They started dating in "Alex's Brother, Maxximan". Dean apparently moved away (though has not been mentioned since "Saving WizTech") and he came back in "Wizards vs. Vampires: Dream Date" (because Alex was using magic to control his dreams to go on dates with him). They broke up because Dean wasn't acting as romantic as he was in his dreams Alex was controlling. When she broke up, at first he acted all cool, but when Alex went into yet another dream, but let Dean control it this time, he says the reason he acted that way was because he was hurt. They break up properly and Dean disappears in his dream. Dean returns in the episode, "Journey To The Center Of Mason".

- **Ronald Longcape, Jr.** (Chad Duell, season 2) – seen in "Saving WizTech". Alex liked Ronald when they met, but she was still in a relationship with Dean. Ronald then shape-shifted into Dean (he froze the real Dean inside gelatin) and broke up with Alex so he could convince Alex into coming to WizTech with him. Ronald used her as part of his evil plan to take over WizTech, but his plan was foiled by Alex's love for Dean.

- **Javier** (Xavier Torres) - seen in *Wizards of Waverly Place: The Movie*. He was a host at the hotel the Russos were staying at in the Caribbean. Alex had a small crush on him, but soon turned him down once she realized how she would rather spend time with her family.

- **Mason Greyback** (Gregg Sulkin, season 3 - 4) - long term; first mentioned in season 2 episode " Future Harper" andfirst seen in "Alex Charms a Boy". He is a transfer student from England, perfect in every way except for his artistic vision. Alex casts a spell on Mason, so that she becomes the inspiration for all the art he creates in their school art class. In "Future Harper", Harper from the future asked Alex if Mason has already broken up with her, but Alex hasn't met him yet. In "Wizards vs. Werewolves", it's revealed that he is a werewolf and he knows Juliet for 300 years and when he sees her, he shouts out that he loves her. After that, Alex is left crying on her family's shoulders. Then he tells her that the necklace shaped in a heart that he gave her it doesn't glow on batteries, but it's magical. So he takes her back to Transylvania, where she threw the necklace. Alex puts the necklace on Mason and the heart glows, which means that he loves her. But it's too late, because he was bitten by Juliet (a vampire), and is transformed to a wolf, forever. It is revealed by Harper in season 3 episode "Alex Russo, Matchmaker?" that he was Alex's longest relationship. He returns in Wizards Unleashed/ Alex Saves Mason because Alex saw him on TV so they get back together when Alex makes him human again, with the help of her brothers. He and Alex stay together. He will also be a main character in season 4. In the "Wizards Season Finale", Mason helps the family when they get locked up by the government and eventually escape.In Season 4, Mason and Alex have to break up due to the fact that Alex gave up in the wizard competition, the werewolf always ends up eating the mortal girlfriend.

- **George** (Austin Butler, season 3) - He appears in the episode "Positive Alex" as the school band leader. He is asked out by Alex, but he refuses because of her negativity. However, he becomes attracted to her when she starts acting positive to prove him wrong. In the end, she became *too* positive because of the magical marker she used, and he was turned off.

- **Zack Martin** (Dylan Sprouse, season 2) - Zack Martin is seen In the On Deck episode "Double Crossed" (part of the "Wizards on Deck With Hannah Montana" special), Zack is seen flirting with Alex. His obsession comes in handy when she needs to hide in his room, to which he responds by looking up to the sky, putting his hands together and saying, "Thank you!" Later on, when he discovered that Alex used him to cover up a prank, he insults her by calling her cunning, sadistic, and cold-hearted, but this was immediately followed by, "Where have you been all my life?" Alex then showed a temporary interest, but then was dragged away by her brother to be punished for the prank.

Reference

[1] *Wizards of Waverly Place* episode: "Quinceañera"

[2] *Wizards of Waverly Place* episode: "The Crazy 10 Minute Sale"

[3] "AOL – Top TV Witches" (http://television.aol.com/photos/tv-witches). .

[4] *Wizards of Waverly Place* episode: "First Kiss"

[5] *Wizards of Waverly Place* episode: *"The Supernatural"*

[6] *Wizards of Waverly Place* episode: *"Alex's Spring Fling"*.(Press on the 9) However, he goes back out with her during the episode. He doesn't appear again though after that, and what happened to him is a mystery.

[7] Wizards of Waverly Place 2nd Season Extended (http://www.dcmedianet.com/DNR/2008/doc/ WizardsOfWaverlyPlace_2ndSeason_Extended.doc)

[8] *"Wizards of Waverly Place*episode: Taxi Dance"

[9] *Wizards of Waverly Place: Alex Does Good*

[10] *Wizards of Waverly Place: Detention Election*

[11] *Wizards of Waverly Place episode: "Art Teacher"*

[12] *Wizards of Waverly Place episode: "Paint By Committee"*

External links

- Alex Russo (http://www.imdb.com/character/ch0033410/) at the Internet Movie Database

Wizards of Waverly Place

Wizards of Waverly Place	
Genre	Teen sitcom Contemporary fantasy Comedy-drama
Created by	Todd J. Greenwald
Starring	Selena Gomez David Henrie Jake T. Austin Jennifer Stone María Canals Barrera David DeLuise
Theme music composer	John Adair and Steve Hampton
Opening theme	"Everything Is Not What It Seems", performed by Selena Gomez
Country of origin	United States
Language(s)	English
No. of seasons	4
No. of episodes	81 (aired) (List of episodes)
Production	
Executive producer(s)	Todd J. Greenwald Peter Murrieta (season 1–3) Vince Cheung Ben Montanio
Location(s)	New York City (setting) Hollywood Center Studios, Hollywood, California (taping location)
Camera setup	Videotape; Multi-camera
Running time	approx. 22–23 minutes
Production company(s)	It's a Laugh Productions
Broadcast	
Original channel	Disney Channel
Picture format	480i, SDTV (seasons 1–2) 720p, HDTV (season 3–present)
Audio format	Stereo
Original run	October 12, 2007 – present

Status	Current (Currently airing: season 4)
External links	
Official website [1]	

Wizards of Waverly Place is a Disney Channel Original television series that premiered on October 12, 2007. It won "Outstanding Children's Program" at the 61st Primetime Emmy Awards in 2009. A film adaptation of the series, *Wizards of Waverly Place: The Movie*, premiered as a Disney Channel Original Movie on August 28, 2009; In 2010, the film adaptation won "Outstanding Children's Program" at the 62nd Primetime Emmy Awards.

The series was created by Todd J. Greenwald, and stars Selena Gomez, David Henrie and Jake T. Austin as three wizard siblings with magical abilities competing to win sole custody of the family powers. Further main cast includes Jennifer Stone, María Canals Barrera and David DeLuise. In June 2010, Disney Channel renewed the show for a fourth season. It also announced plans for a second film based on the series.[2] [3]

Premise

Set on Waverly Place in Manhattan, New York's Greenwich Village neighborhood, *Wizards of Waverly Place* centers on the Italian-Mexican Russo family, which includes Alex (Selena Gomez), her older brother Justin (David Henrie), and their younger brother Max (Jake T. Austin). The three Russo siblings are wizards in training and live with their Italian-American father Jerry (David DeLuise), a former wizard, and their Mexican-American mother, Theresa (María Canals Barrera) who is a mortal. Alex's best friend Harper (Jennifer Stone) also found out about the Russos' wizard powers in Season 2 in the episode "Harper Knows". Bailee Madison will also star as Maxine, a ten year old wizard in the fourth season. The siblings have to keep their secret safe while living in the mortal world. When they all complete their wizard training, the three siblings will have a wizard competition to decide who will become the family wizard of their generation and keep their powers forever while the others will lose their powers for good and become mortal. Because of this, Jerry is always trying to get the kids not to rely on magic, because they might not have it someday. The magical world tends to be very eccentric and surreal. They also learn that keeping a very big secret can sometimes become a challenge.

Production

The series was created and as executive produced by Todd J. Greenwald, who began developing the show after working as a writer and consulting producer during the first season of *Hannah Montana*. The show is produced by It's a Laugh Productions and Disney Channel Original Productions. The theme song, "Everything Is Not What It Seems", written by John Adair and Steve Hampton, is of techno-pop style and is performed by Selena Gomez & the Scene. The series is filmed at Hollywood Center Studios in Hollywood, California.

Opening sequence

In the first three seasons, the same opening sequence is used. It shows the six main characters in the morning with Alex, Justin, Max, and Harper getting ready to go to school. For season four, the opening sequence has been changed. It shows a wizard's crystal ball for the setting. In the crystal ball it features the main cast with clips of episodes from the third and fourth seasons. The opening song, "Everything Is Not What It Seems (Remixed/New Version)" sung by Selena Gomez & the Scene.

Release

The show debuted on Disney Channel on October 12, 2007 after the premiere of *Twitches Too*, gathering 5.9 million viewers.[4] In February 2009, the episode "Helping Hand" broke the record for the largest audience in the 7:00 PM (Eastern Time) time period on the Disney Channel, with a total of 4.5 million viewers.[5] In January 2010, "Wizards vs. Werewolves" one-hour special episode became the series' most-watched episode with 6.2 million viewers,[6] surpassing the 6 million viewers of "Paint By Committee" episode[7] In 2009, the series was the top scripted telecast for teens between the age of 9-14 (1.63 million/6.7 rating) and second in kids 6-11 (1.81 million/7.4 rating), which was only slightly behind "The Suite Life on Deck"(1.82 million/7.4 rating.)[8]

Episodes

Season	Episodes	Originally aired	
		Season premiere	Season finale
1	21	October 12, 2007	August 31, 2008
2	30	September 12, 2008	August 21, 2009
Film		August 28, 2009	
3	28	October 9, 2009	October 15, 2010
4	TBA	November 12, 2010	TBA

Films

Wizards of Waverly Place: The Movie

The Disney Channel Original Movie, based on the series, premiered on August 28, 2009 on Disney Channel. *Wizards of Waverly Place: The Movie* was filmed in Puerto Rico, Los Angeles, and New York City from February 16 to March 27, 2009.[9] The movie received 13.6 million viewers on its premiere,[10] making it the second-most-viewed DCOM premiere in the US after *High School Musical 2*. It was also one of the top scripted telecasts in 2009.[11] It won a Primetime Emmy Award in 2010 for "Outstanding Children's Program".

Wizards of Waverly Place 2: The Next Big Adventure

Development was announced June 2, 2010 by Disney.[3] This has also been confirmed by an interview with Selena Gomez. Dan Berendsen will return as script writer for the film.[12]

Cast

Main

- Selena Gomez as Alexandra "Alex" Russo
- David Henrie as Justin Russo
- Jake T. Austin as Max Russo
- Jennifer Stone as Harper Finkle
- María Canals Barrera as Theresa Russo
- David DeLuise as Jerry Russo

Major recurring

- Gregg Sulkin as Mason Greyback (season 3 - present)
- Dan Benson as Zachary Ezekiel "Zeke" Rosenblatt Beakerman[13] (season 1 - present)
- Bridgit Mendler as Juliet Van Heusen (season 2 -season 3)
- Jeff Garlin as Uncle Kelbo (season 1 - present)
- Ian Abercrombie as Professer Crumbs (season 1-present)
- Bailee Madison as Maxine Joneson (season 4-present)

Recurring

- Josh Sussman as Hugh Normous (season 1-2)
- Daniel Samonas as Dean Moriarty (season 2-4)
- Fred Willard as Mr. Stuffleby (seasons 2-3)
- Moises Arias as Conscience (season 3)
- Daryl Sabara as T.J. Taylor (season 1-2)
- Andy Pessoa as Alfred (season 2)
- Lucy Hale as Miranda Hampson (season 1)
- Skyler Samuels as Gertrude "Gigi" Hollingsworth (season 1-2)
- Paulie Litt as Frankie/Joey (seasons 1 and 3)
- Chad Duell as Ronald Longcape Jr. (season 2)
- Maurice Godin as Ronald Longcape Sr. (season 2)
- Andy Kindler as Chancellor Rudy Tootietooie (season 3-4)
- Octavia Spencer as Dr. Evilini (season 1)
- Belita Moreno as Grandma Russo (season 2)
- Gilland Jones as Jenny Majorheely (season 2-3)
- Hayley Kiyoko as Stevie (season 3)

Season one (L-R): David Henrie as Justin Russo, David DeLuise as Jerry Russo, Selena Gomez as Alex Russo, María Canals Barrera as Theresa Russo and Jake T. Austin as Max Russo. *Absent*: Jennifer Stone as Harper Finkle

Season two (L-R): David Henrie as Justin Russo, Jake T. Austin as Max Russo, Jennifer Stone as Harper Finkle, Selena Gomez as Alex Russo, David DeLuise as Jerry Russo and María Canals Barrera as Theresa Russo.

Season three (L-R): David DeLuise as Jerry Russo, María Canals Barrera as Theresa Russo, David Henrie as Justin Russo, Selena Gomez as Alex Russo, Jake T. Austin as Max Russo, and Jennifer Stone as Harper Finkle..

Merchandise

Soundtrack

The soundtrack album for the hit Disney Channel Original Series of the same name. The album was released as a physical CD, enhanced CD and digital on August 4, 2009, under Walt Disney Records.[14] [15] [16] [17] The album includes songs from and inspired by the TV series and *Wizards of Waverly Place: The Movie*.[17] [18]

In response to the soundtrack, Stephen Thomas Erlewine of Allmusic recognized *Wizards* for its "teen revamps of boomer classics that parents can enjoy too". He also stated that the album is "agreeable" and that Selena Gomez "inevitably stands out from the pack". However, Erlewine said: "the dang-awful version of America's "You Can Do Magic" by Drew Seeley is sunk by its hyper-claustrophobic rhythms, the biggest rearrangement of a tune here and easily the worst cut."[16]

Video game

A video game based on the series was released in August 2009.[19] [20]

DVD releases

Compilations

Name	Episodes	Region 1	Region 2	DVD extras
Wizards of Waverly Place: Wizard School	Wizard School Part 1, Wizard School Part 2, Curb Your Dragon, Disenchanted Evening	July 29, 2008[21]	TBA	Work It Like a Wizard - Selena, Jake and David's favorite things to do.
Wizards of Waverly Place: Supernaturally Stylin'	Credit Check, Smarty Pants, Beware Wolf, Graphic Novel[22]	February 10, 2009[23]	TBA	Fashionista Presto Chango! - Go behind the scenes with the stars for some wardrobe magic!
Wizards on Deck with Hannah Montana	Cast-Away (To Another Show) (Wizards), "Double Crossed" (Suite Life), "Super(stitious) Girl" (Hannah Montana)	September 22, 2009[24]	TBA	Justin's Award Winning Essay - It's A Suite Life Having Fun With Hannah & The Wizards

Season releases

Name	Episodes	Region 2	Region 4	DVD extras
Season 1: Volume 1: Work It Like a Wizard	Crazy 10-Minutes Sale, First Kiss, I Almost Drowned in a Chocolate Fountain, New Employee, Disenchanted Evening, You Can't Always Get What You Carpet, Alex's Choice	October 5, 2009[25]	March 3, 2010[26]	Work It Like a Wizard - Selena, Jake and David's favorite things to do.
Season 1: Volume 2: Magic Training	Curb Your Dragon, Movies, Pop Me and We Both Go Down, Potion Commotion ,Justin's Little Sister, Wizard School Part 1, Wizard School Part 2	October 5, 2009[27]	June 2, 2010[28]	Casting A Spell
Season 1: Volume 3: Stylin' Powers	The Supernatural, Alex in the Middle, Report Card, Credit Check, Alex's Spring Fling, Quinceanera, Art Museum Piece	October 5, 2009[29]	August 2010[30]	Backstage Disney

The show's complete first season was released on September 10, 2009 in Germany,[31] on October 1, 2009 in Spain,[32] on March 3, 2010 in France and on March 12, 2010 in Poland.[33] The first season of the show was released in volumes in Brazil on October 5, 2009.

Awards and nominations

Year	Award	Category	Recipient(s)	Outcome
2008	Alma Award[34]	"Outstanding Male Performance in a Comedy Television Series"	Jake T. Austin	Nominated
		"Outstanding Female Performance in a Comedy Television Series"	Selena Gomez	
	Imagen Award[35]	"Best Actress - Television"		
2009	Image Award[36]	"Outstanding Performance in a Youth/Children's Program - Series or Special"		
	Nickelodeon Kids' Choice Awards[37]	"Favorite TV Actress"		Won
	Young Artist Award[38]	"Best Performance in a TV Series - Leading Young Actress"		Nominated
	Primetime Emmy[39]	"Outstanding Children's Program"	Cast	Won
	Alma Award[40]	"Special Achievement Comedy - Television - Actress"	Selena Gomez	
			María Canals Barrera	Nominated
	Imagen Award[41]	"Best Actress - Television"	Selena Gomez	
2010	Image Award[42]	"Outstanding Performance in a Youth/Children's Program - Series or Special"		
	Nickelodeon Kids' Choice Awards[43]	"Favorite TV Show"	Cast	
		"Favorite TV Actress"	Selena Gomez	Won
	Teen Choice Awards[44] [45]	"Choice TV Actress: Comedy"		
		"Choice TV Show: Comedy"	Cast	Nominated
	Primetime Emmy[46]	"Outstanding Children's Program"	Cast	
		"Outstanding Children's Program" (for Wizards of Waverly Place: The Movie)		Won
	Nickelodeon Australian Kids' Choice Awards[47]	"Fave TV Show"		Nominated
		"Fave TV Star"	Selena Gomez	Won
	British Academy Children's Awards[48]	"BAFTA Kid's Vote: TV"	Cast	

International release

Country/Region	Network(s)	Series premiere	Series Title in Country
Turkey	Digiturk[49]	October 24, 2007	Waverly Büyücüleri
	Disney Channel Turkey[50]	October 12, 2007	*Wizards of Waverly Place*
United States	Disney Channel[51]		
Pakistan	Disney Channel		
Australia	Disney Channel[52]	October 19, 2007	
	Seven Network	October 4, 2008	
New Zealand	Disney Channel New Zealand[52]	October 19, 2007	
	TV3		
United Kingdom	Disney Channel UK & Ireland[53]	November 4, 2007	
Ireland	Disney Channel UK & Ireland and TRTÉ[54]	November 3, 2007	
Canada (English)	Family[55]	October 26, 2007	
India	Disney Channel India[56]	May 5, 2008	
Sri Lanka			
Bangladesh			
Malaysia	Disney Channel Malaysia[57] (Airs in Malay(penyihir tempat Waverly) and English Language)	March 9, 2008	
Arab World	Disney Channel Middle East[58] (Airing with Arabic subtitles)	February 29, 2008	
The Netherlands	Disney Channel (Netherlands & Belgium)[59]	October 3, 2009	
Belgium		November 1, 2009	
Hong Kong	Disney Channel Asia[58] (Airing the show with Indonesian, Malay and Chinese Subtitles) (Dubbed in Hong Kong, Thailand, and South Korea, Vietnam)	March 9, 2008	
Indonesia			
Philippines			
Singapore			
Thailand			
South Korea			우리가족마법사
Vietnam			Những phù thủy xứ Waverly
South Africa	Disney Channel South Africa (airs in English)		
Canada (French)	VRAK.TV[60]	August 24, 2009	*Les Sorciers de Waverly Place*
France	Disney Channel France[61]	January 22, 2008	
	NRJ12[62]	August 31, 2009	
Israel	Disney Channel Israel[63]	June 2008	סיילפ ילרביווט םיפשכמה
Bulgaria	BNT 1	March 28, 2009	*Магьосниците от Уейвърли Плейс*
	Disney Channel Bulgaria	September 19, 2009	

Greece	Disney Channel Greece	November 7, 2009	*Οι Μάγοι του Γουέβερλυ*
	ERT[64]	January 5, 2010	
Italy	Disney Channel Italy[59]	January 26, 2008	*I Maghi Di Waverly*
	Italia 1[65]	January 12, 2010	
Poland	Disney Channel Poland	February 29, 2008	*Czarodzieje z Waverly Place*
	TVP 1	September 12, 2010	
Finland	Disney Channel Scandinavia Nelonen[66]	February 29, 2008	*Waverly Placen velhot*
Denmark[67]			*Magi på Waverly Place*
Sweden[68]			
Norway[69]			*Magikerne på Waverly Place*
Germany	Disney Channel Germany[70]	March 8, 2008	*Die Zauberer vom Waverly Place*
	Super RTL[71]	September 1, 2008	
Switzerland	SF Zwei[72]	April 11, 2009	
Austria	ORF 1[73]	June 20, 2009	
Spain	Disney Channel Spain[74]	January 18, 2008	Los Magos de Waverly Place
	Antena 3[75]		
Portugal	Disney Channel Portugal[76]		*Os Feiticeiros de Waverly Place*
	SIC[77]		
Brazil	Disney Channel Brazil[78]	March 23, 2008 (Advance) April 11, 2008 (Premiere)	
Dominican Republic	Disney Channel Latin America[79]	March 23, 2008 (Advance) April 14, 2008 (Premiere)	*Los Hechiceros de Waverly Place*
Argentina			
Bolivia			
Colombia			
Ecuador			
Haiti			
Mexico			
Panama			
Peru			
Paraguay			
Uruguay			
Venezuela			
Taiwan	Disney Channel Taiwan[80]	March 28, 2008	《少年魔法師》

● Japan	Disney Channel Japan[81]		April 18, 2008	ウェイバリー通りのウィザードたち
■ Albania	Digitalb[82]		July, 2009	Magjistaret e sheshit Uejverli
▀ Chile	Disney Channel Latin America		March 23, 2008 (Advance) April 14, 2008 (Premiere)	*Los Hechiceros de Waverly Place'*
	Canal 13 (Chile)		March 6, 2010	
▐ Romania	Disney Channel Romania[83]		September 19, 2009	Magicienii Din Waverly Place
▀ Czech Republic	Disney Channel (Central and Eastern Europe)[84] [85] [86]		February 2009	*Kouzelníci z Waverly*
▀ Slovakia				
▬ Hungary				*Varázslók a Waverly helyből*
▀ Russia	CTC		November 2, 2009	*Волшебники из Вэйверли Плэйс*
	Disney Channel (Russia)		August 11, 2010	
▓ Serbia	Radio Television of Serbia[87]		June 27, 2010	Чаробњаци са Вејверли плејса
	Disney Channel Serbia[88]			
▀ Slovenia	Kanal A		August 1, 2010	Čarovniki s trga Waverly

References

[1] http://tv.disney.go.com/disneychannel/wizardsofwaverlyplace/index.html

[2] Robert Seidman (June 3, 2010). Disney Channel Renews "Wizards of Waverly Place" for a Fourth and Final Season; Plans Second Movie (http://tvbythenumbers.com/2010/06/03/disney-channel-renews-wizards-of-waverly-place-for-a-fourth-season/53112). TVbytheNumbers. Accessed 2010-11-15.

[3] Disney Orders 4th Season Of "Wizards Of Waverly Place" And Film Sequel (http://www.allheadlinenews.com/articles/7018896380) All Headline News June 4, 2010 12:49 p.m. EST

[4] Levin, Gary (October 18, 2007). "Nielsens: Friday night was 'Murder' on ABC" (http://www.usatoday.com/life/television/news/2007-10-17-nielsens-analysis_N.htm). *USA Today*. .

[5] "Disney Channel Shines with "Night of Stars" Programming Event" (http://tvbythenumbers.com/2009/02/17/disney-channel-shines-with-night-of-stars-programming-event/12981). .

[6] "Disney's "Wizards of Waverly Place" Hits Series Highs with 6.2 Million Viewers" (http://tvbythenumbers.com/2009/02/17/disney-channel-shines-with-night-of-stars-programming-event/12981). .

[7] Princess Protection Program is TV's No. 1 Entertainment Telecast of 2009 in Kids 6-11 and Tweens 9-14 (http://tvbythenumbers.com/2009/06/27/princess-protection-program-is-tvs-no-1-entertainment-telecast-of-2009-in-kids-6-11-and-tweens-9-14/21543)

[8] Seidman, Robert (2009-12-22). "Disney Channel Sets New Viewing Records in 2009" (http://tvbythenumbers.com/2009/12/22/disney-channel-sets-new-viewing-records-in-2009/36997). Tvbythenumbers.com. . Retrieved November 4, 2010.

[9] "Wizards of Waverly Place Movie" (http://www.disneychannelmedianet.com/DNR/2009/doc/WOWP_MoviePremiere.doc). Disney Channel. . Retrieved 2009-07-12.

[10] 'Wizards of Waverly Place: The Movie' Disney Channels Wizards of Waverly Place The Movie scores 11.4 million viewers (http://tvbythenumbers.com/2009/08/29/disney-channels-wizards-of-waverly-place-the-movie-scores-11-4-million-viewers/25660)

[11] Seidman, Robert. "Top 100 Most-Watched Telecasts On Basic Cable For 2009" (http://tvbythenumbers.com/2009/12/29/espn-domination-top-100-most-watched-telecasts-on-basic-cable-for-2009/37284). Tvbythenumbers.com. . Retrieved November 4, 2010.

[12] Disney Channel Renews "Wizards of Waverly Place" for a Fourth Season; Plans Second Movie (http://tvbythenumbers.com/2010/06/03/disney-channel-renews-wizards-of-waverly-place-for-a-fourth-season/53112)

[13] "Smarty Pants", season 2, episode 1 has Zeke in the credits; in "Movies", season 1, episode 9 he is called "Zack".

[14] "Amazon.com: Wizards of Waverly Place" (http://www.amazon.com/Wizards-Waverly-Place-Soundtrack/dp/B002BA9QMK/ref=sr_1_6?ie=UTF8&s=music&qid=1244079309&sr=8-6). Amazon.com. . Retrieved August 3, 2009.

[15] "Target - Wizards of Waverly Place Soundtrack" (http://www.target.com/Wizards-Waverly-Place-Soundtrack/dp/B002BA9QMK). Target.com Merchandise. . Retrieved August 3, 2009.

[16] Thomas Erlewine, Stephen (August 3, 2009). "allmusic {{{Wizards of Waverly Place: Songs from and Inspired by the Hit TV Series > Review}}}" (http://www.allmusic.com/album/r1612628). Allmusic. . Retrieved August 3, 2009.

[17] Kelly Grant, Brenda (July 23, 2009). "SELENA GOMEZ'S "MAGIC" MUSIC VIDEO PREMIERES FRIDAY, JULY 24 ON DISNEY CHANNEL" (http://disneychannelmedianet.com/DNR/2009/doc/MagicVideo_072309.doc). Disney Channel. . Retrieved August 3, 2009.

[18] "Disney 365 - Wizards Soundtrack" (http://disney.go.com/videos/#/videos/musicvideos/&content=358849). Disney.com. . Retrieved August 3, 2009.

[19] "Buy Music CDs, DVDs, Games, Consoles, Blu Ray, MP3s & More - hmv.com - Free Delivery" (http://hmv.com/hmvweb/displayProductDetails.do?ctx=280;-1;-1;-1;-1&sku=11116). hmv.com. 2005-12-15. . Retrieved November 4, 2010.

[20] "Wizards of Waverly Place [SOUNDTRACK (http://www.amazon.com/Wizards-Waverly-Place-Soundtrack/dp/B002BA9QMK/ref=sr_1_6?ie=UTF8&s=music&qid=1244079309&sr=8-6)"]. Amazon.com. . Retrieved 2009-06-09.

[21] Lambert, David (April 26, 2008). "Wizards of Waverly Place - Head to Wizard School this July with the First Release on DVD!" (http://tvshowsondvd.com/news/Wizards-Waverly-Place-Wizard-School/9472). TVShowsOnDVD.com. . Retrieved November 15, 2010.

[22] Sinnott, John (March 26, 2009). "The Wizards of Waverly, Vol. 2: Supernaturally Stylin'" (http://www.dvdtalk.com/reviews/36762/wizards-of-waverly-vol-2-supernaturally-stylin-the/). DVD Talk. . Retrieved November 15, 2010.

[23] Lambert, David (November 10, 2008). "Wizards of Waverly Place - Selena Gomez and the Waverly Place Cast are Supernaturally Stylin' in '09!" (http://tvshowsondvd.com/news/Wizards-Waverly-Place-Volume-2/10848). TVShowsOnDVD.com. . Retrieved November 15, 2010.

[24] DisneyDVD.com: Wizards on Deck with Hannah Montana (http://disneydvd.disney.go.com/wizards-on-deck-with-hannah-montana.html#27848)

[25] "Wizards Of Waverly Place - Series 1 Vol.1 DVD 2007: Amazon.co.uk: Selena Gomez: DVD" (http://www.amazon.co.uk/Wizards-Waverly-Place-Vol-1-DVD/dp/B002OSYFP2/ref=sr_1_1?ie=UTF8&s=dvd&qid=1254668699&sr=1-1). Amazon.co.uk. . Retrieved November 4, 2010.

[26] "From teen wizards to rock stars on Disney". Bribie Weekly: p. 12. January 8, 2010.

[27] "Wizards Of Waverly Place - Series 1 Vol.2 DVD 2007: Amazon.co.uk: Selena Gomez: DVD" (http://www.amazon.co.uk/Wizards-Waverly-Place-Vol-2-DVD/dp/B002OSYFPC/ref=pd_bxgy_d_h__img_b). Amazon.co.uk. . Retrieved November 4, 2010.

[28] "Jonas Thrice the Fun". Sunday Herald Sun: p. 4. May 30, 2010.

[29] "Wizards Of Waverly Place - Series 1 Vol.3 DVD 2007: Amazon.co.uk: Selena Gomez: DVD" (http://www.amazon.co.uk/Wizards-Waverly-Place-Vol-3-DVD/dp/B002OSYFPM/ref=pd_bxgy_d_h__img_c). Amazon.co.uk. . Retrieved November 4, 2010.

[30] "DVDS of the week". The Tweed Daily News: p. 32. August 21, 2010.

[31] "Die Zauberer vom Waverly Place - Die komplette erste Staffel 3 DVDs: Amazon.de: Selena Gomez, David Henrie, Jake T. Austin, John Adair, Steve Hampton, Ryan Elder, Robert Berlinger, Victor Gonzalez, Mark Cendrowski, Fred Savage, Joe Regalbuto, Andrew Tsao, Todd J. Greenwald: DVD & Blu-ray" (http://www.amazon.de/Die-Zauberer-vom-Waverly-Place/dp/B002CO8VF8/ref=sr_1_5?ie=UTF8&s=dvd&qid=1247937808&sr=8-5). Amazon.de. 2009-09-09. . Retrieved November 4, 2010.

[32] "Los Magos de Waverly Place - Primera Temporada DVD" (http://www.zonadvd.com/modules.php?name=News&file=article&sid=23282). ZONADVD.com. . Retrieved November 4, 2010.

[33] "Czarodzieje z Waverly Place sezon 1 [3DVD] za jedyne 99.99 PLN (Wizards of Waverly Place)" (http://www.dvdmax.pl/dvd/art/id/67508). Dvdmax.pl. . Retrieved November 4, 2010.

[34] "Alma Awards 2008" (http://www.almaawards.com/2008-nominees.html). AlmaAward.com. 2008. . Retrieved 2009-10-20.

[35] "Hbo'S Rodrigo Garcia, Ugly Betty'S Tony Plana And Writer Ligiah Villalobos Of La Misma Luna To Receive Top Honors" (http://www.imagen.org/awards/2008/nominees). Imagen.org. 2009. . Retrieved 2009-08-06.

[36] "The 40th NAACP Image Awards" (http://www.naacpimageawards.net/40/win_tv.php). Naacpimageawards.net. 2009. . Retrieved 2009-08-06.

[37] "Nickelodeon Kids' Choice Awards 2009 Press Kit" (http://www.nickkcapress.com/2009KCA/). Nickkcapress.com. 2009-03-30. . Retrieved 2009-08-06.

[38] "30th Annual Young Artist Awards" (http://www.youngartistawards.org/noms30.html). YoungArtistAwards.org. 2009-06-21. . Retrieved 2009-10-20.

[39] "Primetime Emmy Nominees & WinnersClick Drop-Down to Select Category" (http://www.emmys.com/nominations?tid=123). 2009-10-08. . Retrieved 2009-10-08.

[40] "Alma Awards 2009" (http://www.almaawards.com/2009-winners.html). AlmaAward.com. 2009. . Retrieved 2009-10-20.

[41] "Nominees for 24th Annual Imagen Awards Announced" (http://www.imagen.org/awards/2009/nominees). Imagen.org. 2009. . Retrieved 2009-12-21.

[42] "The 41st NAACP Image Awards" (http://www.naacpimageawards.net/41/nominees-and-voting/nominees/). Naacpimageawards.net. 2010. . Retrieved 2010-01-06.

[43] "2010 Nickelodeon Kids' Choice Awards" (http://www.chiff.com/pop-culture/kids-choice-awards.htm). Nickkcapress.com. 2010-02-14. . Retrieved 2010-02-14.

[44] "2010 Teen Choice Award Nominees" (http://www.chiff.com/pop-culture/teen-choice-awards.htm). TeenChoiceAwards.com. 2009-08-11. . Retrieved 2010-06-15.

[45] "2010 Teen Choice Award Nominees" (http://www.teenchoiceawards.com/pdf/TC10-Winners.pdf). TeenChoiceAwards.com. 2009-08-10. . Retrieved 2010-12-01.

[46] "Primetime Emmy Nominees & WinnersClick Drop-Down to Select Category" (http://www.emmys.com/nominations?tid=123). 2010-07-08. . Retrieved 2010-07-08.

[47] David Knox (2010-08-16). "Kid's Choice Awards: 2010 Nominees" (http://au.hadnews.com/kidsâ-choice-awards-2010-nominees.htm). *AU.HADNEWS.COM.* . Retrieved 2010-08-19.

[48] [www.bafta.org/awards/childrens/awards2010,1452,BA.html "The 2010 EA British Academy Children's Awards"]. *www.bafta.org*. 2010. www.bafta.org/awards/childrens/awards2010,1452,BA.html. Retrieved 2010-11-28.

[49] "HATA : 404 - Sayfa Bulunamadı!" (http://www.digiturk.gen.tr/theme/detail.aspx?content=3432). Digiturk. . Retrieved November 4, 2010.

[50] "disney wizards of waverly place" (http://www.disneychannel.com.tr/DisneyChannel/supersites/wizardsofwaverlyplace). Disneychannel.com.tr. . Retrieved November 4, 2010.

[51] "Wizards of Waverly Place | Disney Channel" (http://tv.disney.go.com/disneychannel/wizardsofwaverlyplace/index.html). Tv.disney.go.com. . Retrieved November 4, 2010.

[52] "Wizards of Waverly Place - Disney Channel Australia" (http://www.disney.com.au/DisneyChannel/wizardsofwaverlyplace/?utm_source=hp&utm_medium=charnav&utm_campaign=wizards). Disney.com.au. . Retrieved November 4, 2010.

[53] "Shows | Five" (http://www.five.tv/programmes/teen/wizards-of-waverly-place). Five.tv. . Retrieved November 4, 2010.

[54] "Wizards of Waverly Place - Disney Channel" (http://www2.disney.co.uk/DisneyChannel/supersites/wizardsofwaverlyplace/). .disney.co.uk. . Retrieved November 4, 2010.

[55] "Wizards of Waverly Place" (http://www.family.ca/wizardsofwaverlyplace//). family.ca. . Retrieved November 4, 2010.

[56] "Wizards of Waverly Place - Disney Channel" (http://www.disney.in/DisneyChannel/supersites/wizardsofwaverlyplace//). Disney.in. . Retrieved November 4, 2010.

[57] "Wizards of Waverly Places" (http://www.disneychannel-asia.com/DisneyChannel/supersites/wizardsofwaverlyplace///). Disney Channel Asia. . Retrieved November 4, 2010.

[58] "Wizards of Waverly Places" (http://www.disneychannel-asia.com/DisneyChannel/supersites/wizardsofwaverlyplace/). Disney Channel Asia. . Retrieved November 4, 2010.

[59] "Wizards of Waverly Place - Disney Channel" (http://www.disney.nl/DisneyChannel/supersites/wizardsofwaverlyplace/). Disney.nl. . Retrieved November 4, 2010.

[60] http://www.vrak.tv/emissions/les-sorciers-de-waverly-place/

[61] http://www.disney.fr/DisneyChannel/supersites/wizardsofwaverlyplace/

[62] http://www.nrj12.fr/la-chaine-3282/toutes-les-emissions-et-series-3289/emission/fiche/169-les-sorciers-de-waverly-place-saison-1.html

[63] http://disney.co.il/DisneyChannel/supersites/wizardsofwaverlyplace/

[64] http://tvradio.ert.gr/tv/details.asp?pid=3185795&chid=8

[65] http://www.tv.mediaset.it/italia1/i_maghi_di_waverly_place/index.shtml

[66] http://www.disney.fi/DisneyChannel/supersites/wizardsofwaverlyplace/

[67] http://www.disney.dk/DisneyChannel/supersites/wizardsofwaverlyplace/

[68] http://www.disney.se/DisneyChannel/supersites/wizardsofwaverlyplace/

[69] http://www.disney.no/DisneyChannel/supersites/wizardsofwaverlyplace/

[70] http://www.disney.de/DisneyChannel/supersites/wizardsofwaverlyplace/

[71] http://www.superrtl.de/InfosfürEltern/TOGGOInfosfürEltern/DieZauberervomWaverlyPlace/tabid/551/Default.aspx/

[72] http://www.sf.tv/sendungen/tubii/artikel.php?docid=serie-zauberer&catid=tubiiartikelprogramm

[73] http://okidoki.orf.at/?story=1782

[74] http://www.disney.es/DisneyChannel/supersites/wizardsofwaverlyplace/

[75] http://www.laguiatv.com/actualidad/noticias/41187/reportajes/antena-emitira-los-magos-waverly-place-otros-productos-disney.html/

[76] http://www.disney.pt/DisneyChannel/supersites/wizardsofwaverlyplace//

[77] http://sic.sapo.pt/online/sites+sic/disney+kids/series/feiticeirosdewaverlyplace.htm

[78] http://rd1audienciadatv.wordpress.com/2009/05/09/rede-globo-adquire-os-feiticeiros-de-waverly-place/

[79] http://www.disneylatino.com/disneychannel/wizardsofwaverlyplace/

[80] http://www.disney.com.tw/DisneyChannel/supersites/wizardsofwaverlyplace/

[81] http://www.disney.co.jp/records/wizard/

[82] http://www.digitalb.al/artikull.php?id=4753

[83] http://www.disney.ro/DisneyChannel/originalmovies/wizardsofwaverlyplacethemovie/

[84] http://www.disney.hu/DisneyChannel/originalmovies/wizardsofwaverlyplacethemovie/

[85] http://www.disney.cz/DisneyChannel/originalmovies/wizardsofwaverlyplacethemovie/

[86] http://www.disney.cz/DisneyChannel/originalmovies/wizardsofwaverlyplacethemovie//

[87] http://www.rts.rs/page/tv/ci/story/17/РТС+1/729338/Чаробњаци+са+Вејверли+плејса.html

[88] http://disneyxd.disney.rs/

External links

- Official website (http://tv.disney.go.com/disneychannel/wizardsofwaverlyplace)
- *Wizards of Waverly Place* (http://www.imdb.com/title/tt0799922/) at the Internet Movie Database
- *Wizards of Waverly Place* (http://www.tv.com/show/69866/summary.html) at TV.com
- Wizards of Waverly Place Wiki at Wikia

Another Cinderella Story

Another Cinderella Story	
Directed by	Damon Santostefano
Produced by	Dylan Sellers Damon Santostefano Clifford Werber Neal Dodson Chris Foss Michelle Johnston
Written by	Erik Patterson Jessica Scott
Starring	Selena Gomez Drew Seeley Jane Lynch Katharine Isabelle Emily Perkins Jessica Parker Kennedy Marcus T. Paulk Nicole LaPlaca
Music by	John Paesano Greg Cham Aragorn Wiederhold
Cinematography	Jon Joffin
Editing by	Tony Lombardo
Studio	CS2 Films Dylan Sellers Productions

Distributed by	Warner Bros. Warner Premiere
Release date(s)	September 16, 2008
Running time	88 min.
Country	Canada United States
Language	English
Preceded by	*A Cinderella Story*

Another Cinderella Story is a 2008 romantic comedy directed by Damon Santostefano and starring Selena Gomez and Drew Seeley. The film was released direct-to-DVD by Warner Premiere on September 16, 2008.[1] It was released on DVD in the UK on October 27, 2008.[2] It is a thematic sequel to the 2004 film *A Cinderella Story*, reprising the same themes and situations but not containing any characters from the earlier movie.

The movie was shot in Vancouver, British Columbia, Canada throughout January 2008,[3] and was essentially ignored by critics, but ranked as the number one cable movie in several key demographics when aired on the ABC Family on January 19, 2009. The soundtrack reached number eight on Billboard's soundtrack chart, with one single charting at position 58 on the Billboard Hot 100.

Plot

This movie is a retelling of the Cinderella fairy tale in a modern setting, with Mary Santiago (Selena Gomez), a high school student with ambitions of becoming a dancer, taking the role of Cinderella; Tami (Jessica Parker Kennedy) Mary's best and only friend helps her throughout the movie. Dominique Blatt (Jane Lynch) taking the role of the stepmother; Britt (Emily Perkins) and Bree (Katharine Isabelle) as the two stepsisters; and Joey Parker, (Drew Seeley) now a famous celebrity that has returned to school for his senior year (and also to find a girl to love, which is Mary Santiago), as the prince. A school dance substitutes for the ball, with the role of the glass slippers filled by a Zune.[4]

Cast

Cast	Role	Character Based on
Selena Gomez	Mary Santiago	Cinderella
Drew Seeley	Joey Parker/J.P.	Prince Charming
Jane Lynch	Dominique Blatt	Wicked Stepmother
Katharine Isabelle	Bree Blatt	Evil Stepsister
Emily Perkins	Britt Blatt	Evil Stepsister
Jessica Parker Kennedy	Tami	Fairy Godmother
Marcus T. Paulk	Dustin/The Funk	The Grand Duke
Nicole LaPlaca	Natalia Faroush	Lucifer

Reception

Critics

Amber Wilkinson of *Eye For Film* gave the film four out of five stars, saying that it was better than its predecessor, and praised the musical aspects, saying that "the song and dance numbers are so well-handled and catchy, it's a shame there aren't more of them." However, she also said that the "char[a]cters are so wafer thin they barely cast a shadow."[5] While Wilkinson says that the film is completely different from *A Cinderella Story*, Lacey Walker, reviewing for *Christian Answers*, notes several aspects of the two films that were directly parallel to each other. Walker also gave it three out of five stars, praising the script, saying the writers "peppered this story with a surprising dose of humor and some pleasing plot twists." However, Walker specifically criticized the "glaringly obvious" age difference between the 15 year old Gomez and the 25 year old Seeley.[6]

Ratings

ABC Family presented the television premiere of the film on January 18, 2009.[7] The premiere was watched by 5.3 million viewers. The movie ranked as January 2009's No. 1 cable movie across all key demos: Adults 18-34 (1.0 million, tie), Adults 18-49 (1.9 million) and Viewers 12-34 (2.3 million). In Females 12-34, ABC Family aired January 2009's Top 7 movies on all TV, led by the debut of "Another Cinderella Story" (1.8 million, 1/18/09, 8:00 p.m.) and namesake "A Cinderella Story" (978,000, 1/18/09, 6:00 p.m.). It aired on Disney Channel on July 11.[8] Source: Nielsen Media Research (National Ratings, January 2009: 12/29/08-1/25/09, Most Current: Live + SD, blended with Live + 7, when available).

Soundtrack

The soundtrack was released by Razor & Tie, and reached 116 on the Billboard 200 on Feb 27, 2009. It also reached number eight on Billboard's Soundtrack chart.[9]

Tracklist

No.	Title	Recording artist	Length
1.	"Tell Me Something I Don't Know"	Selena Gomez	3:20
2.	"New Classic (Single Version)"	Drew Seeley, Selena Gomez	3:08
3.	"Hurry Up and Save Me"	Tiffany Giardina	3:50
4.	"Just That Girl"	Drew Seeley	3:17
5.	"Bang a Drum"	Selena Gomez	3:12
6.	"1st Class Girl"	Drew Seeley, Marcus Paulk	3:00
7.	"On Hold 4 You"	Jane Lynch	2:29
8.	"Valentine's Dance Tango"	The Twins	2:12
9.	"No Average Angel"	Tiffany Giardina	2:57
10.	"Don't Be Shy"	Small Change, Lil' JJ, Chani	4:03
11.	"X-Plain it to My Heart"	Drew Seeley	1:15
12.	"New Classic (Live)"	Drew Seeley, Selena Gomez	5:29
13.	"Another Cinderella Story (Score Suite)"	John Paesano	2:39
14.	"New Classic (Acoustic Version)"	Drew Seeley, Selena Gomez	2:41

Tell Me Something I Don't Know

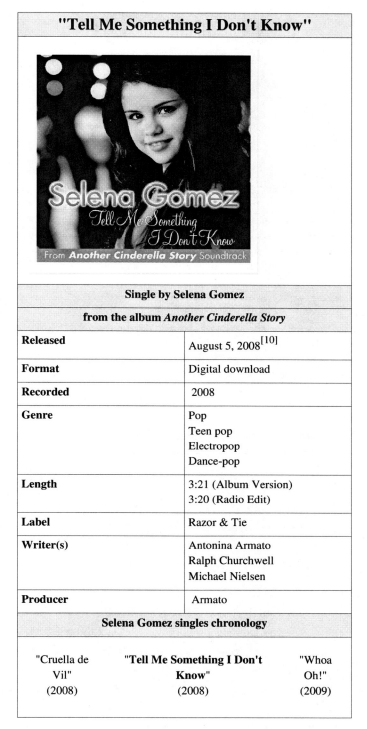

"Tell Me Something I Don't Know"	
Single by Selena Gomez	
from the album *Another Cinderella Story*	
Released	August 5, 2008[10]
Format	Digital download
Recorded	2008
Genre	Pop Teen pop Electropop Dance-pop
Length	3:21 (Album Version) 3:20 (Radio Edit)
Label	Razor & Tie
Writer(s)	Antonina Armato Ralph Churchwell Michael Nielsen
Producer	Armato
Selena Gomez singles chronology	

"Cruella de Vil" (2008)	"Tell Me Something I Don't Know" (2008)	"Whoa Oh!" (2009)

"Tell Me Something I Don't Know" by Selena Gomez was released as a single on August 5, 2008 on iTunes[10] and a Radio Disney version (which removes the Hurricane Katrina reference) was released on September 9, 2008 on iTunes. The song was also featured on the Kidz Bop 15 CD. A new version of the song is featured on Selena Gomez & the Scene's debut album, *Kiss & Tell*.

Music video

The music video starts with scenes reminiscent of (but not from) the film; Gomez cleaning a house and the maid yelling at her. Gomez then leaves the house and does a dance routine with her backup dancers, while the maid watches from the house window. The video also features Gomez in front of a black background with lyrics from the song (such as "I'm ready for it" and "One in a million") flying around her.[11]

Charts

Chart (2008)	Peak position
Australian Hitseekers Singles[12]	13
U.S. *Billboard* Hot 100[13]	58

References

[1] "Andrew Seeley Stars in Another Cinderella Story" (http://www.dvdactive.com/news/releases/another-cinderella-story.html). movieweb.com. .

[2] "Another Cinderella Story" (http://www.dvdactive.com/news/releases/another-cinderella-story2.html). movieweb.com. .

[3] "Drew Seeley Stars in Another Cinderella Story" (http://www.movieweb.com/news/71/25271.php). movieweb.com. .

[4] "Damon Santostefano Brings Us Another Cinderella Story" (http://www.movieweb.com/news/NEF41MHILy5yIO). movieweb.com. .

[5] Eye for Film "Another Cinderella Story Movie Review (2008)" (http://www.eyeforfilm.co.uk/reviews.php?film_id=15319). EyeforFilm.co.uk. Eye for Film.

[6] "Another Cinderella Story Movie Review" (http://www.christiananswers.net/spotlight/movies/2008/anothercinderellastory2008.html). christiananswers.net. .

[7] "ABC Family: Selena Gomez and Drew Seely in Another Cinderella Story" (http://abcfamily.go.com/abcfamily/path/section_Movies+ Another-Cinderella-Story/page_Detail). ABC.com. .

[8] "Battlestar Galactica Flies High, Tween Shows Fly Higher" (http://www.eonline.com/uberblog/ b80120_battlestar_galactica_flies_high_tween.html?utm_source=eonline&utm_medium=rssfeeds&utm_campaign=imdb_topstories). E Online.com. .

[9] Billboard "Another Cinderella Story - Billboard" (http://www.billboard.com/#/album/original-soundtrack/another-cinderella-story/ 1161121). Billboard.com. Billboard.

[10] Tell Me Something I Don't Know - single (http://itunes.apple.com/us/album/tell-me-something-i-dont-know/id286152910)

[11] "*Tell Me Something I Don't Know* Video - Selena Gomez - AOL Music" (http://music.aol.com/video/tell-me-something-i-dont-know/ selena-gomez/2239406). AOL.com. .

[12] "41205 Tell Me Something I Don't Know ARIA Peak Position" (http://pandora.nla.gov.au/pan/23790/20090220-0000/issue988.pdf). pandora.nla.gov.au. .

[13] "Tell Me Something I Don't Know Hot 100 Peak Position" (http://www.billboard.com/bbcom/esearch/chart_display.jsp?cfi=379& cfgn=Singles&cfn=The+Billboard+Hot+100&ci=3106116&cdi=10131142&cid=02/14/2009). billboard.com. .

External links

- Official website (http://http://anothercinderellastory.warnerbros.com)
- *Another Cinderella Story* (http://www.imdb.com/title/tt1071358/) at the Internet Movie Database
- *Another Cinderella Story* (http://www.allmovie.com/work/454235) at Allmovie
- *Another Cinderella Story* (http://www.rottentomatoes.com/m/Another_Cinderella_Story/) at Rotten Tomatoes
- *Another Cinderella Story* (http://tcmdb.com/title/title.jsp?stid=729492) at the TCM Movie Database

Princess Protection Program

Princess Protection Program	
The DVD cover for the film.	
Directed by	Allison Liddi-Brown
Produced by	Douglas Sloan
Written by	Annie DeYoung David Morgasen (Book)
Starring	Demi Lovato Selena Gomez Jamie Chung Samantha Droke Robert Adamson
Music by	John Van Tongeren
Cinematography	David A. Makin
Country	United States
Language	English
Original channel	Disney Channel Family
Release date	May 20, 2009 (France) June 26, 2009 (United States) (Canada)
Running time	88 minutes

Princess Protection Program is a 2009 Disney Channel Original Movie that premiered on June 26, 2009 in the United States and winner of the Teen Choice Awards 2009 for Choice Summer TV Show.[1] The film is directed by Allison Liddi-Brown, filmed in Puerto Rico[2] written by Annie DeYoung[3] and stars Selena Gomez and Demi Lovato. *Princess Protection Program* was watched by 9.8 million viewers, the third-highest premiere for a Disney Channel Original Movie.[4]

Plot

Princess Rosalinda Maria Montoya Fiore (Demi Lovato) is about to be crowned queen of the small nation of Costa Luna, to take her mother's role in sight of her father, the king's, death. General Kane (Johnny Ray Rodriguez), the dictator of neighboring country Costa Estrella, infiltrates her palace with his agents during her coronation rehearsal, and attempts to stage a coup d'etat against the royal family. Joe Mason (Tom Verica), an agent of the Princess Protection Program, a secret organization funded by royal families that looks after endangered princesses, whisks her away to safety via helicopter. Kane's agents succeed in capturing her mother, Queen Sophia.

The Princess Protection Program hides Rosalinda in Mr. Mason's home in Louisiana, where she is to pretend to be a typical American teenager named Rosie Gonzales. She meets Mr. Mason's daughter, Carter Mason (Selena Gomez), whose mother died and is also an insecure girl who works at the family bait shop and dreams of going to the homecoming dance with her crush, Donny (Robert Adamson). Though Carter is at first openly bitter and hostile towards Rosie, she warms up to her after Rosie explains her situation, and the two become close friends. Carter teaches Rosalinda to act like a normal girl and Rosie shows Carter how to disarm those that scorn them by behaving as a princess. Rosie soon becomes popular at their high school.

In an attempt to trick Rosalinda into exposing her location, General Kane announces plans to forcibly marry Rosalinda's mother. Rosalinda is distraught and tells Carter that she has decided to secretly return home. Knowing Costa Luna is still too dangerous, Carter secretly devises a plan to pose as Rosalinda and then use herself as bait to lure Kane into capture. Mr. Elegante, Rosalinda's royal dress maker, tells Kane that Rosalinda will be attending the homecoming dance and will be wearing a blue dress that he actually sends to Carter. In the meantime, Rosalinda agrees to help Carter behave like a princess by helping a group of girls dress up for the dance; The girls all wear masks, which helps Carter disguise herself as Rosalinda.

According to plan, Kane and his agents mistake Carter for Rosie and lead her to Kane's helicopter the night of the dance. However, Rosalinda narrowly discovers and ruins the plan by exposing herself to Kane, insisting that this is not Carter's fight. Fortunately, agents of the Princess Protection Program, including Mr. Mason, have been waiting inside the helicopter and rescue both girls. The PPP agents quickly apprehend Kane and his henchmen and turn them over to the international authorities.

At the end, Carter realizes what a jerk Donny is and goes to the dance with Ed, her best friend who has had a crush on her for a long time. Rosie is crowned Queen of Costa Luna with Carter, Mr. Mason, Ed, Rosalinda's mother, and Mr. Elegante in attendance.

Cast

- Selena Gomez as Carter Mason
- Demi Lovato as Princess Rosalinda
- Tom Verica as Major Mason
- Sully Diaz as Queen Sophia Fiore
- Johnny Ray Rodriguez as General Kane
- Jamie Chung as Chelsea Barnes
- Nicholas Braun as Edwin Tinka
- Robert Adamson as Donny Wilde
- Samantha Droke as Brooke Angels
- Kevin G. Schmidt as Bull Willilger
- Talia Rothenberg as Margaret Algoode
- Dale Dickey as Helen Digenerstet
- Ricardo Alvarez as Mr. Elegante
- Brian Tester as Principal Bull

Demi Lovato and Selena Gomez at the *Princess Protection Program* premiere

Awards

Year	Ceremony	Award	Result
2009	Teen Choice Awards	Choice Summer TV Movie	Won
		Choice Summer TV Star - Female: Selena Gomez	Won
		Choice Summer TV Star - Female: Demi Lovato	Nominated

Promotion

The film introduced two new songs: a duet recorded by Gomez and Lovato called "One And The Same" and a song recorded by Mitchel Musso called "The Girl Can't Help It." Both songs are featured on the Disney compilation album, *Disney Channel Playlist*, which was released on June 9, 2009.[5] The film also includes Lovato's song "Two Worlds Collide" which was first featured on her debut album *Don't Forget*. Disney Channel promoted the movie's premiere weekend by offering never-before-seen episodes of their original series' *Wizards of Waverly Place* and *Sonny With a Chance* as an online reward if viewers can correctly count the number of times the words "princess," "princesses," and "princesa" are spoken during the movie and enter the correct number, 86, into a section on their website.[6]

The DVD was released on June 30, 2009 in the US.[7] It also features the music video for Gomez & Lovato's duet "One and the Same" and a behind-the-scenes look at the movie. The DVD was released on June 18, 2009 in Germany[8] and four days later in the UK.[9]

Sequel

A sequel for the movie is in development and will be relased fall 2012. The plot of the movie will be "an endangered prince need help from the *Princess Protection Program*, this time Rossie and Carter will be the agents responsible for saving the prince". Is unknow if Selena Gomez or Demi Lovato will be reprise her roles, this is the cause for the sequell will be canceled.

Release

Country	Network(s)	Premiere	Movie Title in Country
France	Disney Channel France	May 20, 2009	Princess Protection Program: Mission Rosalinda
Germany	Disney Channel Germany	May 29, 2009	Prinzessinnen Schutzprogramm
	Pro 7	June 14, 2009	
	Super RTL	November 6, 2009	
Italy	Disney Channel Italy	June 8, 2009	Programma Protezione Principesse
	Italia 1	September 26, 2009	
Spain	Disney Channel Spain	June 13, 2009	Programa de Protección de Princesas
United Kingdom	Disney Channel UK	June 19, 2009	Princess Protection Programme
United States		June 26, 2009	Princess Protection Program
Portugal		June 20, 2009	Programa de Proteção de Princesas
Poland	Disney Channel Poland		Program Ochrony Księżniczek
Middle East	Disney Channel Middle East		Princess Protection Program
Latin America	Disney Channel Latin America	July 26, 2009	Programa de Protección para Princesas
Netherlands		October 03, 2009	Princess Protection Program
Australia		July 25, 2009	
Brazil	Disney Channel Latin America	July 26, 2009	Programa de Proteção para Princesas
Japan	Disney Channel Japan	August 15, 2009	プリンセス・プロテクション・プログラム
Estonia		August 28, 2009	
Norway	Disney Channel Scandinavia	August 28, 2009	Prosjekt Prinsesse
Sweden	Disney Channel Scandinavia	August 28, 2009	Projekt Prinsessa

Brunei	Disney Channel Asia	September 6, 2009	
Cambodia			
Hong Kong			
Indonesia			
Laos			
Malaysia			
Philippines			Princess Protection Program
Singapore			
South Korea			공주님은 내친구/프린세스 구출 대작전
Thailand			
Vietnam			Kế hoạch Bảo vệ Công chúa
Israel	Disney Channel Israel	September 9, 2009	תוכנית להגנת נסיכות
Taiwan	Disney Channel Taiwan	September 12, 2009	公主保衛戰
Romania	Disney Channel Romania	September 19, 2009	Programul de Protecţie al Prinţeselor
India	Disney Channel India	November 20, 2009	Princess Protection Program
Canada	Family / VRAK.TV	June 26, 2009 / March 1 2010	Princess Protection Program (English) Mission Rosalinda (French)
New Zealand			Princess Protection Program

References

[1] http://www.teenchoiceawards.com/pdf/TC09WINNERSFINALDB.pdf

[2] "*Princess Protection Program* production credits" (http://tv.nytimes.com/show/194599/Princess-Protection-Program/credits). New York Times. . Retrieved 2009-02-23.

[3] "Annie DeYoung" (http://www.imdb.com/name/nm0223395/). .

[4] "Top 100 Most-Watched Telecasts On Basic Cable For 2009" (http://tvbythenumbers.com/2009/12/29/espn-domination-top-100-most-watched-telecasts-on-basic-cable-for-2009/37284). . Retrieved 2010-09-21.

[5] "Disney Channel Playlist by Various Artists" (http://disneymusic.disney.go.com/albums/dcplaylist.html). Walt Disney Records. . Retrieved 2008-05-25.

[6] "Princess Protection Program - Original Movies - Disney Channel" (http://tv.disney.go.com/disneychannel/originalmovies/princessprotectionprogram/premierestunt/index.html). Disney Channel. . Retrieved 2009-06-28.

[7] "Princess Protection Program - On DVD - WD Home Entertainment" (http://disneydvd.disney.go.com/princess-protection-program.html). Walt Disney Studios Home Entertainment. . Retrieved 2009-06-06.

[8] Amazon.de (http://www.amazon.de/Prinzessinnen-Schutzprogramm-Demi-Lovato/dp/B0026L8M6A/ref=sr_1_1?ie=UTF8&s=dvd&qid=1241525486&sr=8-1)

[9] Play.com (http://www.play.com/DVD/DVD/4-/9292109/Princess-Protection-Program/Product.html)

External links

- Official website (http://http://tv.disney.go.com/disneychannel/originalmovies/princessprotectionprogram/)
- *Princess Protection Program* (http://www.imdb.com/title/tt1196339/) at the Internet Movie Database

Beezus Quimby

First appearance	Beezus and Ramona
Last appearance	Ramona's World
Created by	Beverly Cleary
Portrayed by	Lori Chodos (*Ramona*) Selena Gomez (*Ramona and Beezus*)
Gender	Female
Occupation	Student
Family	Mr. Robert Quimby (Father) Mrs. Dorothy Quimby (Mother) Ramona Quimby (Younger Sister) Roberta Quimby (Youngest Sister) Beatrice (Aunt) Howie Kemp (Cousin) Picky - Picky (Pet Cat)

Beatrice "Beezus" Quimby is a character from the Henry Huggins and Ramona series of books by Beverly Cleary. She is the friend of Henry, Mary Jane, and the older sister of Ramona and Roberta. Beezus earned her nickname from Ramona, who had a hard time saying Beatrice. Beezus' favorite aunt is Aunt Beatrice.

In some of the stories, Beezus is jealous of Ramona because she gets a lot of attention and because her art work is taped on the fridge. Beezus and Ramona is the only story that is written from Beezus' point of view. It is revealed that Beezus is the rightful owner of Picky-picky because she got him before Ramona was born. Beezus can be stubborn, and spends a lot of time looking at herself in the mirror. Beezus tries not to eat chocolate because of her acne.

In some stories, Beezus gets along with Ramona very well. Sometimes, Beezus doesn't. In Ramona's World, Beezus gets her ears pierced without her parents' permission and they let her off with a warning, and she starts to wear make up. She has a crush on Daisy Kidd's older brother Jeremy. Beezus makes her first appearance in the Henry series and continues to appear in the Ramona series. Beezus has a new baby sister named Roberta in Ramona Forever. Beezus loves reading, shown in Beezus and Ramona. Beezus makes a new friend in Ramona's World.

Film And Merchandise

In the 2010 movie *Ramona and Beezus*, Beezus is portrayed by teen star Selena Gomez. Joey King plays Beezus' pest of a sister Ramona Quimby. The film is live action and hit theaters July 23, 2010. The film does not focus on just one book, it goes from one book to another. The movie started filming in April 2009. Selena has made big sisters guides as well and there are also Ramona dolls now available from big companies like Madam Alexander.

In the 1988 Ramona TV show based on the "Ramona" books, Beezus is portrayed by Lori Chodos.

External links

- Beezus Quimby [1] at the Internet Movie Database

References

[1] http://www.imdb.com/character/ch0145900/

Ramona and Beezus

Ramona and Beezus
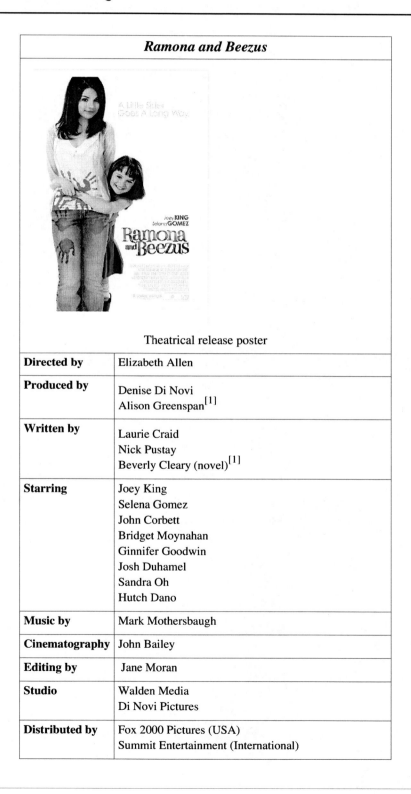 Theatrical release poster

Directed by	Elizabeth Allen
Produced by	Denise Di Novi Alison Greenspan[1]
Written by	Laurie Craid Nick Pustay Beverly Cleary (novel)[1]
Starring	Joey King Selena Gomez John Corbett Bridget Moynahan Ginnifer Goodwin Josh Duhamel Sandra Oh Hutch Dano
Music by	Mark Mothersbaugh
Cinematography	John Bailey
Editing by	Jane Moran
Studio	Walden Media Di Novi Pictures
Distributed by	Fox 2000 Pictures (USA) Summit Entertainment (International)

Release date(s)	July 23, 2010
Running time	104 minutes (57 minutes of Selena Gomez screen time)
Country	United States
Language	English
Budget	$15 million[2]
Gross revenue	$26,642,435[3]

Ramona and Beezus is a 2010 film adaptation of the book "*Beezus and Ramona*" by Beverly Cleary.[4] [5]

Plot

Young third grader Ramona (Joey King) has a vivid imagination, boundless energy, and accident-prone antics that keeps everyone she meets on their toes, especially her older sister Beezus (Selena Gomez) who is trying to get her cute crush, Henry (Hutch Dano), to go out with her. But her irrepressible sense of fun, adventure and mischief come in handy when she puts her mind to helping save her family's home before its too late.

Cast

- Joey King as Ramona Quimby
- Selena Gomez as Beezus Quimby
- Hutch Dano as Henry Huggins
- Ginnifer Goodwin as Aunt Bea
- John Corbett as Robert Quimby
- Bridget Moynahan as Dorothy Quimby
- Josh Duhamel as Hobart
- Jason Spevack as Howie Kemp
- Sandra Oh as Mrs. Meacham
- Aila and Zanti McCubbing as Roberta Quimby
- Sierra McCormick as Susan Kushner
- Patti Allan as Mrs. Pitt
- Lynda Boyd as Triplet mother

Release

Ramona and Beezus was released in theaters on July 23, 2010, by 20th Century Fox and Walden Media to 2,719 theaters nationwide, and was rated G by MPAA, becoming the studio's fourth film to be rated G since 1997's *Anastasia*.

The trailer was released on March 18, 2010, and was shown in theaters along with *How to Train Your Dragon*, *The Last Song*, *Despicable Me*, *Toy Story 3*, and 20th Century Fox's other films, including *Diary of a Wimpy Kid* and *Marmaduke*. The film premiered in New York on July 20, 2010.

It was released in Irish and British cinemas October 22, 2010.

Critical reception

Ramona and Beezus earned generally positive reviews. Review aggregator Rotten Tomatoes reports that 74% of critics have given the film a positive review based on 68 reviews, for an average rating of 6.3/10.[6] Among Rotten Tomatoes' "Top Critics", consisting of notable critics from the top newspapers and websites,[7] the film holds an overall approval rating of 73%, based on a sample of 26 reviews.[8] The film holds a 56 rating on Metacritic, based on 28 reviews.[9] Eric Snider of Film.com said that "The resulting story is a jumble, and there are too many side characters, but golly if it isn't pretty darned infectious."[10] Jason Anderson of the *Toronto Star* gave *Ramona and Beezus* a good review, saying that "(Ramona and Beezus) is a lively affair, largely thanks to the sweet and snappy screenplay by Laurie Craig and Nick Pustay and to the appealing performances by the cast."[11]

Box office

The film opened at #4 on opening day, grossing under $3 million.[12] It would earn altogether $7.8 million on its opening weekend, earning #6 at the box office. Over its first week, it earned nearly $12.7 million.[13] As of November 20, 2010, its total gross stands at $26,645,939,[3] surpassing its $15 million budget. The film made £84,475 on it's first week-end in the UK (information based on the UK film council).

Home media

The film was released on DVD and Blu-ray combo pack on November 9, 2010.

Soundtrack

Currently, there is only one confirmed track for the film's soundtrack entitled "Live Like There's No Tomorrow", performed by Selena Gomez & the Scene. The song was digitally released as a soundtrack single on July 13, 2010.[14] The song is also part of the band's second album, *A Year Without Rain*. It is unknown whether or not there will be a music video. Other songs in the movie, that may be included on the soundtrack, include "A Place in This World" by Taylor Swift, "Say Hey (I Love You)" by Michael Franti & Spearhead, a song from Peter, Paul, and Mary, "Here It Goes Again" by OK Go, a cover of "Walking on Sunshine by Aly & AJ, Eternal Flame by The Bangles and "(Let's Get Movin') Into Action" by Skye Sweetnam featuring Tim Armstrong.

"Live Like There's No Tomorrow"

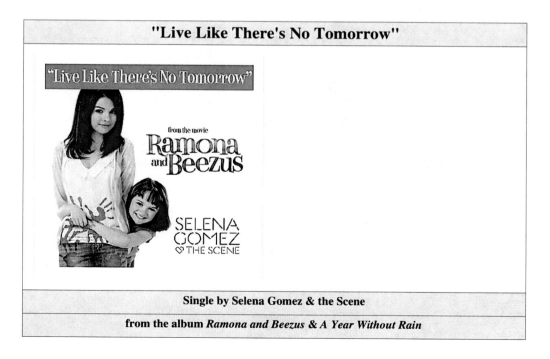

"Live Like There's No Tomorrow"
Single by Selena Gomez & the Scene
from the album *Ramona and Beezus & A Year Without Rain*

Released	July 13, 2010
Format	Digital download
Recorded	2010
Genre	Pop, Soft rock, Ballad
Length	4:07
Writer(s)	Matt Bronleewe, Nicky Chinn, Andrew Fromm, Meghan Kabir
Producer	Superspy

Selena Gomez & the Scene singles chronology		
"Round & Round" (2010)	"Live Like There's No Tomorrow" (2010)	"A Year Without Rain" (2010)

"Live Like There's No Tomorrow" was released as a single from the upcoming *Ramona and Beezus* soundtrack album on July 13, 2010.[14] This is the one confirmed track of the soundtrack thus far. There is currently no music video for the single. It is performed by Selena Gomez & the Scene and also appears on their *A Year Without Rain* album.

References

[1] "Ramona and Beezus - IMDb Credits" (http://www.imdb.com/title/tt0493949/fullcredits). IMDb.com. . Retrieved 2009-06-22.

[2] Siegel, Tatiana (July 17, 2010). "Female power pushes 'Ramona'" (http://www.variety.com/article/VR1118021858. html?categoryid=2520&cs=1). *Variety*. .

[3] "*Ramona and Beezus* (2010)" (http://boxofficemojo.com/movies/?id=ramona.htm). Box Office Mojo. IMDb. October 31, 2010. . Retrieved Noverber 1, 2010.

[4] Vena, Jocelyn. "Selena Gomez To Star In 'Ramona and Beezus' Movie." (http://www.mtv.com/movies/news/articles/1604489/story. jhtml) MTV.com, 2009-02-06.

[5] Kilday, Gregg. "Young actresses cast for 'Beezus and Ramona.'" (http://www.reuters.com/article/filmNews/idUSTRE51515A20090206) Reuters, 2009-02-05.

[6] "Ramona and Beezus (2010)" (http://www.rottentomatoes.com/m/ramona_and_beezus/). *Rotten Tomatoes*. . Retrieved July 31, 2010.

[7] "Rotten Tomatoes FAQ: What is Cream of the Crop" (http://www.rottentomatoes.com/pages/faq#creamofthecrop). *Rotten Tomatoes*. . Retrieved May 7, 2010.

[8] "Ramona and Beezus (2010)" (http://www.rottentomatoes.com/m/ramona_and_beezus/?critic=creamcrop). *Rotten Tomatoes*. . Retrieved May 27, 2010.

[9] Ramona and Beezus Reviews, Ratings, Credits, and More at Metacritic (http://www.metacritic.com/film/titles/ramonaandbeezus)

[10] Review: Ramona and Beezus Pleases - Film.com (http://www.film.com/features/story/review-ramona-and-beezus-pleases/39369882)

[11] Anderson, Jason (July 23, 2010). "Ramona and Beezus: A family film with a dose of reality" (http://www.thestar.com/entertainment/ movies/article/838995--ramona-and-beezus-a-family-film-with-a-dose-of-reality). *The Star* (Toronto). .

[12] Daily Box Office for Friday, July 23, 2010 - Box Office Mojo (http://boxofficemojo.com/daily/chart/?sortdate=2010-07-23&p=.htm)

[13] Ramona and Beezus (2010) - Weekly Box Office Results - Box Office Mojo (http://boxofficemojo.com/movies/?page=weekly& id=ramona.htm)

[14] Live Like There's No Tomorrow (From "Ramona and Beezus") - Single by Selena Gomez & The Scene - Download Live Like There's No Tomorrow (From "Ramona and Beezus") - Single on i... (http://itunes.apple.com/us/album/live-like-theres-no-tomorrow/id380017649)

External links

- Official website (http://http://www.ramonaandbeezus.com/)
- *Ramona and Beezus* (http://www.imdb.com/title/tt0493949/) at the Internet Movie Database
- *Ramona and Beezus* (http://www.boxofficemojo.com/movies/?id=ramona.htm) at Box Office Mojo
- *Ramona and Beezus* (http://www.rottentomatoes.com/m/Ramona_and_Beezus/) at Rotten Tomatoes

Selena Gomez & the Scene

Selena Gomez & the Scene	
Left to right: Ethan Roberts, Joey Clement, Selena Gomez, Dane Forrest, and Greg Garman	
Background information	
Origin	Hollywood, California, United States
Genres	Electropop, Dance-pop[1] Pop rock, Pop-punk[2] , Pop[3]
Years active	2008–present
Labels	Hollywood
Website	http://www.selenagomez.com
Members	
Selena Gomez Greg Garman Joey Clement Ethan Roberts Dane Forrest	
Past members	
Nick Foxer	

Selena Gomez & the Scene is an American pop band from Hollywood, California that formed in 2008. The band consists of Selena Gomez on lead vocals, Ethan Roberts on guitar, Joey Clement on bass, Greg Garman on drums, and Dane Forrest on keyboards.

History

2008–09: Formation and *Kiss & Tell*

During an interview with Jocelyn Vena, of MTV in August 2008, Selena Gomez said of her future music career that: "I'm going to be in a band. I'm not going to be a solo artist...I don't want my name attached to it. I will be singing..."[4] Gomez later announced, via Twitter, that the band would be called The Scene.[5] It is an "ironic jab" at the people who called the frontwoman "wannabe scene."[5] Gomez has also stated that the band name, which was originally intended to be just The Scene, became *Selena Gomez* & The Scene due to complications with Hollywood Records.[6] Due to this, the band is sometimes incorrectly credited as just Selena Gomez. The band released their debut studio album, *Kiss & Tell* on September 29, 2009. The album debuted at number 9 on the U.S. Billboard 200 with sales of 66,000 copies in its first week of release.[7] Gomez has said in several interviews (including one with Z100 New York)[8] that the band was formed through a long, exhausting audition process. She said it was worth it, though, because she has a great band. However, not long after joining the band, keyboardist Nick Foxer left for unknown reasons, and was replaced by Dane Forrest.

Kiss & Tell is the band's debut studio album and was released on September 29, 2009 by Hollywood Records. Gomez worked with several writers and producers on the album including Gina Schock of the Go-Go's. Musically, the album has a combination of different styles, prominently rock, and dance elements.[9] The album debuted at number 9 on the Billboard 200.[7] On March 5, 2010, the album was certified Gold by the RIAA for sales of 500,000 in the US.[10]

Gomez confirmed that she co-wrote one song on the album entitled "I Won't Apologize". The lead single "Falling Down" was released on August 21, 2009. The music video premiered after the world premiere of Gomez' TV-movie *Wizards of Waverly Place: The Movie* on August 28, 2009. It peaked at number 82 on the U.S. Billboard Hot 100 and at number 69 on the Canadian Hot 100.[11] The second single from the album, "Naturally" was released on December 11, 2009 along with a music video for digital download. The music video was shot on November 14, 2009 and premiered on Disney Channel following the premiere of *Phineas and Ferb Christmas Vacation* on December 11, 2009. The single debuted at number 39 and later peaked at number 29 on the Billboard Hot 100 and has peaked at number 18 on the Canadian Hot 100. It is the band's biggest hit to date and first top 40 hit beating out their first single "Falling Down" and also their first number 1 hit on the "Billboard Hot Dance/Club Songs".[12] "Naturally" had its highest peak in Hungary where it peaked at number 4 on the regions chart, becoming the band's first Top Five hit. On July 15, 2010, the single was certified Platinum by the RIAA for sales of 1,000,000 in the US.[10]

The band has gone on a few tours including their House of Blues Tour and Kiss & Tell Tour, and have had a European Promo Tour to promote the album overseas.[13] Gomez and the rest of the band performed on various TV shows and Special events such as on *Dancing with the Stars* season nine,[14] *The Ellen DeGeneres Show*,[15] [16] *Late Night With Jimmy Fallon*,[17] and *Dick Clark's New Year's Rockin' Eve with Ryan Seacrest*[18] among other shows. Selena Gomez & the Scene along with Justin Bieber played at the 2010 Houston Livestock Show and Rodeo, and the band and Justin Bieber also co-headlined Popcon.[19]

Selena Gomez & the Scene contributed to Disney's *All Wrapped Up Vol. 2*. The EP includes the band's cover of "Winter Wonderland" as well as Christmas covers by other successful artists.[20] Their single "Falling Down" was featured on *Radio Disney Jams, Vol. 12*, along with songs by other popular artists. *Jams 12* was officially released on March 30, 2010.[21] On March 9, 2010 The Scene released their EP *Naturally (The Remixes)*. The EP featured remixes of their highest charting single "Naturally" by Dave Audé, Ralphi Rosario, and Disco Fries, as well as the original track.[22]

2010–present: *A Year Without Rain*

The band's second studio album, *A Year Without Rain* was released on September 17, 2010.[23] It debuted on the US Billboard 200 at number 4, with sales of a little over 66,000, barely beating out *Kiss & Tell*. The sophomore effort continues with the Dance-pop/Electronica style of the group's hit single "Naturally". "I think we wanted to do something a little fun. We wanted to do a techno vibe," said lead singer Selena Gomez. Gomez said in an interview with Z100 New York[8] that it would feature some songs that did not make it onto the first album and that the rest of the band would be much more included on it. In an interview with MTV, Gomez said, "I'm really proud of this record, it's very different, and kind of shows my growth a little bit in [our] music... I think if anything the lyrics are more powerful, in a way."

The record's first single, "Round & Round", premiered on June 18, 2010.[24] The accompanying music video, which was filmed in Budapest, premiered two days later.[25] The single was released on June 22, 2010.[26] It debuted at number 24 on Billboard's Hot 100, and 76 on the Canadian Hot 100. It also debuted at number 15 on Billboard's Digital Songs chart[27] and number 47 in the UK. The album's second single "A Year Without Rain" was released on September 7, 2010. The music video premiered on September 3, 2010, after the world premiere of *Camp Rock 2: The Final Jam*. Selena & the Scene have performed "Round & Round" live on *America's Got Talent*, Blue Peter, Daybreak, and MTV's The Seven; "Round & Round" and "A Year Without Rain" live on *Good Morning America*; and "A Year Without Rain" live on *The Ellen DeGeneres Show* and *Lopez Tonight*. On October 27, the band played an acoustic set for charity (Unicef). They will also be playing the Jingle Ball later in the year.

On July 13, Selena Gomez & the Scene's song "Live Like There's No Tomorrow" was released as a single from the forthcoming *Ramona and Beezus* soundtrack.[28] The song is also a track on *A Year Without Rain*.[29] [30] .

Members

Current band members

- Selena Gomez - Lead vocals
- Greg Garman- Drums[31]
- Joey Clement - Bass, backing vocals[32]
- Ethan Roberts - Guitar, vocals[33]
- Dane Forrest - Keyboards, backing vocals

Former band members

- Nick Foxer - Keyboards, backing vocals[34]

Discography

- *Kiss & Tell* (2009)
- *A Year Without Rain* (2010)

Tours

- 2009: House of Blues Tour
- 2009-2010: Kiss & Tell Tour
- 2010: Fairs & Festivals Tour
- 2010-2011: A Year Without Rain Tour

Awards and nominations

Year	Title	Award	Nominated work	Result
2010	Teen Choice Awards	Choice: Music Group[35]	Selena Gomez & the Scene	Won
		Choice: Breakout Artist Female[36]		
	MTV Europe Music Awards	Best Push Act[37]		Nominated
2011	37th People's Choice Awards	Favorite Breakout Artist[38]		Pending

References

[1] http://www.allmusic.com/artist/selena-gomez-p1063097

[2] http://www.allmusic.com/artist/selena-gomez-p1063097

[3] http://www.allmusic.com/artist/selena-gomez-p1063097

[4] Jocelyn Vena (2008-08-07). "Selena Gomez forming a band" (http://www.mtv.com/news/articles/1592286/20080806/id_0.jhtml). *MTV.com*. . Retrieved 2009-10-27.

[5] "Selena Gomez's The Scene And Six More Of The Most Boring Band Names Of All Time » MTV Newsroom" (http://newsroom.mtv.com/2009/08/13/selena-gomez/). Newsroom.mtv.com. 2009-08-13. . Retrieved 2010-03-14.

[6] http://www.youtube.com/watch?v=7B_Xg0ClSwQ

[7] Caulfield, Keith; Herrera, Monica (October 7, 2009). "Barbra Streisand Surprises With Ninth No. 1 On Billboard 200" (http://www.billboard.com/#/news/barbra-streisand-surprises-with-ninth-no-1004019217.story). Billboard. . Retrieved 2009-10-07.

[8] "Media Player" (http://www.z100.com/cc-common/mediaplayer/player.html?redir=yes&mps=jj.php&mid=http://a1135.g.akamai.net/f/1135/18227/1h/cchannel.download.akamai.com/18227/podcast/NEWYORK-NY/WHTZ-FM/Selena int. mp3?CPROG=PCAST?CCOMRRMID&CPROG=RICHMEDIA&MARKET=NEWYORK-NY&NG_FORMAT=chr&NG_ID=whtz100fm&OR_NEWSFORMAT=&OWNER=&SERVER_NAME=www.z100.com&SITE_ID=1793&STATION_ID=WHTZ-FM&TRACK=). Z100.com. . Retrieved 2010-03-14.

[9] "Kiss and Tell: Selena Gomez and the Scene: Music" (http://www.amazon.com/Kiss-Tell-Selena-Gomez-Scene/dp/B001QXE0OC). Amazon.com. . Retrieved 2010-03-14.

[10] RIAA - GOLD & PLATINUM (http://www.riaa.com/goldandplatinumdata.php?resultpage=1&table=SEARCH_RESULTS&action=&title=&artist=selena gomez &format=&debutLP=&category=&sex=&releaseDate=&requestNo=&type=&level=&label=&company=&certificationDate=&awardDescription=&catalogNo=&aSex=&rec_id=&charField=&gold=&platinum=&multiPlat=&level2=&certDate=&album=&id=&after=on&before=on&startMonth=1&endMonth=8&startYear=1958&endYear=2010&sort=Artist&perPage=25)

[11] "Selena Gomez & The Scene - Falling Down - Music Charts" (http://acharts.us/song/49198). Acharts.us. . Retrieved 2010-03-14.

[12] "Selena Gomez & The Scene - Naturally - Music Charts" (http://acharts.us/song/52715). Acharts.us. . Retrieved 2010-03-14.

[13] "Selena Gomez op MySpace Music – Gratis gestreamde MP3's, foto's en Videoclips" (http://www.myspace.com/selenagomez). Myspace.com. 1992-07-22. . Retrieved 2010-03-14.

[14] September 29, 2009 (2009-09-29). "Selena Gomez & The Scene Perform On Dancing With The Stars Results Show | Neon Limelight - Exclusive Music News, Artist Interviews, Reviews, Photos!" (http://neonlimelight.com/2009/09/29/selena-gomez-the-scene-perform-on-dancing-with-the-stars-results-show/). Neon Limelight. . Retrieved 2010-05-29.

[15] "Watch Selena Gomez & The Scene Perform "Naturally" -- and More!" (http://ellen.warnerbros.com/2009/12/selena_gomez_the_scene_1211.php?adid=selena_gomez_the_scene_1211_sphere_ellen). *The Ellen DeGeneres Show*. Warner Bros. 2009-12-11. . Retrieved 2010-01-19.

[16] "Ellen's Music: Selena Gomez" (http://ellen.warnerbros.com/music/selena-gomez.php). *The Ellen DeGeneres Show*. Warner Bros. 2009-12-11. . Retrieved 2010-01-19.

[17] "Selena Gomez Interview (2/12/10) - Video - NBC.com" (http://www.latenightwithjimmyfallon.com/video/selena-gomez-interview-21210/1201192/). Late Night with Jimmy Fallon. . Retrieved 2010-05-29.

[18] "DICK CLARK'S NEW YEAR'S ROCKIN' EVE (12/31) : J!-ENT entertainment news pop culture TV music DVD Blu-ray reviews fashion celebrity USA Asia UK" (http://www.nt2099.com/J-ENT/news/american-entertainment/dick-clarks-new-years-rockin-eve-1231/). Nt2099.com. 2009-12-08. . Retrieved 2010-03-14.

[19] "Selena Gomez & Justin Beiber Houston Livestock Show & Rodeo" (http://www.rodeohouston.com/concerts/selena-gomez-justin-bieber.aspx). Rodeohouston.com. 2010-03-21. . Retrieved 2010-05-29.

[20] "All Wrapped Up, Vol. 2: Jordan Pruitt, Jesse McCartney, Jonas Brothers, Honor Society, Selena Gomez & the Scene, Steve Rushton, Anna Margaret: Music" (http://www.amazon.com/All-Wrapped-Up-Vol-2/dp/B002SQJ3ZW). Amazon.com. . Retrieved 2010-03-14.

[21] "Radio Disney Jams 12: Various Artists: Music" (http://www.amazon.com/gp/product/B0038M61CS). Amazon.com. . Retrieved 2010-05-29.

[22] "Selena Gomez & The Scene – Naturally (Remixes) (Promo CDM)-2010" (http://www.hiphopforfree.com/2010/01/25/selena-gomez-the-scene-naturally-remixes-promo-cdm-2010/). Hiphopforfree.Com. 2010-01-25. . Retrieved 2010-05-29.

[23] "Year Without Rain PL Wykonawca:Gomez Selena Data ([[Polish language|Polish (http://www.empik.com/year-without-rain-pl-gomez-selena,prod58634942,muzyka-p)])"]. . Retrieved 2010-09-21.

[24] "Selena Gomez ROUND AND ROUND" (http://www.oceanup.com/2010/05/26/selena-gomez-round-and-round). oceanUP.com. . Retrieved 2010-05-29.

[25] "Selena Gomez - Selena Gomez - Round & Round Sneakpeak 3" (http://www.twitvid.com/TGCOF). TwitVid. . Retrieved 2010-09-12.

[26] "Round & Round - Single by Selena Gomez & the Scene" (http://itunes.apple.com/us/album/round-round-single/id376899592). *iTunes*. . Retrieved 2010-06-30.

[27] "Top 100 Music Hits, Top 100 Music Charts, Top 100 Songs & The Hot 100" (http://www.billboard.com/charts/hot-100?tag=chscr1#/artist/selena-gomez/1011432). Billboard.com. . Retrieved 2010-09-12.

[28] "Live Like There's No Tomorrow (From "Ramona and Beezus") - Single by Selena Gomez & The Scene - Download Live Like There's No Tomorrow (From "Ramona and Beezus") - Single on iTunes" (http://itunes.apple.com/us/album/live-like-theres-no-tomorrow/ id380017649). Itunes.apple.com. 2010-07-13. . Retrieved 2010-09-12.

[29] "A Year Without Rain: Selena Gomez & The Scene: Music" (http://www.amazon.com/Year-Without-Selena-Gomez-Scene/dp/ B003YCI1PM/). Amazon.com. 2009-09-09. . Retrieved 2010-09-12.

[30] "A Year Without Rain [Deluxe Edition]: Selena Gomez & The Scene: Music" (http://www.amazon.com/Year-Without-Rain-Deluxe/dp/ B003Y66MTA/). Amazon.com. 2009-09-09. . Retrieved 2010-09-12.

[31] Artist Feature: Greg Garman of Selena Gomez and The Scene (2010-03-23). "Artist Feature: Greg Garman of Selena Gomez and The Scene" (http://boomdrum.com/artist-feature/artist-feature-greg-garman-selena-gomez-scene). Boom Drum. . Retrieved 2010-09-12.

[32] http://www.takamine.com/?fa=artist&id=977

[33] http://www.takamine.com/?fa=artist&id=974

[34] by Idolator. "Selena Gomez & The Scene" (http://soundmaven.com/artist/Selena+Gomez+%26+The+Scene/). soundmaven.com. . Retrieved 2010-09-12.

[35] "Teen Choice Awards 2010 - Music "Your Choice, Your Voice!"" (http://www.teenchoiceawards.com/vote-music.php). Teenchoiceawards.com. . Retrieved 2010-09-12.

[36] "Teen Choice Awards 2010 - Music "Your Choice, Your Voice!"" (http://www.teenchoiceawards.com/vote-music.php). Teenchoiceawards.com. . Retrieved 2010-09-12.

[37] "MTV EMA 2010 Artists Selena Gomez and the Scene" (http://ema.mtv.co.uk/artists/selena-gomez-scene). MTV EMA. . Retrieved 2010-09-19.

[38] "Favorite Breakout Artist" (http://www.peopleschoice.com/pca/vote/votenow.jsp). http://www.peopleschoice.com/pca/. . Retrieved 2010-11-09.

Barney & Friends

Barney & Friends	
 Barney & Friends season 3 logo	
Format	Children's television series
Created by	Sheryl Leach[1]
Starring	David Joyner, Carey Stinson, and Josh Martin (Barney suit) Bob West and Dean Wendt (Barney voice) Jeff Ayers (Baby Bop suit) Julie Johnson (Baby Bop voice) Patty Wirtz (B.J. voice) Kyle Nelson (B.J. suit) Adam Brown (Riff suit) Michaela Dietz (Riff voice)
Country of origin	United States
Language(s)	English
No. of episodes	248 (List of episodes)
Production	
Running time	30 Minutes
Production company(s)	The Lyons Group (1992–2001) HiT Entertainment[2] (2001–present) Connecticut Public Television(1992–2005) WNET New York (2006–present)
Broadcast	
Original channel	PBS[3]
Picture format	NTSC (480i) (1992-2008) HDTV (1080i) (2009-present)
Original airing	April 6, 1992
Status	On Hiatus
Chronology	
Preceded by	Barney and the Backyard Gang

Barney & Friends is an independent children's television show produced in the United States, aimed at very young children ages 1–8. The series, which first aired in 1992, features the title character *Barney*, a purple anthropomorphic *Tyrannosaurus rex* who conveys learning through songs and small dance routines with a friendly, optimistic attitude.[4] [5] [6] [7]

Origin and development

Barney & Friends season 1 title card.

Barney was created in 1987 by Sheryl Leach of Dallas, Texas.[8] She came up with the idea for the program while considering TV shows that she felt would be educational and appeal to her son. Leach then brought together a team who created a series of home videos, *Barney and the Backyard Gang*, which also starred actress Sandy Duncan in the first 3 videos.[9] Later, Barney was joined by the characters *Baby Bop*, *BJ*, and *Riff*.

Although the original videos were only a modest success outside of Texas, Barney became a major success only when the character and format were revamped for the television series and were picked up by the Public Broadcasting Service (PBS), debuting as *Barney & Friends* in 1992.[10] The series was produced by Lyrick Studios (bought by HIT Entertainment) and Connecticut Public Television.[11] For several years, the show was taped at the ColorDynamics Studios facility at Greenville Avenue & Bethany Drive in Allen, after which it moved to *The Studios at Las Colinas* in Dallas, Texas. Currently, the series is produced in Carrollton, Texas, a suburb of Dallas. The TV series and videos are currently distributed by HiT Entertainment and Lionsgate, while the TV series has been produced by WNET since 2006. Sheryl Leach left the show in 2002 after HIT Entertainment bought Lyrick Studios.

Formula of the program

Each episode follows the same sequence.

Opening sequence

The series opens with the theme song (complete with clips from various episodes) and the title card before it dissolves into the school. The stuffed Barney doll, who is interacted on by the children, dissolves into the 'real' Barney with imagination with him jumping to the floor and the children yelling "Barney".

Main sequence

Here, the main plot of the episode takes place. Barney and the children learn about the subject, with Baby Bop, BJ or Riff appearing at random points within the episode and numerous songs themed to the subject featured in the series. The roles of Baby Bop, BJ and Riff have grown larger in later seasons and later episodes venture outside of the school to other places within the neighborhood and to other countries around the world in Season 13.

Closing sequence

Barney closes up with "I Love You" before he dissolves back into his original stuffed form. After the children discuss a bit about what they had learned, the sequence cuts to *Barney Says* where Barney, who is off-screen, goes over what he and his friends had done that day, along with still snapshots from the episode. Then Barney, himself, appears on-screen saying "And remember, I love you" before the credits role.

Criticism

Although the show has been criticized for its lack of educational value,[12] Yale researchers Dorothy and Jerome Singer have concluded that episodes contain a great deal of age-appropriate educational material, calling the program a *"model of what preschool television should be."*[13]

One specific criticism is:

[H]is shows do not assist children in learning to deal with negative feelings and emotions. As one commentator puts it, the real danger from Barney is denial: the refusal to recognize the existence of unpleasant realities. For along with his steady diet of giggles and unconditional love, Barney offers our children a one-dimensional world where everyone must be happy and everything must be resolved right away.[14]

It is ranked on TV Guide's List of the 50 Worst TV Shows of All Time at #50.[15]

Cast

Dinosaurs

Barney the Dinosaur

The protagonist is a purple and green Tyrannosaurus Rex in stuffed animal likeness, who comes to life through a child's imagination. His theme song is "Barney Is a Dinosaur," which is sung to the tune of "Yankee Doodle". Barney often quotes things as being "Super dee-duper". Episodes frequently end with the song "I Love You", sung to the tune of "This Old Man", which happens to be Barney's favorite song of all time. Despite being a *carnivorous* type dinosaur, Barney likes many different foods such as fruits and vegetables, but his main favorite is a peanut butter and jelly sandwich with a glass of milk. He also loves Marching bands and parades.

Baby Bop

A three-year-old green Triceratops, Baby Bop has been on the show since July 29, 1991 (from the video "Barney in Concert"). She carries a yellow blanket, and sings the song "My Yellow Blankey" to show how much it means to her. She refers to herself as 3 years old. She likes to eat macaroni and cheese and pizza. She wears a pink bow and pink ballet slippers. She is B.J.'s little sister. When she first debuted on the series, she was just about the same size (in height) as Barney.

B.J.

A seven-year-old yellow Protoceratops, B.J. has been on the show since September 27, 1993. His theme song is "B.J.'s Song". He wears a red baseball cap and red sneakers (as heard in the lyrics of his theme). He has lost his hat in the episode *Hats Off to B.J.!* and sometimes says stuff to hide fears (like in the episode *Barney's Halloween Party*, he was shocked by the paper spiders and after learning they were fake, he said "I knew that, sort of."). Pickles are his favorite food and because of that, he actually has had them in different ways like pickles (also with pepperoni, peppers, pineapple and peanut butter) on a pizza (in the episode *Barney's Adventure Bus*). He is Baby Bop's older brother. When he first debuted on the series, he was just about the same size (in height) as Barney and had a slightly deeper voice.

Riff

Referred as *Cousin Riff* by Baby Bop, he is an orange six-year-old hadrosaur, who is Baby Bop and B.J.'s cousin. He has been on the show since September 18, 2006. He wears green sneakers. His theme music is "I Hear Music Everywhere." Riff loves music and it's in almost everything he does. In the episode *Barney – Let's Go to the Firehouse*, it was revealed that Riff also likes to invent things; he created a four-sound smoke detector (the first three were different alarm sounds and the final one his own voice). He even likes Marching bands and Parades as much as Barney does, himself.

Adults

The adults on the show are usually one or two time guest actors who portray teachers, storytellers, or other characters.

One-time guests

Role	Real Name	Episode/Description
Aunt Rachel	Saint Adeogba	Ashley and Alissa's Aunt from the episode *Aunt Rachel is Here*.
Aunt Molly	Mary Ann Brewer	Julie's aunt who appeared in the episode *The Alphabet Zoo*.
Firefighter Frank	Frank Crim	A real firefighter who appeared in the episode *I Can Be a Firefighter!*
Mr. Tenagain	R. Bruce Elliott	A close friend of Barney's, who loves anything to do with the number 10. He appeared in the episode *Having Tens of Fun!*
Teri Garr	Teri Garr	She was a guest in *Barney's First Adventures*.
Melissa Gilbert	Melissa Gilbert	She was a guest in *Barney's First Adventures*.
Rebecca Garcia	Rebecca Garcia	A Mexican dancer who appeared in the episode *Hola México*.
Ella Jenkins	Ella Jenkins	A famous children's singer and a friend of Barney's who appeared in the episode *A Very Special Delivery*.
Captain Kangaroo	John McDonough	The famous children's TV host was a guest in the special *Barney's First Adventures*.
Mr. Delivery Man	Mark S. Bernthal	A delivery man who has delivered a package to Barney in the episode *Everyone Is Special*. Apparently, he cannot tell kids in disguise from adults. In real life, Mark was one of the show's writers, along with Stephen White.
Tosha's mom	J.D. Mosley	Tosha's mother, who brought her twins with her father in the episode *A Very Special Delivery*. She reappeared in the special *Barney's Imagination Island*.
Tina's mom	Sonya Resendeze	She appeared in *Barney's Campfire Sing-Along*.
Joe Scruggs	Joe Scruggs	A famous children's music singer who appeared in the episode *The Exercise Circus*. Lyrick Studios owned the rights to his music in the mid-late 90's.
James Turner	James Turner	A singer who appeared in the episode *Eat, Drink and Be Healthy!*
Farmer Henderson	Max Vaughan	Barney's farmer friend who appeared in the episode *Down on Barney's Farm* with a whole bunch of animals.
Rainbowbeard the Pirate	Stephen White	A mysterious pirate who left his treasure for Barney and the kids to find in the episode *Treasure of Rainbowbeard*.
Princess Zulie	Alexander Hairston	The princess of the Land of Make Believe, who Barney and the kids have to return home in the video *The Land Of Make Believe*.
Patty	Donna Kraft	Luci's blind friend from the episode *1-2-3-4-5 Senses*.
Nana	Jane Hall	Kathy's grandmother who appeared in the episode *Grandparents Are Grand!*
Granddad Richards	Cliff Porter	Derek's grandfather from the episode *Grandparents Are Grand!*
Tosha's dad	David J. Courtney	Tosha's father, who brought her twin baby brothers in the episode *A Very Special Delivery*, along with Tosha's mom. He makes a brief appearance in the special *Barney's Imagination Island*.
Doug and Becky	Doug and Becky from Kathy Burk's marionettes	Marionette performers who guest appeared in the episode *Grown Ups For A Day*.
Joe Ferguson	Joe Ferguson	A storyteller who comes to visit in the episode *My Favorite Things*.
Old King Cole	DeWayne Hambrick	One of Barney's friends who lives in a castle. He comes to visit the treehouse in the episode *A Royal Welcome* and makes an appearance in the stage show *Barney's Big Surprise*.

| Colleen | Claire Burdett | Mr. Grady Boyd's niece, who come in town for a visit. Colleen is a congenital amputee born without her right hand, as is her actress. She appeared in two episodes, *A New Friend!* and *A Perfectly Purple Day.* |
| Dorothy the Dinosaur | Samantha Hibburt (costume) Anna-Lee Robertson (voice) | Dorothy the Dinosaur is seen with Barney in a PBS Kids Sprout Valentine's Day Special: "Sprout's Dino-Mite Valentine's Sing-A-Long". |

Multiple appearances

Role	Real Name	Description and Appearances
Mother Goose	Sandy Walper, Michelle McCarel, Julie Johnson	The rhyme master herself appears in the episodes *Let's Help Mother Goose, Honk! Honk! A Goose On The Loose, A Little Mother Goose, Barney's Big Surprise*, and *Mother Goose/Fairy Tales.*
Stella	Phyllis Cicero	*Stella the Storyteller* travels all around the world, collecting new stories to tell Barney and friends, among other people. She appeared in several episodes from Season 3 to Season 6. Stella reappeared in the video *The Best of Barney*, where she gave Barney a photo album of his friends (most of the TV show cast) over the years she made herself.
Professor Tinkerputt	Barry Pearl	He appeared in *Barney's Imagination Island* and in the *Barney's Big Surprise* stage show tour. Professor Tinkerputt didn't want to share his invented toys, until Barney and the kids showed him that good things happen when you share. For this reason, Tinkerputt left Imagination Island with Barney and the others and started a new toy factory.
Tomie dePaola	Tomie dePaola	The famous children's author is also good friends with Barney and usually meets his friends in the episodes he appears in. He appeared in the episodes *Picture This, It's Raining, It's Pouring*, and *Oh Brother, She's my Sister.*
Mom	Sandy Duncan	Michael and Amy's mom in the early *Barney and the Backyard Gang* videos.
Mr. Boyd	Robert Sweatman	His full name is Grady Boyd and has a niece named Colleen. First worked as a janitor in Seasons 3–6 and worked as a park keeper in Seasons 7 and 8. Like Stella, Mr. Boyd reappeared in the episode *The Best of Barney*, taking pictures in the park. He also took the latest picture in Barney's new photo album from Stella.

Children

Over the years, more than one hundred children have appeared as cast members on the show. *Barney & Friends* mostly uses local talent based in and around North Texas and the Dallas – Fort Worth Metroplex. Some notable children who have appeared on *Barney & Friends* and in other Barney media include:

- Debby Ryan (teenager on *Barney: Let's Go to the Firehouse*)
- Selena Gomez (Gianna on *Barney & Friends*)
- Tory Green (Sarah in *Barney's Colorful World*)
- Demi Lovato (Angela on *Barney & Friends*)
- Trevor Morgan (Cody in *Barney's Great Adventure*)
- Madison Pettis (Bridget)
- Kyla Pratt (Mindy on *Barney & Friends*, Marcella in *Barney's Great Adventure*)
- Nonnie (Halle "Guest Star")
- Erica Rhodes (Kim on *Barney & Friends*) - She auditioned for *American Idol* season 9, but was cut in the Hollywood round.

Crew

- Sheryl Leach (creator)
- Kathy Parker (producer)
- Dennis DeShazer (director)
- Mark S. Bernthal (writer)
- Stephen White (writer)

Movies and specials

- *Barney's Great Adventure* (1998) (Theatrical Movie, starring Trevor Morgan and Kyla Pratt)
- *Barney's Imagination Island* (1994)
- *Barney Live In New York City* (1994)

Airings

Besides the United States, the TV show has aired in Canada, Mexico and Latin America, France, Ireland, Italy, Spain, the United Kingdom, Japan (On English-based DVDs under the name "Let's Play with Barney in English! (バーニーと英語であそぼう！ *Bānī to Eigo de asobō!*)" and on television as simply "Barney & Friends (バーニー＆フレンズ *Bānī ando Furenzu!*)"), the Philippines, Turkey, Australia, and New Zealand, among others. Two known co-productions of Barney & Friends have been produced outside of the US. The Israeli co-production (ינרב לש םירבחה *Hachaverim shel Barney* (The Friends of Barney)) produced from 1997–1999 in Tel Aviv, Israel, was the first of these. Rather than dubbing the original American episodes from Seasons 1–3, the episodes are adapted with a unique set and exclusive child actors.>[16] The other co-production was one shot in South Korea from 2001–2003, airing on KBS (under the name "바니와 친구들" (*Baniwa Chingudeul* (Barney and Friends)). This one, however, adapted the first six seasons (including the first three that the Israel co-production did). It was done in a similar manner as the Israel production.

Music

A majority of the albums of Barney and Friends feature Bob West's voice as the voice of Barney, though the recent album *The Land of Make-Believe* (like every album starting with *Start Singing with Barney*) has Dean Wendt's voice.

Barney's famous song "I Love You" (as well as songs from Sesame Street and Metallica) has been used by interrogators at Guantanamo Bay, Cuba to coerce the detainees.[17]

References

[1] Hofmeister, Sallie (October 20, 1994). "A Blue Year for the Purple-and-Green Dinosaur" (http://www.nytimes.com/1994/10/20/business/a-blue-year-for-the-purple-and-green-dinosaur.html?scp=1&sq=Sheryl Leach&st=cse). *The New York Times*. . Retrieved 2010-08-14.

[2] "Richard Leach; Bankrolled Creation of 'Barney' Dinosaur" (http://articles.latimes.com/2001/jun/02/local/me-5526). Los Angeles TImes. June 2, 2001. . Retrieved 2010-09-09.

[3] Carter, Bill (March 21, 1994). "A Cable Challenger for PBS As King of the Preschool Hill" (http://www.nytimes.com/1994/03/21/business/a-cable-challenger-for-pbs-as-king-of-the-preschool-hill.html?scp=2&sq=Barney &Friends&st=cse). *The New York Times*. . Retrieved 2010-08-14.

[4] Gorman, James (April 11, 1993). "TELEVISION VIEW; Of Dinosaurs Why Must This One Thrive?" (http://www.nytimes.com/1993/04/11/arts/television-view-of-dinosaurs-why-must-this-one-thrive.html?scp=3&sq=Barney &Friends&st=cse). *The New York Times*. . Retrieved 2010-08-14.

[5] "Stuuuupendous!" (http://www.time.com/time/magazine/article/0,9171,977303,00.html). *Time*. December 21, 1992. . Retrieved 2010-08-14.

[6] Cerone, Daniel (April 3, 1993). "Dinosaur Is a Star, Spreading Love With Hugs, Kisses, Songs" (http://articles.latimes.com/1993-04-03/entertainment/ca-18599_1_hug-barney). LA Times. . Retrieved 2010-08-24.

[7] "Barney the launching pad" (http://articles.latimes.com/2009/jan/30/entertainment/et-barney30). LA Times. January 30, 2009. .
     Retrieved 2010-08-24.

[8] Lev, Michael A (December 10, 1992). "Barney! Barney! He`s Kid Dinomite" (http://articles.chicagotribune.com/1992-12-10/news/
     9204220357_1_barney-friends-barney-costume-barney-doll/3). Chicago Tribune. . Retrieved 2010-09-09.

[9] Lawson, Carol (December 3, 1992). "Why Young Children Scream" (http://www.nytimes.com/1992/12/03/garden/
     why-young-children-scream.html?scp=10&sq=Barney &Friends&st=cse). *The New York Times*. . Retrieved 2010-08-14.

[10] Heffley, Lynne (April 6, 1992). "Dinosaur 'Barney' to Join PBS Gang" (http://articles.latimes.com/1992-04-06/entertainment/
     ca-387_1_barney-bag). LA Times. . Retrieved 2010-08-24.

[11] Heffley, Lynne (March 28, 2008). "Barney is far from extinct" (http://articles.latimes.com/2008/mar/28/entertainment/et-barney28).
     Los Angeles TImes. . Retrieved 2010-09-09.

[12] "Advertising; Barney's Image Gets Makeover For New Crop Of Toddlers" (http://www.nytimes.com/2002/08/12/business/
     advertising-barney-s-image-gets-makeover-for-new-crop-of-toddlers.html?scp=8&sq=Barney &Friends&st=cse). *The New York Times*.
     August 12, 2002. . Retrieved 2010-08-14.

[13] IPTV (http://www.iptv.org/kids/grownups/resources/ResearchItem10.cfm)

[14] Lyons Partnership v. Ted Giannoulas, 179 F.3d 384, 386 (5th Cir. 1999) (http://bulk.resource.org/courts.gov/c/F3/179/179.F3d.384.
     98-11003.html), citing Chala Willig Levy, "The Bad News About Barney", *Parents*, Feb. 1994, at 191–92 (136–39).

[15] TV Guide (http://www.cbsnews.com/stories/2002/07/12/entertainment/main515057.shtml)

[16] Zacharia, Janine (December 25, 1997). "Why Barney Doesn't Wear a Yarmulke". Jerusalem Report.

[17] Sesame Street breaks Iraqi POWs (http://news.bbc.co.uk/2/hi/middle_east/3042907.stm)

External links

- HIT Entertainment official website (http://www.hitentertainment.com/barney/index2.asp)
- Barney & Friends on PBS Kids (http://pbskids.org/barney/index.htm)
- Barney & Friends on Treehouse (http://treehousetv.com/watch/shows/Barney/default.aspx)
- Barney & Friends on Sprout (http://www.sproutonline.com/sprout/characters/?preset=barney)
- *Barney & Friends* (http://imdb.com/title/tt0144701/) at the Internet Movie Database

Tinker Bell (film)

<table>
<tr><td colspan="2" align="center">***Tinker Bell***</td></tr>
<tr><td colspan="2" align="center">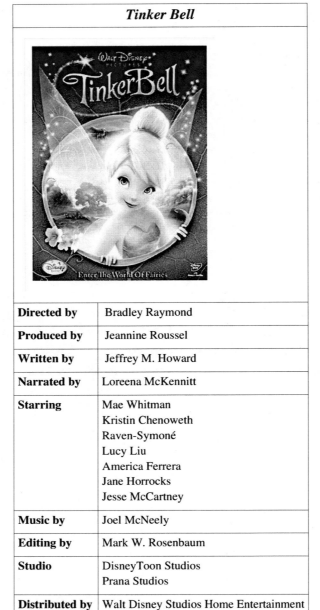</td></tr>
<tr><td>Directed by</td><td>Bradley Raymond</td></tr>
<tr><td>Produced by</td><td>Jeannine Roussel</td></tr>
<tr><td>Written by</td><td>Jeffrey M. Howard</td></tr>
<tr><td>Narrated by</td><td>Loreena McKennitt</td></tr>
<tr><td>Starring</td><td>Mae Whitman
Kristin Chenoweth
Raven-Symoné
Lucy Liu
America Ferrera
Jane Horrocks
Jesse McCartney</td></tr>
<tr><td>Music by</td><td>Joel McNeely</td></tr>
<tr><td>Editing by</td><td>Mark W. Rosenbaum</td></tr>
<tr><td>Studio</td><td>DisneyToon Studios
Prana Studios</td></tr>
<tr><td>Distributed by</td><td>Walt Disney Studios Home Entertainment</td></tr>
<tr><td>Release date(s)</td><td>September 18, 2008[1]</td></tr>
<tr><td>Running time</td><td>78 minutes</td></tr>
<tr><td>Country</td><td>United States</td></tr>
<tr><td>Language</td><td>English</td></tr>
<tr><td>Gross revenue</td><td>$52,201,882[2]</td></tr>
<tr><td>Followed by</td><td>*Tinker Bell and the Lost Treasure*</td></tr>
</table>

Tinker Bell is a 2008 computer animated film based on the *Disney Fairies* franchise produced by DisneyToon Studios. It revolves around Tinker Bell, a fairy character created by J. M. Barrie in his play *Peter Pan, or The Boy Who Wouldn't Grow Up*, and featured in the 1953 Disney animated film, *Peter Pan* and its 2002 sequel *Return to Never Land*. Unlike Disney's two Peter Pan films featuring the character, which were produced primarily using traditional animation, *Tinker Bell* was produced using digital 3D modeling. The film was released on DVD and Blu-Ray by Walt Disney Home Video on September 18, 2008.[1]

Plot

Tinker Bell (Mae Whitman) is born from the first laugh of a baby, and is brought by the winds to Pixie Hollow (which is part of the island of Never Land). She learns that her talent is to be one of the tinkers, the fairies who make and fix things. Two other tinker fairies, Bobble (Rob Paulsen) and Clank (Jeff Bennett), teach her their craft, and tell her about the fairies who visit the mainland to bring each season. Tinker Bell is thrilled and can't wait to go to the mainland for spring.

While out working, she meets Silvermist (Lucy Liu), a water fairy; Rosetta (Kristin Chenoweth), a garden fairy; Iridessa (Raven-Symoné), a light fairy; and Fawn (America Ferrera), an animal fairy. After meeting them, she notices Vidia (Pamela Adlon), a fast-flying fairy who immediately dislikes her because of her unusually strong talent. Vidia challenges her to prove she'll be able to go to the mainland, and Tinker Bell creates several inventions, which she shows to the Minister of Spring (Steve Valentine). But Tinker Bell soon learns from Queen Clarion (Anjelica Huston) that only nature-talent fairies visit the mainland.

She tries her hand at nature skills; making dewdrops with Silvermist, lighting fireflies with Iridessa, and trying with Fawn to teach baby birds to fly, but she fails miserably at all of these. Meanwhile, Bobble and Clank cover for Tinker Bell when questioned by Fairy Mary (Jane Horrocks), the tinker fairy overseer. When Tinker Bell returns, she tries to explain, but Mary simply responds that she knows, and expresses her disappointment with Tinker Bell's actions.

On the beach, Tinker Bell finds parts of a music box and figures out how to put them together. Iridessa, Fawn, Silvermist, and Rosetta witness her doing this, then tell her that she was tinkering and that she should be proud of her talent--if this is what she's good at, the mainland shouldn't matter. But Tinker Bell still wants to go to the mainland. She asks Rosetta if she'll still teach her to be a garden fairy, but Rosetta says she thinks that tinkering is Tinker Bell's talent.

As a last resort, Tinker Bell asks Vidia for help in becoming a garden fairy. Vidia craftily tells her that capturing the sprinting thistles would prove her worth. However, once she sees Tinker Bell making progress, she lets the captured thistles loose, and in attempting to recapture them, Tinker Bell destroys all the preparations for spring. Tinker Bell decides to leave, but after talking with the light-keeper Terence (Jesse McCartney) about how important his job is, she realizes the importance of a tinker.

Tinker Bell redeems herself by inventing machines that quicken the process of decorating flowers, ladybugs, etc. This allows the other fairies to get back on schedule, thus saving the arrival of spring. Vidia is punished for prompting her to cause the chaos, and Queen Clarion allows Tinker Bell to join the nature-talent fairies when they bring spring to the mainland. Tinker Bell is given the task of delivering the music box to its original owner (shown to be Wendy Darling). The narrator ends by saying that when lost toys are found or a broken clock starts to work, "it all means that one very special fairy might be near."

Cast

- Mae Whitman as Tinker Bell, a tinker fairy born of a baby's first laugh. She is fascinated by stories about the mainland, and is thus discouraged to learn that tinkers don't go there. She tries to learn various other skills before finally accepting, with the help of her friends, that she truly is a tinker. She helps to repair the massive damage she created and is rewarded, as she is allowed to join the nature fairies on their trip, where she delivers Wendy her lost toy.
- Kristin Chenoweth as Rosetta, a garden fairy who at first agrees to teach Tinker Bell how to garden, but later d changes her mind after seeing Tinker Bell fix a music box.

- Raven-Symoné as Iridessa, a light fairy who tries to teach Tinker Bell to light fireflies. She is often the first to voice discomfort about Tinker Bell not wanting to accept her job as a tinker.
- Lucy Liu as Silvermist, a water fairy who tries to teach Tinker Bell to make dewdrops. She is possessed of a sassy sense of humor.
- America Ferrera as Fawn, an animal fairy who tries to teach Tinker Bell to get baby birds to fly. She is the closest to Tinker Bell, and expresses her desire for her to be happy, which she suggests is in tinkering.
- Jane Horrocks as Fairy Mary, the overseer of the tinker fairies, who expresses high hope for Tinker Bell. She is greatly disappointed to learn that Tinker Bell doesn't like being a tinker, but is pleased to see her accept her job and help repair the damage caused to Spring. Mary charges her with delivering the toy she repaired after she becomes a nature fairy.
- Jesse McCartney as Terence, the pixie-dust keeper, who is surprised to find out that Tinker Bell knows his name. In mentioning how his job is unimportant, he causes Tinker Bell to remark just how important it is, and realize her own importance.
- Jeff Bennett as Clank, a large tinker fairy with a booming voice. He is usually found with Bobble or Tinker Bell.
- Rob Paulsen as Bobble, a wispy tinker fairy with large glasses who helps Tink out; he is usually found with Clank or with Cheese, a mouse.
- Pamela Adlon as Vidia, a fast-flying fairy, Tinker Bell's rival and the film's main antagonist. She is humiliated by Tinker Bell when they both choose the same hiding space from a hawk, and Vidia has a load of berries fall on her. When Tinker Bell comes to her for help, Vidia craftily suggests that Tink capture sprinting thistles. Vidia is later punished for her part in this.
- Anjelica Huston as Queen Clarion, the queen of all Pixie Hollow, who gives Tinker Bell her job and oversees the four seasons. She is wary of Tinker Bell's eagerness and is proved correctly so after she destroys the preparations for spring. She nonetheless forgives her after Tinker Bell helps repair the damage done, and rewards Tinker Bell by allowing her to go to the mainland.
- Loreena McKennitt as The Narrator, who relates the importance of fairies as it applies to reality.
- Steve Valentine as The Minister of Spring, the grand master of spring, who makes sure everything is finished in time.
- Kathy Najimy as The Minister of Summer
- Richard Portnow as The Minister of Autumn
- Gail Borges as The Minister of Winter
- America Young as Wendy Darling, the girl whose toy Tinker Bell repaired. She is given it back at the end of the film.
- Kathryn Cressida as Mrs. Darling
- Bob Bergen as Firelfies

Crew

- Director - Bradley Raymond[3]
- Writer - Jeffrey M. Howard

Production

Tinker Bell is the first Disney film to feature Tinker Bell in a speaking role. Late actress Brittany Murphy was originally selected for the part, before the role went to Mae Whitman.[4] Planned for release in fall 2007, the movie experienced delays in connection with personnel changes in Disney management.[5] According to a June 2007 article in *Variety*, Sharon Morrill, the head of DisneyToons direct-to-DVD division since 1994, was removed from this position due to problems with this film, including a budget that had expanded to almost $50 million, and "close to two dozen versions of the script and a dozen different directors." Pixar Animation executives John Lasseter and Ed

Catmull were given leadership of Walt Disney Feature Animation after Disney purchased Pixar in early 2006, and although DisneyToons is not under their management, "they are said to have gotten increasingly involved in the unit's operations."[6] Lasseter reportedly said that the film was at that time "virtually unwatchable"[7] and that it would hurt both Walt Disney Feature Animation as well as the Disney Consumer Products line it was meant to support.[8] Morill was moved to "special projects" and the status of the movie was seriously in doubt.[9] Disney observer Jim Hill reported at the time that the complications surrounding this movie had resulted in a decision that Disney would no longer produce straight-to-DVD sequels to its feature films.[10]

Music

The score to the film was composed by Joel McNeely, who recorded the music with an 88-piece ensemble of the Hollywood Studio Symphony and Celtic violin soloist Máiréad Nesbitt at the Sony Scoring Stage.[11]

Soundtrack

The movie's soundtrack was released on October 14, 2008, a week before the DVD release and contains songs from and inspired by the film.

1. "To the Fairies They Draw Near" - Loreena McKennitt
2. "Fly to Your Heart" - Selena Gomez
3. "How to Believe" - Ruby Summer
4. "Let Your Heart Sing" - Katharine McPhee
5. "Be True" - Jonatha Brooke
6. "To the Fairies They Draw Near, Part II" - Loreena McKennitt
7. "Shine" - Tiffany Giardina
8. "Fly With Me" - Kari Kimmel
9. "Wonder of It All" - Scottie Haskell
10. "End Credit Score Suite" - Joel McNeely[12]

Marketing

The digitally animated character of Tinker Bell and other fairies appearing in the film were featured in Disney Channel bumpers in which they would draw the channel's logo with their wands. Rosetta's represents her webisode. Marketing efforts for the film included a tie-in with Southwest Airlines, decorating and naming a Boeing 737 "Tinker Bell One". Flight attendants wore fairy wings and awarded prizes to passengers who correctly answered trivia questions about the Tinker Bell character.[13]

Frank Nissen, the director of *Cinderella III: A Twist in Time* directed a series of webisodes to promote the film[3] on the "Fairies" channel of the Disney XD web site.[14] Except for a few vocal effects, only one contains dialogue.

Title	Description
Tink and the Bell	Tinker Bell finds a silver jingle bell, makes funny faces at her reflection in it, and then gets stuck in it.
Tink and the Pepper Shaker	Tinker Bell finds a pepper shaker and plays with it.
Fawn and the Log	Fawn attempts to wake some sleepy squirrels in a log.
Fawn and the Butterfly	Fawn attempts to help a butterfly which is having trouble getting out of its chrysalis.
Silvermist and the Fish	Silvermist helps a baby fish get over a waterfall so that it can be with its family.
Iridessa and the Light Bugs	With the help of Pixie Dust, Iridessa helps make lightning bugs glow.
Rosetta and the Flower	Rosetta has some trouble in attempting to get a stubborn flower bud to open up. (This is the only webisode with two versions: one with dialogue and one without.)
Tink and the Bird	This one was shown once on ABC in their special airing of Walt Disney's *Peter Pan*.

Reception

The film saw a brief theatrical release at the El Capitan Theatre between September 19 and October 2.[15] It was shown on the Disney Channel on November 30 as part of "New in November". It was well-received by critics, with Rotten Tomatoes giving it an 86% approval rating.[16] The film was released on DVD and Blu-ray Disc on October 28, 2008.[17] In North America, 668,000 copies were sold on its first day of release, about 22 percent above previous estimations.[18]

DVD sales brought in $52,201,882 in revenue for 3,347,686 units sold.[2] At the time they also announced three direct-to-DVD sequels to follow this film, also digitally animated, with a fourth added to the list in 2009- *Tinker Bell and the Lost Treasure* (Autumn 2009), *Tinker Bell and the Great Fairy Rescue* (Autumn 2010), *Tinker Bell and the Mysterious Winter Woods* (Winter 2011) and *Tinker Bell: Race Through the Seasons* (working title, Winter 2012).[19]

References

[1] *Disney A to Z* Supplement (http://adisney.go.com/vault/supplement.pdf), dated May 1, 2009, page 47. Accessed May 26, 2009.

[2] http://www.the-numbers.com/movies/2008/0TIBE-DVD.php

[3] "Director Frank Nissen on *Cinderella III*" (http://animated-views.com/2007/director-frank-nissen-on-cinderella-iii-a-twist-in-time/). Animated-Views.com. January 23, 2007. Retrieved January 28, 2007.

[4] Disney (20 June 2006). "Brittany Murphy Gives Tinker Bell Her Voice" (https://licensing.disney.com/Home/display. jsp?contentId=dcp_home_pressroom_pressreleases_dcp_home_pr_us_fairies_tink_voice_062006&forPrint=false&language=ja& preview=true&imageShow=0&pressRoom=ES&translationOf=null&region=0&ccPK=dcp_home_pressroom_press_room_all_US). Press release. . Retrieved 2010-07-02.

[5] Joseph Menn (21 December 2006). "Merchandise has less magic with delay of 'Tinker Bell'" (http://articles.latimes.com/2006/dec/21/ business/fi-tinkerbell21). *Los Angeles Times*. .

[6] "Variety.com" (http://www.variety.com/article/VR1117967400.html?categoryid=20&cs=1)

[7] IMDB news (http://imdb.com/news/sb/2007-06-21/)

[8] o-meon: Tinker Bell: Return of the Dark Fairy By C. W. Oberleitner (http://www.o-meon.com/pages/news&features/n&f_2007/n& f_02-27-07.htm)

[9] "Tinkerbell Straight-To-DVD Release in Limbo" (http://www.movieweb.com/dvd/news/77/20677.php). .

[10] Jim Hill (http://jimhillmedia.com/blogs/jim_hill/archive/2007/06/21/ say-so-long-to-direct-to-video-sequels-disneytoon-studios-tunes-out-sharon-morrill.aspx)

[11] Dan Goldwasser (2008-07-09). "Joel McNeely scores *Tinker Bell*" (http://www.scoringsessions.com/news/142). ScoringSessions.com. . Retrieved 2008-07-09.

[12] DisneyShopping.com (http://disneyshopping.go.com/webapp/wcs/stores/servlet/DSIProductDisplay?catalogId=10002& storeId=10051&productId=1235225&langId=-1&categoryId=14737)

[13] Ted Jackovics (1 November 2008). "Southwest Adds Pixie Dust In Deal With Disney" (http://www2.tbo.com/content/2008/nov/01/ 010000/bz-southwest-adds-pixie-dust-in-deal-with-disney/). *Tampa Tribune*. .

[14] http://www.disney.go.com/dxd

[15] *Disney A to Z* Supplement (http://adisney.go.com/vault/supplement.pdf), dated May 1, 2009, page 47. Accessed May 26, 2009.

[16] http://www.rottentomatoes.com/m/tinker_bell/

[17] http://corporate.disney.go.com/news/corporate/2008/2008_0408_animation_roll_out.html Disney Animation plans 2008-2012

[18] http://thedisneyblog.com/2008/10/31/sales-of-tinker-bell-movie-outperforming-expectations/

[19] http://www.ultimatedisney.com/tinkerbell-losttreasure-pressrelease-1027.html

External links

- Official website (http://http://www.disneyfairies.com/)
- *Tinker Bell* (http://www.allmovie.com/work/353383) at Allmovie
- *Tinker Bell* (http://www.bcdb.com/bcdb/cartoon.cgi?film=86713/) at the Big Cartoon DataBase
- *Tinker Bell* (http://www.imdb.com/title/tt0823671/) at the Internet Movie Database
- Scoring Session Photo Gallery at ScoringSessions.com (http://www.scoringsessions.com/sessions/26276)
- Independent Review of Tinker-Bell (http://www.moviefilmreview.com/tinker-bell.php)

Spy Kids 3-D: Game Over

Spy Kids 3-D: Game Over	
Theatrical release poster	
Directed by	Robert Rodriguez
Produced by	Robert Rodriguez Elizabeth Avellan Harvey Weinstein Bob Weinstein
Written by	Robert Rodriguez

Starring	Alexa Vega
	Daryl Sabara
	Sylvester Stallone
	Antonio Banderas
	Carla Gugino
	Ricardo Montalbán
	George Clooney
	Salma Hayek
	George Hurst
	Selena Gomez
	Mike Judge
Music by	Robert Rodriguez
Cinematography	Robert Rodriguez
Editing by	Robert Rodriguez
Studio	Troublemaker Studios
Distributed by	Dimension Films
Release date(s)	July 25, 2003
Running time	82 minutes
Country	United States
Language	English
Budget	$38 million
Gross revenue	$197,011,982[1]
Preceded by	*Spy Kids 2: The Island of Lost Dreams*
Followed by	*Spy Kids 4: All the Time in the World*

Spy Kids 3-D: Game Over is a 2003 American action-adventure family film directed by Robert Rodriguez and the third film in the *Spy Kids* series. It was released in the United States on July 25, 2003. The film featured the return of many cast members from the past two films, although most were in minor roles and cameo appearances. The film was to be the last in the trilogy,[2] but director Robert Rodriguez is currently writing a *Spy Kids 4* due out August 19, 2011.

Plot

Juni Cortez, a former agent of the OSS, now works as a private detective but gets little profit for his work. He is contacted by the OSS and informed that his sister, Carmen Cortez, is missing. He is reunited with Donnogan Giggles and his wife Francesca, who explain that Carmen was captured by the Toymaker (Sylvester Stallone), a villain. The Toymaker was imprisoned in cyberspace by the OSS, but he has since created "Game Over", a virtual reality-based video game which he intends on using to escape cyberspace via players that reach the unbeatable Level 5. Juni agrees to venture into the game, save Carmen, and shut down the game.

In the game, which takes place in a full 3D environment, Juni finds the challenges difficult. He finds three beta-testers, Francis, Arnold and Rez, who launch him to the moon so that they'll have less competition on the way to Level 5. On the moon, Juni receives an opportunity to bring in a fellow ally to assist him, selecting his grandfather Valentin (Ricardo Montalbán), who has been looking for the Toymaker for years. He receives a power-up which gives him a robotic suit allowing him to walk. Juni ventures into a robot battle arena where he fights a girl named Demetra in order to return to Earth and Level 2. He meets the beta-testers again who believe he is a player named The Guy who can beat Level 5. Rez is unconvinced and challenges Juni to a race involving a multitude of different vehicles. Juni wins the race with help from Valentin, and Demetra joins the group, she and Juni displaying romantic feelings for each other. Arnold and Juni are forced to battle each other in level 3, the loser getting an immediate game over. Demetra swaps places with Juni and is defeated, seemingly getting a game over, much to Juni's sadness.

The group get to Level 4 where Juni finds Carmen, released by the Toymaker, who leads the group on. Juni follows a map given to him by Demetra to a lava-filled gorge. The group surf their way through the lava but Donnogan attempts to prevent them from reaching Level 5 to save them, but this fails. Outside the door to Level 5, the real "Guy" appears and opens the door only to get a game over by an electrical shock. Demetra appears, claiming to have got back into the game via a glitch but Carmen identifies her as The Deceiver, a program used to fool players. Demetra confirms this and apologizes to Juni. The Toymaker attacks the group with giant robot, Demetra shedding a single tear and shutting the game down so Juni and the others can return to reality. However, it is revealed that Valentin released the Toymaker, the villain's army of robots attacking a nearby city.

Juni and Carmen summon their family members: Parents Gregorio and Ingrid, Gregorio's brother Machete, their Grandma, and Uncle Felix. With too many robots to handle, Juni calls out to their "extended" family, summoning characters from the first two films (including Fegan Floop and Alexander Minion, Dinky Winks and his son, scientist Romero, and Gary and Gerty Giggles). The robots are destroyed except the Toymaker's. Valentin confronts Sebastian the Toymaker and reveals that it was he who put him in the wheelchair, but forgives Sebastian the Toymaker for his actions, which is why he was perching on his shoulders all those years. Sebastian the Toymaker shuts down his robot and joins the rest of the Cortez family and their friends to celebrate their family.

Cast

- Alexa Vega as Carmen Cortez
- Daryl Sabara as Juni Cortez
- Ricardo Montalbán as Valentin Grandfather
- Ryan Pinkston as Arnold
- Robert Vito as Rez
- Bobby Edner as Francis
- Antonio Banderas as Gregorio Cortez
- Carla Gugino as Ingrid Cortez
- Emily Osment as Gerti Giggles
- Matt O'Leary as Gary Giggles
- Sylvester Stallone as Sebastian the Toymaker
- Mike Judge as Donnagon Giggles
- Salma Hayek as Francesca Giggles
- George Clooney as Devlin, the President of the United States
- Holland Taylor as Grandma
- Courtney Jines as Demetra
- Cheech Marin as Felix
- Danny Trejo as Isador "Machete" Cortez
- Alan Cumming as Fegan Floop
- Steve Buscemi as Romero
- Bill Paxton as Dinky Winks
- Tony Shalhoub as Alexander Minion
- Elijah Wood as The Guy
- Selena Gomez as Waterpark Girl
- George Hurst as Uncle Gomez
- James Paxton as Little Dink/Dinky Winks Jr.

Soundtrack

Music from the Motion Picture Spy Kids 3-D: Game Over	
Soundtrack by Robert Rodriguez	
Released	July 22, 2003
Genre	Soundtrack, pop rock
Length	47:15
Label	Milan Records
Professional reviews	
• Allmusic ★ ★ ★ ★ ★ Link [3] • Filmtracks [4] ★ ★ ★ ★ ★ • SoundtrackNet [5] ★ ★ ★ ★ ★	
Robert Rodriguez film soundtrack chronology	
Spy Kids 2: The Island of Lost Dreams (2002) ***Spy Kids 3D: Game Over*** (2003) *Once Upon a Time in Mexico* (2003)	

The film score was composed by Robert Rodriguez and is the first score for which he takes solo credit. Rodriguez also performs in the "Game Over" band, playing guitar, bass, keyboard and drums, including the title track, "Game Over", performed by Alexa Vega.[6]

Track listing

All selections composed by Robert Rodriguez and performed by Texas Philharmonic Orchestra, conducted by George Oldziey and Rodriguez.

1. "Game Over" (title track, vocals by Alexa Vega)
2. "Thumb Thumbs"
3. "Pogoland"
4. "Robot Arena"
5. "Metal Battle"
6. "Toy Maker"
7. "Mega Racer"
8. "Programmerz"
9. "Bonus Life"
10. "Cyber Staff Battle"
11. "Tinker Toys"
12. "Lava Monster Rock"
13. "The Real Guy"
14. "Orbit"
15. "Welcome to the Game"
16. "Heart Drive" (performed by Bobby Edner and Alexa Vega) and
17. "Video Girl"
18. "Isle of Dreams (Cortez Mix)"
    - Tracks 17-18 produced by Dave Curtin for DeepMix

Recorded but not in film

1. "Superstar" Recorded By Selena Gomez

Reception

The response to the film was mainly mixed. Many critics stated that the glasses give a headache.[7] [8] Bob Longino of the Atlanta Journal-Constitution wrote that "the 3D process will hurt your eyes", but also stated that it helped mask what he deemed as an overall lack of a story.[9] Jim Lane of Sacramento News and Review called the 3D scenes "murky and purple like a window smeared with grape jell-o."[10] Roger Ebert suggested that perhaps Rodriguez was held back by the film's technical constraints. Ebert also admitted to showing disdain for the 3D gimmick, saying that the picture quality is more murky and washed out than the crisper and more colorful 2D films.[11] Mick LaSalle of the San Francisco Chronicle noted Carmen's absence for much of the film and criticized the plot's repeated scenes of Juni attempting over and over again to reach Level Five.[12] Kimberly Jones of the Austin City Chronicle praised the visuals but called the plot twig-thin and stated that the parents' near absence in the story makes Rodriguez' continuing theme of family ties seem much less resonant than in the other films.[13] Actor Sylvester Stallone earned the Razzie Award for Worst Supporting Actor for his performance.

The film opened with a surprising $33.4 million, but didn't quite live up to the first *Spy Kids* film. In the end, it grossed $111 million in North America. However, its overseas intake was double that of either of the first two *Spy Kids* films at $85.3 million, grossing a worldwide total of $197,011,982, making it the highest grossing film in the series. The film had a 3D effect which was not removable in the DVD, but only for some European DVD releases. A set of four 3D glasses, made of cardboard (Silver Screen Retail), was included with the DVD, although some DVDs did not have it.

Sequel

Spy Kids 4 is set to be released on August 19, 2011. the story revolves around two twins who cannot get along with their stepmother Marissa Cortez Wilson who married their father, Wilbur, a spy-hunting reporter. However unbeknownst to them, Marissa is a retired spy for the OSS (Organization of Super Spies) which has since become the world's top spy agency and former headquarters of the now-defunct Spy Kids division.

References

[1] http://www.boxofficemojo.com/movies/?id=spykids3.htm

[2] Harrison, Eric (2004-05-12). "Spy Kids 3-D: Game Over" (http://www.chron.com/disp/story.mpl/ae/movies/reviews/2010392.html). The Houston Chronicle. . Retrieved 2009-10-22.

[3] http://www.allmusic.com/album/r649483

[4] http://www.filmtracks.com/titles/spy_kids3.html

[5] http://www.soundtrack.net/albums/database/?id=3327

[6] SoundtrackNet: Spy Kids 3D: Game Over Soundtrack (http://www.soundtrack.net/albums/database/?id=3327)

[7] "Spy Kids (2001)" (http://www.rottentomatoes.com/m/spy_kids/). *Rotten Tomatoes*. IGN Entertainment, Inc. . Retrieved 2009-10-30.

[8] "Spy Kids 2: Island of Lost Dreams (2002)" (http://www.rottentomatoes.com/m/spy_kids_2_island_of_lost_dreams/). *Rotten Tomatoes*. IGN Entertainment, Inc. . Retrieved 2009-10-30.

[9] Longino, Bob. "Spy Kids 3D: Game Over" (http://www.accessatlanta.com/movies/content/shared/movies/reviews/S/spykids3.html). *accessAtlanta*. The Atlanta Journal-Constitution. . Retrieved 2009-10-28.

[10] Lane, Jim (2003-07-31). "Film>Short Reviews: Spy Kids 3-D: Game Over" (http://www.newsreview.com/sacramento/content?oid=15568). *Sacramento News and Review*. Chico Community Publishing, Inc. . Retrieved 2009-10-28.

[11] Ebert, Roger (2003-07-25). "Spy Kids 3-D: Game Over" (http://rogerebert.suntimes.com/apps/pbcs.dll/article?AID=/20030725/REVIEWS/307250305/1023). rogerebert.com. . Retrieved 2009-10-28.

[12] LaSalle, Mick (2003-07-25). "Game's over for latest 'Spy Kids'" (http://www.sfgate.com/cgi-bin/article.cgi?f=/c/a/2003/07/25/DD255460.DTL). *SFGate: Home of the San Francisco Chronicle*. Hearst Communications Inc. . Retrieved 2009-10-22.

[13] Jones, Kimberly (2003-07-25). "Spy Kids 3-D: Game Over" (http://www.austinchronicle.com/gyrobase/Calendar/Film?Film=oid:169586). Austin Chronicle Corp. . Retrieved 2009-10-28.

External links

- *Spy Kids 3-D: Game Over* (http://www.imdb.com/title/tt0338459/) at the Internet Movie Database
- *Spy Kids 3-D: Game Over* (http://www.boxofficemojo.com/movies/?id=spykids3.htm) at Box Office Mojo

Horton Hears a Who! (film)

Dr. Seuss' Horton Hears a Who!	
Theatrical release poster	
Directed by	Jimmy Hayward Steve Martino
Produced by	Bob Gordon Bruce Anderson
Written by	Cinco Paul Ken Daurio Mike Reiss [uncredited]
Based on	*Horton Hears a Who!* by Dr. Seuss
Narrated by	Charles Osgood
Starring	Jim Carrey Steve Carell Carol Burnett Seth Rogen Jesse McCartney Will Arnett Dan Fogler Isla Fisher Amy Poehler Selena Gomez
Music by	John Powell
Editing by	Tim Nordquist
Studio	Blue Sky Studios
Distributed by	20th Century Fox

Release date(s)	March 14, 2008
Running time	94 minutes
Country	United States
Language	English
Budget	$85 million
Gross revenue	$297,679,954

Horton Hears a Who!, also known as ***Dr. Seuss' Horton Hears a Who!***, is a 2008 American CGI-animated feature film based on the Dr. Seuss book of the same name. It is the fourth feature film from Blue Sky Studios, and the third Dr. Seuss-based feature film, following *How the Grinch Stole Christmas* and *The Cat in the Hat*.

It is the first Dr. Seuss adaptation fully animated using CGI technology.

Plot

The film opens in the Jungle of Nool, where a drop of water falls off a leaf, causing a chain reaction. The small flower is crushed by a bur and a tiny dust speck is pushed off the flower and into the jungle. Meanwhile, a caring, imaginative elephant named Horton (Jim Carrey), the jungle's nature teacher, takes a dip in the pool. The dust speck floats past him in the air, and he hears a tiny yelp coming from it. Believing that an entire family of microscopic creatures are living on that speck, he places it on top of a pink clover that he holds in his trunk. Horton finds out the speck harbors the city of Who-ville and its inhabitants, led by Mayor Ned McDodd (Steve Carell). He has a wife, Sally (Amy Poehler), 96 daughters (Selena Gomez) who all have names that start with the letter H, and one teenage son named JoJo (Jesse McCartney). Despite being next in line for the mayoral position, JoJo refuses to become mayor of the city.

The Mayor finds out from Dr. LaRue (Isla Fisher) that Who-ville will be destroyed if Horton does not find a "safer more stable home." Horton resolves to place the speck atop Mt. Nool, the safest place in the jungle. This outlook earns Horton nothing but ridicule from the inhabitants of Nool, especially from the leader of the jungle, the Sour Kangaroo (Carol Burnett). The Kangaroo tries to get Horton to give up the speck, so as not to put supposedly ridiculous ideas into the heads of the children. Ever faithful to his two mottos, "A person's a person, no matter how small," and "I meant what I said, and I said what I meant, an Elephant's faithful 100%" (a reference to his other story *Horton Hatches the Egg*), Horton refuses. Also taking force toward Horton are the Wickersham brothers (Frank Welker and Dan Castellaneta), a group of bullying monkeys who love making misery.

The other Whos become suspicious of the various phenomena in their world (actually caused by Horton's various mishaps), the Mayor finally reveals the truth, but at first, the Whos do not believe him any more than the animals believe Horton. The Kangaroo enlists a buzzard named Vlad Vladikoff (Will Arnett) to get rid of the speck by force. Vlad manages to steal the clover with the speck on it, flee from a chasing Horton and drop it from hundreds of feet into a valley full of nearly identical clovers. The impact destroys Who-ville. Horton picks clovers through the field and finally finds it "on the 3 millionth flower." The city's destruction, combined with hearing Horton's voice through the drain pipe, is enough to convince the rest of the Whos that the mayor is not crazy, and they all tell Horton they believe in him.

The Kangaroo finds out that Horton still has the speck, and decides to rally the jungle community into confronting Horton. The Kangaroo offers Horton to give up the speck. Unable to convince Horton, she orders the animals to rope and cage him, and that the speck be burned in a pot of boiling "beezlenut" oil.

The Mayor enlists all of his people to make noise by shouting, "We are here," as well as playing a variety of instruments, so the animals can hear them. Horton is caged, and the Kangaroo takes the clover and drops it into the oil. At the last minute, JoJo grabs the horn used to project Horton's voice, runs up the highest tower and yells "YOP!" Just before the speck hits the oil, Jojo's sound causes their noise to be heard.

Hearing the Whos' cries, Rudy (Josh Flitter), the Kangaroo's son, grabs the clover and returns it to Horton, refusing his mother's orders to return to her pouch. The animals realize their mistake. While being praised for his integrity by his neighbors, Horton forgives the Kangaroo and she accepts his friendship. She and the animals resolve to join Horton in returning the clover to Mount Nool. Here the people of Who-ville and the animals of Nool gather in song and recite the chorus from "Can't Fight This Feeling", and begin walking the final stretch to the mountain. The film ends with the narrator revealing that the jungle of Nool is just one speck among numerous others.

Cast

- Horton the Elephant, voiced by Jim Carrey, has an imagination since his childhood. He serves as the main protagonist of the film. It was that imagination along with his unwavering dedication that makes Horton a great teacher, unconditional friend and a force to be reckoned with.
- Ned McDodd, the Mayor of Whoville, voiced by Steve Carell, is the mayor of a microscopic world, and father of ninety-six daughters and a son named JoJo. He is the deuteragonist of the film. He is very proud and formal and cares very much for his city and its people, but when he starts hearing the voice of Horton, whom he cannot see, things begin to unravel for the Mayor. It is noted that the name of the character wasn't revealed until the theatrical release. He can be described as "The mayor of Who-ville, a man named McDodd, was devoted, fair, and a little bit odd." However as smoothly as he runs the town, at the beginning of the movie, his relationship with his son JoJo is very strained, as JoJo doesn't talk to him.
- Sour Kangaroo, voiced by Carol Burnett, is a busybody and creator of the jungle's laws who is skeptical about the existence of the Whos and Whoville on a dust speck. She serves as the main antagonist of the film. As Horton's claims begin to drive her towards darkness, she believes that once other people start listening to Horton, they'll start to come to her with questions she won't be able to answer. In order to avoid this, she begins making deals with the Wickershams and the vulture hitman Vlad Vladikoff. As the film progresses, her aims start to shift towards crushing Horton's spirit and building up her own reputation. The Kangaroo is too dismissive of the products of imagination and creativity, even to the point where she keeps her son Rudy jammed inside her pouch. She believes that outside the "comfort" her ideas provide him, non-conformity and anarchy are minutes away from turning their ordered life into chaos. Yet, in the end, Horton's convincing changes her mindset.
- JoJo McDodd is voiced by Jesse McCartney. JoJo is the Mayor's only son and the eldest of the mayor's children. He is the film's tritagonist. Since he is the oldest, JoJo is next in line to become the Mayor of Whoville, though he doesn't want to follow in his father's footsteps. He doesn't want his Dad to know because he thinks he'll let his dad down. He never speaks to his father because of this, although from the deleted scenes commentary it is implied that he does speak, but since his scenes are mostly with his father, we don't hear him speak until he shouts "YoP" and saves the town. After this he begins speaking to multiple characters, and even sings at the end to cap off the camera going into Whoville. He also shows a surprising talent for inventions and is somewhat of a prodigy and a musician. In fact, he turns the inside of Whoville's abandoned observatory into a giant mechanical musical instrument called the "Symphoniphone". In the deleted scenes commentary, it is revealed that at the time of the "Horton Incident," JoJo was 14.
- Rudy is voiced by Josh Flitter. Rudy is Kangaroo's young joey. He lives in his mother's pouch. Over the course of the movie, he starts to question his mother's ethics as she continually tries to demolish the clover on which Horton has caught the Whos' speck of dust. But his stifling environment can't contain his free-thinking spirit, and Rudy is ready to take the next step, even if it's his first.
- Morton the Mouse is voiced by Seth Rogen. Morton the mouse is Horton's best friend who makes up in speed what he lacks in size. He's smaller than the elephant's big toe, but when Morton speaks, Horton listens. Morton will endure Horton's whims, but when the elephant takes off on flights of fancy, Morton knows it's his job to bring him back to earth. He's successful, most of the time. Morton also acts as a messenger for Horton, bringing him news about Vlad, and says, "If you don't like the idea of his claws ripping your flesh, leave the flower and keep your eyes open!"

- Sally O'Malley McDodd is voiced by Amy Poehler. Sally is the Mayor's wife and mother of 96 daughters and one son named JoJo. With all of these children, Sally's responsibilities dwarf even those of her husband. Still, she's able to juggle them with the grace of a first lady. The last thing she needs is another problem child with an overactive imagination, but when her husband starts hearing voices, that's exactly what she gets. It's a situation even her sharp wit and pointed sarcasm can't defuse, but when the truth is revealed, she's willing to give it her all to help her husband save Whoville. Sally deeply cares for her husband and children.
- Dr. Mary Lou LaRue is voiced by Isla Fisher. Dr. LaRue is an eccentric Whoville scientist who can be a bit scatterbrained at times. However, being the smartest of the staff at Who University, she is willing to help the Mayor find out how they can preserve the peace that holds their town together. She is one of the first Whos to believe that the Mayor was right about Whoville being a speck. She speaks with a lateral lisp.
- Vlad Vladikoff is voiced by Will Arnett He is the vulture in the scene where he tries to get the clover. There is a confusing matter about a good Vlad is a rabbit (which bakes cookies) and a bad Vlad. Vlad is a reclusive vulture who lives in a tree stump in a swamp surrounded by thorns and snakes, feasting on a zebra carcass and shooing a jackal. The Sour Kangaroo hires him to get rid of Horton's clover. At first, he agrees to do it in exchange for her son Rudy, but he stated a brand new pair of objects never specified beforehand. After "thinking" it over, she uses reverse psychology to get him to do it for free. He speaks in a thick Russian accent and is extremely theatrical in his wickedness to the point of embarrassing himself.
- Yummo is voiced by Dan Fogler. Yummo is the rumbling leader of the Wickersham brothers who serves as a bully for Horton, as he sees him as an annoyance. He's hot-tempered, power-hungry, and just plain hungry. He helps with the capture of Horton because he agreed that Horton was poisoning the youth of the jungle, first said by Kangaroo.
- Mrs. Quilligan is voiced by Jaime Pressly. Mrs. Quilligan is a jungle bird that is a two-faced and easily influenced busybody. She sways with public opinion and everybody knows it. It's not unusual for her to be caught flip-flopping and backtracking to cover herself, keeping her firmly entrenched in the" in crowd".
- Jessica Quilligan is voiced by Laura Ortiz. Like any teenager, Jessica might be embarrassed by her mother's busybody behavior, but it's obvious to everyone else in the community that she's Mrs. Quilligan's mini-clone. She views herself as an independent thinker, but since conformity leads to acceptance, she's just another cog in the wheel. She is vain. When she and her classmates tell Horton about their clovers with worlds, Jessica states that her world is called Jessica-Land, where everyone worships her, Queen Jessica, because she is so beautiful.
- Tommy is voiced by Jonah Hill. Tommy is an orange wombat-like creature that is one of the children of the Jungle of Nool that looks up to and views Horton as a teacher. He seems to have somewhat of a frat boy/smart aleck persona, but truly believes in what Horton is trying to do, even if he is being ridiculed for it. He tends to get out of the way of trouble, such as the time when Sour Kangaroo approaches them after hearing "nonsense" about the clover worlds, he says, "Oh, um... You guys with worlds are in trouble!"
- Katie is voiced by Joey King. Katie is a small baby yak with strange mannerisms and abilities. Aside from saying "ahhh" on a few occasions, her only lines in the film are when Horton's students create worlds of their own on their own flowers: Katie explains that everyone in her world is a pony that eats rainbows, and excretes butterflies and in the tree when she says "horton" and "yeah". She also has a frog's tongue, and the ability to float, which she demonstrates at the end of the film. Katie is one of the female pupils of Horton. On the special features, it is revealed that the character of Katie was created to be creepy, and that she thinks of herself as a huge, demonic being. In a deleted scene, she is shown as huge, and terrorizing a village and consuming villagers.
- Miss Yelp, voiced by Niecy Nash, is the Mayor's assistant. She talks in a bored voice, and does all her tasks mechanically, before she is asked. She has a MySpace profile (named Whospace in the film), which she mostly spends her time on during work.
- The Chairman, voiced by Dan Fogler, is the head of the Whoville City Council and views the Mayor as a 'blathering boob', and appears to have more power than him. It is Horton who takes him down a peg or two. He and his cronies all have blue or green hair and skin, black suits and resemble The Grinch. It is said in the DVD

commentary that the last one is named Pugerson and he can't fly his box kite very well.

- The Wickersham Brothers, voiced by Frank Welker and Dan Castellaneta, are a group of vicious monkeys who serve as bullies for Horton. They have a very large family consisting of many members who help bind Horton. When Horton speaks up to all the animals of Nool about his protected speck, the Wickershams actually take pity on him, only to be forced by Sour Kangaroo to rope and cage him, but after a while, the Wickershams realize they do hear the people on the speck, and they also reject the still-resenting Sour Kangaroo. They serve as minor antagonists in the film.
- The Narrator, voiced by Charles Osgood. Osgood reads the book throughout the film.

Soundtrack

The original score for the film's soundtrack album was composed by John Powell. Near the end of the picture, the cast comes together and sings the song, "Can't Fight This Feeling" by REO Speedwagon. This version of the song was not featured on the soundtrack. The song used in the theatrical advertisements was the theme to *Beetlejuice*.

Reaction

Critical reception

The film received generally positive reviews from film critics. As of May 8, 2008, the review aggregator Rotten Tomatoes reported that 78% of critics gave the film positive reviews, based on 123 reviews, and an even better 84% rating from the top critics on the site based on 31 reviews, both classifying the film as "Certified Fresh", and making it by far the most favorably reviewed Dr. Seuss film adaptation on the site.[1] Metacritic reported the film had an average score of 71 out of 100, indicating "generally favorable reviews", based on 31 reviews, also the most favorably reviewed Dr. Seuss film on the site.[2] Brian Eggert of Deep Focus Review gave it one and a half stars out of four, criticizing its numerous pop-culture references, calling it a "mish-mash of incoherent babble" and claiming it ends up "reducing Seuss' otherwise admirable message to ordinary storytelling, when Seuss' work is anything but."

Box office

In its opening weekend, the film grossed $45,012,998 in 3,954 theaters, averaging $11,384 per theater in the United States and Canada, and ranking #1 at the box office.[3] The film previously had the 7th largest opening weekend in March, behind *Ice Age*, *Ice Age: The Meltdown* and *300*. It is now the 7th largest opening weekend in March behind *Monsters vs. Aliens* and *Alice in Wonderland*.[4] In the United States and Canada, *Horton Hears a Who* was also the #1 film its second weekend of release, grossing $24,590,596 over the Easter frame, in 3,961 theaters and averaging $6,208 per venue. It dropped to #2 in its third weekend grossing $17,740,106 in 3,826 theaters and averaging $4,637 per venue. Its fourth weekend ranked at #4 grossing $9,115,987 in 3,571 theaters and averaging $2,553 per venue. Its fifth weekend ranked at #6, grossing $5,920,566 in 3,209 theaters and averaging $1,845 per venue.

As of July 20, 2008, it has grossed a total of $295,133,433 worldwide; $154,245,889 in the United States and Canada and $140,887,544 in other territories.[5]

Home media release

Dr. Seuss' Horton Hears a Who! was released on DVD and Blu-ray on December 9, 2008. Three versions of the DVD are available: a single disc edition, a two-disc special edition, and a gift set packaged with a Horton plush.

The DVD and Blu-ray Disc were released in the UK on October 20, 2008 and in Australia on September 20, 2008.

References

[1] "Dr. Seuss' Horton Hears a Who Movie Reviews, Pictures - Rotten Tomatoes" (http://www.rottentomatoes.com/m/ horton-hears-a-who2008/). Rotten Tomatoes. . Retrieved 2008-04-14.

[2] "Horton Hears a Who! (2008): Reviews" (http://www.metacritic.com/film/titles/hortonhears). Metacritic. . Retrieved 2008-03-14.

[3] "Dr. Seuss' Horton Hears a Who! (2008) - Weekend Box Office Results" (http://www.boxofficemojo.com/movies/?page=weekend& id=hortonhearsawho.htm). Box Office Mojo. . Retrieved 2008-03-16.

[4] "Top March Opening Weekends at the Box Office" (http://boxofficemojo.com/alltime/weekends/month/?mo=03&p=.htm). Box Office Mojo. . Retrieved 2008-03-16.

[5] "Dr. Seuss' Horton Hears a Who! (2008)" (http://www.boxofficemojo.com/movies/?page=main&id=hortonhearsawho.htm). Box Office Mojo. . Retrieved 2008-03-24.

External links

- Official website (http://http://www.hortonmovie.com/)
- *Horton Hears a Who!* (http://www.bcdb.com/bcdb/cartoon.cgi?film=87576/) at the Big Cartoon DataBase
- *Horton Hears a Who!* (http://www.imdb.com/title/tt0451079/) at the Internet Movie Database
- *Horton Hears a Who!* (http://www.allmovie.com/work/361176) at Allmovie
- *Horton Hears a Who!* (http://www.boxofficemojo.com/movies/?id=hortonhearsawho.htm) at Box Office Mojo
- *Horton Hears a Who!* (http://www.rottentomatoes.com/m/horton-hears-a-who2008/) at Rotten Tomatoes
- *Horton Hears a Who!* (http://www.metacritic.com/film/titles/hortonhears) at Metacritic

Arthur and the Vengeance of Maltazard

Arthur and the Revenge of Maltazard	
 Teaser poster	
Directed by	Luc Besson
Written by	Luc Besson
Starring	Freddie Highmore Mia Farrow Selena Gomez
Cinematography	Thierry Arbogast
Editing by	Fili Genes
Studio	EuropaCorp
Distributed by	MGM/The Weinstein Company (North America/Mexico) Momentum Pictures (United Kingdom) Asmik Ace (Japan)
Release date(s)	26 November 2009 (Germany) 2 December 2009 (France)
Running time	93 minutes
Country	France
Language	English
Budget	€ 64 240 000
Gross revenue	€ 51 000 000
Preceded by	*Arthur and the Invisibles*
Followed by	*Arthur and the War of the Two Worlds*

Arthur and the Revenge of Maltazard is a part-animated, part-live action feature film written and directed by Luc Besson, and starring Freddie Highmore and Mia Farrow. EuropaCorp is producing the film which is a sequel to *Arthur and the Invisibles*.

Plot

In 1963, 13-year-old Arthur stays with his grandparents in the holidays. He is befriended with a Maasai-like tribe called the Bogo Matassalai and with the Minimoys, tooth-sized, elfin beings, who all live there in the garden. The Bogo Matassalai grant Arthur a distinction regarding being one with nature, after succeeding in a series of tests, such as hugging a tree for hours, sleeping with a wild animal, and eating grass.

The Bogo Matassalai are capable of transforming a person to a Minimoy. It is only possible every tenth full moon, at midnight. Arthur is about to undergo this procedure, to visit the Minimoys (who are expecting him and preparing a party for him), and especially the Minimoys' princess Selenia. A spider delivers to Arthur a grain of rice with the message "help", which must come from the Minimoys, and makes it even more important for him to visit them.

Arthur's father wants to kill bees, since Arthur is allergic to the stings. However, his grandfather Archibald objects because of his respect for nature. Therefore Arthur's father wants to take him home earlier than planned. At a gas station Arthur escapes from the car and returns to his grandparents' house. The Bogo Matassalai attempt to transform him using a telescope, but this method fails due to clouds covering the full moon. Therefore Arthur asks the Bogo Matassalai to apply the alternative method, even though it is more dangerous. They agree. Arthur is wound into ropes, which are pulled more and more tight. The procedure is successful.

In the end Selenia and Arthur share a kiss before Maltazard explains.

It turns out that Maltazard sent the message to lure Arthur, so that Maltazard can use the passage back, which is available at the next noon. Thus he arrives in the world of humans, enlarged to their size. He is pleased to see that animals are afraid of him.

Arthur is stuck in small size in the Minimoy kingdom, because the telescope to be used for his return has been destroyed by the passage of Maltazard. This could mean that he can only return after ten months.

The film ends abruptly, with the sound of The Minimoys Band singing "Poker Face", with the hook "ma-ma-ma-ma" in the opening of the song is replaced by "ma-ma-ma-ma... Maltazard". The plot is continued in the following film, *Arthur and the War of Two Worlds*. The teaser at the end of the film shows a human Arthur being pursued by Maltazard's soldiers in a grocery store, who he trips up by tipping a display of oranges down the aisle.

Cast

Characters are animated, live action, or each partly. Correspondingly the actor provides a voice only, or is visually present in the film.

Character	Film		
	Arthur and the Invisibles	*Arthur and the Revenge of Maltazard*	*Arthur and the War of Two Worlds*
Arthur	Freddie Highmore		
Grandma Daisy	Mia Farrow		
Grandpa Archibald	Ron Crawford		
Armand, Arthur's Dad	Doug Rand	Robert Stanton	
Rose, Arthur's Mother	Penny Balfour		
Chief Matassalai	Jean Bejote Njamba		
Ernesto Davido	Adam LeFevre		
Princess Selenia	Madonna	Selena Gomez	
Prince Betameche	Jimmy Fallon	Doug Rand	
Minimoy King	Robert De Niro	David Gasman	
Miro	Harvey Keitel	Paul Bandey	

Mino	Erik Per Sullivan		
Max	Snoop Dogg		
Snow		Will.i.am	
Replay		Stacy Ferguson	
Travel Agent	Chazz Palminteri		
Ferryman	Emilio Estevez	Leslie Clack	
Jake		Logan Miller	
Maltazard	David Bowie	Lou Reed	

Internet

The Arthur web portal gives access to the films' official websites as well as an entry to an Arthur's Virtual World designed for children. The teaser trailer has been released for the film.[1] [2] [3] [4]

Within the website of *Arthur and the Revenge of Maltazard*, a web application in real-time 3D enables viewers to create a virtual avatar from a photo or a webcam, to customize it and to share it among contacts. This user experience was developed through a strategic partnership with Dassault Systemes and uses the Virtools technology.

American release

4Kids Entertainment and The Weinstein Company. Notably, the actors who provided voices in the first film, with the exception of Snoop Dogg and those who had live-action roles have been recast.

UK release

The UK version will be released on December 17th 2010. The films title has been changed to Arthur and the Great Adventure in the UK and Ireland.

Japanese release

Asmik Ace handles the official Japanese dubbed version of the movie and it's released on April 29, 2010. The dubbed version will feature famous J-pop artist Gackt as the voice of Maltazard. IMALU is also confirmed to sing the movie's opening song titled **"Uh Uh"**.

References

[1] http://www.youtube.com/watch?v=noHozne8_oQ
[2] http://www.youtube.com/watch?v=FmLaqGOEkJ8
[3] http://www.youtube.com/watch?v=pBffj9Gji5g
[4] http://www.youtube.com/watch?v=0qa0K7P_qio

External links

- Official website (http://http://www.arthuretlesminimoys.com/arthur2/index.html)
- *Arthur et la vengeance de Maltazard* (http://www.bcdb.com/bcdb/cartoon.cgi?film=114041/) at the Big Cartoon DataBase
- *Arthur et la vengeance de Maltazard* (http://www.imdb.com/title/tt0940657/) at the Internet Movie Database

Monte Carlo (2011 film)

Monte Carlo	
Directed by	Tom Bezucha
Produced by	Nicole Kidman Denise Di Novi Alison Greenspan
Written by	Tom Bezucha April Blair
Starring	Selena Gomez Katie Cassidy Leighton Meester Catherine Tate Cory Monteith Andie MacDowell Pierre Boulanger Luke Bracey Brett Cullen
Editing by	Jeffrey Ford
Studio	New Regency Productions Regency Enterprises Dune Entertainment Walden Media
Distributed by	20th Century Fox
Release date(s)	July 1, 2011
Country	United States
Language	English

Monte Carlo is an upcoming American romantic comedy film, coming out July 1, 2011, directed by Tom Bezucha. Nicole Kidman, Denise Di Novi and Alison Greenspan are producing the film for 20th Century Fox and Walden Media, New Regency Productions, Regency Enterprises.[1] It is loosely based on the novel *Headhunters* by Jules Bass. It began production in Budapest on May 5, 2010.[2] *Monte Carlo* stars Selena Gomez, Katie Cassidy and Leighton Meester[1] as three friends posing as wealthy socialites in Monaco.[3] The film will be released on July 1, 2011.[4] Allison Iraheta sings the movie's theme song, "Don't Waste the Pretty," which features Orianthi.

Plot

Three young girls (Selena Gomez, Leighton Meester, Katie Cassidy) use their savings for a dream trip to Paris, which turns out to be a big disaster. When they decide to take a break from their lousy tour and sneak into the lobby of a 5-star hotel, one of the girls is mistaken for a spoiled British heiress. Before they get the chance to reveal their true identities, the girls are wrapped up in a whirlwind of paparazzi, private planes, couture gowns, storybook romances, and living the glamorous life in Monte Carlo.

Cast

- Selena Gomez as Grace, a young girl who goes on vacation with Emma and her future step-sister.[5]
- Katie Cassidy as Emma,[6] a "high school dropout who wants to see what the world has to offer."[7]
- Leighton Meester as Meg, Grace's future step-sister.[8]
- Cory Monteith as Owen, Emma's love interest, a truck-driving football player who follows her to Europe.[9]
- Andie MacDowell as Grace's mother.[7]
- Luke Bracey as Riley, Meg's love interest.[6]
- Pierre Boulanger as Theo, Grace's love interest.[10]
- Brett Cullen as a love interest.[6]
- Carlos Alvarez as Grace's little brother

Production

Monte Carlo is loosely based on the novel *Headhunters* by Jules Bass. The novel tells the story of four middle-aged New Jersey women who pretend to be wealthy heiresses while searching for rich potential husbands in Monte Carlo. There, they meet four gigolos posing as wealthy playboys. Fox bought the film rights to the novel in 1999, three years prior to the novel's publication.[11] In 2005, Hollywood trade magazine *Variety* announced that siblings Jez and John Henry Butterworth would be writing the script. It also reported that actress Nicole Kidman had signed on to play the lead as well as produce the film with Rick Schwartz.[11]

Gomez during filming in Paris(beautiful day) on June 21, 2010.

The Butterworths were later fired because of irresponsibility and Tom Bezucha was hired to direct and co-write *Monte Carlo*. Bezucha and Maria Maggenti turned in a draft of the screenplay by July 2007; it starred Kidman as "one of three Midwestern schoolteachers who decide to ditch a disappointing no-frills holiday in Paris and pose as wealthy women vacationing in Monaco".[12] However, in 2010, executives had the film rewritten again after deciding that the film should be made more youthful. Also Carlos Alvarez said that the updated script was co-written by Bezucha and April Blair and changed the three schoolteachers to two college students and a recent high-school graduate.[11] *Monte Carlo* was shot in Budapest, Hungary, Paris, France and Monaco.[12] It began filming in Budapest on May 5, 2010 and finished filming on July 7, 2010. It was planned for a February 11th release date, but on November 28, it was revealed the film was pushed to a July 1, 2011 Summer July 4th weekend release to appear to a wider audience.[2] It is the first film to use the film studio Raleigh Studios Budapest.[13]

Casting

In March 2010, it was announced Selena Gomez has been cast as one of the film's leads following the script's rewrite.[8] For the role, Gomez spent several weeks learning to play polo and to fake an English accent.[2] Leighton Meester also negotiated a deal to one of the leads in March, and Katie Cassidy was cast as Emma in April.[7] French actor Pierre Boulanger will make his American film debut as the love interest of Gomez's character.[10]

References

[1] McClintock, Pamela (2010-03-03). "Fox, New Regency head to 'Monte Carlo'" (http://www.variety.com/article/VR1118016027.html). *Variety*. . Retrieved 2010-05-10.

[2] Gomez, Selena (05-06-2010). "Note from Selena!" (http://selenagomez.com/news/note-selena). *SelenaGomez.com*. . Retrieved 05-07-2010.

[3] Los Angeles Production Listings (http://www.backstage.com/bso/production-listings/los-angeles-production-listings-1004086063.story)

[4] http://boxofficemojo.com/movies/?id=montecarlo.htm

[5] "Selena Gomez Describes Her 'Monte Carlo' Character, Is 'Thrilled' To Star With Leighton Meester » Hollywood Crush" (http:// hollywoodcrush.mtv.com/2010/04/01/selena-gomez-monte-carlo). *HollywoodCrush.MTV.com*. 2010-03-30. . Retrieved 2010-05-10.

[6] "Selena Gomez's 'Monte Carlo' Boyfriend Found: French Actor Pierre Boulanger » Hollywood Crush" (http://hollywoodcrush.mtv.com/ ?p=33722). *HollywoodCrush.MTV.com*. 2010-04-26. . Retrieved 2010-05-10.

[7] Kit, Borys (2010-04-09). "Two teens plan trip to Monaco" (http://www.hollywoodreporter.com/hr/content_display/news/ e3i8351d327c2b5b41eaae88e5c016a2123). *The Hollywood Reporter*: pp. 1, 13. . Retrieved 2010-05-10.

[8] McClintock, Pamela (2010-04-08). "Cassidy set for 'Monte Carlo'" (http://www.variety.com/article/VR1118017429.html). *Variety*. . Retrieved 2010-05-10.

[9] "'Glee' Star Cory Monteith Giddy About His 'Monte Carlo' Movie Role: Love Interest To Katie Cassidy » Hollywood Crush" (http:// hollywoodcrush.mtv.com/2010/04/14/cory-monteith-monte-carlo). *HollywoodCrush.MTV.com*. 2010-04-14. . Retrieved 2010-05-10.

[10] McClintock, Pamela (2010-04-26). "French actor makes English debut" (http://www.variety.com/article/VR1118018295.html). *Variety*. . Retrieved 2010-05-10.

[11] Mohr, Ian (2005-09-25). "'Head' games at Fox 2000" (http://www.variety.com/article/VR1117929656.html). *Variety.com*. . Retrieved 2010-05-10.

[12] Fleming, Michael (2007-07-09). "Kidman to star in 'Monte Carlo'" (http://www.variety.com/article/VR1117968258.html). *Variety.com*. . Retrieved 2010-05-07.

[13] (2010-05-07). Hollywood style film studio opens in Budapest (http://news.xinhuanet.com/english2010/entertainment/2010-05/07/ c_13281446.htm). Retrieved 2010-11-20.

External links

- Monte Carlo (http://www.imdb.com/title/tt1067774/) at the Internet Movie Database

Wizards of Waverly Place: The Movie

Wizards of Waverly Place: The Movie	
	Extended Edition DVD Cover
Genre	Fantasy, comedy-drama
Distributed by	Disney Channel Original Movie
Directed by	Lev L. Spiro
Produced by	Kevin Lafferty Todd J. Greenwald Peter Murrieta
Written by	Dan Berendsen
Starring	Selena Gomez David Henrie Jake T. Austin Jennifer Stone Maria Canals-Barrera Steve Valentine Xavier Torres Jennifer Alden David DeLuise
Music by	Keith Burgomaster
Editing by	Matthew Colonna
Country	United States
Language	English
Original channel	Disney Channel
Release date	August 28, 2009[1]
Running time	98 minutes
Followed by	*Wizards of Waverly Place 2: The Next Big Adventure*[2]

Wizards of Waverly Place: The Movie is a 2009 American television film adaptation of the Disney Channel Original Series, *Wizards of Waverly Place*. Filmed primarily in San Juan, Puerto Rico in February and March 2009, it premiered on August 28, 2009 on Disney Channel in the United States.[3] The film received 13.4 million viewers at its premiere,[4] making it the second-most-viewed DCOM (Disney Channel Original Movie) premiere at that time, after *High School Musical 2*. It was also cable's No. 1 scripted telecast of 2009 in total viewers.[5] The film received generally positive reviews. The review aggregate website Rotten Tomatoes reported that 62% of RT Community gave the film positive reviews, based on 2693 reviews, with an average score of 7.2/10.[6]

The film won the 2010 Primetime Emmy Award for Best Children Program.[7] The film was directed by Lev L. Spiro, and premiered on Disney Channel in the UK and Ireland on October 23, 2009 as part of Wiz-Tober 2009.

The full cast of the series starred in the film, except for Jennifer Stone, who only had a small role in the film. The DVD was released on December 15, 2009 as an *Extended Edition*. The film focuses on the Russo family taking a vacation to the Carribean.

Plot

The entire Russo family, except Alex (Selena Gomez), who is to be staying with her best friend Harper Finkle (Jennifer Stone), are preparing for a vacation to Puerto Rico. Alex decides to sneak a peek at Justin (David Henrie)'s personal belongings when his enchanted backpack attacks Alex trapping her as Justin had planned. When her father, Jerry (David DeLuise) comes down to help he accidentally speaks of the forbidden book of spells and how he let Justin borrow it, which Alex takes when no one is looking. Alex wants to go to a party with Harper but her mother, Theresa (Maria Canals Barrera) tells her she can not go to the party because its all the way in Brooklyn and she doesn't know the girls' parents.

After her parents go out, and her brothers are not in sight, Alex puts a spell on the subway train so it will take them to the party (without actually leaving the building since her parents told her she wasn't allowed to), but Alex and Harper miss the party after almost getting killed by a real subway train and running into a dead end tunnel, only to be saved by Justin. Unfortunately, the side frame of the subway car falls off, just as their parents come back. Because of this, Alex is forced to go on vacation with the rest of the family to Puerto Rico, the kids having their wands confiscated. Along the way they meet a street magician and former wizard (Steve Valentine) (who lost the full-wizard contest to his older brother) named Archie who wants to turn his girlfriend, Giselle, from a parrot back into a human by finding the Stone of Dreams, which has the power to grant any wish or reverse any spell. Jerry considers it crazy since many wizards have gone on the quest and never returned.

Later, after Alex was about to use a spell on her mother to convince her to let Alex hang out with a boy but doesn't work because she does not have the full wand, she gets caught, grounded and forbidden to use magic that means no dates no parties and no magic. After a heated argument with Theresa, Alex, in a fit of rage, wishes that her parents had never met; unfortunately, the smuggled full-wizard wand and spell book, which Alex was holding at the time, grants her wish. As a result, Jerry and Theresa do not remember Justin, Alex and Max (Jake T. Austin) or each other. The children will gradually forget their past as a result, and then disappear forever. After consulting Jerry, Justin and Alex set off to find the Stone of Dreams, guided by Archie. Eventually, Alex and Justin succeed in finding the Stone of Dreams, but Giselle steals the stone. The kids tell Theresa and Jerry their story. Theresa doesn't believe them because she thinks she would never forget her own children. While trying to figure out how to reverse the spell without the stone of dreams, Jerry mentions that if one of the kids was a full wizard, they might be able to cast a spell to reverse it. While preparing to begin the full-wizard contest, Max finally loses all memory of who he is and gets sucked into the vortex of non-existence. Theresa remembers him slightly, and realizes that they were telling the truth. Realizing they must work quickly, Alex and Justin are transported to an ancient battlefield, where the contest will be held. Jerry explains that they will only be allowed to use spells involving the four elements (earth, water, fire, and air). The winner will become a full wizard, and the loser gets nothing while losing their powers forever. Alex and Justin engage in what turns out to be an intense battle, and Alex narrowly wins.

In trying to come up with a spell to fix everything, she turns to Justin for help. However, Justin has lost all his memory and is sucked into the same vortex that Max was. Desperate, Alex tries to cast a reversal spell, but Jerry tells her it may be too late. Alex then wishes that everything go back to the way it was before, and time rewinds back to the beginning of the argument between Alex and Theresa that started all the trouble, which is quickly stopped when Alex apologizes and accepts her punishments with grace; while Theresa and Jerry remember nothing about the ordeal, Alex, Justin, and Max do.

Cast

- Selena Gomez as Alex Russo
- David Henrie as Justin Russo
- Jake T. Austin as Max Russo
- Maria Canals-Barrera as Theresa Russo
- David DeLuise as Jerry Russo
- Jennifer Stone as Harper Finkle
- Steve Valentine as Archie
- Jennifer Alden as Giselle
- Xavier Enrique Torres as Javier
- Johnathan Dwayne as Activities director
- Jazmín Caratini as Bartender
- Marise Alvarez as Greeter
- Bettina Mercado as Woman in Village #1
- Veraalba Santa as Woman in Village #2
- Gabriela Alejandra Rosario as Village Girl
- Ruby as Giselle the Parrot (uncredited)

Production

Casting

The full cast of the Disney Channel Original Series *Wizards of Waverly Place* starred in the film.

Filming

Wizards of Waverly Place: The Movie was filmed primarily in San Juan, Puerto Rico in February and March 2009. Hotel scenes were shot at the Caribe Hilton in San Juan. The *Wizards of Waverly Place The Movie: What's What Edition* shows where the film was shot. On their way to Puerto Rico it says that Selena Gomez's face was really a bored looking face, that she wasn't acting in that scene, she actually meant it.

Also during filming the Director, Lev L. Spiro found a spider on the cave where the Stone of Dreams is, and that the bats were real, but Gomez and Henrie had to be careful to not wake them up. The subway scene where we see the train from the platform was shot in Toronto, despite the series being based in New York.

Promotion

Selena Gomez recorded a "Magic" cover for the film that is featured on the soundtrack for the film and television show.[8] A sneak peek of the film aired during the conclusion of the four-part "Wizards vs. Vampires" event on Disney Channel on August 8, 2009 and on Family Channel during the week of August 24, 2009. The What's What Edition of the film premiered on October 24, 2009 on Disney Channel.[9]

DCOM extras

The DCOM extras of the film aired on Disney Channel before the premiering of the film. It shows behind the scenes features of the movie and interviews of the cast. A total of 4 DCOM extras premiered on Disney Channel. DCOM extras stands for Disney Channel Original Movie Extras.

Release

The film premiered on Disney Channel as a Disney Channel Original Movie on August 28, 2009, with 13.6 million viewers that night making the TV-film a success. The film premiered in the UK and Ireland on October 23, 2009 as part of Wiz-Tober 2009. The film premiered in Spain on October 11, 2009 as part of Magoctubre 2009 in Spain.

Reception

The film received generally positive reviews. The review aggregate website Rotten Tomatoes reported that 62% of RT Community gave the film positive reviews, based on 2693 reviews, with an average score of 7.2/10.[6]

Ratings

The film garnered 13.5 million viewers on its premiere night,[4] making it cable's No. 1 scripted telecast of 2009 and Disney Channel's second most-viewed film premiere after *High School Musical 2*.[10] On its second night, the film's second showing received 5.8 million viewers. The next day, the film's third showing got 4.3 million viewers, and its fourth showing received 4.7 million viewers.[11] [12] When the film premiered in the UK, as part of Wiz-tober, the film received 1.04 million viewers, which made it the 7th most watched program on multi-channel viewing for that week, and the second highest views watched on Disney Channel UK.[13]

What's What Edition

The "What's What Edition" of the film premiered on October 24, 2009 on Disney Channel, part of a *Wizards of Waverly Place* marathon. The "What's What Edition" features exclusive behind the scenes information on the film during the presentation.

Soundtrack

In an interview with Disney Channel's commercial-segment, *Disney 365*, Selena Gomez discussed her interpretations of the songs on the soundtrack saying: "'Disappear' is more of a romantic song. It's basically talking about how a girl likes a guy and they [she] don't want him to disappear, and then 'Magical' is about casting a spell on a guy and this song, 'Magic', ties in to *Wizards of Waverly Place: The Movie*".[14] Although recorded for an episode, "Make it Happen" doesn't appear on the album, for an unknown reason. The album includes songs from and inspired by the TV series and *Wizards of Waverly Place: The Movie*.[14] [15] "Magic" by Selena Gomez is a digital single on the iTunes Store. The song was released on July 21, 2009 as part of the Radio Disney iTunes Pass.[16] "Magic" premiered on Radio Disney and a music video to Disney Channel on July 24. The song's music video has Gomez singing into a microphone with bright and flamboyant background, as well as including clips from *Wizards of Waverly Place: The Movie*.[15] [17] "Magic" debuted at no. 61 in the *Billboard* Hot 100 with 42,000 downloads.[18]

Track listing

Standard Edition[19]			
No.	Title	Recording Artist(s)	Length
1.	"Disappear"	Selena Gomez	3:39
2.	"Magical"	Selena Gomez	2:54
3.	"Magic" (Originally by Pilot)	Selena Gomez	2:49
4.	"Strange Magic" (Originally by Electric Light Orchestra)	Steve Rushton	3:20
5.	"Magic" (Originally by The Cars)	Honor Society	3:51
6.	"Every Little Thing She Does Is Magic" (Originally by The Police)	Mitchel Musso	3:44
7.	"Magic Carpet Ride" (Originally by Steppenwolf)	KSM	2:57
8.	"Magic" (Originally by Olivia Newton-John)	Meaghan Jette Martin	4:08
9.	"You Can Do Magic" (Originally by America)	Drew Seeley	3:33
10.	"Some Call It Magic"	Raven-Symoné	3:13
11.	"Do You Believe in Magic" (Originally by The Lovin' Spoonful)	78violet	2:13
12.	"Everything Is Not As It Seems" (Theme song)	Selena Gomez	0:51

Home video release

The film was released on DVD in the United States and Canada on December 15, 2009 as an "Extended Edition", which also came with a replica of the Stone of Dreams in a necklace. The film is in English, French and Spanish, and has subtitles in the same languages. The film was also released on DVD in Australia on December 15, 2009, in Germany and France on December 2, 2009, and in the United Kingdom on February 22, 2010. Though, The film was not released on Blu-ray disc.

Awards and nominations

Year	Award	Category	Result
2010	62nd Primetime Emmy Awards	Outstanding Children's Program	**Won**
	Image Awards	Outstanding Children's Program	Nominated
	Golden Reel Award	Best Sound Editing	Nominated

Marketing

The film's first teaser trailer of the was released on Disney Channel on June 17, 2009. The full-length trailer was released on June 26, 2009, during the premiere of Selena Gomez's other Disney Channel Original Movie, Princess Protection Program.[9]

Worldwide release

Country / Region	Network(s)	Premiere	Movie title in country
United States (including Puerto Rico)	Disney Channel	August 28, 2009	Wizards of Waverly Place: The Movie
Canada	Family		
Latin America	Disney Channel Latin America	October 11, 2009 (as a part of Abracadubre 2009)	Los Hechiceros de Waverly Place: La Película
Spain	Disney Channel Spain	October 17, 2009 (as a part of Magoctubre 2009)	Los Magos de Waverly Place: Vacaciones en el Caribe
	Cuatro	December 2, 2009	
Portugal	Disney Channel Portugal	October 17, 2009 (as part of Feitiçoutubro 2009)	Os Feiticeiros de Waverly Place: Férias nas Caraíbas
	SIC	December 24, 2009	
UK	Disney Channel (UK and Ireland)	October 23, 2009 (as a part of Wiz-tober 2009)	Wizards of Waverly Place: The Movie
Ireland			
Brazil	Disney Channel Brazil	October 25, 2009 (as a part of Abracadubro 2009)	Os Feiticeiros de Waverly Place: O Filme
France	Disney Channel France	October 27, 2009	Les Sorciers de Waverly Place: Le Film
Québec	VRAK.TV	December 21, 2009	
Germany	Disney Channel Germany	October 30, 2009	Die Zauberer vom Waverly Place − Der Film
	Pro 7	November 29, 2009	
Switzerland	SF ZWEI Aired in Dual Audio Channel - English & German		
Austria	ORF 1		
Greece	ET1 (Greece)	December 5, 2009	Οι Μάγοι του Γουέιβερλυ − Η Ταινία
Cyprus	Disney Channel (Greece)	September 28,2010	
Northern Cyprus	Disney Channel (Greece)	September 28,2010	
Netherlands	Disney Channel (Netherlands/Flanders)	December 24, 2009 (as a part of WishCember)	Wizards of Waverly Place: The Movie
Belgium			
Italy	Disney Channel Italy	October 30, 2009 (as a part of Magottobre 2009)	I Maghi di Waverly − The Movie
	Italia 1	January 6, 2010	
Poland	Disney Channel Poland Disney XD Poland	October 31, 2009 (as a part of Magic October 2009),2010	Czarodzieje z Waverly Place − Film
Taiwan	Disney Channel Taiwan	December 25, 2009	少年魔法師:電影版
Denmark	Disney Channel Scandinavia	October 30, 2009	Magi på Waverly Place: Filmen
Sweden			Magi på Waverly Place - The Movie
Czech Republic	Disney Channel (Hungary, the Czech Republic, Slovakia)	October 31, 2009 (Wiz-tober 2009)	Kouzelníci z Waverly - Film
Slovakia			
Hungary			Varázslók a Waverly helyből - A Film
Romania	Disney Channel Romania	October 31, 2009 (as part of Un Octombrie Magic	Magicienii din Waverly Place: Filmul

▭ Israel	Disney Channel Israel	November 26, 2009	מכשפים מווברלי פלייס: הסרט
◉ Arab World	Disney Channel Middle East	October 31, 2009 (as a part of Wiz-tober 2009)	Wizards of Waverly Place: The Movie
● Japan	Disney Channel Japan	March 19, 2010	ウェイバリー通りのウィザードたち ザ ム――ビ――
▤ Russia	Disney Channel Russia	October 31,2010	Волшебники из Вейверли Плейс: кино

References

[1] "Wizards of Waverly Place The Movie at Disneychannel.com" (http://tv.disney.go.com/disneychannel/originalmovies/ wizardsofwaverlyplacethemovie/). Disney Channel. . Retrieved 2009-08-03.

[2] Disney Channel Renews "Wizards of Waverly Place" for a Fourth Season; Plans Second Movie (http://tvbythenumbers.com/2010/06/03/ disney-channel-renews-wizards-of-waverly-place-for-a-fourth-season/53112) Posted on 03 June 2010 by Robert Seidman of TVbytheNumbers

[3] Disney Channel (July 13, 2009). "Hit Comedy Series Inspires an Adventure-Themed Disney Channel Original Movie, "Wizards of Waverly Place The Movie," Premiering Friday, August 28 on Disney Channel" (http://www.webcitation.org/5m9v6eTQ4). Press release. Archived from the original (http://disneychannelmedianet.com/DNR/2009/doc/WOWP_MoviePremiere.doc) on December 20, 2009. . Retrieved August 3, 2009.

[4] "Top 100 Most-Watched Telecasts On Basic Cable For 2009" (http://tvbythenumbers.com/2009/12/29/ espn-domination-top-100-most-watched-telecasts-on-basic-cable-for-2009/37284). . Retrieved 2010-09-21.

[5] name="tvbythenumbers.com">http://tvbythenumbers.com/2009/12/29/ espn-domination-top-100-most-watched-telecasts-on-basic-cable-for-2009/37284

[6] Wizards of Waverly Place: The Movie (http://www.rottentomatoes.com/m/wizards_of_waverly_place_the_movie/reviews_users.php) on Rotten Tomatoes

[7] "Nominations: Official Primetime Emmy Award Nominations 2010" (http://www.emmys.com/nominations?tid=123). Academy of Television Arts & Sciences. 2010-07-08. . Retrieved 2010-07-08.

[8] "SELENA GOMEZ'S "MAGIC" MUSIC VIDEO PREMIERES FRIDAY, JULY 24 ON DISNEY CHANNEL" (http://www. disneychannelmedianet.com/DNR/2009/doc/MagicVideo_072309.doc). Disney Channel. 2009-07-23. . Retrieved 2009-08-03.

[9] "Full-Length Trailer of 'Wizards of Waverly Place: The Movie'". Aceshowbiz. 2009-06-27.

[10] http://tvbythenumbers.com/2009/12/29/espn-domination-top-100-most-watched-telecasts-on-basic-cable-for-2009/37284

[11] http://disneychannelmedianet.com/DNR/2009/html/DC_Aug24_30_09.html

[12] http://tvbythenumbers.com/2009/09/01/cable-ratings-wizards-of-waverly-place-the-closer-wwe-raw-royal-pains/25880

[13] http://www.barb.co.uk/

[14] "Disney 365 - Wizards Soundtrack" (http://disney.go.com/videos/#/videos/musicvideos/&content=358849). Disney.com. . Retrieved August 3, 2009.

[15] Kelly Grant, Brenda (July 23, 2009). "SELENA GOMEZ'S "MAGIC" MUSIC VIDEO PREMIERES FRIDAY, JULY 24 ON DISNEY CHANNEL" (http://disneychannelmedianet.com/DNR/2009/doc/MagicVideo_072309.doc). Disney Channel. . Retrieved August 3, 2009.

[16] "Radio Disney iTunes Pass" (http://radio.disney.go.com/music/itunes.html). Apple (iTunes Store). . Retrieved August 3, 2009.

[17] "Disney.com: Selena Gomez - Magic" (http://disney.go.com/videos/#/videos/musicvideos/&content=363566). Disney.com. . Retrieved August 3, 2009.

[18] Ben-Yehuda, Ayala & Trust, Gary (August 13, 2009). "Black Eyed Peas, Jason Mraz Tie Records on Billboard Hot 100" (http://www. billboard.com/#/news/black-eyed-peas-jason-mraz-tie-records-on-1004002946.story). *Billboard*. . Retrieved August 14, 2009.

[19] "Amazon.com: Wizards of Waverly Place" (http://www.amazon.com/Wizards-Waverly-Place-Soundtrack/dp/B002BA9QMK/ ref=sr_1_6?ie=UTF8&s=music&qid=1244079309&sr=8-6). Amazon.com. . Retrieved August 3, 2009.

External links

- Official website (http://http://www.disneychannel.com/wizardsmovie)
- *Wizards of Waverly Place: The Movie* (http://www.imdb.com/title/tt1369845/) at the Internet Movie Database

List of *The Suite Life of Zack & Cody* episodes

The following is an episode list for the Disney Channel situation comedy, *The Suite Life of Zack & Cody*.

Series overview

Season	Episodes	Originally aired (U.S. dates)	
		Season premiere	Season finale
1	26	March 18, 2005	January 27, 2006
2	39	February 3, 2006	June 2, 2007
3	22	June 23, 2007	September 1, 2008

Season 1: 2005–06

- Season 1 consisted of 26 episodes.
- This season was filmed from September 2004 - May 2005.

Series #	Season #	Title	Directed by	Written by	Original U.S. air date	Production code
1	1	"Hotel Hangout"	Rich Correll	Jeny Quine	March 18, 2005	102

Zack and Cody meet Max and Tapeworm and invite them over, but when the Drew Crew finds out that they live in the Tipton Hotel, they suddenly want to hang out with the twins instead, leaving Max and Tapeworm behind. Meanwhile, Maddie tutors London in Math, and London gives Maddie advice on how to talk to the hotel lifeguard, Lance.

Guest stars: Adrian R'Mante as Esteban, Dennis Bendersky as Tapeworm, Jascha Washington as Drew, Alyson Stoner as Max, Aaron Musicant as Lance

2	2	"The Fairest of Them All"	Rich Correll	Valerie Ahern Christian McLaughlin	March 18, 2005	104

A beauty pageant checks into the Tipton to participate in a beauty contest. Cody bumps into a girl named Rebecca and finds that he likes her. When he accidentally enters the beauty pageant, Zack convinces him to stay in so they can win the 2,000 dollar prize so they can buy bikes, which they couldn't afford.

Guest stars: Stephanie Hodge as Brianna's mom, Victoria Justice as Rebecca, Lisa Long as Bev, Skyler Samuels as Brianna, Matt Winston as Tim
Co-stars: Paige Hurd as Tiffany, Camille Smith as Tyreesha, Virginia Watson as Tyreesha's Mom

3	3	"Maddie Checks In"	Rich Correll	Danny Kallis Jim Geoghan	March 25, 2005	103

A hotel guest named Jason checks into the Tipton Hotel, and Maddie seems to like him very much. When London invites her and Jason to see a concert, she asks Maddie to play along for one night and act rich. This backfires when Jason and his parents stay another night in Boston, and when Zack and Cody get involved. They get her into the imperial suite, but another guest, the Amputator, checks into Maddie's suite, so the boys must dismantle the suite in order for the wrestler to check out of the hotel.

4	4	"Hotel Inspector"	Henry Chan	Marc Flanagan	April 1, 2005	107

Mr. Moseby gives Zack and Cody tickets to a baseball game while the health inspector arrives at the Tipton. Unfortunately, the boys arrive before the inspector does and due to Zack's rat (and Cody's, which he stole as part of their science project), it causes chaos in the hotel, getting Mr. Moseby fired in the process. Together, they must devise a way to get Mr. Moseby back.

Guest stars: Caroline Rhea as Ilsa, Adrian R'Mante as Esteban

5	5	"Grounded on the 23rd Floor"	Lee Shallat-Chemel	Danny Kallis Jim Geoghan	April 8, 2005	101

Zack and Cody get grounded for rollerblading in the lobby, injuring Mr. Moseby in the process. When they find out a famous couple is getting married at the hotel, they buy a camera off Maddie to take a picture of the kiss that was rumored to be selling for 20,000 dollars. Zack sneaks into the wedding and takes the picture, only for Maddie, Cody, and Zack to be busted by Mr. Moseby. The boys are grounded again for another week after Carey finds out.

Note: This was originally the first episode of the entire series, as the episode style and layout was that of a pilot episode and many of the props used in the episode (such as Maddie's uniform or some furniture in the Martins' suite) were not used in future episodes. Additionally, Maddie has brown hair in this episode. An alternate version of this episode also aired with different cuts and extended scenes, including an an extended scene after Maddie and London talk and London says "Hold that elevator!" and more conversations between Zack and Cody when they are observing armpit hairs and when Carrie refers to the previous hotel accident.

6	6	**"The Prince & The Plunger"**	Andrew Tsao	Adam Lapidus	April 15, 2005	106

Arwin, the hotel engineer, sends Carey flowers and a poem. However, she thinks they were sent by Serge the concierge, who when asked, lied to Carey about the flowers and poem. When Zack and Cody find out, they help Arwin tell Carey that it was him who sent the flowers. Meanwhile, London's father (the owner of the Tipton) is attending her father-daughter dance, but he fails to show due to usual circumstances.

7	7	**"Footloser"**	Rich Correll	Bill Freiberger	April 22, 2005	105

Zack and Max enter GoDance USA, a dance contest. However, when Zack hurts his ankle by jumping off the bed, Cody has to take his place for him, despite being a terrible dancer. Meanwhile, London lends Maddie money for her parents' trip to Paris, but then to pay back the favor, Maddie becomes her servant until London is paid back.

Note: Cody makes a reference to the Missy Elliott video for "I'm Really Hot," which guest-starred Alyson Stoner

Guest star: Alyson Stoner as Max

8	8	**"A Prom Story"**	Jim Drake	Jeny Quine	May 6, 2005	111

Maddie's high school prom is coming up, and Zack finds out by throwing it at the Tipton. When he overhears her saying that she likes a guy who has an age difference from her by three years, he thought it was him, not Jeff (the guy she liked). Meanwhile, a circus comes to the Tipton, prompting Cody to act like a mime. When Zack gets his heart broken by Maddie, she gets her heart broken by Jeff, who has a college girlfriend. Maddie then agrees to dance with Zack.

Note: In the end of this episode, Maddie makes a deal with Zack. She tells him that she will dance with him at his prom, if he dances with her at her prom.

Guest star: Monique Coleman

9	9	**"Band in Boston"**	Rich Correll	Billy Riback	May 20, 2005	112

Zack, Cody, Max, and Tapeworm organize a band called Rock Squared for battle of the bands, but due to fighting, Zack and Cody quit the band at different times. On the day of the event, Max locks the twins in their closet, but they find their own way there, provided by Arwin. Meanwhile, Maddie and Lance's band Waterworks for battle of the bands instruments' are funded by London after they promise she can be a back-up singer, but she is a terrible singer.

Guest stars: Alyson Stoner as Max, Dennis Bendersky as Tapeworm

10	10	**"Cody Goes to Camp"**	Rich Correll	Jim Geoghan	June 6, 2005	113

Cody and Tapeworm go to math camp for a week, leaving Zack on his own for a few days. Meanwhile, London gets her learner's permit and while Mr. Moseby teaches her how to drive, her car ends up in the Tipton hotel wall. When Zack starts to miss Cody, he persuades London, Maddie, and Muriel to drive up to camp to check on Cody with him.

11	11	**"To Catch a Thief"**	Jeff McCracken	Ross Brown	June 18, 2005	108

Esteban is accused of a jewelry theft after someone's jewelry was stolen. Zack and Cody try to prove it wasn't him, but they end up crashing a Bar Mitzvah, for which they get punished. Meanwhile, London can't bring her dog onto her dad's ship, so Maddie takes care of Ivana (the dog) while she's gone. When Zack and Cody overhear the real thieves talking about heading up to London's suite, the twins, Esteban, and Maddie all set a trap to catch the real thieves.

Note: This is the first time we see the "S.S. Tipton" when London is on the phone with Maddie. The life preserver says "S.S. Tipton."

12	12	**"It's a Mad, Mad, Mad Hotel"**	Lex Passaris	Howard Nemetz	July 17, 2005	114

When Zack and Cody's football breaks a painting hung up in the hallway, they find an article on the back saying that someone was coming back for his treasure. Desperate, Zack, Cody, Maddie, London, and Esteban all imagine what their life would be like if they found the treasure, despite London already rich. They all search frantically for the treasure, but they end up breaking into the bank of Boston. In the end, the real treasure was Muriel.

13	13	"Poor Little Rich Girl"	Dana deVally Piazza	Lloyd Garver	July 22, 2005	110

Zack and Cody watch a video of them being born, but in the video, their mom might have mistaken them for each other, so they become the complete opposite of theirselves. Meanwhile, London becomes poor after finding out her father went bankrupt from a failed investment of diamonds, so she stays with Maddie until her father can find a place for her to stay.

14	14	"Cookin' with Romeo and Juliet"	Jim Drake	Jeny Quine Adam Lapidus	July 22, 2005	115

Ilsa, the hotel inspector who attempted to replace Mr. Moseby as manager of the Tipton (see episode 4), returns and informs Mr. Moseby that she is the manager of the hotel across the street. The son of the rival hotel owner likes London but the owners of the hotel hate each other. Maddie helps them meet behind everyone's back. Zack tries to make money from Cody's cookies which are the best some people have ever tasted.

Guest stars: Caroline Rhea as Ilsa, Ben Ziff as Todd

15	15	"Rumors"	Rich Correll	Bernadette Luckett	August 14, 2005	116

London starts a rumor about Maddie and Lance that angers Maddie, eventually leading her into accidentally beginning a rumor about London that she has real fox fur in her closet. It turns out that she pronounced "faux" as "fox," which caused Maddie to think she had real animal furs. Cody tries to make himself look less like Zack by dyeing his hair, it accidentally turned red and he asks Zack to take his place in an interview.

16	16	"Big Hair & Baseball"	Rich Correll	Pamela Eells O'Connell	August 28, 2005	117

Mr. Moseby takes Zack and Cody to a baseball game, but when he accidentally catches a baseball that makes the Boston Red Sox lose the game, everyone in Boston hates him. Maddie attempts to stop her hair from frizzing before going to a blind date London set up for her with a boy who sweats when he's nervous.

Guest star: Chad Broskey as Gavin

17	17	"Rock Star in the House"	Kelly Sandefur	Jeny Quine Howard Nemetz	September 18, 2005	122

Jesse McCartney stays at the Tipton. London and Maddie try to see him while Zack obtains souvenirs to auction off to other fans. Cody works on his science project, a high frequency laser, and Arwin helps him even though it is against the rules.

Guest stars: Jesse McCartney as Himself, Sophie Oda as Barbara Brownstein

18	18	"Smart & Smarterer"	Rich Correll	Danny Kallis Adam Lapidus	October 10, 2005	125

Zack gets a bad grade in school and Carey says he will have to go to summer school if he can't keep his grades up. However, after he finds out that Bob gets more time to complete tests because he has dyslexia, Zack pretends that he has dyslexia too. Mr. Moseby loses his voice, causing havoc in the hotel. London and Maddie play chess but London keeps winning so they keep playing until Maddie wins. When she can't, London eventually lets Maddie win.

Guest star: Charlie Stewart as Bob

19	19	"The Ghost of Suite 613"	Rich Correll	Danny Kallis Jim Geoghan	October 14, 2005	109

A rumor is circulating around the Tipton Hotel that Suite 613 is haunted by a ghost named Irene, whose husband left her for an Italian women during World War II. Meanwhile, Zack plays practical jokes on everyone, embarrassing them among other people. Later, when they hear that London has dropped her purse with a thousand dollars in Suite 613, Maddie, London, Zack, and Cody all run up to get it. On the way, Muriel tells them about Irene, then leaves. When Mr. Moseby finds them in the suite later on, he tells them of the experience he had with suite 613 when he was only a bellhop in the hotel. Then Zack dares Cody to spend a night at 613 and the person who runs out first owes the other five dollars.

20	20	"Dad's Back"	Rich Correll	Jim Geoghan	November 26, 2005	119

The boys' father Kurt (played by Robert Torti) returns. Zack gets tired of living by his mother's boring rules, so Zack sneaks onto his father's bus the day he leaves. Carey decides to become the "fun" parent while Kurt becomes the responsible one. London trains Maddie because of her lack of strength for gym class.

21	21	"Christmas at the Tipton"	Danny Kallis	Danny Kallis Jim Geoghan	December 10, 2005	123

Everyone's plans for Christmas are cancelled when a snowstorm traps everyone in the Tipton. Carey and the boys are stuck with Kurt. After Cody sees Carey and Kurt hugging he thinks they are getting back together. Maddie tries to get an expensive present from London by writing her name on all the Secret Santa slips, and asking London to pick. In the end though, Maddie is disappointed when London gives her a sweater that she sewed herself, with no hole for the head because there is a third arm instead. Mr. Moseby has to have Arwin's help to keep everyone in the hotel warm by firing up a furnace with ripped-up furniture. While this is happening, a couple named Joseph and Mary (who is expecting a baby) come to stay at the Tipton on Christmas Eve, and she goes into labor, but can't make it to the hospital because the roads are closed. Finally, Mary must give birth to a beautiful baby girl in the Elevator.

Guest star: Robert Torti as Kurt Martin, Adrian R'Mante as Esteban

22	22	"Kisses & Basketball"	Lex Passaris	Danny Kallis Jim Geoghan	January 1, 2006	120

Max kisses Zack after they win a basketball game, then Zack insults Max because she feels bad that she really likes him. The basketball team then makes him go on a date with her so that she'll feel better, but then the date goes horribly wrong, with Zack revealing it wasn't his own decision to come, and Max feels worse than ever. Maddie helps London with her shopping problems.

Guest stars: Alyson Stoner as Max, Dennis Bendersky as Tapeworm

23	23	"Pilot Your Own Life"	Lee Shallat-Chemel	Danny Kallis	January 6, 2006	118

Maddie and London compete with each other to get on the cover of a teen magazine. Cody convinces Moseby's employees to "pilot their own lives," which causes a lot of chaos.

24	24	"Crushed"	Rich Correll	Pamela Eells O'Connell Adam Lapidus	January 13, 2006	121

A classmate named Agnes (Allie Grant) falls in love with Cody because he is the only pupil who isn't mean to her. She asks him out on a date, and Cody gets Zack to go on the date and revolt her. Agnes finds out it's really Zack, not Cody, on the date, and begins to like him, too. London sets up her dog Ivana on a date with another rich dog. Ivana doesn't like the other dog, and falls in love with Maddie's dog, Scamp.

Guest stars: Allie Grant as Agnes, Emma Stone as the voice of Ivana

25	25	"Commercial Breaks"	Rich Correll	Danny Kallis	January 20, 2006	126

A commercial for the Tipton is being shot at the hotel. All of the employees have to audition. The director didn't like anybody who auditioned, but picked London just to suck up to Mr. Tipton. London is horrible, so she is fired and replaced by Mr. Moseby who trips and breaks his leg, so Carey (who had previously dated the director) does the commercial.

Guest star: Steve Hytner

26	26	"Boston Holiday"	Lex Passaris	Pamela Eells O'Connell	January 27, 2006	124

Prince Sanjay, The Prince of Ishkabar stays at the Tipton and becomes friends with Zack and Cody. He tells them he just wants to be a normal child and Zack takes him to the mall while Cody takes his place in a meeting with the mayor (Cody wears a Shabalakaba which is a worn on occasions in Sanjay's culture it covers the face so nobody could tell it was Cody). While trying to impress girls, Sanjay accidentally steals clothes while thinking that it was ok and that his people will pay for it. Zack and Sanjay end up in mall jail. Meanwhile, London thinks she has spotted a UFO and Maddie helps her because London keeps ordering delicious and expensive food. In the end it turns out to be a mylar balloon from London's birthday party caught on a TV antenna.

Season 2: 2006–07

- Season 2 consisted of 39 episodes.
- Brenda Song is absent for two episodes.
- Ashley Tisdale is absent for one episode.
- This season was filmed from September 2005 – August 2006.

Series #	Season #	Title	Directed by	Written by	Original U.S. air date	Production code
27	1	"Odd Couples"	Danny Kallis	Adam Lapidus	February 3, 2006	203

London likes a merit scholar (Zac Efron), and Maddie helps her to trick him into thinking she is smart. Cody moves into a coat closet because Zack is too messy and doesn't clean his side of the room. To Zack's surprise, Cody makes the room more "home" like by putting in a flat-screen TV and more.

Guest star: Zac Efron as Trevor

| 28 | 2 | "French 101" | Rich Correll | Jim Geoghan | February 10, 2006 | 201 |

The French Ambassador and his daughter visits the Tipton Hotel, and both Zack and Cody develop a crush on the daughter, although neither of them knows French. Following his mom's advice, Cody locks Zack in a coat closet, then hires Mr. Moseby to translate for him. He eventually gets to dance with the daughter, but while doing so, Zack arrives with a card full of 'compliments' for Cody to say to the daughter. They are actually insults and the daughter goes to Zack. It is Bob, who speaks fluent French, who gets the daughter at the end. Meanwhile, Esteban is upset when London can beat a street thief but he can't. To cheer him up, Maddie arranges a plan for Arwin to pretend to be a thief and let Esteban defeat him. Things go wrong when Arwin forgets about the plan and Esteban must fight a real thief instead.

Guest star: Katelyn Pippy

| 29 | 3 | "Day Care" | Jim Drake | Jeff Hodsden | February 17, 2006 | 204 |

Maddie requires Zack and Cody's help to run a day care center. London takes Mr. Moseby and Carey to yoga lessons, but when London doesn't like the yoga teacher, she decides to be the teacher.

Co-star: Amita Balla as Tia
Guest stars: Moises Arias as Randall, Wynter Daggs as Brandi, Logan Grove as Johnny, Joey King as Emily, Adrian R'Mante as Esteban, Cheryl Rusa as Woman in hotel, Sara Christine Smith as Randall's Mom

| 30 | 4 | "Heck's Kitchen" | Rich Correll | Pamela Eells O'Connell | February 24, 2006 | 207 |

Mr. Moseby receives information that a food critic called Bernard Burnaise is coming to the Tipton to try out the food. He is told that Burnaise has three different disguises: A middle-aged woman, a Chinese man with a long beard, and a cowboy. Mr. Moseby then hires Zack and Cody to sneak around the hotel and find out who exactly is Burnaise. They conclude that a Texan cowboy is actually Burnaise and Mr. Moseby orders Chef Paolo to cook a wonderful meal for him. Things take a turn for the worse when Chef Paolo quits after being insulted, and Cody must take over, having London, Maddie, and Zack as his kitchen staff. What they don't know is that although the cowboy is impressed with his meal, he is actually not the real food critic, who suddenly appears to give the Tipton another chance when he realizes the situation and the struggle to serve the cowboy. Chef Paolo then decides to go back to work at the Tipton, where his being in charge assures that the Tipton will get good reviews.

| 31 | 5 | "Free Tippy" | Rich Correll | Jeny Quine | March 3, 2006 | 202 |

Zack and Cody try to save the Tipton's carriage horse (Tippy) from being sold to a mean lumberjack when the horse carriage driver Henry gets retired. London borrows Maddie's great grandma's brooch, but when she loses it, Maddie makes her feel bad. Mr. Moseby arranges a banquet with Mrs. Delecourt. The boys sneak Tippy into the hotel and have him stay with Arwin, but then Tippy escapes so the boys look all around the hotel. London tells Carey that the broach is in the trash but she's not looking there. But Carey tells her that a good friend would help look for it. So Arwin and London look for it in the dumpster and run into a homeless guy. At the end, Mrs. Delecourt convinces Mr. Tipton not to retire Henry, and the homeless man comes to the hotel with Maddie's brooch.

| 32 | 6 | "Forever Plaid" | Jim Drake | Tim Pollock | March 20, 2006 | 205 |

London has transferred to Maddie's school and causes her to get a detention, later they pretend to be nuns from Finland. Zack and Cody make a hole in a wall, and Arwin helps them fix it. Zack and Cody then discover that they can see soccer girls in the next room, so they invite their friends to look in the hole too. They later get found out by Mr. Moseby and Carey and they all end up with a sore eye.

Guest stars: Vanessa Hudgens, Monique Coleman

| 33 | 7 | "Election" | Rich Correll | Howard Nemetz | March 21, 2006 | 206 |

Zack and Cody both run in a school election, and London and Maddie take sides: Maddie tries to help Cody and London tries to help Zack. At first, Zack was getting more attention (by making lies that the students will get ice cream and a skate park if he is president). Later, Cody gets the attention after Zack drops out because he thought that Cody's ideas were better and he would want him to be president.

Guest stars: Alyson Stoner as Max, Allie Grant as Agnes

34	8	"Moseby's Big Brother"	Rich Correll	Howard Nemetz	March 22, 2006	212

Mr. Moseby's smaller-in-size but older-in-age brother comes to the Tipton. He is very rich and they do not really like each other much. Zack and Cody get one bicycle together because they do not have enough money to get their own (one each). However, Zack begins to keep the bike all for himself which makes Cody angry. Maddie and Esteban send London fake horoscopes to take advantage of her, which backfires when London finds out.

35	9	"Books & Birdhouses"	Rich Correll	Jim Geoghan	March 23, 2006	214

London steals Maddie's idea for a school assignment and turns it into a famous book. When London's theft backfires because Maddie's idea violated a copyright law from a previous book, she is sued for a million dollars. Meanwhile, Cody signs up for an advanced Calculus Math Class covering tables, Conversion and Convergences, but no one, even the teacher, shows up. Cody is jealous that Zack is acing woodshop, and signs up for it instead. He does not know anything about wood and ends up getting his first demerit and C.

Note: In an earlier episode of the show, *Smart and Smarterer*, when Cody gets his report card back, Carey reads his card and it says he is great at woodshop, and in this episode he is bad at it.

Guest stars: Phil Abrams, Patricia Bethune, Max Burkholder, Lauren Cohn, Chris Dollard, D. C. Douglas, Joey King, Marianne Muellerleile, Charlie Stewart

36	10	"Not So Suite 16"	Rich Correll	Adam Lapidus	March 24, 2006	213

Maddie and London's 16th birthday parties are scheduled on the same day, even though London's birthday was 6 months ago. London refuses to change her date out of selfishness and bribes people with gifts if they come to her party. Cody gets Maddie the perfect gift. Zack wants it, but Cody won't give it to him; he instead helps find Zack a suitable gift. Aside from her family, only Zack shows up at Maddie's party while everyone else goes to London's, thus earning a hug. Maddie and London both have a miserable time and in the end, reconcile and merge parties.

Guest stars: Vanessa Hudgens, Monique Coleman, Bernie Kopell, Kathryn Joosten

37	11	"Twins at the Tipton"	Rich Correll	Pamela Eells O'Connell	March 31, 2006	215

The Tipton is having a twin convention. Zack forces Cody, who was recently dumped by his girlfriend Irma, to go out on a double date with Janice and Jessica (Camilla and Rebecca Rosso), who are British identical twins. Maddie and London also go on a double date with twins, and Maddie ends up dating the geek twin who is really smart, yet disturbing; while London gets the handsome twin who is just as dumb as she is.

Note: When Bob tells Cody that he has been dumped by Irma, he says "Irma told Kim who told Phill who told Ashley who told Brenda who told Dylan who told Cole who told me." The names used are the first names of the cast members in the reverse of the sequence shown in the opening credits.

Guest stars: Rebecca Rosso as Jessica, Camilla Rosso as Janice, Scott Halberstadt as Dirk, Jake Abel as Kirk

38	12	"Neither a Borrower nor a Speller Bee"	Lex Passaris	Lloyd Garver	April 14, 2006	209

Zack wants Cody to drop out of the junior spelling bee because he owes the $30 to his competitor. London and Maddie do community service. London sees that her friend got in the newspaper, so London brings the paparazzi with her. Sister Dominique also gives all the credit to London while Maddie, Corrie, and Mary-Margaret are the ones doing ALL the work, and Maddie becomes infuriated as a result.

Guest stars: Vanessa Hudgens, Monique Coleman

39	13	"Bowling"	Rich Correll	Danny Kallis	April 28, 2006	208

When the Tipton staff keeps losing at sports against Ilsa and the St. Mark crew, Zack tells them he is a good bowler, so they decide to play bowling against them. Arwin, however, has a fear of bowling, and quits. Zack is the best bowler on the Tipton team, but gets grounded for playing a mean trick on Cody and can't help his team in a bowling contest against the St. Mark hotel, so Arwin has to fill in for him, regardless of a bowling accident that he experienced years ago.

Guest stars: Caroline Rhea, Dot Jones

40	14	"Kept Man"	Jim Drake	Jeff Hodsden Tim Pollock	May 19, 2006	216

Zack befriends a rich boy named Theo who gives him expensive items in order to buy his friendship. Meanwhile, London and Maddie have to take care of a baby simulator for school, which keeps them up all night. Maddie mainly does all the work, while London does hardly any except buying him expensive clothing and giving Esteban the position of a nanny.

Guest stars: Vanessa Hudgens, Monique Coleman, Mike Weinberg

Note: In the UK airings of this episode, the scene where the doll simulator is thrown out the window is cut. The following scene, where Esteban is talking to Norman, is shortened and does not show the doll hit him on the head. Also, the scene in which Mr. Moseby throws the doll against the couch is also cut. However in "Mr. Tipton Comes to Visit," these scenes are left in.

41	15	"The Suite Smell of Excess"	Kelly Sandefur	Billy Riback	June 2, 2006	210

Arwin builds a machine called the P.U. (Parallel Universalizer) that can take you to an alternate universe. Zack and Cody use the machine to travel to a universe where everything is how they like it, but completely opposite of the normal universe: Paris Hilton is President, George Clooney is on the quarter, The Tipton hotel is the Fitzpatrick hotel because Maddie is the one who is rich, and not London. Carey is a successful singer, with Arwin being her producer (Carey is the one who has a crush on Arwin in the parellel Universe, not the other way around). Mr. Moseby's nickname is 'M' and he loves playing in the lobby and disturbing the guests. Lastly, Esteban is a cleaning lady. After spending a few days there, they become tired of it and return to the real universe.

Co-stars: Mary Kate McGeehan as the Automated Voice, Adam Tait as the Radio Announcer

42	16	"Going for the Gold"	Rich Correll	Adam Lapidus	June 10, 2006	221

Arwin enters the Hotel Engineers' competition which is taking place at the Tipton. Zack and Cody find out that one of the competitors, Irv Weldon, is cheating, so they try to help Arwin win. London opens her own store and hires Maddie to be in it.

43	17	"Boston Tea Party"	Rich Correll	Pamela Eells O'Connell	June 30, 2006	222

When Zack and Cody visit the park, they find out it is being cordoned off. Then a construction worker tells them they're going to knock down the tree of liberty and pave the park over into a parking lot. Cody writes an eighteen page letter to convince city hall not to pave the park, but they don't listen. Zack has a dream about the Boston Tea Party and finds out Liberty Park is where they planned it. This gives the construction workers reason to not pave it over. At the end, Mr. Moseby gets a restraining order not to tear down the park. Meanwhile, Esteban is taking a test to become a citizen of the United States.

44	18	"Have a Nice Trip"	Rich Correll	Jeny Quine	July 7, 2006	219

A hotel patron claims he fell on Zack's skateboard. Zack and Cody find out that he faked the accident to get free things from the Tipton. The Tipton staff have to serve their "injured" guest with the best service they have, or risk the hotel's reputation being trashed by the man. (Cody says that his mom got the twins skateboards at a garage sale. In the episode Kept Man, he says she got them for free at Cheap Charlie's).

Absent: Brenda Song as London Tipton

Guest stars: Sammi Hanratty, Eric Lutes

45	19	"Ask Zack"	Eric Dean Seaton	Billy Riback	July 15, 2006	224

Zack wants a job on the school paper because the only other job was on the band. He then uses his part of the paper (the "Ask Shirley" column) to get a girl named Darlene. London has trouble getting to sleep because there are diamond dust bunnies under her mattress.

Guest stars: Camilla Rosso, Rebecca Rosso, Nicki Prian

46	20	"That's So Suite Life of Hannah Montana" (Part two of "That's So Suite Life of Hannah Montana")	Rich Correll	Howard Nemetz	July 28, 2006	218

Raven Baxter visits the Tipton and has a vision that Carey's birthday party will be full of chaos. Maddie tries to get London to wear Raven's dress but London doesn't want to wear it, as it was not made by someone famous. Maddie tricks London into wearing the dress but London finds out, soon Hannah Montana shows up at the hotel and also wants the dress, so she fights for it with London.

Guest stars: Raven-Symoné as Raven Baxter, Miley Cyrus as Miley Stewart/Hannah Montana

47	21	"What the Hey?"	Lex Passaris	Danny Kallis	August 5, 2006	217

After they miss the bus, Zack convinces Cody to skip school and go to the mall where they (along with Bob) meet Cody's favorite band, "Everything Stinks," who are shooting a music video. Cody wins a contest to have a part in the video as "Wing Lee", but before the shoot, Carey comes to the mall for shopping and Zack, Cody and Bob try to keep her from seeing them. Meanwhile, London and her new step-mother have trouble getting along.

Guest stars: T Lopez, Monet Lerner

48	22	"A Midsummer's Nightmare"	Lex Passaris	Jeny Quine	August 11, 2006	211

Zack and Cody are in a school play. Cody and a girl named Gwen (Selena Gomez) are going out and Zack likes Vanessa. Zack gets a role in the play where he has to kiss Gwen. When they are practicing the kiss, Gwen starts to like Zack. Zack doesn't like her back. Vanessa likes Cody. Cody changes the kissing scene with help from Agnes (because she couldn't stand to see Zack kiss another girl). London changes the look of the hotel to bring good luck Feng Shui,the arrangement causes more trouble than good. At first, Maddie finds a $100 bill, Esteban's parents get rich, and Moseby gets an exotic vehicle because his breaks down. But, Maddie is arrested since the bill was a fake, Esteban's parents go bankrupt, and Moseby's "exotic vehicle" is a bike.

Guest stars: Chris Doyle as Messenger, Gage Golightly as Vanessa, Selena Gomez as Gwen, Allie Grant as Agnes, Ernie Grunwald as Mr. Forgess, Asante Jones as G-Man, Loren Lester as Man, Adrian R'Mante as Esteban, Charlie Stewart as Bob

49	23	"Lost in Translation"	Rich Correll	Danny Kallis	August 19, 2006	223

It is International Week at Zack and Cody's school. A Japanese singer (Kumiko Mori as herself) visits the Tipton, and Zack uses her for his school project. Meanwhile, London gets stuck in her closet with Maddie. When Zack loses the singer at school, Carey, Cody, and Zack end up performing for a large Japanese audience, until Kumiko returns.

50	24	"Volley Dad"	Kelly Sandefur	Adam Lapidus	September 8, 2006	227

Cody is concerned about his mom's new boyfriend, so he calls his father to the Tipton. Maddie plays a trick on London to get her to play volleyball well.

Guest stars: Monique Coleman, Kaycee Stroh, Mindy Sterling

51	25	"Loosely Ballroom"	Rich Correll	Jeny Quine	September 22, 2006	225

Esteban starts a ballroom dancing class to help earn money for his sister's quinceañera (15th birthday party, similar to a 'sweet 16'). Mr. Moseby schedules a ballroom dancing competition at the Tipton. The gang enters to win money for Esteban's sister's quinceañera.

Note: Jared Murillo, Ashley Tisdale's then-boyfriend, has a cameo in this episode. He is seen in the dance competition, but is not credited.
Absent: Ashley Tisdale as Maddie Fitzpatrick
Guest stars: Camilla Rosso, Rebecca Rosso, Rip Taylor, Ashly DelGrosso, Louis van Amstel, Cheryl Burke, Alaina Reed Hall

52	26	"Scary Movie"	Rich Correll	Pamela Eells O'Connell	October 13, 2006	228

Zack gets scared by a horror film about zombies, which their mother has told them not to see, and Zack starts to pile furniture against the hotel door in the lobby when he's sleepwalking. London pretends to be poor to impress a boy.

Guest stars: Tahj Mowry, Camilla and Rebecca Rosso

53	27	"Ah! Wilderness!"	Rich Correll	Danny Kallis Jim Geoghan	November 10, 2006	230

The boys become Wilderness Scouts, with Mr. Moseby as their leader. When all of their food disappears, Zack saves the team from starvation by finding wild food. Cody is jealous, and when he meets an old man (Tom Poston) who gives him food, Cody lies to the team and says that he found it himself. While the boys are away, Carey tries to have free time, but Maddie and London keep bothering her about a guy Maddie is dating. The guy is London's old boyfriend and she still likes him.

Note: This was Tom Poston's last acting role before his death.
Guest star: Tom Poston

54	28	"Birdman of Boston"	Rich Correll	Jim Geoghan	November 24, 2006	220

A hawk makes a nest at the Tipton and causes havoc, so Mr. Moseby scares it away. When Cody finds that the hawk laid an egg, he cares for it while Zack films the hatching of the egg to sell on the internet. Cody continues to care for the baby hawk after the egg hatches, but when the baby hawk is ready to be released into the wild, Cody has a difficult time letting go.

Absent: Brenda Song as London Tipton
Note: The name of the Hawk, "Bubba," is also the name of Dylan and Cole Sprouse's dog.

55	29	"Nurse Zack"	Rich Correll	Danny Kallis	December 8, 2006	229

Cody takes care of Carey when she is sick, but when Cody also falls ill, Zack needs to take care of them both. All of the employees at the Tipton try to win Employee of the Month by sabotaging all of the other employees' stations.						
56	30	**"Club Twin"**	Lex Passaris	Howard Nemetz	January 7, 2007	231
Zack and Cody try to find summer jobs, so they convince Moseby to let them have the lounge on Monday nights, and they start an underage club. London gives Maddie some of her homemade beauty products called Simply London, but turns out to have a side effect. **Guest star**: Alyson Stoner as Max						
57	31	**"Risk It All"**	Rich Correll	Danny Kallis Jim Geoghan	January 27, 2007	234
Zack and Cody enter a game show called "Risk It All." Maddie tries to retrieve an angry email that London accidentally sent to Mr. Moseby - which she didn't intend to send at all.						
58	32	**"A Nugget of History"**	Danny Kallis	Dan Signer	February 23, 2007	236
Moseby's grandmother, Rose Moseby (Phill Lewis in a dual role), comes to visit, and helps Zack with his history paper. But, when Zack gets a "D" and a week of detention, Zack gets help from Grandma Moseby to prove Zack's history teacher was wrong. Meanwhile, London gets a job at Cluck Bucket with Maddie. When London causes Maddie to get her old job back as "Hillary Hen", Maddie becomes furious; but when London is in trouble, it's up to a reluctant Maddie to save her. **Guest star**: Oliver Muirhead						
59	33	**"Miniature Golf"**	Jim Drake	Jeny Quine	March 2, 2007	232
Zack & Cody go on a double date at mini golf. Zack stinks at it, but his date is great. Soon, Zack tries to get help from Mr. Moseby, who was an expert at mini golf. Zack returns to the mini golf course and proceeds to beat everyone sorely. London joins a book club and Carey tries to live a healthier life. **Guest stars**: Alexa Nikolas as Tiffany, Brittany Curran as Chelsea						
60	34	**"Health and Fitness"**	Rich Correll	Howard Nemetz	March 16, 2007	226
Every employee at the Tipton must take a Cholesteral test and Mr. Moseby is afraid of the needle. Cody tries to get Chef Paolo to eat healthily after bacon bits were found in his blood after a Cholesteral Check. After looking in a slanted mirror that distorts images, London is worried about being overweight, and Maddie is worried about being too thin. London starts to exercise and not eat while Maddie tries to eat a lot. Carey tries to stop Zack from eating too much candy and gives him a healthy diet.						
61	35	**"Back in the Game"**	Rich Correll	Pamela Eells O'Connell Adam Lapidus	April 6, 2007	237
A wheelchair basketball team is staying at the Tipton, giving Zack the opportunity to persuade his friend Jamie, now permanently using a wheelchair, to start playing the sport again. Maddie tries to make a film for her school project starring London and Lance. **Guest stars**: Nathan Kress, Daryl "Chill" Mitchell						
62	36	**"The Suite Life Goes Hollywood, Part 1"**	Rich Correll	Danny Kallis Jim Geoghan	April 20, 2007	238
Two television writers discover about the life of Zack & Cody, and sells a sitcom about the show, and everyone gets to go there to watch it. Although, when Zack and Cody's actors don't work out, Zack and Cody are offered to take their place. **Guest stars**: Jennifer Tisdale, Nikki Soohoo, Dante Basco, Sam McMurray, The Veronicas						
63	37	**"The Suite Life Goes Hollywood, Part 2"**	Rich Correll	Danny Kallis Jim Geoghan	April 20, 2007	239
Zack and Cody accept the offer to become the stars of the television show, although Cody gets stage fright and can't act, leading to a fight, so Carey gives them a timeout. During the timeout, some twins (guest stars The Veronicas) sing in front of the audience, and the writers fire Zack & Cody and hire them. Meanwhile, London and Maddie sneak onto a movie set to see a cute actor, and the director mistakes them for stunt doubles. **Note**: The Veronicas perform their song "Cry" when asked to sing in front of the audience. **Guest stars**: Jennifer Tisdale, Nikki Soohoo, Dante Basco, Sam McMurray, The Veronicas						
64	38	**"I Want My Mummy"**	Phill Lewis	Pamela Eells O'Connell	May 18, 2007	235

When London comes back from Peru, she brings back a lot of artifacts, including an ancient necklace and a mummy, which Esteban says is cursed. Zack and Cody want to see the mummy, so they sneak into the suite to see it, but accidentally push it out of the window. As a result, Zack disguises Cody as the mummy until Zack can get the real one. However, Maddie and Esteban feel the mummy should go back where it came from, so they dress up one of Maddie's old dolls to look like the mummy and switch with the one on display (which is really Cody). Eventually, they all find out the original mummy is a fake.

Note: This episode marked Phill Lewis' directorial debut.

65	39	"Aptitude"	Danny Kallis	Adam Lapidus	June 2, 2007	233

Zack and Cody are surprised by their aptitude test scores: Zack is told he will be a CEO, while Cody is going to turn out as a sanitation engineer (garbage man). Zack soon starts acting smart, while Cody starts to have a negative attitude. Meanwhile, Maddie saves the life of a Moroccan ambassador, and later London. She becomes famous for a little while and London doesn't like it. But eventually new news comes and Maddie is sad to find out that her 15 minutes of fame are over.

Season 3: 2007–08

- Season 3 consisted of 22 episodes.
- Ashley Tisdale is absent for eleven episodes.
- This season was shot from February-August 2007.
- This is the final season of the series.

Series #	Season #	Title	Directed by	Written by	Original U.S. air date	Production code
66	1	"Graduation"	Rich Correll	Danny Kallis Adam Lapidus	June 23, 2007	301

Zack finds out he has failed English, unable to graduate so he has to attend summer school. He lies to his parents, making them believe that he passed. However, at the party they throw for the boys' graduation, he is overcome with guilt and announces in front of everyone that he failed. Maddie becomes a camp counselor and finds that she needs to spend the summer with a group of juvenile girls including Holly, the little girl who hustled Maddie out of her candy (and almost her watch) in "Have a Nice Trip."

Guest star: Robert Torti as Kurt Martin

67	2	"Summer of Our Discontent"	Rich Correll	Dan Signer	June 30, 2007	302

Cody searches for a summer job, and finds a "help wanted" sign at the local mini-mart. When the owner realizes Cody is friends with London, he will only hire Cody if he will set him up on a date with her. When Zack discovers he is the smartest student in his summer school class, all the other kids give him three hanging wedgies but in the end he tutors them too.

Title reference: The phrase "Now is the winter of our discontent," from Shakespeare's *Richard III*
Guest stars: Tara Lynne Barr as Haley, Adam Cagley as Brick, Jareb Dauplaise as Wayne Wormser, Mary Scheer as Mrs. Bird, Tyler Steelman as Mark, Kara Taitz as Millicent
Absent: Ashley Tisdale as Maddie Fitzpatrick

68	3	"Sink or Swim"	Rich Correll	Jeny Quine Dan Signer	July 8, 2007	303

Since Zack is done with summer school, Carey asks him if he wants to find a summer job. When the girls at camp overhear Maddie on the phone with London, they report the latest juicy gossip to the tabloids. Since all the news is saying that London can't swim, she starts taking swim lessons with Lance. After he "saves her" from drowning in a shallow pool, she falls in love with him. Arwin takes Zack in as his assistant, but Zack doesn't want to do all the required dirty work, so he hides in the mini-mart.

69	4	"Super Twins"	Rich Correll	Jim Geoghan	July 13, 2007	305

Zack and Cody wish for superhero powers when they see a shooting star. Their wish comes true; Zack gets super speed, and Cody gets telekinesis and can read minds. They learn that Mr. Moseby is a super-villain, whose evil plot is to turn all kids into mini adults with the help of his minions, Arwin (the Engineer), Esteban (Bellboy), and London, who is hypnotized into giving her diamonds to Moseby. At the end, Zack realizes it was all a dream he had after eating three slices of cold pizza before bed.

Guest stars: Charlie Stewart as Bob, Brian Stepanek as Arwin, Adrian R'Mante as Esteban
Note: This episode was part of Disney Channel's "Wish Gone Amiss Weekend"

70	5	"Who's the Boss?"	Rich Correll	Danny Kallis Adam Lapidus	July 22, 2007	304

At the mini-mart, Cody does all the work but Zack gets all the credit. With the help of Arwin, Cody gets a machine to help him with his job. But when things go wrong, Cody gets fired, and Zack tries to help Cody get his job back. Meanwhile, London doesn't know how to present Lance to her friends, because Lance embarrasses her constantly.

Guest stars: Alexa Nikolas as Tiffany, Brittany Curran as Chelsea

71	6	"Baggage"	Rich Correll	Pamela Eells O'Connell Jim Geoghan	July 22, 2007	306

A competing mini-mart issues a competition to see who can bag items faster. Meanwhile, Mr. Moseby's niece, Nia (Giovonnie Samuels), comes to the Tipton and works as the candy counter girl in Maddie's absence. Instead of preparing for the challenge, Zack and Cody are goofing off at a party with London and Nia.

Guest star: Giovonnie Samuels as Nia

Absent: Ashley Tisdale as Maddie Fitzpatrick

72	7	"Sleepover Suite"	Danny Kallis	Adam Lapidus	July 28, 2007	307

To impress Stacey (Meaghan Jette Martin), Cody tells her that she can have her birthday slumber party in London's hotel suite while she's in Scotland but, when London comes home early, Zack, Cody, and Nia must find a way to keep London out of the suite. Meanwhile, Carey is constantly pursued by a barbershop quartet named The Mellow Notes because she is so beautiful.

Guest stars: Giovonnie Samuels as Nia, Meaghan Jette Martin as Stacey

Absent: Ashley Tisdale as Maddie Fitzpatrick

73	8	"The Arwin That Came to Dinner"	Rich Correll	Jeny Quine	August 5, 2007	308

Arwin couldn't fix things right because his mother re-married and moved out. When Zack and Cody invite Arwin over for dinner and stay over night, he won't seem to leave, because he doesn't want to be alone. Carey is getting annoyed at him so she forces Zack and Cody to make him go. Meanwhile, Lance dumps London and she wants to find a way to get back with him.

Guest stars: Samantha Droke as Wanda, Megan Hilty as Enid

Absent: Ashley Tisdale as Maddie Fitzpatrick

74	9	"Lip Synchin' in the Rain"	Rich Correll	Danny Kallis Dan Signer	August 12, 2007	318

London (even though she can't sing or dance) gets the role of Sharpay in their school production of *High School Musical* instead of Maddie because Mr. Tipton is financing the director's play "Floss" on Broadway. Zack has to work backstage for detention and Cody gets the part of Troy.

Guest stars: Mitchell Whitfield as Mr. Blaine, Mark Indelicato as Antonio

Co-stars: Emily Morris as Kelsi, Adam Tait as Mr.Tipton **Note**: Maddie references Ashley Tisdale (who actually plays Maddie in the series) a few times by saying that she looks like Sharpay (which Ashley Tisdale also played in *High School Musical*), though no other character on the show seems to agree.

75	10	"First Day of High School"	Lex Passaris	Howard Nemetz	August 26, 2007	310

It's the first day of high school for Zack and Cody. Zack finds a new crush, Amber, (Kay Panabaker). Cody saves Bob from Vance, the school bully, Nia gets in trouble for defending Zack, and Mark (from summer school) gets Cody's help to learn to be a geek. London attends public school for the first time (after being expelled again from Our Lady of Perpetual Sorrow), in which she is out to tear down lockers for her own personal lounge.

Guest stars: Kay Panabaker as Amber, Blythe Auffarth as Ellen, Kathy Najimy as the principal, Giovonnie Samuels as Nia

Absent: Ashley Tisdale as Maddie Fitzpatrick

76	11	"Of Clocks and Contracts"	Rich Correll	Tim Pollock	September 15, 2007	309

Zack tries to negotiate a better contract for Carey as the Tipton's nightly singer to Mr. Moseby so they could stay at the Tipton. After losing her science tutor, London asks and pays Cody to help her with her project. Nia also wants Cody's help and bribes him with concert tickets to Yo Yo Ma. Cody quits and London and Nia combine their machines, inventing a French Fry maker.

Guest star: Giovonnie Samuels as Nia

Absent: Ashley Tisdale as Maddie Fitzpatrick

77	12	"Arwinstein"	Rich Correll	Pamela Eells O'Connell	September 30, 2007	313

It's Halloween at the Tipton. When looking for Arwin, Zack and Cody accidentally release a robot Frankenstein monster (created by Arwin), who is almost an exact replica of Arwin. The employees think 'Arwinstein' is Arwin in his costume for Halloween. Meanwhile, London is hosting a Halloween party at the Tipton, which has a costume contest, and the winner gets diamonds. Arwinstein shows up at the party and becomes the winner of London's costume contest. Soon, Arwinstein kidnaps Carey and everyone finds out that Arwinstein is a monster.

Absent: Ashley Tisdale as Maddie Fitzpatrick

78	13	"Team Tipton"	Rich Correll	Howard Nemetz	October 27, 2007	312

Maddie returns and does not get along with Nia at all, while Esteban and Patrick are also fighting. Carey then gets into an argument with Patrick, after saying he was making noise during her performance. Meanwhile, when Zack causes some customers to leave, he and Cody schedule a bug convention at the Tipton to make it up to Mr. Moseby. However, due to his fear of bugs, Zack accidentally releases the bugs into the Tipton. Mr. Moseby make arrangements for a seminar to be held at the Tipton for himself, Arwin, Esteban, Patrick, Carey, Millicent, Maddie, London, and Nia to help them to learn to respect their co-workers.

Guest stars: Giovonnie Samuels as Nia and Pat Finn as Sandy Butteaux

79	14	"Orchestra"	Rich Correll	Jeff Hodsden	November 10, 2007	311

Cody becomes jealous of the new violinist Sergay, a Russian professional. When Sergay starts to flirt with Barbara, the girl Cody likes, Cody becomes jealous and is determined to win her back. Meanwhile, London wants to learn the business of the Tipton hotel, so she shadows all the jobs in the Tipton including the bellboy and maid and causes chaos for the guests and all the employees. But when she goes for Mr. Moseby's job, she realizes all the nasty things the workers at the tipton have to say about her. Meanwhile, the orchestra has a performance at the Tipton and Cody desperately tries to win Barbara back.

Note: This episode was part of Disney Channel's November 2007 "Night of Premieres."
Absent: Ashley Tisdale as Maddie Fitzpatrick

80	15	"A Tale of Two Houses"	Rich Correll	Jim Geoghan	November 17, 2007	314

Zack and Cody each invite a girl over at their dad's empty apartment at the same time without the other knowing it. Meanwhile, London teaches Esteban how to act rich because his family inherits the throne to his country, but ends up ruining everything for Esteban and when a military coup d'etat has overthrown Esteban's royal family, all his luxury items are subject to repossession, forcing Esteban to go back to his old job as a bellhop.

Absent: Ashley Tisdale as Maddie Fitzpatrick

81	16	"Tiptonline"	Rich Correll	Dan Signer	December 15, 2007	315

Cody helps London with her website Yay Me! Starring London Tipton [1] and produces a video on her site. Zack gets addicted to Medieval Magic Quest [2], an online game. Mr. Moseby is playing the game too, so they become friends online. Cody is tired of all the things London makes him do (wearing high heels, etc.), so he quits. London's site then starts to get less viewers and she apologizes to Cody, inviting him back to be the producer. Meanwhile, Zack and Mr. Moseby discover each others identity in the game and they later try to quit because the game proves to be addictive.

Guest star: Brittany Curran as Chelsea
Absent: Ashley Tisdale as Maddie Fitzpatrick

82	17	"Foiled Again"	Danny Kallis	Billy Riback	February 1, 2008	319

Tony Hawk checks into the Tipton; Maddie and London each have a crush on their fencing instructor. While Zack and Cody are doing their science project, the problem is that Cody has a fear of germs, and when Zack makes a mistake when analyzing a germ from the kitchen and thinks it's a toxic type of black mold, the rumor spreads through the hotel and everyone starts panicking. Cody gets over his fear after he realizes that he can't go skateboarding with Tony Hawk wearing an anti-germs suit.

Guest star: Tony Hawk as himself

83	18	"Romancing the Phone"	Rich Correll	Danny Kallis Pamela Eells O'Connell	April 19, 2008	317

Zack and Cody befriend Travis, a kid whom they rope into helping them impress their dates because his dad works on a cruise ship. They then bail on Travis and go out with their dates, but lets Travis go with the girls instead. Maddie finds a stranger's phone whom she thinks is her crush (because she and the stranger have many of the same interests, which she found out on the lost phone). At the end, the owner of the phone was an old man, but Maddie takes an interest in the old man's grandson named Geoffey.

Guest stars: Jaden Smith as Travis, Drew Seeley as Geoffrey, William Schallert as David

84	19	"Benchwarmers"	Jim Drake	Danny Kallis	July 19, 2008	316

Zack tries out for the high school basketball team but realizes there's some stiff competition, the kind he didn't face in middle school, and worse yet, the giant, in-your-face Coach Little (Michael Clarke Duncan). Meanwhile, when they're rejected as cheerleaders, Cody and London form their own cheer-leading squad with the help of Mr. Moseby, who ends up doing a jumping cheer and landing right into the arms of a gruff Coach Little.

Guest stars: Sophie Tamiko Oda as Barbara, Giovonnie Samuels as Nia, Kaycee Stroh as Leslie, Tara Lynne Barr as Haley, Camilla and Rebecca Rosso as Janice and Jessica Ellis, Daniella Monet as Dana, Michael Clarke Duncan as Coach Little

Absent: Ashley Tisdale as Maddie Fitzpatrick

85	20	**"Doin' Time in Suite 2330"**	Rich Correll	Jeny Quine Adam Lapidus	August 9, 2008	320

When Zack and Cody are grounded and forbidden to leave their suite, Maddie steps in for Cody as the producer of London's Internet show. In order to win the Golden Netty award, Cody sneaks out and gets The Cheetah Girls as guest stars for London's show but is surprised when he finds out that Maddie has already booked Chris Brown as a guest star. In the end Carey finds out and goes on a rampage against the blatant disobedience of her sons, scaring Chris, the Cheetah Girls, and the live audience, and grounds Zack and Cody in rage. It ends up that Maddie and Cody both win the Golden Netty and Zack and Cody's mother was the top download of the week.

Guest stars: Chris Brown as himself, The Cheetah Girls as themselves

86	21	**"Let Us Entertain You"**	Rich Correll	Danny Kallis Pamela Eells O'Connell	August 16, 2008	322

Zack and Cody get an offer to stay in the King Neptune suite on the SS Tipton with their mother if she will sing, however, they don't to tell her that she will have to sing, and after a couple hours she finds out herself. Since Carey does not think it is a vaccation if she has to work, she offers to pay for her room herself, although the only room she can afford is the *"Sardine Suite"* in other words the storage room. Also, Sardine Suite members only get fed one small plate of food a day. Carey finally gives in and agree's to sing. Unfortunately, she falls asleep in the sun and gets a sunburn, no longer able to perform. Zack and Cody then perform in her place, stating that because their mother has made so many sacrifices for them, it is time they made a sacrifice for her. When the uppity cruise director says this is not authorized, the audience applauds Zack and Cody and says they put on a great show. Meanwhile in Boston, London is hosting a 24-hour telethon during her "Yay Me!" Staring London Tipton" broadcast. In this episode of "Yay Me" London takes Maddies advice to raise money for the less fortunate through phone pledges. They plan to have special guests come in from around the world and perform to help the cause. However, a blizzard occurs, which prevents any of London's guests for her broadcast to get to the hotel (since the roads have all been closed). Therefore, they are forced to improvise, which include Mr. Moseby jumping through a hoop like a dog, Maddie and London performing a ventriloquist act, and London spinning plates. After almost the full 24 hours, London gets tired and decides to log off. Then they realize that their internet connection has been lost for over twenty three hours and that all their performances had been for nothing. Instead, they decide to give the left-over food from the Tipton to the food shelter once or twice a week.

Note: The same cruise set (the S.S. Tipton) is used in The Suite Life on Deck. The cityscape background seen throughout the episode is that of the Miami skyline.

Also, this is the last episode of The Suite Life of Zack and Cody, before the season finale. After that, they set sail on a new show The Suite Life on Deck premiering on September 26, 2008. **Guest star**: Nicole Sullivan as Miss Klotz

87	22	**"Mr. Tipton Comes to Visit"**	Lex Passaris	Jim Geoghan	September 1, 2008	321

The news of a visit from Mr. Tipton gets the employees excited and they start reminiscing about their good deeds, while thinking about who deserves a possible $50,000 bonus. When Mr. Tipton arrives he is in a bad mood, which means somebody will be fired and nobody will get the raise. All fingers point to Carey because of the boys' mishaps, but Zack & Cody come up with a plan, involving Muriel, to protect their mother. Muriel makes a mistake in front of Mr. Tipton and he fires her, not realizing that she had already retired some time ago.

Notes: This is the last episode of *The Suite Life of Zack & Cody*, before the premiere of *The Suite Life on Deck*. This is a flashback episode and aired during "The Suite Life and Times of London Tipton [3]" marathon.

Guest stars: Estelle Harris as Muriel, Brian Stepanek as Arwin, Bob Joles as Mr. Tipton

References

[1] http://tv.disney.go.com/disneychannel/suitelife/yaymestarringlondontipton/

[2] http://tv.disney.go.com/disneychannel/suitelifeondeck/cds/yous/games/medievalquest/index.html

[3] http://tv.disney.go.com/disneychannel/schedule/londontipton/

General references

- "Suite Life of Zack & Cody Episodes" (http://www.tvguide.com/detail/tv-show.aspx?tvobjectid=194675& more=ucepisodelist). TV Guide. Retrieved June 21, 2010.

- "The Suite Life of Zack & Cody: Episode Guide" (http://tv.msn.com/tv/series-episodes/ the-suite-life-of-zack-and-cody). MSN TV. Retrieved June 21, 2010.

External links

- List of *The Suite Life of Zack & Cody* episodes (http://www.tv.com/the-suite-life-of-zack-and-cody/show/ 28842/episode.html?season=All) at TV.com

- List of *The Suite Life of Zack & Cody* episodes (http://www.imdb.com/title/tt0426371/episodes) at the Internet Movie Database

- List of The Suite Life of Zack & Cody episodes (http://tvlistings.zap2it.com/tvlistings/ZCSC. do;jsessionid=5416F0D7A3CB27F09E3B530BD3A31F16?t=The+Suite+Life+of+Zack+&+Cody& sId=EP00730224&method=getEpisodesForShow) at Zap2it

- List of The Suite Life of Zack & Cody episodes (http://television.aol.com/show/ the-suite-life-of-zack-and-cody/168929/episodes) at AOL Television

- List of The Suite Life of Zack & Cody episodes (http://tv.yahoo.com/the-suite-life-of-zack-cody/show/36370/ season/56821;_ylt=ArUu0vYJJid_G7gEexbVGEOSo9EF) at Yahoo! TV

- List of The Suite Life of Zack & Cody episodes (http://sharetv.org/shows/the_suite_life_of_zack_and_cody/ episodes) at shareTV (http://sharetv.org/)

- List of The Suite Life of Zack & Cody episodes (http://www.fancast.com/tv/The-Suite-Life-of-Zack-&-Cody/ 12140/episodes) at Fancast

- List of The Suite Life of Zack & Cody episodes (http://www.pazsaz.com/suitel.html) at Paszas Entertainment Network (http://www.pazsaz.com/)

List of *Hannah Montana* episodes

The following is a list of episodes of the Disney Channel Original Series **Hannah Montana**, which debuted on the Disney Channel on March 24, 2006. Created by Michael Poryes, Richard Correll and Barry O'Brien, the program follows the life of a teenage girl who lives a double life as an average teenage school girl named Miley Stewart (played by Miley Cyrus) by day and a famous pop singer named Hannah Montana by night, concealing her real identity from everyone else, except for her family and a few close friends.

Season 4 premiered on July 11, 2010. As of 5 December 2010, 95 original episodes of the series have aired.

Series overview

Season	Episodes	Originally aired (U.S. dates)		Notes
		Season premiere	**Season finale**	
1	26	March 24, 2006	March 30, 2007	
2	29	April 23, 2007	October 12, 2008	A 30th episode, titled "No Sugar, Sugar" was produced, but never aired in the United States.
3	30	November 2, 2008	March 14, 2010	
4	N/A	July 11, 2010	Spring 2011[1]	
Films	2 films	N/A		

Season 1: 2006–07

Series #	Season #	Title	Directed by	Written by	Original air date	Prod. code	Viewers (millions)
1	1	"Lilly, Do You Want to Know a Secret?"	Lee Shallat-Chemel	Michael Poryes Rich Correll Barry O'Brien	March 24, 2006	101	5.4[2] [3] [4]
2	2	"Miley Get Your Gum"	David Kendall	Michael Poryes	March 31, 2006	103	N/A
3	3	"She's a Supersneak"	David Kendall	Kim Friese	April 7, 2006	105	N/A
4	4	"I Can't Make You Love Hannah if You Don't"	Roger S. Christansen	Kim Friese	April 14, 2006	108	N/A
5	5	"It's My Party and I'll Lie if I Want To"	Roger S. Christiansen	Douglas Lieblein	April 21, 2006	102	N/A
6	6	"Grandma Don't Let Your Babies Grow Up to Play Favorites"	Roger S. Christiansen	Douglas Lieblein	April 28, 2006	109	N/A
7	7	"It's a Mannequin's World"	Roger S. Christiansen	Howard Meyers	May 12, 2006	110	N/A
8	8	"Mascot Love"	Roger S. Christiansen	Sally Lapiduss	May 26, 2006	111	N/A
9	9	"Ooo, Ooo, Itchy Woman"	David Kendall	Gary Dontzig Steven Peterman	June 10, 2006	104	N/A
10	10	"O Say, Can You Remember the Words?"	Lee Shallat-Chemel	Sally Lapiduss	June 30, 2006	113	N/A

11	11	"Oops! I Meddled Again!"	Chip Hurd	Lisa Albert	July 15, 2006	107	N/A
12	12	"On the Road Again?" (Part three of "That's So Suite Life of Hannah Montana")	Roger S. Christiansen	Steven James Meyer	July 28, 2006	112	7.1[5]
13	13	"You're So Vain, You Probably Think This Zit is About You"	Chip Hurd	Todd J. Greenwald	August 12, 2006	106	N/A
14	14	"New Kid in School"	Kenneth Shapiro	Todd J. Greenwald	August 18, 2006	114	N/A
15	15	"More Than a Zombie to Me"	Roger S. Christiansen	Steven Peterman	September 8, 2006	116	N/A
16	16	"Good Golly, Miss Dolly"	Roger S. Christiansen	Sally Lapiduss	September 29, 2006	118	N/A
17	17	"Torn Between Two Hannahs"	Roger S. Christiansen	Todd J. Greenwald (Teleplay) Valerie Ahern & Christian McLaughlin (Story)	October 14, 2006	126	N/A
18	18	"People Who Use People"	Shannon Flynn	Michael Poryes	November 3, 2006	119	N/A
19	19	"Money for Nothing, Guilt for Free"	Roger S. Christiansen	Heather Wordham	November 26, 2006	115	N/A
20	20	"Debt It Be"	Roger S. Christiansen	Heather Wordham Sally Lapiduss	December 1, 2006	120	N/A
21	21	"My Boyfriend's Jackson and There's Gonna Be Trouble"	Roger S. Christiansen	Andrew Green Sally Lapiduss	January 1, 2007	124	N/A
22	22	"We Are Family---Now Get Me Some Water!"	Roger S. Christiansen	Jay J. Demopoulos Andrew Green	January 7, 2007	122	N/A
23	23	"Schooly Bully"	Roger S. Christiansen	Douglas Lieblein Heather Wordham	January 19, 2007	125	N/A
24	24	"The Idol Side of Me"	Fred Savage	Douglas Lieblein	February 9, 2007	117	N/A
25	25	"Smells Like Teen Sellout"	Sheldon Epps	Heather Wordham	March 2, 2007	123	N/A
26	26	"Bad Moose Rising"	Roger S. Christiansen	Douglas Lieblein Steven James Meyer	March 30, 2007	121	N/A

Season 2: 2007–08

Series #	Season #	Title	Directed by	Written by	Original air date	Prod. code	Viewers (millions)
27	1	"Me and Rico Down by the Schoolyard"	Roger S. Christansen	Heather Wordham	April 23, 2007	203	3.51[6]
28	2	"Cuffs Will Keep Us Together"	Roger S. Christiansen	Steven Peterman	April 24, 2007	201	3.51[6]
29	3	"You Are So Sue-able to Me"	Roger S. Christiansen	Sally Lapiduss	April 25, 2007	202	3.91[6]
30	4	"Get Down, Study-udy-udy"	Roger S. Christiansen	Andrew Green	April 26, 2007	204	3.69[6]
31	5	"I Am Hannah, Hear Me Croak"	Roger S. Christiansen	Michael Poryes	April 27, 2007	206	3.54[6]
32	6	"You Gotta Not Fight for Your Right to Party"	Jody Margolin Hahn	Steven James Meyer	May 4, 2007	207	2.9[7]
33	7	"My Best Friend's Boyfriend"	Roger S. Christiansen	Jay J. Demopoulos	May 18, 2007	209	4.5[8]
34	8	"Take This Job and Love It"	Roger S. Christiansen	Sally Lapiduss	June 16, 2007	210	N/A
35	9	"Achy Jakey Heart (Part 1)"	Rich Correll	Douglas Lieblein	June 24, 2007	211	7.38[9][10]
36	10	"Achy Jakey Heart (Part 2)"	Rich Correll	Douglas Lieblein	June 24, 2007	212	N/A
37	11	"Sleepwalk This Way"	Roger S. Christiansen	Heather Wordham	July 7, 2007	213	N/A
38	12	"When You Wish You Were the Star"	Roger S. Christiansen	Douglas Lieblein	July 14, 2007	205	5.1[11]
39	13	"I Want You to Want Me... to Go to Florida"	Roger S. Christiansen	Michael Poryes	July 14, 2007	208	3.0[12]
40	14	"Everybody Was Best-Friend Fighting"	Jody Margolin Hahn	Sally Lapiduss	July 29, 2007	215	3.6[13]
41	15	"Song Sung Bad"	Roger S. Christiansen	Ingrid Escajeda	August 4, 2007	214	N/A
42	16	"Me and Mr. Jonas and Mr. Jonas and Mr. Jonas"	Mark Cendrowski	Douglas Lieblein	August 17, 2007	217	10.7[14]
43	17	"Don't Stop 'Til You Get the Phone"	Rich Correll	Michael Poryes	September 21, 2007	222	5.1[15]
44	18	"That's What Friends Are For?"	Mark Cendrowski	Douglas Lieblein	October 19, 2007	224	N/A
45	19	"Lilly's Mom Has Got It Goin' On"	Jody Margolin Hahn	Norm Gunzenhauser	November 10, 2007	216	N/A
46	20	"I Will Always Loathe You"	Roger S. Christiansen	Michael Poryes	December 7, 2007	218	N/A
47	21	"Bye Bye Ball"	Sean Lambert	Heather Wordham	January 13, 2008	220	N/A
48	22	"(We're So Sorry) Uncle Earl"	Rich Correll	Robin J. Stein	March 21, 2008	226	N/A
49	23	"The Way We Almost Weren't"	Rich Correll	Andrew Green	May 4, 2008	219	3.1[16]
50	24	"You Didn't Say It Was Your Birthday"	Rich Correll	Heather Wordham	July 6, 2008	225	5.1[16]

51	25	"Hannah in the Streets with Diamonds"	Roger S. Christiansen	Jay J. Demopoulos Steven James Meyer	July 20, 2008	228	3.8[16]
52	26	"Yet Another Side of Me"	Shannon Flynn	Andrew Green Sally Lapiduss (Teleplay) Heather Wordham (Story)	August 3, 2008	229	4.6[16]
53	27	"The Test of My Love"	Rich Correll	Jay J. Demopoulos	August 31, 2008	221	N/A
54	28	"Joannie B. Goode"	Rondell Sheridan	Andrew Green	September 14, 2008	227	N/A
55	29	"We're All on This Date Together"	Roger S. Christiansen	Steven Peterman	October 12, 2008	230	N/A
-	30	"No Sugar, Sugar"	Art Manke	Sally Lapiduss	Unaired[17]	223	

Season 3: 2008–10

Series #	Season #	Title	Directed by	Written by	Original air date	Prod. code	Viewers (millions)
56	1	"He Ain't a Hottie, He's My Brother"	Rich Correll	Steven James Meyer	November 2, 2008	302	5.5[18]
57	2	"Ready, Set, Don't Drive"	Rich Correll	Jay J. Demopoulos	November 9, 2008	301	4.9[19]
58	3	"Don't Go Breaking My Tooth"	Rich Correll	Michael Poryes	November 16, 2008	303	4.6[20]
59	4	"You Never Give Me My Money"	Roger S. Christansen	Andrew Green	November 23, 2008	305	4.6[21]
60	5	"Killing Me Softly with His Height"	Rich Correll	Steven Peterman	December 14, 2008	306	N/A
61	6	"Would I Lie to You, Lilly?"	Shelley Jensen	Michael Poryes	January 11, 2009	308	3.7[22]
62	7	"You Gotta Lose That Job"	Steve Zuckerman	Heather Wordham	February 16, 2009	307	4.4[22]
63	8	"Welcome to the Bungle"	Shelley Jensen	Steven Peterman	March 1, 2009	309	4.1[23]
64	9	"Papa's Got a Brand New Friend"	Shelley Jensen	Maria Brown-Gallenberg	March 8, 2009	310	4.2[24]
65	10	"Cheat It"	Shannon Flynn	Jay J. Demopoulos Steven James Meyer	March 15, 2009	311	4.4[25]
66	11	"Knock Knock Knockin' on Jackson's Head"	Rich Correll	Andrew Green	March 22, 2009	312	4.5[26]
67	12	"You Give Lunch a Bad Name"	Rich Correll	Heather Wordham	March 29, 2009	314	3.4[27]
68	13	"What I Don't Like About You"	Rich Correll	Douglas Lieblein	April 19, 2009	315	4.8[28]
69	14	"Promma Mia"	Rich Correll	Heather Wordham	May 3, 2009	320	4.5[29]
70	15	"Once, Twice, Three Times Afraidy"	Shannon Flynn	Jay J. Demopoulos Steven James Meyer	May 17, 2009	317	3.4[16]

71	16	"Jake... Another Little Piece of My Heart"	Roger S. Christiansen	Douglas Lieblein	June 7, 2009	304	4.1[30]
72	17	"Miley Hurt the Feelings of the Radio Star"	Rich Correll	Maria Brown-Gallenberg	June 14, 2009	313	3.5[31]
73	18	"He Could Be the One"[32]	Rich Correll	Maria Brown-Gallenberg Heather Wordham	July 5, 2009	326/327	7.9[33]
74	19	"Super(stitious) Girl" (Part three of "Wizards on Deck with Hannah Montana")	Rich Correll	Michael Poryes Steven Peterman	July 17, 2009	316	10.6[33]
75	20	"I Honestly Love You (No, Not You)"	Shannon Flynn	Andrew Green	July 26, 2009	318	3.9[34]
76	21	"For (Give) a Little Bit"	Rich Correll	Maria Brown-Gallenberg	August 9, 2009	319	N/A
77	22	"B-B-B-Bad to the Chrome"	Shannon Flynn	Jay J. Demopoulos Steven James Meyer	August 23, 2009	322	4.0[35]
78	23	"Uptight (Oliver's Alright)"	Art Manke	Sally Lapiduss	September 20, 2009	223	5.0[36]
79	24	"Judge Me Tender"	Bob Koherr	Andrew Green	October 18, 2009	323	5.7[37]
80	25	"Can't Get Home to You Girl"	Bob Koherr	Tom Seeley	November 8, 2009	324	N/A
81	26	"Come Fail Away"	Rich Correll	Douglas Lieblein	December 6, 2009	325	N/A
82	27	"Got to Get Her Out of My House"	Rich Correll	Douglas Lieblein	January 10, 2010	321	3.9[38]
83	28	"The Wheel Near My Bed (Keeps on Turnin')"	Bob Koherr	Jay J. Demopoulos Steven James Meyer	February 21, 2010	328	4.5[39]
84	29	"Miley Says Goodbye? Part 1"	Rich Correll	Michael Poryes Steven Peterman	March 7, 2010	329	7.0[40]
85	30	"Miley Says Goodbye? Part 2"	Rich Correll	Michael Poryes Steven Peterman	March 14, 2010	330	7.6[40]

Season 4: 2010–11

Series #	Season #	Title	Directed by	Written by	Original air date	Prod. code	Viewers (millions)
86	1	"Sweet Home Hannah Montana"	Bob Koherr	Michael Poryes Steven Peterman	July 11, 2010	402	5.7[41]
87	2	"Hannah Montana to the Principal's Office"	Bob Koherr	Steven James Meyer	July 18, 2010	401	5.4[42]
88	3	"California Screamin'"	Bob Koherr	Jay J. Demopoulos	July 25, 2010	403	4.2[43]
89	4	"De-Do-Do-Do, Da-Don't-Don't, Don't, Tell My Secret"	Adam Weissman	Andrew Green	August 1, 2010	404	5.7[44]
90	5	"It's the End of the Jake as We Know It"	Shannon Flynn	Maria Brown-Gallenberg	August 8, 2010	405	4.7[45]
91	6	"Been Here All Along"	Adam Weissman	Douglas Lieblein	August 22, 2010	407	4.6[46]

92	7	"Love That Let's Go"	Adam Weissman	Heather Wordham	September 12, 2010	406	4.5[47]
93	8	"Hannah's Gonna Get This"	Bob Koherr	Steven James Meyer (Teleplay) Donna Jatho (Story)	October 3, 2010	408	4.1[48]
94	9	"I'll Always Remember You"	Bob Koherr (Part 1) Shannon Flynn (Part 2)	Andrew Green Maria Brown-Gallenberg	November 7, 2010	409-410	7.1[49] [50]
95	10	"Can You See the Real Me?"	John D'Incecco	Douglas Lieblein	December 5, 2010	411	4.9[51]
96	11	"Kiss It All Goodbye"[52]			December 19, 2010	412	
97	12	"I Am Mamaw, Hear Me Roar!"[53]			January 30, 2011	413	

Films

Title	Directed by	Written by	Release date
"Hannah Montana & Miley Cyrus: Best of Both Worlds Concert"	Bruce Hendricks	N/A	February 1, 2008
"Hannah Montana: The Movie"	Peter Chelsom	Dan Berendsen	April 10, 2009

References

[1] "Hannah Montana Season 4" (http://www.disneychannelmedianet.com/DNR/2010/doc/HMA_011510.doc). Disney Channel Media Net. January 15, 2010. . Retrieved June 24, 2010.

[2] Oldenburg, Ann (January 14, 2007). "Miley Cyrus fulfills her destiny" (http://www.usatoday.com/life/television/news/2007-01-10-miley-cyrus_x.htm). *Usatoday.Com*. . Retrieved August 6, 2010.

[3] Cutler, Jacqueline. "Tween Queen Rules 'Hannah Montana'" (http://www.zap2it.com/tv/zap-story-hannahmontana-mileycyrus,0,3032407. story). Zap2it. . Retrieved August 6, 2010.

[4] Azote, Abigail. "Media Life Magazine" (http://www.medialifemagazine.com/cgi-bin/artman/exec/view.cgi?archive=170&num=3813). Media Life Magazine. . Retrieved August 6, 2010.

[5] "That's So Suite Life of Hannah Montana - Zap2it Forums: Talk About TV, Movies and More" (http://tvbb.zap2it.com/ubbthreads.php/ topics/507617/That_s_So_Suite_Life_of_Hannah). *Tvbb.zap2it.com*. . Retrieved August 6, 2010.

[6] "HBO's 'The Sopranos' Takes Top Spot In Nielsen Cable Rankings For The Week Of April 23–29" (http://www.starpulse.com/news/ index.php/2007/05/03/hbo_s_the_sopranos_takes_top_spot_in_nie_29). *Nielsen Media Research*. . Retrieved July 24, 2007.

[7] "CableFAX Magazine" (http://www.cable360.net/cableworld/departments/ratings/24029.html). *Cable360.net*. June 18, 2007. . Retrieved August 4, 2010.

[8] "Nielsens ratings for July 16–22" (http://www.usatoday.com/life/television/news/nielsens-charts.htm). *USA Today*. . Retrieved July 31, 2007.

[9] "'Hannah Montana' Soars in the Ratings and Everywhere Else" (http://www.buddytv.com/articles/hannah-montana/ hannah-montana-soars-in-the-ra-7892.aspx). . Retrieved July 28, 2007.

[10] "TNT, Disney Top Cable Ratings: June 18–24" (http://www.cable360.net/programming/ratings/24328.html). . Retrieved July 28, 2007.

[11] "'Cory in the House' and Other Disney Shows Soar in Ratings" (http://www.buddytv.com/articles/cory-in-the-house/ cory-in-the-house-and-other-di-8883.aspx). *Buddytv.com*. July 31, 2007. . Retrieved August 6, 2010.

[12] "Weekly Ratings Highlights for July 16–22, 2007" (http://disneychannelmedianet.com/DNR/2007/doc/DCJuly_16_22_07.doc). . Retrieved August 8, 2007.

[13] "CableFAX Magazine" (http://cable360.net/cableworld/programming/ratings/25280.html). *Cable360.net*. August 27, 2007. . Retrieved August 4, 2010.

[14] Joal Ryan (August 18, 2007). "High School Musical 2 Big 2 B Ignored" (http://www.eonline.com/news/article/index. jsp?uuid=65b1c9d5-4091-4fab-a0f9-e79fb8969b13). *E! News*. .

[15] "Nielsen ratings for week of April 19" (http://www.usatoday.com/life/television/news/nielsens-charts.htm). *USA Today*. April 28, 2010. . Retrieved May 4, 2010.

[16] "Multichannel News" (http://www.multichannel.com/article/CA6586001.html). . Retrieved September 8, 2008.

[17] ""Hannah Montana" Diabetes Episode Pulled ("No Sugar, Sugar")" (http://www.popcrunch.com/ hannah-montana-diabetes-episode-pulled-no-sugar-sugar/). . Retrieved November 9, 2008.

[18] "'Hannah' Hands Disney Channel 5.5 Million Viewers - 2008-11-04 15:30:00 | Multichannel News" (http://www.multichannel.com/ article/CA6611537.html). *Multichannel.com*. . Retrieved August 3, 2010.

[19] "Ratings Highlights For 2008" (http://www.disneychannelmedianet.com/DNR/2008/html/dc_nov3-9_08.html). *Disneychannelmedianet.com*. November 11, 2008. . Retrieved August 3, 2010.

[20] "Ratings Highlights For 2008" (http://www.disneychannelmedianet.com/DNR/2008/html/DC_Nov10_16_2008.html). *Disneychannelmedianet.com*. November 18, 2008. . Retrieved August 3, 2010.

[21] "Ratings Highlights For 2008" (http://www.disneychannelmedianet.com/DNR/2008/html/DC_Nov_17-23_2008.html). *Disneychannelmedianet.com*. November 25, 2008. . Retrieved August 3, 2010.

[22] "Ratings Highlights For 2008" (http://www.disneychannelmedianet.com/DNR/2009/html/DC_Night_of_Stars021609.html). *Disneychannelmedianet.com*. . Retrieved August 3, 2010.

[23] WWE RAW, The Closer and President Obama lead cable viewing (http://tvbythenumbers.com/2009/03/03/ wwe-raw-the-closer-and-president-obama-lead-cable-viewing/13835) Posted on 03 March 2009 by Robert Seidman

[24] iCarly, Burn Notice and WWE RAW top cable charts (http://tvbythenumbers.com/2009/03/10/ icarly-burn-notice-and-wwe-raw-top-cable-charts/14228) Posted on 10 March 2009 by Robert Seidman

[25] "Ratings Highlights For 2008" (http://www.disneychannelmedianet.com/DNR/2009/html/DC_Mar9_15_2009.html). *Disneychannelmedianet.com*. March 17, 2009. . Retrieved August 3, 2010.

[26] "Ratings Highlights For 2008" (http://www.disneychannelmedianet.com/DNR/2009/html/DC_Mar16_22_2009.html). *Disneychannelmedianet.com*. March 24, 2009. . Retrieved August 3, 2010.

[27] Kids' Choice Awards, Penguins of Madagascar and WWE RAW lead cable (http://tvbythenumbers.com/2009/03/31/ kids-choice-awards-penguins-of-madagascar-and-wwe-raw-lead-cable/15549) Posted on 31 March 2009 by Robert Seidman

[28] "Ratings Highlights For 2008" (http://www.disneychannelmedianet.com/DNR/2009/html/DC_April_13_19_2009.html). *Disneychannelmedianet.com*. April 21, 2009. . Retrieved August 3, 2010.

[29] "Ratings Highlights For 2008" (http://www.disneychannelmedianet.com/DNR/2009/html/DC_April27-May3_9.html). *Disneychannelmedianet.com*. . Retrieved August 3, 2010.

[30] Corrected: Burn Notice, Jon & Kate Plus 8 and Royal Pains lead cable (http://tvbythenumbers.com/2009/06/09/ nba-playoffs-jon-kate-plus-8-and-2009-mtv-movie-awards-lead-cable/20342) Posted on 09 June 2009 by Robert Seidman

[31] "Disney Channel Ratings" (http://www.disneychannelmedianet.com/DNR/2009/html/DC_June8-14_2009.html). *Disneychannelmedianet.com*. . Retrieved August 3, 2010.

[32] NSumski (June 18, 2009). "Brooke Shields and Cody Linley Guest Star in a One-Hour Special of "Hannah Montana," Premiering Sunday, July 5 On Disney Channel" (http://www.disneychannelmedianet.com/DNR/2009/doc/HNM_061809.doc) (DOC). The Walt Disney Company. . Retrieved November 9, 2010.

[33] "Top 100 Most-Watched Telecasts On Basic Cable For 2009" (http://tvbythenumbers.com/2009/12/29/ espn-domination-top-100-most-watched-telecasts-on-basic-cable-for-2009/37284). . Retrieved 2010-09-21.

[34] "Top Cable Shows For the Week Ending August, 2009; Burn Notice, The Closer, Next Food Network Star, Royal Pains, SpongeBob Squarepants, WWE Raw, NCIS" (http://tvbythenumbers.com/2009/08/04/the-closer-burn-notice-royal-pains-top-weeks-cable-shows/ 24119). *Tvbythenumbers.com*. . Retrieved August 3, 2010.

[35] Updated: The Closer, WWE RAW, & True Blood Top Week's Cable Shows (http://tvbythenumbers.com/2009/08/25/ the-closer-wwe-raw-royal-pains-nascar-monk-top-weeks-cable-shows/25330) Posted on 25 August 2009 by Robert Seidman

[36] Cable ratings: Monday Night Football, WWE RAW, Hannah Montana and Monk... (http://tvbythenumbers.com/2009/09/22/ cable-ratings-monday-night-football-vmas-icarly-and-true-blood-finale/28024) Posted on 22 September 2009 by Robert Seidman

[37] (http://www.disneydreaming.com/category/hannah-montana-miley-cyrus)

[38] Cable ratings: WWE RAW, NCIS, SpongeBob, Secret Life and iCarly Top Weekly Cable Charts (http://tvbythenumbers.com/2010/01/ 12/cable-ratings-wwe-raw-ncis-spongebob-secret-life-and-icarly-top-weekly-cable-charts/38551) Posted on 12 January 2010 by Robert Seidman

[39] "Disney Channel is TV's No. 1 Network in Tweens 9-14; Fueled by "Hannah Montana" and "StarStruck"" (http://tvbythenumbers.com/ 2010/02/23/disney-channel-is-tvâs-no-1-network-in-tweens-9-14-fueled-by-hannah-montana-and-starstruck/42774). *Tvbythenumbers.com*. . Retrieved August 3, 2010.

[40] "Disney Channel Claims its Most-Watched March Ever in Total Day in Total Viewers, Kids 6-11 and Tweens 9-14" (http:// tvbythenumbers.com/2010/03/30/ disney-channel-claims-its-most-watched-march-ever-in-total-day-in-total-viewers-kids-6-11-and-tweens-9-14/46716). *Tvbythenumbers.com*. March 30, 2010. . Retrieved August 3, 2010.

[41] "Cable TV Top 25: LeBron, Pawn Stars, Hannah Montana Forever, Deadliest Catch Top Week's Viewership" (http://tvbythenumbers.com/ 2010/07/13/cable-tv-top-25-lebron-pawn-stars-royal-pains-deadliest-catch-top-weeks-viewership/56943). *Tvbythenumbers.com*. July 13, 2010. . Retrieved July 28, 2010.

[42] "Cable Top 25: Deadliest Catch, The Closer, Rizzoli & Isles & Home Run Derby Top Week's Viewership" (http://tvbythenumbers.com/ 2010/07/20/cable-top-25-deadliest-catch-the-closer-rizzoli-isles-home-run-derby-top-weeks-viewership/57704). *Tvbythenumbers.com*. July

20, 2010. . Retrieved July 28, 2010.

[43] "Cable Top 25: Rizzoli & Isles, The Closer, Burn Notice & Brickyard 400 Top Week's Viewership" (http://tvbythenumbers.com/2010/07/27/cable-top-25-rizzoli-isles-the-closer-burn-notice-brickyard-400-top-weekâ s-viewership/58279). *Tvbythenumbers.com*. July 27, 2010. . Retrieved July 28, 2010.

[44] "Cable Top 25: iCarly Tops Hannah Montana; Snooki Edges Sookie" (http://tvbythenumbers.com/2010/08/03/cable-top-25-icarly-tops-hannah-montana-snooki-edges-sookie/58915). *Tvbythenumbers.com*. July 30, 2010. . Retrieved August 4, 2010.

[45] "Cable Top 25: The Closer, Rizzoli & Isles, Burn Notice, Royal Pains, Covert Affairs Top Week's Cable Viewing" (http://tvbythenumbers.com/2010/08/10/cable-top-25-scripted-dramas-the-closer-rizzoli-isles-burn-notice-royal-pains-covert-affairs-top-weeks-cable-viewing/59604). *Robert Seidman*. August 10, 2010. . Retrieved August 10, 2010.

[46] "Cable Top 25: The Closer, Rizzoli & Isles, Pawn Stars, NFL & Jersey Shore Top Week's Cable Viewing" (http://tvbythenumbers.com/2010/08/24/cable-top-25-the-closer-rizzoli-isles-pawn-stars-nfl-jersey-shore-top-weekâ s-cable-viewing/60881). *Tvbythenumbers.com*. August 24, 2010. . Retrieved August 25, 2010.

[47] "Cable Top 25: VMAs, Boise State, The Closer & Rizzoli & Isles Top Week's Cable Viewing" (http://tvbythenumbers.com/2010/09/14/cable-top-25-vmas-boise-state-the-closer-rizzoli-isles-top-weekâ s-cable-viewing/63194/2). *Tvbythenumbers.com*. September 14, 2010. . Retrieved September 14, 2010.

[48] Cable Top 25: 'Monday Night Football,' 'Jersey Shore,' Wizards of Waverly Place,' 'Phineas and Ferb' Top Week's Cable Viewing (http://tvbythenumbers.com/2010/10/05/cable-top-25-monday-night-football-jersey-shore-wizards-of-waverly-place-phineas-and-ferb-top-weekâ s-cable-viewing/66700) By Robert Seidman— October 5, 2010

[49] clord (November 9, 2010). ""Hannah Montana" (7:30-8:30 p.m.)" (http://www.disneychannelmedianet.com/DNR/2010/doc/DC_Ratings_110810.doc). *Ratings Highlights for Sunday, November 7, 2010 Preliminary National Ratings*. The Walt Disney Company. . Retrieved November 9, 2010.

[50] Gorman, Bill (November 8, 2010). ""Shake it Up" Averages 6.2 Million Viewers; Disney Channel's #2 Highest Rated Series Premiere Of All Time" (http://tvbythenumbers.com/2010/11/08/shake-it-up-averages-6-2-million-viewers-disney-channels-2-highest-rated-series-premiere-of-all-time/71247). . Retrieved November 9, 2010.

[51] Cable Top 25: NFL, Lebron's Return to Cleveland, The Walking Dead, Big Time Rush and WWE RAW Top Week's Cable Viewing (http://tvbythenumbers.zap2it.com/2010/12/07/cable-top-25-nfl-lebrons-return-to-cleveland-the-walking-dead-big-time-rush-and-wwe-raw-top-weeks-cable-viewing/74610) By Robert Seidman— December 7, 2010

[52] "*Hannah Montana* Episode: "Kiss It All Goodbye"" (http://www.tvguide.com/tvshows/hannah-montana-2010/episode-11-season-4/kiss-goodbye/278865). *Hannah Montana Episodes on Disney*. TV Guide. . Retrieved December 2, 2010.

[53] "*Hannah Montana* Episode: "I Am Mamaw, Hear Me Roar!"" (http://www.tvguide.com/tvshows/hannah-montana-2011/episode-12-season-4/mamaw-hear-roar/278865). *Hannah Montana Episodes on Disney*. TV Guide. . Retrieved December 11, 2010.

List of *Sonny with a Chance* episodes

The following is an **episode list** for the Disney Channel Original Series, *Sonny with a Chance*. It premiered on February 8, 2009 and is currently in its second season.

Created by Steve Marmel, the series revolves around Sonny Munroe (Demi Lovato), a teenage comedian who wins the chance of starring in the fictional children's sketch comedy series, *So Random!*. She is assisted by fellow cast members and new friends Tawni Hart (Tiffany Thornton), Nico Harris (Brandon Mychal Smith), Grady Mitchell (Doug Brochu) and Zora Lancaster (Allisyn Ashley Arm), along with Chad Dylan Cooper (Sterling Knight), the star of *Mackenzie Falls*, the rival tween TV show of *So Random!*.

Series overview

Seasons	Episodes	First air date	Last air date
1	21	February 8, 2009	November 22, 2009
2	26	March 14, 2010	January 9, 2011

Season 1: 2009

Series #	Season #	Title	Directed by	Written by	U.S. viewers (millions)	Original air date	Prod. code
1	1	"Sketchy Beginnings"	David Trainer	Michael Feldman Steve Marmel	4.1[1]	February 8, 2009	101

Sonny Munroe enters the set, not knowing that she is in for a difficult time with Tawni Hart. When Sonny changes Tawni's "Queen Bee" sketch, Tawni becomes jealous; the situation does not improve when Sonny and Tawni have to share a dressing room. Sonny's mother advises her to talk to Tawni. Things get worse when Sonny tries to help Tawni, as she accidentally shreds Tawni's favorite stuffed animal. Then, when Tawni talks to Marshall, Sonny decides she doesn't care what Tawni thinks anymore and makes the One Bad Bee sketch to get back at her.

***So Random!* sketches:**

"Dolphin Boy": Grady plays the main character, "Dolphin Boy", who is half-dolphin and half-boy. Nico plays Dolphin Boy's friend and Tawni plays a cheerleader whom Grady wants to ask out. The sketch's tagline is "Who da mammal?"

"One Bad Bee": Sonny writes this sketch, which is entirely rapped with Zora as the DJ. Sonny plays the main rapping bee. All the cast but Tawni are backup bees.

"'Bumbling Bee": Sonny writes this sketch that takes the place of Tawni's sketch; it features flowers and a woman with a big butt.

"Queen Bee": Tawni writes this sketch which is replaced by Sonny's "Clumsy Bee" sketch. Tawni plays the queen bee and the other cast play worker bees.

"Barf Sketch": This sketch was not seen but parts of it are mentioned. Nico played the stomach, Grady played the barf, and Zora played the toilet.

"Mother and Baby sketch": This sketch was also never seen but was mentioned. Nico played the mother and Grady was the baby.

"Chicken Sketch": The sketch was also never seen, but Nico and Grady in the costumes were seen. Nico was a chicken and Grady was an egg.

Special Guest Star: Nancy McKeon as Connie Munroe
Guest Starring: Michael Kostroff as Marshall
Absent: Sterling Knight as Chad Dylan Cooper, as he wasn't introduced until the second episode which aired immediately after this episode.

| 2 | 2 | "**West Coast Story**" | David Trainer | Michael Feldman Steve Marmel | 4.0[1] | February 8, 2009 | 104 |

Sonny meets Chad Dylan Cooper, the star of *Mackenzie Falls,* and is starstruck until she realizes that *Mackenzie Falls* and *So Random!* are rivals. This apparently stems from a Tween Choice Award *Mackenzie Falls* won two years ago, when Chad mocked *So Random!* in his acceptance speech. Sonny decides to hold a peace picnic to dissolve the rivalry, but her plan backfires, resulting in the entire So Random! cast being stuck to their seats. In Grady's attempts to free himself, he rips his pants, after which video of the incident is posted to the internet. Sonny laughs it off until she realizes that video of her getting egg salad tossed in her face is also on the internet. Angry, Sonny challenges Chad to a Musical Chairs competition. The stakes are as follows: If *So Random!* loses, the show will say something nice about *Mackenzie Falls*; if they win, *Mackenzie Falls* must say something good about *So Random!*. In the end, Sonny tricks Chad with a fake injury, winning the game of musical chairs. Chad compliments her on her acting skills and asks her to join his show (offering to have Portlyn disappear in a ballooning accident), but she declines the offer. As his part of the agreement, Chad later says, on camera, that *So Random!* is his favorite show.

Note: A clip of Sonny and Chad in this episode is later used against them in "Sonny: So Far". Supposedly someone on Mackenzie Falls taped it and sent it to the talk show that Sonny and Chad guest starred on to humiliate Sonny, and possibly Chad.

***So Random!* sketches:**

"Fasty's Really Fast Food": A restaurant-based sketch where the food items ordered and mentioned are thrown abruptly at the customers. Sonny and Tawni play customers, Grady plays fast food worker, and Nico plays the manager.

"Madge the Waitress": Sonny dresses up as a fat waitress with a Brooklyn accent who takes people's orders. Tawni mocks Sonny's outfit, asking her, "You're in a fat suit?"

First appearance: Sterling Knight as Chad Dylan Cooper
Guest Starring: Jillian Murray as Portlyn
Title Reference: *West Side Story*

3	3	**"Sonny at The Falls"**	Eric Dean Seaton	Phil Baker Drew Vaupen	3.5[2]	February 15, 2009	112

The cast members of *So Random!* get jealous when they're served bad cafeteria food while *Mackenzie Falls* cast members are dining on lobster and steak; this is because *Mackenzie Falls* is the lunch lady's favorite show. After hearing that *So Random!* has become more popular with Sonny as a cast member, Chad devises a plan to steal Sonny from them so that *Mackenzie Falls* can become popular. Things take a turn for the worse when Sonny gets her sketch rejected by her castmates, and her fellow co-stars hurt Sonny's feelings so much that she quits *So Random!* and joins the cast of *Mackenzie Falls* for comfort and support. In order to get Sonny back, the *So Random!* cast dresses up as characters from Sonny's rejected sketch. Sonny is so touched (and angry at Chad's admission that he was using her for ratings) that she joins the *So Random!* cast again. The cast is later seen doing "Loser Force Five" as an apology to Sonny.

***So Random!* sketch:**

"Loser Force Four": Sonny wrote this sketch about four pathetic superheroes, but it was rejected by the others, though they later agree to do it as "Loser Force Five" in order to get Sonny back on *So Random!*

Guest stars: Jillian Murray as Portlyn and Wendy Worthington as Brenda

4	4	**"You've Got Fan Mail"**	Philip Charles MacKenzie	Phil Baker Drew Vaupen	3.7[3]	February 22, 2009	107

Sonny is the only cast member who hasn't been getting any fan mail. Tawni rubs it in Sonny's face every chance she gets, but Sonny pretends she doesn't care. Finally, sick of Tawni's bragging, Sonny writes herself her own fan letter using the name "Eric," but when Marshall invites Eric to meet Sonny, she has to pretend to be him to hide her lie. Sonny dresses up as Eric, with a fake beard, a hoodie, and two broken arms. Tawni pulls "Eric" into her dressing room as Josh, the mail man, walks in and hands Tawni some of Sonny's fanmail. Tawni stuffs it under her seat cushion, and it turns out she had been hiding fanmail from Sonny all along. Sonny, upset, pulls off her disguise to yell at Tawni. When Tawni finds out that Sonny is pretending to be her own fan, she suggests to Marshall that Sonny should meet Eric on stage after the live *So Random!* taping. Chad also finds out that Sonny is *Weird Beard* (Chad and Josh's nickname for Eric) and decides to help Sonny out by dressing up as Eric, showing that he cares about her. Meanwhile, Nico and Grady try and intercept a package meant for Zora, but she manages to get the last laugh.

So Random! **sketches:**

"So You Think You Can PP Dance?": A parody of the reality show *So You Think You Can Dance?*, featuring contestants dancing whilst holding in a full bladder, which is made even harder by the fact that the announcer repeatedly makes double entendres related to urinating. Sonny plays the announcer while the other castmates play the contestants.

"Baby Waa Waa": This sketch is not seen, but parts of it are mentioned. It is said that it involves Sonny spitting up on the changing table while getting her diaper changed. Her catch phrase is "Waa Waa Waa." She is seen wearing a bonnet, carrying a giant baby bottle and (not seen) wearing a diaper.

Guest Starring: Michael Kostroff as Marshall, Brent Tarnol as Josh

Title Reference: *You've Got Mail*

Other References: Sonny, dressed as Eric, paraphrases a line from the song "Blackbird" by The Beatles, by saying 'Time to take these broken wings and fly'.

Note: In this episode Sonny says she got a new cellphone, but in the previous episode 'Sonny at the Falls' is seen with the same cellphone; this is because this episode was filmed before "Sonny at the Falls".

5	5	"Cheater Girls"	Eric Dean Seaton	Dava Savel	3.0[4]	March 1, 2009	105

Sonny and Tawni are working on a new sketch called the "Check It Out Girls", which they're very excited about. But when Sonny's mother, Connie, finds out about her 'D' in Geometry, she threatens to pull Sonny from the show unless she passes a major test to prove that she can pull her grade up. Tawni tells Sonny to cheat but she refuses; instead, she recruits Zora to help her, but is too preoccupied with the "Check It Out Girls" to pay attention. Zora finally gives up, and Sonny ends up writing the answers on her hand. However, when she is about to take the test, she repeatedly mishears words as "cheat" or "cheating", so she confesses. Marshall then bans Sonny and Tawni from the Check-It-Out girls sketch (because Sonny almost cheated and Tawni told Sonny to cheat) until they retake and pass the test without cheating. Meanwhile, Nico and Grady buy a snake to impress a pretty girl on the set, but chaos abounds when the snake escapes. At the end, Nico decides to just talk to the girl, but is horrified to discover that she has a manly voice.

So Random! **sketch:**

"Check It Out Girls": A sketch written by Sonny and Tawni based in a grocery store where Tawni and Sonny play valley girls and use the phrase "Check out his/her..." to insult various people.

Special Guest Star: Nancy McKeon as Connie Munroe

Guest-starring: Michael Kostroff as Marshall, Vicki Lewis as Mrs. Bitterman

Absent: Sterling Knight as Chad Dylan Cooper

Title Reference: *The Cheetah Girls*

Note: After Zora tells Nico and Grady that she would like to borrow them her snake, she disappears behind some clothes. After someone comes and takes the clothes, Zora can be seen walking behind the clothes.

6	6	"Three's Not Company"	Eric Dean Seaton	Amy Engelberg Wendy Engelberg	3.8[5]	March 8, 2009	106

Sonny's best friend Lucy visits from Wisconsin but when Tawni tags along with them, Lucy enjoys Tawni more and Sonny gets jealous. Lucy wants to go to Chad's birthday party, but Sonny lies and says she was not invited. Tawni turns up to Sonny's apartment to take them both to the party, therefore telling Lucy the truth. Sonny tries to get into to Chad's birthday, but because she said 'no' to his invitation she is not allowed in. She sneaks in anyway and ends up being chased by security guards. She eventually manages to apologize to Lucy in front of everyone but when Lucy hugs Sonny, the two back up and all the card board cut-outs of Chad falls but then the largest one falls and Chad gets knocked into the cake. Meanwhile, Nico and Grady devise a plan to get revenge on the security guard, Murphy, who keeps stealing their pizza, and he ends up in the hospital. The guilt-stricken boys go and visit Murphy, and he gets back at them.

So Random! **sketches:**

"The Bully-Proof Backpack": A mock commercial marketing a school backpack equipped with "patented cartoon violence technology" to fight back against school bullies. Grady plays the pitchman, and Sonny plays the bully, with Tawni and Nico as the potential victims who use the backpacks.

"The Hair Salon": This is a sketch based on a hair salon worker from Wisconsin.

Guest stars: Eden Sher as Lucy, Steve Hytner as Murphy and Johari Johnson as Clipboard Girl

Absent: Allisyn Ashley Arm as Zora Lancaster

Title Reference: *Three's Company*, the 1977-1983 American sitcom

7	7	"Poll'd Apart"	David Trainer	Amy Engelberg Wendy Engelberg	3.9[6]	March 15, 2009	110

Gossip blogger Sharona targets Sonny and Tawni, but when Sharona keeps on saying bad stuff about Tawni, Sonny tries to tell Sharona to stop blogging about Tawni. Tawni wore a bald cap because Sharona said Sonny's hair was better than Tawni's. Sonny tried to make things better, but like usual, it turns out even worse; Sonny accidentally told Sharona about Tawni was wearing the bald cap. But Sharona wrote on her gossip blog that Tawni was bald. Sonny makes a mean sketch, which name is Wicked Witch of the Web resemble *Wizard of Oz* that hurts Sharona's feelings. Sharona threatens them with meat so they won't come to the Oh No You Di'nt Awards. The cast goes anyway and gets revenge wearing the same clothes as Sharona, making her mad and she falls into a pond. Meanwhile, Nico and Grady try to persuade Chad to drive them to the awards ceremony in his new car by bribing him. Chad takes their gifts and leaves them without a ride. To get back at him Nico and Grady take the battery out of Chad's car and replace it with a plate of doughnuts.

So Random! **sketch:**

"The Wicked Witch of the Web": A *Wizard of Oz* parody that makes fun of Sharona and hurts her feelings.

Guest stars: Elisa Donovan as Sharona, Lily Holleman as Sharona's assistant

8	8	**"Fast Friends"**	David Trainer	Michael Feldman Steve Marmel	3.2[7]	March 29, 2009	102

When Sonny is interviewed by Tween Weekly TV, Chad immediately steps in and uses Sonny to make himself look better. When Sonny realizes this, she gets frustrated with Chad and the cameras witness the interaction, making everyone hate her. Sonny sees herself getting angry with Chad on TV and decides to talk to him and clear her name. But Chad refuses to help Sonny's reputation so she fights fire with fire and catches Chad being a jerk on a hidden camera in her hat. Impressed, Chad gives Sonny 'props' and says they should hang out sometime, and Sonny says he can stop acting since the camera is off. Chad says he knows, implying that he likes her. Sonny smiles at him and nods, and Chad smiles back. Meanwhile, Nico and Grady sort through Tawni's trash to sell it online, but are caught and punished by Tawni by having to feed her and apply lip gloss whenever she tells them to.

So Random! **sketch:**

"Granny Slam!": A fake wrestling match between grandmas played by Nico and Grady; Tawni plays the referee.

Absent: Allisyn Ashley Arm as Zora Lancaster

9	9	**"Sonny with a Chance of Dating"**	Eric Dean Seaton	Cindy Caponera	N/A	April 12, 2009	111

When Sonny is asked out by Tawni's ex-boyfriend James Conroy (who is guest-starring on "Mackenzie Falls"), Tawni tries to convince her out it by telling Sonny that her "best friend" (who is Tawni) dated James and was left heartbroken. However, Sonny ignores Tawni's advice and goes out with James anyway. Tawni asks Chad to tell James to back off of Sonny; the reason being that she doesn't want Sonny to be left so heartbroken. Chad claims that he doesn't care but Tawni sees that he also wants James to back off Sonny. At Sonny and James' date, Tawni and Chad interrupt them (Tawni, because she doesn't want Sonny to be left heartbroken and Chad, because he has a crush on Sonny and can't get used to the fact of Sonny going out with another guy. He also tells James he thinks Sonny is cute.) and Tawni tries to convince Sonny to leave. That's when Sonny discovers Tawni is the one left heartbroken by James when they were arguing while playing air hockey. The next day, James sends Tawni flowers to ask her out, dumping Sonny. The girls decide to get him back. To do so, Sonny goes on fake date with Chad to make James jealous. Just when Chad and Sonny are beginning to enjoy the fake date, James tries dump Tawni for Sonny, and when he overhears Nico and Grady saying that the date is fake, and confronts Sonny and Chad. To convince James that the date is real, Sonny fake-kisses Chad. Convinced, James says he wants Sonny back, but then Sonny and Tawni both dump him. Meanwhile, Nico and Grady are banned from the cafeteria by Murphy, the security guard, so Zora convinces them to let her be their lawyer, with unsuccessful results.

So Random! **sketch:**

"Sally Jenson: Kid Lawyer": Zora mentions this character she played a couple of times when trying to convince Nico and Grady to make her their lawyer.

"Life of the Boston Tea Party": Chad guesses this right before James asks Sonny out. In this sketch, Sonny is a tea pot.

Mackenzie Falls **episode:**

:"Christmas Episode" - Chad mentioned this episode is the one James Conroy guest-stars in. In the end, he realizes he had a wonderful life.

Guest Stars: Kelly Blatz as James Conroy and Steve Hytner as Murphy

10	10	**"Sonny and the Studio Brat"**	Eric Dean Seaton	Amy Engelberg Wendy Engelberg	N/A	April 26, 2009	114

Sonny gives a tour to a under-privileged girl named Dakota. She claims she is from the Children Having A Dream Foundation. Zora points out in the beginning that Dakota was evil but no one believes her. At the prop house, Sonny decides to continue the tour but Dakota demands to see Chad and ties Sonny up. It was then revealed that Dakota really is evil, everyone found out that she's the daughter of Mr. Condor and the Children Having A Dream Foundation really stands for 'CHAD'. They have to keep her happy or her dad could cancel So Random! Dakota forces the cast of So Random! to get Chad to meet her so Sonny talks to him but Chad won't do it unless he can go to "The Basement," a fake club Tawni, Nico and Grady created. Sonny took Dakota and Tawni took Chad to "The Basement". Sonny introduces Dakota to Chad and he decided to hang out with her but due to her annoying behavior, he ends up yelling at her. When Mr. Condor shows up, he gets mad at Sonny for bringing Dakota to a Hollywood club and Chad for yelling at her. Sonny and Chad back up and breaks down the club and Sonny is seen clutching Chad for dear life as Chad holds hands with Mr. Condor and all embarrassingly stop. Everyone in the club finds out the club is fake. Sonny and Chad work it out with Mr. Condor and then everything turns out alright. Chad takes pictures of the fake club, but Tawni stops him from sending the pictures by showing pictures of Chad and Dakota (and Sonny) dancing (She took the picture when Sonny was holding Dakota and Sonny said that she felt a little third-wheel-ish). Sonny makes them both delete the pictures. Since Mr. Condor didn't really like what Chad did, he was forced to do whatever Dakota wants him to do. At the end, Chad and Dakota are each wearing a *Mackenzie Falls* blue robe, with Dakota presumably ordering him around.

So Random! **sketch:**

"The Basement": Nico mentions it when Tawni says they're going to use the set to pretend that they got invited to a hot, teen club opening.

"Cheese Pants": There is a picture of Nico and Grady wearing cheese pants and Nico says it's from a sketch.

Guest Starring: G. Hannelius as Dakota, Daniel Roebuck as Mr. Condor
Note: "Gnomy the Gnome" was broken by Dakota in this episode but reappeared in "Tales from the House" when Chad said "Start with the gnome. He continued to appear in all other episodes.
Also: Demi Lovato's sister, Dallas Lovato, appears as the actress dancing with Nico.

11	11	"Promises, Prom-misses"	David Trainer	Dava Savel	4.1[8]	May 3, 2009	109

After Sonny is upset about missing her prom in Wisconsin, she asks Marshall if she can have a prom for all the shows on the lot on the So Random! set. After he refuses, they send him on a wild goose chase with his GPS and throw the prom in secret. Sonny un-invites Chad because he says the idea of a prom is dumb. Meanwhile, to prepare for their prom, Nico teaches Grady how to slow dance, and Tawni wants to be prom queen. Unfortunately, at the actual prom, Sonny is too busy running around to actually enjoy it. She first gets stuck in Marshall's office, food was out, and the mustard got on her dress so she had to find the different one. When Marshall finds out that Zora has been the voice on his GPS because of Nico, he tells her that he's going back. Before Sonny can go in, Zora tells men that Marshall was coming and even though Sonny didn't want to miss the prom, she tells the So Random! cast to clean everything up. When Marshall gets there he sees the cast practicing for the supposed 'Prom Sketch'. Then Marshall changes his mind and says that they can have a real prom. Sonny gets upset that she missed the prom she created. Afterward, Chad waits behind for Sonny and comes out and asks her to dance with him, which she thinks is sweet. She remarks "I thought you would be the first to go". Chad replies "Which is exactly why I had to be the last to go". They even share a special moment as they slow dance for a few short seconds. At the end everyone is dancing except Marshall trying to find the bathroom.

So Random! **sketches**:

"The Prom": Marshall guesses that Sonny is thinking of doing a prom sketch when he sees her twirling around in a pretty dress. Sonny and the rest of the cast later actually think of doing a prom sketch.

"Princess Girl": This is the dress Sonny wears that angers Tawni.

"Mermaid Girl": This is the dress Sonny wears to keep Tawni happy.

Guest Star: Michael Kostroff as Marshall Pike

12	12	"The Heartbreak Kids"	Eric Dean Seaton	Cindy Caponera	3.4[9]	May 17, 2009	103

When Sonny sees that Marshall and Ms. Bitterman are both lonely, she arranges a date for them. However, Ms. Bitterman gets too involved with *So Random!*, changing Grady's "Scotland's Top Model" sketch and coming up with sketches that aren't funny. Ms. Bitterman writes a sketch about Sonny having to eat real worms and she realizes that it was a huge mistake to bring Marshall and Bitterman together. Ms. Bitterman even gives Sonny, Tawni, Nico, and Grady A's on their test without grading them to direct the show. Sonny asks Chad for help, but Chad says he will only do it if she goes to "Lookout Mountain," with him and without a choice, Sonny and Chad go to Lookout Mountain. Sonny and Chad starts to show their signs of having feelings for each other. Just when they are getting close, Bigfoot (Nico & Grady) jumps out and scares them, and both Sonny and Chad got so scared they grab each other's hands. In the end, with Nico, Grady and Chad's help, they use material from Episode 319 of Mackenzie Falls (called "Bigfoot Gets the Girl") to try and break them up. Much to their dismay, it just brings Marshall and Ms. Bitterman closer. Ms. Bitterman beats up "Bigfoot" to protect Marshall. At the end, she finds out that she beat up Nico and Grady and shows the two her "12 Angry Men" video she starred in when she was in the Navy.

So Random! **sketches**:

"Scotland's Top Model": This is the sketch where Sonny, Tawni, Nico are dressed up in kilts and Grady is the announcer.

Mackenzie Falls **episode** "Episode 319 - Bigfoot Gets the Girl" - This is the episode Chad, Nico, and Grady use to break Marshall and Ms. Bitterman up. The episode is about Bigfoot wanting to get this girl, and he scares her boyfriend away to get her.

Absent: Allisyn Ashley Arm as Zora Lancaster

Guest Starring: Michael Kostroff as Marshall Pike and Vicki Lewis as Ms. Bitterman

13	13	**"Battle of the Networks' Stars"**	Eric Dean Seaton	Michael Feldman Steve Marmel	4.0[10]	June 7, 2009	116

Chad is filming a movie about his life: *Chad Dylan Cooper: The Chad Dylan Cooper Story*. Chad decides to have the real *So Random!* cast to play their parts except for Sonny because he thinks she is difficult to work with. So, he decides to hire Selena Gomez to play the part instead. Selena sees that Chad and Sonny like each other, but when they both deny it, she uses reverse psychology to get them to admit that they do. When Chad and Sonny had a enough of Selena saying they like each other (even though she is right), Sonny ends up admitting she thinks Chad has sparkly eyes and Chad ends up admitting that he thinks Sonny has pretty hair when they get into to a fight. In the end, Selena leaves with anger, saying that they are perfect for each other and she doesn't have to do Chad's movie because she was in Camp Hip Hop (A parody of *Camp Rock*). Chad then gives Sonny the part. Meanwhile, Nico and Grady hangs out with the lookalikes of themselves, but get into hot water with Tawni when Grady's alter-ego tries to hit on her.

So Random! **sketches:**

"Gassie the Toot'n Pooch": A sketch following the adventures of a dog who speaks by farting.

Also:

"Chad Dylan Cooper: The Chad Dylan Cooper Story" - A movie about Chad's life. Directed by Chad, stars Chad, Sonny, Tawni, Nico, and Grady.

"Camp Hip Hop": Selena plays a character similar to Mitchie in *Camp Rock*, who was played by Demi Lovato.

Absent: Allisyn Ashley Arm as Zora Lancaster

Special Guest Star: Selena Gomez as Herself

References Made: *Camp Rock*, Mitchie Torres (from *Camp Rock*), Jonas Brothers, Robert Feggans, *Harry Potter*, *Wizards of Waverly Place*, *Lassie*, *Hannah Montana* Sonny thinking Selena being a "relationship wizard" is a reference to "Wizards of Waverly Place", in which Selena Gomez plays Alex Russo, a wizard. **Note:** In the end, Chad tells Sonny and her friends that his movie is on, but it appears to be the same day because they are all wearing the same clothing. Which is strange, because Chad tells Sonny that they will start tomorrow.

14	14	**"Prank'd"**	Carl Lauten	Kevin Kopelow Heath Seifert	5.1[11]	July 5, 2009	115

Chad is the host of a new prank show and Sonny fears she is his next target when Chad arranges a movie audition for her that happens to be for the role of Sonny's favorite superhero "Fashionita". Sonny pulls a prank on the casting director before Grady can warn her that the audition is real. The audition being real is some sort of sign that Chad likes Sonny. Sonny feels embarrassed and apologizes to Chad and he forgives her. Since Sonny pranked Chad's friend, director of "Fashionita", he tells the whole cast of *So Random!* that he's going to do something 100 times worse than he planned it to do before and tells them to watch out. When Tawni wants to audition for *Fashonita*, she talks to Chad and bribes him. Chad calls the director but when Tawni listens to it, Nico and Grady thinks Tawni is the co-host with Chad so the two sets a prank for Tawni. When Nico and Grady accidentally traps themselves in a net, they told Sonny that Tawni is the co-host with Chad and thinks Sonny is with them because she didn't say anything. Sonny calls Chad and tells him to stop, but realizes it's too late when Chad explains that he set up a prank audition for Tawni for the same role. When Chad runs in to witness the aftermath of his prank, things didn't work the way he planned. Zora shows up and tells Chad that he was being prank'd and that she is actually the host of Celebrity Practical Jok'd and pranked Chad into thinking he was the host. That was not the end of the prank though. She also glued his feet to the floor, put elephant manure in his convertible, and glued his face to the window. At the end, Tawni and Gassie were rehearsing but Gassie messes up and Tawni gets upset.

So Random! **sketches:**

"Gassie the Toot 'n Pooch": A sketch following the adventures of a dog who speaks by farting. In this sketch the mayor visits.

'*Also:*

"Fashionita": The movie that Sonny and Tawni both want to audition for, but in the end it turned out to be a prank audition.

"Celebrity Practical Jok'd": The show Zora is the host of, but pranks Chad into thinking he's the host.

"Young Lincoln": The one man show the casting director mentions he is a part of.

Guest Starring: Andrew Abelson as Director

Note: This was one of the episodes that were on unlocked on DisneyChannel.com by counting how many times they say "princess" (or variations of the word) during the presentation of *Princess Protection Program*

Title Reference: *Punk'd*

15	15	"Tales From the Prop House"	Eric Dean Seaton	Dava Savel	3.9[12]	August 2, 2009	117

The *So Random!* cast attempt to prevent their prop house from being taken away and used as a meditation room for the *Mackenzie Falls* cast. The number one show gets any room in the building according to the contract. After remembering all the good memories about sketches they have done (like *Dolphin Boy* and the *Check It Out Girls*), they hand-cuff themselves to the prop house. After two hours of being hand-cuffed they decide to fight back. They chase away the cast of *Mackenzie Falls* by cutting a hole in the ceiling and annoying them by throwing objects on their heads. The whole cast of *Mackenzie Falls* except for Chad runs away and says he won't be driven away, but as he starts meditating in the photo booth, he runs away because of a rat. The *So Random* cast get their prop house back. Chad comes back and brings gifts to everyone in order to say he is sorry because he didn't know how much the prop house meant to them. He gives Tawni a Bedazzled lip gloss case, Zora a night light for the sarcophagus, and lastly gives an autograph picture of himself to Sonny that says "To my biggest fan, I'm sorry, TV's Chad Dylan Cooper." Then Sonny says she is touched. Suddenly, Nico and Grady blast through the wall, riding the forklift, after Chad tells the girls that he let them ride it as a gift after Sonny freaks out saying "You Let Them Do What On The Who Now?!".

So Random! **sketches:**

"Dolphin Boy (from Episode 1)": The story of "Dolphin Boy" who is half-dolphin and half-boy.

"Annoying Girl": A girl who always annoys the people around her.

"Check It Out Girls: First Fight": A continuation of the "Check It Out Girls" sketch where they get into the first argument.

Guest Starring: Michael Kostroff as Marshall Pike, Jillian Murray as Portlyn

16	16	"Sonny in the Kitchen with Dinner"	Linda Mendoza	Danny Warren	N/A	August 16, 2009	118

Sonny tries to help Tawni have a good date with an intern Hayden (Robert Adamson). Sonny begs Chad for Laker Tickets for herself, Tawni, and Hayden which she got after saying three nice things about him. Meanwhile, Nico and Grady try to create a sandwich to be named after, after seeing the sandwich Chad got named after. At the date, Tawni leaves for a moment and the kiss cam zooms in on Sonny and Hayden. Under the pressure, Sonny and Hayden are forced to kiss, making Tawni furious. Chad gets upset because he trusted Sonny to use his tickets "responsibly", but instead he saw the kiss on "Tween Weekly" magazine. Both Chad and Tawni blames Sonny so to make it up to Tawni, Sonny gets her a second chance with Hayden. Hayden wants the date to be a home cooked meal at Tawni's apartment. Since Tawni doesn't know how to cook and uses her kitchen as a closet, the date will be at Sonny's and Sonny will cook the meal. At the apartment, Sonny's oven is not working, so Nico and Grady sends over sandwich to serve. Not only that, but Sonny drops her phone down the drain and Tawni accidentally destroys it by turning on the garbage disposal and then Sonny's phone somehow calls Chad, Tawni loses her contact lens when the sandwich hit her, and Sonny gets locked out after Hayden comes in to the kitchen. Nico and Grady come into the apartment to help Sonny get back in. Chad breaks open Sonny's door and accidentally damages it when he heard a phone call from Sonny (this happened when her phone went down the drain). Then, Sonny gets back in and Tawni tells Hayden the truth. In the end, Nico, Grady, Hayden, and Chad all end up retching because they ate the sandwich Nico and Grady accidentally left out in the sun for 12 hours. Then Sonny's new blarmie end up with a gross sandwich that Tawni retched on when it showed up in the mail at Sonny's apartment.

Absent: Allisyn Ashley Arm as Zora Lancaster

Guest Starring: Robert Adamson as Hayden, Lanny Horn as Howie, Max Williger as Delivery Guy

Notes: This is the first episode not to feature or make reference of a *So Random!* sketch. Also, this was Demi Lovato's first on-screen kiss.

References: There's someone who appears to look like Jack Nicholson at the Lakers game, a reference to the well known actor, who is a great fan of the Los Angeles Lakers. "Blarmie" is a spoof of a real-life blanket with sleeves called "Snuggie". **Title Reference:** Someone's in the Kitchen with Dinah (a line from the song: "I've Been Working on the Railroad")

17	17	"Guess Who's Coming to Guest Star"	Eric Dean Seaton	Michael Feldman Steve Marmel	4.1[13]	September 27, 2009	108

When Jackson Tyler from *Tridark* (parody of Robert Pattinson in *Twilight*) cancels to be on So random, Marshall hires Chad Dylan Cooper to be the replacement guest. But when Sonny finds out she has to do the sketch with Chad, Chad tells Sonny that she is going to fall in love with him. He tells her that she'll stumble at first, and get all nervous and then dream about him and get lost in his eyes. And when all those things start to happen to Sonny, she decides she has to do everything she can not to look into Chad's eyes. So she wears a hat to rehearsal and when Marshall asks why, Sonny says she thought the sketch was missing something. But she ends up making things worse, when Marshall says Sonny and Chad have to kiss. Meanwhile, Marshall let's Nico and Grady use his office while Chad using their dressing room. But when Nico and Grady take advantage of the office, and are brought a pig wrapped in a blanket, out of confusion. On the night of the show, Nico and Grady make Marshall hold the pig when they go apologize. When Sonny and Chad are about to kiss, the pig lands in Sonny's lap and she lets the pig kiss Chad.

So Random! **sketch:**

> "Hot E.M.T": Sonny plays a girl who pretends to get hurt so she can see the paramedic played by Chad Dylan Cooper. They are supposed to kiss but just before they do a pig falls into Sonny's lap and she lets the pig kiss Chad instead.

Also:

> "The Goody Gang": The show Tawni and Chad were on when they were young.

Absent: Allisyn Ashley Arm as Zora Lancaster
Guest Starring: Michael Kostroff as Marshall, David Magidoff as Dave (the assistant), Paul Butler as Young Chad, True Bella as Young Tawni.
Title Reference: *Guess Who's Coming to Dinner*
Note: This episode premiered on Disney Channel Latin America on August 8. This episode is also known as "Sonny with a Chad" as it was called in its promo.

18	18	**"Hart to Hart"**	Eric Dean Seaton	Lanny Horn Josh Silverstein	4.1[14]	November 1, 2009	119

Sonny convinces Tawni to fire her overbearing manager, not realizing it is Tawni's mother. When Tawni fires her mom as a manager, she also fires her mom as a mom. Sonny allows Tawni to stay at her home, but Tawni quickly begins to take advantage of Sonny's hospitality, doing nothing but lie around on the couch and turning Sonny into her domestic slave, which prompts Sonny and Connie to devise a plan to get Tawni and her mom back together. Meanwhile, Nico and Grady try to get past the new security guard Jeff's dummy Walter (who appears to have a mind of his own) so they can use Chad's private bathroom. Chad discovers this and Jeff later confesses to using the bathroom because of Walter's fan devotion to Chad.

So Random! **sketches:**

> "Dumb Blond": Tawni is the only So Random! actor/actress seen rehearsing this sketch. Tawni plays a dumb blond with her own television cooking show in this offensive sketch.

> "Pinata sketch": Not shown, but described as having Tawni playing a pinata, and Grady hitting her with a stick.

Absent: Allisyn Ashley Arm as Zora Lancaster
Special Guest Star: Nancy McKeon as Connie Munroe
Guest Stars: Christina Moore as Tammi Hart, Jeff Dunham as Jeff

19	19	**"Sonny in the Middle"**	Eric Dean Seaton	Lanny Horn Josh Silverstein	N/A	November 8, 2009	113

Sonny gives Nico and Grady a video game chair for their birthday. Right after she gives them this gift, Nico and Grady start fighting over it because only one person can sit on the chair at a time. Nico and Grady both get so mad that they declare that they are "Not friends anymore", and both try to hang out with Sonny instead. Sonny gets annoyed with them not being friends and trying to replace each other with her. Meanwhile, Zora pretends to be upset and convinces Tawni to take her to see 'Giraffes on Ice' which Tawni figures out is an Animal Morgue. She later tricks Chad to take her also. Sonny finally decides to make Nico and Grady miss each other by taking them to movies that they don't want to see (Grady to "Five Weddings and a Wedding", and Nico to "Sisterhood of the Traveling Secret Princesses") instead of Monkey Cars 3D, the movie they both wanted to see. While watching their movies, they each realize that they miss each other, make up and go to Monkey Cars 3D where the whole cast of *So Random!* and Chad is seen watching "Monkey Cars 3D". At the end in the cafeteria, Nico and Grady pull a prank on Sonny that they had done before, but things backfire when Sonny thinks that a man with the actual name of "Rip a big one" is another prank and laughs, leaving Nico and Grady disgusted and Sonny herself embarrassed.

'So Random! *sketches:*

> "Garry and Larry": Nico and Grady play two friends who have their own talk show in their basement. Also, the set of "Garry and Larry" was also the set for "The Basement" in "Sonny and the Studio Brat".

Guest Starring: Lanny Horn as Howie
Note: This episode can be seen on the DVD "Sonny's Big Break" that was released on August 25th, as a bonus feature, and was also recorded to show on online flights with Delta Airlines. This episode premiered in Disney Channel India on November 6th 2009.

20	20	**"Cookie Monsters"**	Eric Dean Seaton	Cindy Caponera (Story) Kevin Kopelow Heath Seifert (Teleplay)	N/A	November 15, 2009	120

Zora gets challenged by the studio head's daughter, Dakota, to sell the most Blossom Scout cookies ever, and Sonny steps in to help Zora win. However, Chad helps Dakota sell more cookies as she threatens him to get her dad to close down Mackenzie Falls. It turns out that the scout master is Sonny's old Scout Master from Wisconsin, which gets Sonny scared because of memories of being rejected. Both of the teams try to sell the cookies by bribing the customers. At one stage Zora gets kicked out of the Blossom Scouts but knows how to wrap up a twisted ankle when the Scout master's leg gets hurt. Then she is offered her badge sash again. In the end, they tie, but there is one box left. Sonny, Zora, and Dakota want it, but Chad eats it, and chokes. Sonny saves him, and she gets her merit badge that prohibited her from becoming a Blossom Scout ever since she was eight years old. Then, while trying to hold back Dakota and Zora, Sonny and Chad start arguing, which leads to them literally fighting with Zora holding Sonny back and Dakota holding back Chad. Meanwhile, Nico and Grady come up with a scent to attract girls (which attracts a few too many), and Tawni promises not to look in the mirror for two days, which at first makes her slightly eccentric, then daunting, and then she looks like The Joker.

Title Reference: the Cookie Monster from *Sesame Street*

Guest-starring: G. Hannelius as Dakota, Patricia Bethune as Mrs. Montecore, Madison De La Garza as eight-year-old Sonny (in flashbacks).

Note: Madison De La Garza is Demi Lovato's younger sister.

21	21	"Sonny: So Far"	Eric Dean Seaton	Michael Feldman Steve Marmel	3.7[15]	November 22, 2009	121

When Sonny and Tawni are guests on "Gotcha with Gilroy Smith," they are excited at first. But then Gilroy shows them the promo, saying he hopes the girls will reveal something personal and embarrassing. To prevent this from happening, they make a pact backstage to have each other's back so that neither of them will get embarrassed. But Tawni then breaks the pact after Gilroy shows a backstage footage of her and Sonny making the pact. As the show continues, Sonny's mind wanders and she starts to think about Chad Dylan Cooper after Gilroy says, "Do they, Sonny? Do they really?" which is Chad's catchphrase. Sonny starts to think about the time when she danced with Chad for about 10 seconds at the prom ("Promises, Prom-misses"). Gilroy sees her expression, can tell she's thinking about a boy, and starts questioning her on some of the boys she associates with and her feelings toward them. When he brings up Chad Dylan Cooper, and when Sonny seems to be nervous about it, he brings Chad onto the show. Gilroy shows rare footage of Sonny and Chad from episode 2 ("West Coast Story"). Afterwards, Sonny pulls Chad backstage, completely unaware about the fact that Gilroy has a hidden camera backstage and he's showing it to the audience. Tawni, who remembers all the things Sonny has done for her and doesn't want Sonny to get embarrassed in front of everyone, turns off the screen right before Sonny and Chad tell each other how they really feel. We don't hear them say they like each other, but it is assumed that they do like each other, based on what they say before and after Tawni turns off the screen (and how they acted towards each other earlier in the season). Gilroy grabs the remote back and turns the T.V. back on. We see Sonny talking to Chad ("That was...so much easier to say than I thought it would be.") and then she walks away.

Absent: Brandon Mychal Smith as Nico Harris, Doug Brochu as Grady Mitchel and Allisyn Ashley Arm as Zora Lancaster

Guest Star: Eric Toms as Gilroy Smith **Note:** Although not in the episode, Nico Harris, Grady Mitchel and Zora Lancaster were shown in clips from previous episodes.

Season 2: 2010-2011

Series #	Season #	Title	Directed by	Written by	U.S. viewers (millions)	Original air date	Prod. code
22	1	"Walk a Mile in My Pants"	Eric Dean Seaton	Amy Engelberg Wendy Engelberg	6.30[16]	March 14, 2010	202

Sonny is hosting a "Walk-a-Thon For Books", where the participants will be wearing Tawni's Extreme Skinny Jeans. When Chad hears of this, he is inspired to host a "Walk-a-Thon Against Books", where the contenders will also wear Tawni's Extreme Skinny Jeans. On the day of both Walk-A-Thons, Tawni cannot move, and is carried to the hospital, and Sonny follows. Soon after, the TV at the hospital is showing a channel which is broadcasting both Walk-a-Thon events, and the people on the screen all fall down, as a result of SPS (Skinny Pants Syndrome), where skinny jeans cut off blood circulation to your legs. Everyone is brought to the hospital, and gets their pants cut off, much to Tawni's dismay. Later, Tawni has to wear balloon pants, which is her medicine until her legs heal. Tawni decides to not wear them, and continues wearing skinny jeans. But when she sees her fans with SPS in the studio audience, she is inspired to make a music video to raise awareness for SPS.

"Sicky Vicky": Sonny plays Vicky, a sick girl who hosts a TV show from her bed giving tips about fun things to do when you are sick.

Untitled Hula Sketch: The cast rehearses a hula sketch.

"Stop SPS": The casts of *So Random!* and *Mackenzie Falls* unite to film the music video to stop Skinny Pants Syndrome.

Absent: Allisyn Ashley Arm as Zora

Note: On this episode's first broadcast, the 16:9 widescreen picture seen on Disney Channel HD was mistakenly compressed into the 4:3 center cut picture on Disney Channel's SD feed; the rebroadcast on March 21, 2010 corrected this. This is the first episode broadcast that was taped at Hollywood Center Studios, joining *Wizards of Waverly Place*, *The Suite Life on Deck* and *Jonas* at the lot; the series was shot at NBC Studios in Burbank for the first season. The series' record breaking season premiere was lead in by the season finale for *Hannah Montana*, which topped the week with 7.6 million viewers. [17]

| 23 | 2 | "Sonny Get Your Goat" | Eric Dean Seaton | Dava Savel | N/A | March 21, 2010 | 204 |

Sonny and Tawni are invited on an exchange program to Glendovia because of the success of their "Check-it-Out Girls" sketch, but refuse to go together due to an unknown argument. When Tawni goes she is shocked to discover that it is a cultural wasteland and that the Glendovians think the characters are real check out girls. Meanwhile, an exchange student impresses a girl Nico and Grady like, and they both think it is because of his mustache. They then wear a mustache trying to impress her, but they get themselves stuck in their own mustaches because of the glue.

So Random! sketch:

"The Check-it-out Girls": A popular sketch which was a recurring segment in Season 1.

Guest Stars: Michael Kostroff as Marshall, Sam Lerner as Dinka

Absent: Allisyn Ashley Arm as Zora **Title Reference:** *Annie Get Your Gun*

| 24 | 3 | "Gassie Passes" | Eric Dean Seaton | Dava Savel | N/A | March 28, 2010 | 205 |

Feeling that Gassie doesn't get the affection that he deserves, Sonny takes it upon herself to show the dog love, love that it doesn't get from its trainer. Sonny then finds out that giving the dog affection effects Gassie's mood to flatulate on command when filming the "Gassie" sketches as well jeopardizing the feature film "Gassie & We". Sonny then gives Gassie too many dog treats that may have killed him. In the end it turns out Gassie was in shock from too many meatball treats and gets the love he deserves, also putting Chad into shock by pretending to be dead. Meanwhile, Nico and Grady borrow money from Dakota Condor to invest in fart noise lunch boxes for "Gassie & We".

So Random! sketch:

"Gassie the Toot'n Pooch"

Guest Star: G. Hannelius as Dakota Condor and Siobhan Fallon Hogan as Bella, Gassie's trainer

| 25 | 4 | "Sonny with a Song" | John Fortenberry | Michael Feldman Steve Marmel | N/A | April 11, 2010 | 209 |

Sonny's favorite musician, Trey Brothers, is visiting and she would like to spend time with him to show him some songs she has written. However, Tawni likes Trey and thinks Sonny is trying to steal him from her. So she says that Sonny's song is her song. But then things get more complicated when Trey steals "Tawni's song". Meanwhile, Nico and Grady try to find out how to work a magic box.

Guest Stars: Guy Burnet as Trey Brothers, Michael Kostroff as Marshall Pike
Absent: Allisyn Ashley Arm as Zora

| 26 | 5 | "High School Miserable" | Carl Lauten | Michael Feldman Steve Marmel | N/A | April 18, 2010 | 206 |

Sonny and her fellow cast members are disappointed with their studio perks, they then write a letter to Mr. Condor expressing their dissatisfaction. Mr. Condor becomes upset by this and fires the cast forcing them to attend public high school and hires his daughter Dakota as the one and only star of *So Random!*.

Title Reference: *High School Musical*

So Random! sketches:

- "The Real Princesses of New Jersey": A parody of both *The Real Housewives of New Jersey* reality-show and the Disney Princess franchise, performed by Sonny (Snow-White/"Snowy"), Tawni (Cinderella/"Cindy"), Zora (Sleeping-Beauty/"Beauty"), and Grady (the Magic Mirror).
- "Sally Jenson: Kid Lawyer": The cast rehearses this sketch, with Dakota later replacing Zora.
- "Rappin' Pirate": A sketch mentioned by the other cast members, normally performed by Nico, later replaced by Dakota.

Guest Stars: Michael Kostroff as Marshall Pike, G. Hannelius as Dakota Condor and E. E. Bell as Principal

| 27 | 6 | "Legend of Candy Face" | Eric Dean Seaton | Dan Cohen F.J. Pratt | N/A | May 2, 2010 | 203 |

When the casts of *So Random!* and *Mackenzie Falls* keep doing ridiculous things to each other, Ms. Bitterman decides do take them to the woods so they can start trusting each other. While on a team building retreat in the woods, Ms. Bitterman tells the group about the legend of "Candyface". When mysterious events start happening and personal items are found broken, the *So Random!* cast is convinced that "Candyface" is responsible.

So Random! **sketch:**

"Mackenzie Stalls": The cast of *So Random!* parody *Mackenzie Falls*, but instead of the setting being by a waterfall, the setting of the sketch is in a school bathroom.

Guest Stars: Vicki Lewis as Ms. Bitterman, William Jonathan Georges as Devon, Leslie-Anne Huff as Penelope, Ashley Jackson as Chloe and DeVaughn Nixon as Trevor

28	7	"Gummy with a Chance"	Carl Lauten	Josh Herman Adam Schwartz	3.4[18]	May 9, 2010	207

Tawni bans gum from the set after "almost dying" from tripping over Sonny's leftover pieces. Even though Sonny has a ritual of chewing gum just before going on stage and feels she can't be funny without it. Meanwhile, Chad invites Nico and Grady to exercise in his personal gym as a ploy to use their workouts to power his new "green" dressing room.

So Random! **sketches:** "Sicky Vicky" and "Toe-nail Fairy" (played by Tawni)

29	8	"Random Acts of Disrespect"	Leslie Kolins Small	Dan Cohen F.J. Pratt	N/A	May 16, 2010	208

When Grace, an elderly woman, wins the "Be So Random! for a Day" contest, the *So Random!* cast ends up planning an "old geezer" sketch that not only offends Grace and her entire retirement home, but all elderly people. Grace and her friends turn the tables and play a practical joke on the cast. Meanwhile, Chad attempts to help a group of kids with their fear of clowns and ends up looking like one himself.

References

- During one sketch, other Disney Channel shows are (verbally) parodied, including *That's So Raven*, *Wizards of Waverly Place*, and *Hannah Montana*.
- The end-credits sequence features parodies of routines from *The Benny Hill Show* (the "Yakety Sax" chase-sequences, and patting Jackie Wright's bald head), and *Rowan & Martin's Laugh-In* (Arte Johnson's "man on a tricycle").

Guest Stars: Estelle Harris as Grace Gallagher, Carol Locatell as Edith and Larry Gelman as Buddy **Absent:** Allisyn Ashley Arm as Zora

30	9	"Grady with a Chance of Sonny"	Eric Dean Seaton	Lanny Horn Josh Silverstein	N/A	May 23, 2010	216

When Grady's brother, Grant, makes fun of him for not having a girlfriend, Sonny steps in and pretends to be his girlfriend. They try and keep the act going when Grant visits and Sonny tries to squeeze in a date with *Tridark*, star Blake Radisson. Meanwhile, Nico and Tawni pull a prank on Chad just before he gets ready to shoot a commercial for his self-titled energy bar.

Guest Star: Preston Jones as Grant **Absent:** Allisyn Ashley Arm as Zora

31	10	"Falling for the Falls (Part 1)"	Eric Dean Seaton	Michael Feldman Steve Marmel	3.60[19]	June 13, 2010	201

Sonny and her mom start watching *Mackenzie Falls* and eventually become addicted to it. When the season finale is coming up, Sonny can't wait for it and just asks Chad what happens between Mackenzie and Chloe in the finale, though she words it as if she wants him to ask her out instead, which he does. When the other the *So Random!* cast members finds out Sonny is watching *Mackenzie Falls*, they disapprove and Sonny is afraid to tell them about her and Chad. Meanwhile, the cast are working on Astronomy projects and Grady and Nico try to find a way to get Sonny to do it for them.

Special Guest Star: Nancy McKeon as Connie Munroe

32	11	"Falling for the Falls (Part 2)"	Eric Dean Seaton	Michael Feldman Steve Marmel	3.82[20]	June 20, 2010	217

Sonny and Chad try to keep their relationship a secret from their fellow *So Random!* and *Mackenzie Falls* cast members. However, they keep slipping up and saying the words "Chad" and "Sonny" during their rehearsals. This makes the cast members of both shows suspicious. When they go on their first date, Chad messes up because he is nervous and ends up spitting water on Sonny. The cast of *So Random!* then finds out about their date when the incident is posted on the cover of "Tween Weekly" magazine. Chad blames Sonny for what happened and Sonny, infuriated, "breaks up" with him. He then climbs through her window into her house to apologize, and shows Sonny a billboard he had made that says he is a fool for her. They then restart their relationship and have a "second first date" as the rest of *So Random!* watches angrily.

Special Guest Star: Nancy McKeon as Connie Munroe

33-34	12-13	"Sonny with a Secret"	Eric Dean Seaton	Michael Feldman Steve Marmel	6.1[21]	July 18, 2010	212-213

Sonny celebrating her one-year anniversary with *So Random!* is hindered when is she accused of being of thief. From stealing a necklace at a department store, to stealing Nico and Grady's gold coin and possibly stealing the idea of the "Sicky Vicky" sketch. When proof of the contrary is to no avail, she is fired from the show. Meanwhile, Tawni is annoyed at the fact that she is constantly ignored.

Absent: Allisyn Ashley Arm as Zora (in part one only)
Guest Stars: Michael Kostroff as Marshall Pike, Leslie-Anne Huff as Penelope and Regan Burns as Ryan Loughlin
Note: This episode was broadcast in a 4:3 letterbox format on Disney Channel's standard definition feed.

35	14	"The Problem with Pauly"	Shelley Jensen	Josh Herman Adam Schwartz	4.47[22]	August 8, 2010	214

Sonny meets Pauly the star of their favorite childhood show, *Pauly and Pals*. She agrees to wear the Pauly suit at fan meet and greet so that Hank, the actor that plays Pauly, can get a break. But Sonny's commitment to being Pauly hinders a seven week anniversary date she planned with Chad, in addition Hank does not want to return to his job.

Absent: Allisyn Ashley Arm as Zora **Guest Stars:** Vicki Lewis as Ms. Bitterman, Bobby Slayton as Hank and Daniel Roebuck as Mr. Condor

36	15	"That's So Sonny"	Eric Dean Seaton	Dava Savel	4.0[23]	August 29, 2010	215

Chad is upset that he does not have 1,000,000 fans on Flitter (a parody of Twitter) and things get worse when they start to decrease. Sonny enlists the help of Amber Algoode, the president of his fan club and a master of disguise to fix things. Amber uses her disguises to spy on the other *So Random!* cast members to hear what they think of Chad. When she finds out that they like Chad now that he is dating Sonny, Amber insists that Chad dump Sonny, so that people will find him interesting again and to reach his 1,000,000 fans mark.

Absent: Allisyn Ashley Arm as Zora **Special Guest Star:** Raven-Symoné as Amber Algoode

37	16	"Chad without a Chance"	Eric Dean Seaton	Amy Engelberg Wendy Engelberg	N/A	September 19, 2010	210

When Sonny catches the flu, Chad agrees to substitute for her with other *So Random!* cast members. The cast members have arranged a daily chart in which they are allowed to spend individual time with Sonny. With Chad substituting he agrees to dump Tawni's dates over the phone, help Nico get a date with the studio masseuse, assist Zora with her martial arts and offers to be Grady's therapist, all leading to disastrous results.

So Random! **sketch:** "Sicky Vicky": In this sketch Sicky Vicky talks to the audience about ways to have fun when you are sick with Pink eye.

38	17	"My Two Chads"	Eric Dean Seaton	Dan Cohen F.J. Pratt	4.0[24]	September 26, 2010	211

Sonny finds out that Chad has sent his stunt double Chaz on every "dangerous" date with her, so she breaks up with him. Nico and Grady worry about being bored all the time. Tawni becomes the celebrity host of a pirate-themed friendship game show with Sonny pairing with Chad and Nico pairing with Grady.

Absent: Allisyn Ashley Arm as Zora **Special Guest Star:** Lou Ferrigno as Himself

39	18	"A So Random! Halloween Special"	Eric Dean Seaton	Josh Herman Adam Schwartz	4.0[25]	October 17, 2010	226

The first of two specials in the season, the show features a full episode of the show within a show, *So Random!*. Segments include "Check Me Out Girls", "Halloween Do's and Don'ts" and "Roadkill McGill's Roadside Diner". The show also features musical performances from Sonny Munroe and Allstar Weekend; and celebrity host, Shaquille O'Neal.

So Random! **sketches:**

- "Check-it-out girls"
- "The Monster Under My Bed": A sketch from the Halloween Special. Sonny plays a mother and Zora is her daughter who gets attacked by a monster under her bed (Grady).
- "Halloween Party Do's and Dont's": A Halloween sketch with all the casts being at a Halloween Party, saying good and bad things.
- "Roadkill McGrill's Roadside Diner": Sonny and Nico are eating animal food from two country people (Tawni and Grady).
- "Making Babies Cry": A videoclip with the *So Random!* cast with Nico playing Romeo Baby Smooth, a singer that likes making babies cry.

Special Guest Stars: Shaquille O'Neal as Himself and Allstar Weekend as Themselves

40	19	"Sonny with a 100% Chance of Meddling"	Ron Mosely	Lanny Horn Josh Silverstein	N/A	October 24, 2010	219

Sonny sees that Zora was attracted to Wesley Willilger, a child actor guest starring on *Mackenzie Falls*. Sonny tries to set a date for Wesley and Zora and went on a group date with Sonny, Tawni, Nico and Grady. Wesley then gets the wrong message that the date was arranged for him and Sonny to get to together. Meanwhile, Nico and Grady enter a cell phone film festival with Dakota Condor as the star of their film, but Dakota's usual unruly behavior drives the guys crazy.

So Random! sketch: "Counselor Jenny and Dan Dan the Guitar Man": A sketch about camp counselors selling insensitive camp songs for a television commercial, the same songs that got fired from numerous summer camps.

Guest Stars: G. Hannelius as Dakota Condor and Billy Unger as Wesley Willilger

41	20	"Dakota's Revenge"	Eric Dean Seaton	Dava Savel	3.7[26]	November 14, 2010	223

Dakota's new bike gets run over accidentally by Tawni and Sonny and Tawni try desperately to get Izzy the show's prop master to fix it. Meanwhile, Chad writes Dakota a song for her birthday, But Grady and Nico plan on pulling a prank on him to ruin his moment.

Guest Stars: G. Hannelius as Dakota Condor, Daniel Roebuck as Mr. Condor, Steve Hytner as Murphy and Richard Libertini as Izzy

42	21	"Sonny with a Kiss"	Eric Dean Seaton	Ellen Byron Lissa Kapstrom	3.6[27]	November 21, 2010	220

When revealed in an interview that they have yet to share a kiss, Sonny and Chad start to feel pressured by their friends and fans to make it happen. After coming to the realization that there was a lot less pressure when they were just friends, Sonny and Chad decide to break up, they then have their first kiss, then they finally decide to get back together. Meanwhile, Nico and Grady believe their temporary dressing room is being haunted by a dead comedian.

So Random! sketch: "The Toilet Genie and the Nerd": Grady plays The Toilet Genie, a genie from a high school bathroom toilet who grants wishes to nerd Nico.

Absent: Allisyn Ashley Arm as Zora

Guest Stars: Michael Kostroff as Marshall Pike and Johari Johnson as Tia

43	22	"A So Random! Holiday Special"	Eric Dean Seaton	Michael Feldman Steve Marmel	3.7[28]	November 28, 2010	218

Chad Dylan Cooper hosts a fully-produced, jolly-themed "So Random!" holiday special, with special musical guest Joe Jonas. Sketches include "A Jonas for Christmas", "The 12 Days of Sickmas with Sicky Vicky", "Holiday Cooking with Roadkill McGill" and "Christmas with the Real Princesses of New Jersey".

Special Guest Star: Joe Jonas as Himself

44	23	"Sonny with a Grant"	Eric Dean Seaton	Michael Feldman Steve Marmel	4.0[29]	December 5, 2010	221

Grady's older brother Grant makes another visit into town just when Grady was about to spend some alone time alone while the other cast members are on vacation, except for Tawni. Chad is fired from "Mackenzie Falls" with Grant being as the new Mackenzie.

Guest Stars: Preston Jones as Grant and Daniel Roebuck as Mr. Condor
Absent: Brandon Mychal Smith as Nico and Allisyn Ashley Arm as Zora, but their names are both mentioned.
Note: This second time that Brandon Mychal Smith was absent for an episode. He was absent for only one episode in the first season.

45	24	"Marshall with a Chance"[30]	TBA	TBA	N/A	December 12, 2010	224

Absent: Sterling Knight as Chad Dylan Cooper **Note:** This is the third time that Sterling was absent for an episode and his only time being absent this season.

46	25	"Sonny with a Choice"[30]	Eric Dean Seaton	TBA	N/A	December 19, 2010	222

Sonny is forced to choose between So Random and Chad.

47	26	"New Girl"[30]	TBA	TBA	N/A	January 9, 2011	225

References

[1] Sergio Ibarra (February 10, 2009). "'Sonny' Lights Up Sunday for Disney Channel" (http://www.tvweek.com/news/2009/02/ sonny_lights_up_sunday_for_dis.php). TVWeek.com. . Retrieved 2009-02-13.

[2] Disney Channel weekly ratings highlights (http://tvbythenumbers.com/2009/02/18/disney-channel-weekly-ratings-highlights/13057) - tvbythenumbers.com

[3] WWE RAW, The Closer and Monk lead weekly cable viewing (http://tvbythenumbers.com/2009/02/24/ wwe-raw-the-closer-and-monk-lead-weekly-cable-viewing/13386) Posted on 24 February 2009 by Robert Seidman

[4] WWE RAW, The Closer and President Obama lead cable viewing (http://tvbythenumbers.com/2009/03/03/ wwe-raw-the-closer-and-president-obama-lead-cable-viewing/13835) - tvbythenumbers.com

[5] iCarly, Burn Notice and WWE RAW top cable charts (http://tvbythenumbers.com/2009/03/10/ icarly-burn-notice-and-wwe-raw-top-cable-charts/14228) Posted on 10 March 2009 by Robert Seidman

[6] WWE RAW, Cars, Hannah Montana and SpongeBob Lead Weekly Cable Viewing (http://tvbythenumbers.com/2009/03/17/ wwe-raw-cars-hannah-montana-and-spongebob-lead-weekly-cable-viewing/14680) - tvbythenumbers

[7] Kids' Choice Awards, Penguins of Madagascar and WWE RAW lead cable (http://tvbythenumbers.com/2009/03/31/ kids-choice-awards-penguins-of-madagascar-and-wwe-raw-lead-cable/15549) - tvbythebumbers.com

[8] Bulls vs. Celtics, WWE RAW and NCIS lead cable shows (http://tvbythenumbers.com/2009/05/06/ bulls-vs-celtics-wwe-raw-and-ncis-lead-cable-shows/18138) Posted on 06 May 2009 by Robert Seidman

[9] NBA Playoffs, NASCAR and WWE RAW lead cable (http://tvbythenumbers.com/2009/05/19/nba-playoffs-nascar-and-wwe-raw/19069) Posted on 19 May 2009 by Robert Seidman

[10] Corrected: Burn Notice, Jon & Kate Plus 8 and Royal Pains lead cable (http://tvbythenumbers.com/2009/06/09/ nba-playoffs-jon-kate-plus-8-and-2009-mtv-movie-awards-lead-cable/20342) Posted on 09 June 2009 by Robert Seidman

[11] Hannah Montana Tops Cable Shows, SpongeBob Casts A Big, Square Shadow (http://tvbythenumbers.com/2009/07/07/ hannah-montana-the-closer-top-cable-shows-spongebob-casts-a-big-square-shadow/22447) Posted on 07 July 2009 by Bill Gorman

[12] Updated:The Closer, Burn Notice, Royal Pains Top Week's Cable Shows (http://tvbythenumbers.com/2009/08/04/ the-closer-burn-notice-royal-pains-top-weeks-cable-shows/24119) - tvbythebumbers.com

[13] Cable ratings: Monday Night Football, WWE RAW, Monk top weekly cable chart (http://tvbythenumbers.com/2009/09/29/ cable-ratings-monday-night-football-wwe-raw-monk-top-weekly-cable-chart/28807#comment-127818) - tvbythebumbers.com

[14] Cable ratings: Monday Night Football, RAW, White Collar and Monk top weekly cable chart (http://tvbythenumbers.com/2009/11/03/ cable-ratings-monday-night-football-raw-white-collar-and-monk-top-weekly-cable-chart/32402) - tvbythebumbers.com

[15] Cable ratings: NFL, Sons of Anarchy, Monk, WWE RAW and White Collar top weekly cable charts (http://tvbythenumbers.com/2009/ 11/24/cable-ratings-nfl-sons-of-anarchy-monk-wwe-raw-and-white-collar-top-weekly-cable-charts/34438) - tvbythebumbers.com

[16] Disney Channel Claims its Most-Watched March Ever in Total Day in Total Viewers, Kids 6-11 and Tweens 9-14 (http://tvbythenumbers. com/2010/03/30/disney-channel-claims-its-most-watched-march-ever-in-total-day-in-total-viewers-kids-6-11-and-tweens-9-14/46716) - tvbythebumbers.com

[17] Disney Channel Claims its Most-Watched March Ever in Total Day in Total Viewers, Kids 6-11 and Tweens 9-14 (http://tvbythenumbers. com/2010/03/30/disney-channel-claims-its-most-watched-march-ever-in-total-day-in-total-viewers-kids-6-11-and-tweens-9-14/46716) Posted on 30 March 2010 by Bill Gorman

[18] Cable Top 25: NBA Playoffs, WWE RAW and iCarly Top Weekly Cable Viewing (http://tvbythenumbers.zap2it.com/2010/05/11/ cable-top-25-nba-playoffs-wwe-raw-and-icarly-top-weekly-cable-viewing/51073) By Robert Seidman– May 11, 2010

[19] Cable TV Top 25: Disney's Toy Story 2 Tops Burn Notice, Royal Pains, Pawn Stars, True Blood (http://tvbythenumbers.com/2010/06/ 15/cable-tv-top-25-disneys-toy-story-2-tops-burn-notice-royal-pains-pawn-stars-true-blood/54150) - tvbythebumbers.com

[20] Sunday Cable Ratings: Leverage, True Blood, Army Wives, Drop Dead Diva & Much More (http://tvbythenumbers.com/2010/06/22/ sunday-cable-ratings-leverage-true-blood-army-wives-drop-dead-diva-much-more/54986) - tvbythebumbers.com

[21] Cable Top 25: Deadliest Catch, The Closer, Rizzoli & Isles & Home Run Derby Top Week's Viewership (http://tvbythenumbers.zap2it. com/2010/07/20/cable-top-25-deadliest-catch-the-closer-rizzoli-isles-home-run-derby-top-weeks-viewership/57704) By Robert Seidman– July 20, 2010

[22] Cable Top 25: The Closer, Rizzoli & Isles, Burn Notice, Royal Pains, Covert Affairs Top Week's Cable Viewing (http://tvbythenumbers. com/2010/08/10/cable-top-25-scripted-dramas-the-closer-rizzoli-isles-burn-notice-royal-pains-covert-affairs-top-weeks-cable-viewing/ 59604) Posted on 10 August 2010 by Robert Seidman

[23] Cable Top 25: The Closer, Rizzoli & Isles, Burn Notice, Royal Pains, Covert Affairs Top Week's Cable Viewing (http://tvbythenumbers. com/2010/08/31/cable-top-25-the-closer-rizzoli-isles-burn-notice-royal-pains-covert-affairs-top-weeks-cable-viewing/61626) Posted on 31 August 2010 by Robert Seidman

[24] Cable Top 25: 'Monday Night Football,' 'Jersey Shore,' 'iCarly,' 'SpongeBob,' 'Pawn Stars' Top Week's Cable Viewing (http:// tvbythenumbers.com/2010/09/28/ cable-top-25-monday-night-football-jersey-shore-icarly-spongebob-pawn-stars-top-weekâs-cable-viewing/65516) By Robert Seidman– September 28, 2010

[25] Cable Top 25: Brett Favre, New York Yankees, Badgers – Buckeyes, Chilean Miners Rescue & 'iCarly' Top Week's Cable Viewing (http:// tvbythenumbers.com/2010/10/19/

cable-top-25-brett-favre-new-york-yankees-badgers-buckeyes-chilean-miners-rescue-icarly-top-weeks-cable-viewing/68598) By Robert Seidman – OCTOBER 19, 2010 - tvbythenumbers.com

[26] Sunday Cable Ratings: The Walking Dead, Sarah Palin (again, still); Boardwalk Empire Drops; Real Housewives, Sonny With a Chance, Kendra & Much More (http://tvbythenumbers.zap2it.com/2010/11/16/ sunday-cable-ratings-the-walking-dead-sarah-palin-again-still-boardwalk-empire-drops-real-housewives-sonny-with-a-chance-kendra-much-more/ 72307) By Robert Seidman – November 16, 2010 - tvbythenumbers.com

[27] Sunday Cable Ratings: Sarah Palin's Alaska Falls; The Walking Dead(again, still); Boardwalk Empire; Real Housewives, Sonny With a Chance, Kendra & Much More (http://tvbythenumbers.zap2it.com/2010/11/23/ sunday-cable-ratings-sarah-palins-alaska-falls-the-walking-deadagain-still-boardwalk-empire-drops-real-housewives-sonny-with-a-chance-kendra-much-more/ 73243) By Bill Gorman – November 23, 2010 - tvbythenumbers.com

[28] Sunday Cable Ratings: Boardwalk Empire Dips; Soul Train Awards, Real Housewives, Dexter, Top Gear & More (http://tvbythenumbers. zap2it.com/2010/11/30/sunday-cable-ratings-boardwalk-empiredips-soul-train-awards-real-housewives-dexter-top-gear-more/73858) By Bill Gorman – November 30, 2010 - tvbythenumbers.com

[29] Cable Top 25: NFL, Lebron's Return to Cleveland, The Walking Dead, Big Time Rush and WWE RAW Top Week's Cable Viewing (http:// tvbythenumbers.zap2it.com/2010/12/07/ cable-top-25-nfl-lebrons-return-to-cleveland-the-walking-dead-big-time-rush-and-wwe-raw-top-weeks-cable-viewing/74610) By Robert Seidman– December 7, 2010

[30] "MSN.TV: Sonny with a Chance Episodes" (http://tv.msn.com/tv/series-episodes/sonny-with-a-chance/?ipp=25). MSN.TV. . Retrieved February 11, 2010.

External links

- List of *Sonny With a Chance* episodes (http://www.tv.com/sonny-with-a-chance/show/75677/episode. html?tag=list_header;paginator;All&season=All) at TV.com
- List of *Sonny With a Chance* episodes at Zap2it.com (http://tvlistings.zap2it.com/tv/sonny-with-a-chance/ episode-guide/EP01126807)

List of *The Suite Life on Deck* episodes

This is a list of episodes for the Disney Channel original series ***The Suite Life on Deck***. Disney Channel is currently airing the third season.

Series overview

Season	Episodes	Originally aired (U.S. dates)		DVD release date		
		Season premiere	Season finale	Region 1	Region 2	Region 4
1	21	September 26, 2008	July 17, 2009	N/A	N/A	N/A
2	28	August 7, 2009	June 18, 2010	N/A	N/A	N/A
3	TBA	July 2, 2010	TBA	N/A	N/A	N/A

Season 1: 2008–09

- Season 1 consisted of 21 episodes.
- Debby Ryan and Phill Lewis are absent for five episodes each.
- Kim Rhodes reprises her *The Suite Life of Zack & Cody* main role as Carey Martin for two episodes.
- Ashley Tisdale reprises her *The Suite Life of Zack & Cody* main role as Maddie Fitzpatrick for one episode.
- Brian Stepanek, Brittany Curran, Sophie Oda, Charlie Stewart, and Robert Torti reprise their *The Suite Life of Zack & Cody* recurring roles for one episode each.

Overall episode #	Season episode #	Title	Directed by	Written by	Original U.S. air date	Prod. code	Viewers (millions)
1	1	"The Suite Life Sets Sail"	Jim Drake	Danny Kallis Pamela Eells O'Connell	September 26, 2008	101	5.7[1]

Zack, Cody, London, and Mr. Moseby set sail on the SS *Tipton* for their semester at sea. London uses jewelry to bribe her cabin-mate, Padma, to leave the ship so she can have a cabin to herself. Cody finds himself sharing a cabin with Woody, who is very messy. Zack shares a cabin with Bailey, who is a neat freak. Nobody knows that Bailey is a girl who disguised herself a boy in order to gain a position on the ship after she found out that there were no more vacancies for girls. Zack and Cody agree to switch cabin-mates, but Zack changes his mind after he finds out that Bailey is a girl. After everyone else eventually finds this out, Bailey is allowed to stay, filling the position vacated by London's ex-cabin-mate, and Bailey becomes London's new cabin-mate. This is the last straw for London and she escapes to Parrot Island via helicopter.

Co-stars: Ginette Rhodes as Bailey's mother
Guest stars: Erin Cardillo as Emma Tutweiller, Tiya Sircar as Padma, Matthew Timmons as Woody Fink
Special guest star: Kim Rhodes as Carey Martin

| 2 | 2 | "Parrot Island" | Rich Correll | Danny Kallis Pamela Eells O'Connell | September 27, 2008 | 107 | 5.6[2] |

When the SS *Tipton* makes a special trip to pick up London from Parrot Island, Bailey, Moseby, and Woody end up in the island's jail because all of the parrots left for Seal Island after Tipton Industries cut down all the trees. Zack and Cody attempt to get them released from jail, but the twins are incarcerated along with the others and Bailey has to use her pig, Porkers, to rescue them. Zack and Cody fight over Bailey, but Zack lets Cody have her after finding out about her ex-boyfriend Moose and seeing she has too much "baggage," while Zack wants a girl who is just a "carry on."

Guest stars: Erin Cardillo as Emma Tutweiller, Matthew Timmons as Woody Fink, Stuart Pankin as Simms

| 3 | 3 | "Broke 'N' Yo-Yo" | Jim Drake | Jeny Quine Adam Lapidus | October 3, 2008 | 102 | 4.0[3] |

Bailey is mad that London is hogging all the space in their cabin, so she decides to trick her with the myth of the "Sea Snark." She later feels guilty and tells her the truth. Meanwhile, when Zack uses up both his and Cody's meal cards buying things for all of the girls on the ship, they run out of money. Moseby puts them to work so they can earn their keep. Cody decides to enter a yo-yo contest to make some money and Zack agrees to take over both his and Cody's jobs on the ship so Cody can prefect his yo-yo trick. To keep up with both jobs, Zack uses a towel thrower to get the towels to the passengers. Cody finds himself up against yo-yo champion Johan Yo. Johan wins the yo-yo competition, but after Bailey tells Cody that Johan is a professional, he is disqualified and Cody is declared the winner because the competition was only for amateurs. Despite winning, Zack and Cody do not keep the money. Instead, Moseby keeps the money to pay for the damage done by Zack's thrower.

Guest star: Grant Johnson as Johan Yo

| 4 | 4 | "The Kidney of the Sea" | Ellen Gittelsohn | Jeff Hodsden Tim Pollock | October 10, 2008 | 103 | N/A |

Zack has a crush on a cute passenger named Violet, but must deal with her wealthy "boyfriend", Ashton, and snooty mother who will do anything to keep Zack and Violet apart, especially after Ashton gives her an expensive jewelry piece. Meanwhile, Cody referees an intelligence test between London's dog, Ivana, and Bailey's pet pig, Porkers. Bailey tries to take advantage of Cody's crush and London tries to bribe Cody. At the end, the competition ends in a draw. Ashton accuses Zack of stealing the "Kidney of the Sea" necklace. London's dog, Ivana, proves Ashton wrong. Ashton had hidden the jewel in his pocket and then he admits the truth in a grudging tone.

Guest stars: Christa B. Allen as Violet, Shannon Holt as Mrs. Berg, Aaron Perilo as Ashton
Note: The episode is a parody of the 1997 film *Titanic*.

| 5 | 5 | "Showgirls" "Show & Tell" | Shelley Jensen | Howard Nemetz Dan Signer | October 17, 2008 | 104 | N/A |

London and Bailey are on a mission to prove that Miss Tutweiller is dating Mr. Moseby after overhearing a conversation between the two. Meanwhile, Zack convinces Cody to sneak out after curfew to catch the Starlight Follies burlesque show on the ship. When they finally make it past the security guard and into the show, they become convinced that their teacher, Miss Tutweiller, is one of the showgirls after seeing her heart shaped anklet in the show and during class. So, Zack sends Bailey and London undercover as two showgirls to find out. But eventually thanks to Woody ratting them out, Zack, Cody, London & Bailey get caught sneaking into the Starlight Follies on a school night & get detention.

Co-stars: Michael B. Levin as Ira Dinkelman

Guest stars: Erin Cardillo as Emma Tutweiller, Matthew Timmons as Woody Fink, Windell D. Middlebrooks as Kirby

Note: This episode is listed on various media sources under both titles.

6	6	"International Dateline"	Ellen Gittelsohn	Jeny Quine Dan Signer	October 24, 2008	105	N/A

In a fashion similar to *Groundhog Day*, Cody tries to impress Bailey at their school dance, but he fails and finds himself stuck in a time loop while everyone is oblivious to what is happening. Cody believes the time loop is caused by fate giving him another chance with Bailey, but eventually realizes that lightning striking the ship as it crossed the International Date Line was what caused the time reversal, so he reduces the ship's speed to break the time loop. In the end, he still fails to impress Bailey.

Absent: Phill Lewis as Mr. Moseby

Guest stars: Erin Cardillo as Emma Tutweiller, Matthew Timmons as Woody Fink, Steve Monroe as Haggis, Chad Duell as Holden, Rachael Bell as Addison

7	7	"It's All Greek to Me"	Shelley Jensen	Jim Geoghan	November 7, 2008	106	N/A

The SS *Tipton* visits Greece. While they are there, Bailey crushes on the tour guide, which makes Cody jealous. To impress her, Arwin's cousin, Milos, gives him a replica of the ancient amulet of the Greek goddess Aphrodite to give as a gift to her, but in a mix up, he ends up getting the real one. Meanwhile, London has to write a speech for her father, who is funding a new exhibit, but finds it very difficult, but then has a dream about Greek history, which inspires her.

Guest stars: Adam Bay as Adonis, Erin Cardillo as Emma Tutweiller, John Kapelos as Elias, Brian Stepanek as Arwin/Milos

8	8	"Sea Monster Mash"	Rich Correll	Adam Lapidus	November 14, 2008	108	4.4[4]

The class has a school project to complete and Cody chooses Bailey to be his partner, disappointing Zack who had hoped to get Cody to complete his and Woody's project for them. After Bailey tells London that she has partnered with Cody, London teams up with Zack and Woody. Cody is trying to catch a famous sea monster, but keeps failing and disappointing Bailey. Zack tries to sabotage Cody's project. However, his own project turns into a monster when London pours a smoothie into their plant project, causing it to grow and eventually trapping Zack, Woody, and London. The sea monster shows up at the end of the episode.

Guest star: Matthew Timmons as Woody Fink

9	9	"Flowers and Chocolate"	Rich Correll	Danny Kallis Jim Geoghan	November 21, 2008	109	4.07[5]

Chelsea, Barbara, and Bob visit the SS *Tipton*. Cody is worried about how he's going to tell Barbara about his feelings for Bailey, but Barbara has to dump Cody because she and Bob are now dating. Right before Cody tells her about Bailey, Barbara tells him about her and Bob. To make Barbara jealous, Cody tells her that he and Bailey are also dating, thinking he can get away with the lie because Bailey is off the ship, but she returns early. London tells Chelsea that her cabin is her shoe closet, and that Woody is her servant. Woody agrees to help her because he has a crush on Chelsea. During movie night, Cody tries to make Barbara think that he and Bailey are dating, but Bailey eventually finds out. Cody apologizes and Bailey forgives him and says if he wanted her to be his pretend girlfriend, all he had to do is ask. To show it, she tickles him, wraps her arms around him, and finishes with a kiss on the cheek (causing Cody to faint) saying that would have made Barbara really jealous. Chelsea finds out that London is just a regular student, but instead of telling everyone, tells London she will tell everyone that London was "abducted by aliens" instead.

Absent: Phill Lewis as Mr. Moseby

Guest stars: Brittany Curran as Chelsea Brimmer, Sophie Oda as Barbara Brownstein, Jennifer Tisdale as Activities Coordinator Connie, Charlie Stewart as Bob, Matthew Timmons as Woody Fink

Note: London's plot is similar to the *Yay Me* [1] episode, "London in London," in which London and Chelsea meet and London tells her that Bailey is her shoe closet maid.

10	10	"Boo You"	Phill Lewis	Jeff Hodsden	December 5, 2008	110	4.3[6] [7]

When Cody and Kirby don't allow Zack to bungee-jump off the side of the ship, the brothers accidentally knock Kirby off the ship, but Kirby, who is by then attached to the bungee cord, gets pulled back and, after a short flight, lands in the hot tub. To make it up to him, Zack and Cody tutor Kirby so he can pass his high school equivalency exam to earn a promotion. Meanwhile, London embarrasses Bailey on her internet show in a new segment called "Boo You!"

Absent: Phill Lewis as Mr. Moseby

Guest stars: Erin Cardillo as Emma Tutweiller, Windell D. Middlebrooks as Kirby, Chad Duell as Holden

Note: London first mentioned her "Boo You" frown right before her 24-hour *Yay Me* broadcast in "Let Us Entertain You," a season 3 episode of *The Suite Life of Zack & Cody*.

11	11	"seaHarmony"	Lex Passaris	Billy Riback	December 12, 2008	111	4.2[6]

Zack and London play matchmaker for Mr. Moseby and Ms. Tutweiller, but with little success. Eventually, they get Moseby and Tutweiller together, and although they have an argument, they remain together. Meanwhile, Cody tries to impress Bailey by acting like someone else based on her dating test results. However, what Cody doesn't know is that some of her answers were for fun, while others were true.

Guest star: Erin Cardillo as Emma Tutweiller

Title Reference: An online match maker, eHarmony

12	12	"The Mommy and the Swami"	Lex Passaris	Dan Signer Jeny Quine	January 9, 2009	115	N/A

When the ship stops in India, Cody takes Zack with him to visit his guru, a Swami who lives in the top of a mountain who charges high prices for everything he sells. Eventually, Zack and Cody run out of money and join the Swami's worldwide call center. Meanwhile, Mr. Moseby is having computer problems and is trying to contact the call center for help, but without any success. Padma, who was originally London's cabin-mate on the ship, but left after London bribed her, asks London to help convince her mother that she was still at sea. It is later shown that the help center Moseby was calling was run by the Swami, who used an American accent.

Absent: Debby Ryan as Bailey Pickett

Guest stars: Rizwan Manji as the Swami, Tiya Sircar as Padma, Sarah Ripard as Gitanjali/Buffy

13	13	"Maddie on Deck"	Rich Correll	Jeff Hodsden Tim Pollock	January 16, 2009	112	4.1[8]

Maddie Fitzpatrick visits the SS *Tipton* and gains a new friend in Bailey. Prince Jeffy of Linchtenstamp, who is only 8 years old, falls in love with Maddie and forces her to marry him. However, Zack challenges the Prince to a joust, with Maddie being the prize. Zack beats Prince Jeffy on a bouncing ball and using a water noodle weapon. Also, Zack finally gets his long-awaited kiss from Maddie.

Guest stars: Uriah Shelton as Prince Jeffy, Cale Hoelzman as Prince Timmy, Scott Dreier as Harold The Herald

Special guest star: Ashley Tisdale as Maddie Fitzpatrick

14	14	"When in Rome..."	Rich Correll	Jeff Hodsden Tim Pollock	January 23, 2009	113	N/A

The ship docks near Rome and London falls for a handsome musician named Luca while he performs in the streets. Later, as Bailey searches for her money belt key, she overhears that Luca and his uncle, Marco, are actually con men and had already conned London for $20,000. Bailey talks to Luca and finds out that he actually doesn't want to be a con man and really likes London. So, they hatch a plan to get the money back from his uncle that involves Bailey dressing up as Naomi Wyoming, a parody of Hannah Montana. Meanwhile, Zack and Cody get themselves hired by Chef Gigi so they can eat at her restaurant. At the end, Cody is fired, but Zack enjoys a delicious meal with Gigi.

Guest stars: Jacopo Sarno as Luca, Joe Nipote as Marco, Sandra Purpurou as Gigi

Note: The song that Luca performs is the Italian version of "Could You Be the One?" from Disney Channel's short series *As the Bell Rings*.

15	15	"Shipnotized"	Shelley Jensen	Jim Geoghan	January 30, 2009	114	4.0[9] [10]

A famous hypnotist visits the SS *Tipton* and accidentally hypnotizes London to act like Bailey, which gets her really annoyed. Meanwhile, Harvard's Dean of Admissions, Monroe Cabbit, is also visiting with his daughter Olivia. Cabbit is fond of Cody, but thinks lowly of Zack, although Zack wants to date Olivia. Since Cabbit does not approve of the relationship, Zack and Cody concoct a plan where Cody will pretend to date Olivia, which Cabbit approves of, but Zack will actually be the one who goes on the date.

Absent: Phill Lewis as Mr. Moseby

Guest stars: Gilland Jones as Olivia, Hamilton Mitchell as Cabot, Alec Ledd as Enzo Biscotti

16	16	"Mom and Dad on Deck"	Ellen Gittelsohn	Danny Kallis Jim Geoghan	February 20, 2009	117	5.3[11]

Zack and Cody plan to have an all-guys weekend with their father, but a surprise visit from their mother ruins their plans. When Kurt and Carey get a show on the ship, Mr. Moseby says they can stay on board permanently, but worried their parents will stay on the ship, the twins hatch a plan to sabotage their parents' show. Meanwhile, London tries to find the perfect belated birthday gift for Mr. Moseby by following him around all day. In the end, London makes Mr. Moseby very happy that he got a present from her because even his own mother forgot his birthday.

Absent: Debby Ryan as Bailey Pickett
Guest star: Robert Torti as Kurt Martin
Special guest star: Kim Rhodes as Carey Martin
Note: Zack and Cody's father's name is Kurt Martin, but the credits at the end of the show address him as Rick Martin.

17	17	"The Wrong Stuff"	Ellen Gittelsohn	Jeny Quine Adam Lapidus	March 27, 2009	118	3.4[12]

London holds a competition between Cody and Woody to decide which one of them will accompany her on her trip to the Tipton Space Station. Desperate to win, Cody and Woody each try to sabotage the other during the competition. Meanwhile, Zack is in charge of the senior citizen's activities and meets a passenger who is unwilling to participate in any of the activities. Zack makes multiple attempts to find something he wants to do and finally discovers that he enjoys playing pranks on other people. Together, they try to pull off a series of pranks on the other passengers.

Absent: Phill Lewis as Mr. Moseby and Debby Ryan as Bailey Pickett
Guest stars: Lillian Adams as Mrs. Pepperman, Gavin MacLeod as Barker, Matthew Timmons as Woody Fink

18	18	"Splash & Trash"	Rich Correll	Pamela Eells O'Connell Dan Signer	April 17, 2009	119	N/A

Zack and Woody are convinced that a girl the SS *Tipton* rescued from the ocean is actually a mermaid. They make multiple attempts to prove it, but are unsuccessful. Upon her telling Zack that she is really a competitive swimmer and extremely busy training for the Olympics, Zack decides to teach her how to relax. Meanwhile, Cody is fired as the ship's towel boy after he doesn't allow passengers to use multiple towels in an attempt to protect the environment. He also puts up a show to portray the future of the Earth if this kind of overuse continues, which ultimately gets him re-hired as towel boy.

Absent: Debby Ryan as Bailey Pickett
Guest stars: Allie Gonino as Marissa, Matthew Timmons as Woody Fink

19	19	"Mulch Ado About Nothing"	Danny Kallis	Pamela Eells O'Connell	May 1, 2009	116	N/A

When Bailey starts feeling homesick, Cody decides to recreate her hometown festival. However, thanks to London, Bailey's hometown boyfriend, Moose, shows up. He and Cody compete in corn bobbin', arm wrestling, and chess to win Bailey's heart, but Cody loses every competition. Moose asks Bailey to come home, so she asks Cody what to do. Cody says to follow her heart and Bailey stays because she would miss her friends. At the end, Bailey hints that she likes Cody after the pair share a hug.

Guest stars: Hutch Dano as Moose, Matthew Timmons as Woody Fink

20	20	"Cruisin' for a Bruisin'"	Lex Passaris	Danny Kallis	June 5, 2009	121	N/A

Zack puts ice cream on Cody's report. Fed up, Cody throws the ice cream to the floor. Moseby slips on the ice cream. Kirby tries to save him, but ends up injuring him. Connie takes over Moseby's work and breaks a boat in a bottle intended as a gift for the captain. Everyone tries to comfort Moseby, but none of them do any good. Moseby overhears mention of a problem with the boat and thinks there is a problem with the full-size ship. London eventually fixes the boat in a bottle. Moseby falls down the stairs and injures everyone except London. Finally, Moseby accidentally breaks the boat and doesn't have enough time to repair it.

Absent: Debby Ryan as Bailey Pickett
Guest stars: Jennifer Tisdale as Connie, Windell D. Middlebrooks as Kirby

21	21	"Double-Crossed" (Part two of "Wizards on Deck with Hannah Montana")	Rich Correll	Danny Kallis Pamela Eells O'Connell	July 17, 2009	120	10.6[13]

Hannah Montana boards the SS *Tipton* on her way to a concert performance in Honolulu. To impress Bailey, Cody desperately tries to get tickets to the show. Meanwhile, the Russo's are still aboard the ship on their vacation in which Alex pulls a prank on Justin by putting blue dye in the hot tub, making him turn blue, for which Mr. Moseby blames Zack, while Max tries to impress London with his magical suitcase. In the end, Alex is grounded for pranking Justin, and Mr. Moseby apologizes to Zack for blaming him; and Hannah Montana arrives in the lobby and recognizes Cody because of the cake on his shirt, she then gives Bailey & Cody tickets to her concert plus backstage passes, Bailey then tells Cody that "this is going to be the best date ever", and that Cody is "her guy" which ends in Bailey finally kisses Cody on the lips, starting their anticipated relationship.

Guest stars: Matthew Timmons as Woody Fink, Windell D. Middlebrooks as Kirby
Special guest stars: Jake T. Austin as Max Russo, Miley Cyrus as Miley Stewart/Hannah Montana, Selena Gomez as Alex Russo, David Henrie as Justin Russo, Emily Osment as Lilly Truscott/Lola Luftnagle
Notes: This episode is a crossover that features the casts of *Wizards of Waverly Place* and *Hannah Montana* coming aboard the SS *Tipton*. This is the second time Miley Cyrus has worked as *Hannah Montana* on a *Suite Life* show. The first time was in the episode for the *That's So Raven/The Suite Life of Zack & Cody/Hannah Montana* episode called *That's So Suite Life of Hannah Montana*. This is also the second time Selena Gomez has worked on a *Suite Life* show. The first time was in *The Suite Life of Zack & Cody* episode "A Midsummer's Nightmare" when she played a classmate named Gwen.

Season 2: 2009–10

- Season 2 consisted of 28 episodes.
- Doc Shaw is absent for one episode after joining the cast as Marcus Little in the episode "Roomies."
- Debby Ryan is absent for one episode.
- Phill Lewis is absent for six episodes.
- Adrian R'Mante, Camilla Rosso, and Rebecca Rosso reprise their *The Suite Life of Zack & Cody* recurring roles for one episode each.

Overall episode #	Season episode #	Title	Directed by	Written by	Original U.S. air date	Prod. code	Viewers (millions)
22	1	"The Spy Who Shoved Me"	Shelley Jensen	Jim Geoghan	August 7, 2009	205	4.9[14]

A microchip with secret information on it goes missing and the twins help a spy recover it. Cody gives the chip to Bailey, telling her to hide it and not to look at what's in it, but Bailey looks it up on her computer anyway. When Cody finds out that Bailey ignored him, breaking her promise, he has mixed emotions. Bailey kisses Cody on the lips as a way of telling him he can trust her, so he forgives her.

Guest stars: Gildart Jackson as James Smith, Sara Erikson as Red Finger
Notes: This is the first episode of the series to be broadcast in High Definition, and the show now utilizes a 'filmized' appearance (though it is still shot on videotape, as is standard with Disney Channel sitcoms).

23	2	"Ala-ka-scram!"	Shelley Jensen	Billy Riback	August 14, 2009	206	4.1[15]

London develops a crush on the ship's magician. Meanwhile, Zack tries to hang out with Cody and Bailey, much to their annoyance, so to get him off their back, they invite Woody to hang out with Zack for an upcoming Air Band contest.

Guest stars: Matthew Timmons as Woody Fink, Savannah Jayde as Tanya, Briana Lane as Karina, Justin Kredible as Armando
Notes: The song Zack sings, "Hot December Snow," is a parody of Guns N' Roses' "November Rain," with Zack as Jim Gillette of Nitro and Woody as Slash.

24	3	"In the Line of Duty"	Rich Correll	Jeff Hodsden Tim Pollock	August 21, 2009	203	4.3[16]

After Zack gets in trouble with Ms. Tutwieller by setting off a stink cloud, she suggests that he becomes the hall monitor, but it soon gets out of hand when he puts all of his classmates in detention. Meanwhile, Cody and Bailey find it increasingly harder to spend time with each other. In addition, Bailey gets a job at London's new boutique, which is actually a secret closet to store the rest of her extensive collection of clothes.

Guest stars: Matthew Timmons as Woody Fink, Erin Cardillo as Emma Tutweiller, Marisa Theodore as Cara, Windell D. Middlebrooks as Kirby

25	4	"Kitchen Casanova"	Rich Correll	Jeny Quine Dan Signer	September 4, 2009	202	3.7[17]

Cody's teacher is chopping onions and cuts herself so Cody fills in for her. But, when he becomes the center of attention, Bailey starts to get jealous and makes a plan with Woody to get him back. Meanwhile, London is selling Zack's paintings' (sneezed food) for $30,000. Then, Zack finds out and tries to sell them on his own, but people only like them because London did.

Absent: Phill Lewis as Mr. Moseby
Guest stars: Matthew Timmons as Woody Fink, Rachael Bell as Addison, Jennifer Rhodes as Mrs. McCracken, Leslie-Anne Huff as Reina

26	5	"Smarticle Particles"	Rich Correll	Adam Lapidus	September 11, 2009	201	4.0[18]

To win a bet with Cody, Bailey convinces London that a perfume will make her smarter. Meanwhile, Zack asks out the captain of the boys wrestling team, who is a girl, after accidentally dropping freezing cold ocean water on her, that he had meant to drop on Woody.

Guest stars: Matthew Timmons as Woody Fink, Staci Pratt as Becky

27	6	"Family Thais"	Rich Correll	Jeff Hodsden Tim Pollock	September 18, 2009	209	4.5[19]

Bailey and London go to Thailand to meet London's Grandmother and discover that she is a poor farmer so London gives her Grandmother and her hut a makeover. Meanwhile, Zack asks Cody to be his wingman because he likes a girl, although he wants to be faithful to Bailey. In the end, the girl ends up liking Cody.

Absent: Phill Lewis as Mr. Moseby
Guest stars: Erica Aulds as Sasha, Ashley Farley as Hilary, Elizabeth Sung as Khun Yai

28	7	"Goin' Bananas"	Phill Lewis	Jeny Quine Dan Signer	September 25, 2009	204	4.0[20]

Zack turns in one of Cody's old term papers as his own, without realizing Cody applied to a bizarre passage about a fictional banana-phobia, so Mrs. Tutweiller sends him to see a counsellor, ending with Zack taking his anger out on his brother. Meanwhile, London goes through withdrawal when her cellphone is taken away after she is caught texting during class, prompting Bailey to find a new thing that she can do to keep her hands busy. In addition, Woody spends all of his time playing as an avatar named Brock in a virtual reality game called "Better Life" in which he even has a girlfriend called Peaches, who turns out to Addison, but Cody tells him he can't live his whole life through a virtual reality game.

Absent: Phill Lewis as Mr. Moseby
Guest stars: Matthew Timmons as Woody Fink, Rachael Bell as Addison, Erin Cardillo as Emma Tutweiller, Michael Hitchcock as Mr. Blanket
Note: This is the first episode of the series to have two sub-plots.

29	8	"Lost at Sea"	Rich Correll	Danny Kallis Pamela Eells O'Connell	October 2, 2009	207-208	6.8[21] [22]

Shortly after the start of a new semester on the ship, Zack, Cody, London, Bailey, and Woody are all cast-away on a life boat London was using as a closet and eventually find their way onto a deserted island. Cody's relationship with Bailey starts falling apart after an argument over wind patterns emerges and causes a fall out with the remainder of the group. Back on deck, Ms. Tutwieller and Mr. Moseby are put in exactly the same predicament as the others and even have the same disagreement over control of the operations. Cody and Bailey mend their relationship at the end of the episode.

Guest stars: Matthew Timmons as Woody Fink, Erin Cardillo as Emma Tutweiller, Michelle DeFraites as Jenna
Note: This is a one-hour episode and was broadcast in 4:3 letterbox on Disney Channel's standard-definition feed (the first episode of a Disney Channel series to be shown in this format on the SD feed). All previous and subsequent episodes are shown in a 4:3 full-screen pan and scan picture format on the SD feed.

30	9	"Roomies"	Danny Kallis	Danny Kallis Pamela Eells O'Connell	October 16, 2009	210	4.7[23]

Marcus Little, a former child singer, arrives on the SS *Tipton* and is assigned to share a cabin with Zack, who is trying to figure out Marcus' true identity. Meanwhile, Cody and Bailey play against each other in a series of friendly competitions.

Co-stars: Jill Basey as Widow, Veronica Dunne as Tiffany
Guest star: Matthew Timmons as Woody Fink
Note: Doc Shaw joins the cast as Marcus Little.

31	10	"Crossing Jordin"	Mark Cendrowski	Jeff Hodsden Tim Pollock	October 23, 2009	213	5.2[24]

Zack, Cody, and Marcus attempt to write a song for the ship's guest singer, Jordin Sparks, to perform, but with less than her best interests in mind. Meanwhile, London meets the winner of a contest where a contestant gets to be London's best friend for a week on the ship, but the winner acts like a brat and also steals London's identity.

Guest stars: Cameron Escalante as Alyssa, Dave Secor as George
Special guest star: Jordin Sparks as herself
Note: Jordin Sparks performs the song "Battlefield" from her 2009 album of the same name.

32	11	"Bermuda Triangle"	Phill Lewis	Adam Lapidus Jeny Quine	November 13, 2009	211	4.8[25]

Zack and Cody receive a $200 check from their parents for their 16th birthday, but have an argument about how to spend it and end up ripping it in half. Following this, Zack wishes he was an only child and Cody wishes for the same, saying that nothing would make him happier. Once the ship enters the Bermuda Triangle, their wish comes true; the twins were split up at birth, with Zack growing up with just their mom and Cody growing up with just their dad.

Co-stars: Aileen Hurtado as Flamenco Dancer

Guest star: Matthew Timmons as Woody Fink

Note: This is the first episode of the series that Phill Lewis both directs and appears in. Lewis was absent from all prior episodes that he directed.

33	12	**"The Beauty and the Fleeced"**	Lex Passaris	Dan Signer	November 20, 2009	212	4.8[26]

Zack, Marcus, and Woody create a fake beauty pageant so they can meet girls. When Mr. Moseby learns of their plans, he punishes them by forcing them to see it through. Meanwhile, London intimidates Bailey by bragging about her previous success in beauty pageants, as a result Bailey enters the SS *Tipton*'s pageant to try to beat London and hires Cody as her coach.

Guest stars: Matthew Timmons as Woody Fink, Brittany Ross as Capri

Note: When Cody tells Bailey that he has been in a beauty pageant before, this is a reference to *The Suite Life of Zack & Cody* episode, "The Fairest of Them All." It also references the pilot where Bailey disguised as a boy.

34	13	**"The Swede Life"**	Ellen Gittelsohn	Jeff Hodsden Tim Pollock	December 4, 2009	215	N/A

Zack, Cody, London, and Bailey visit Martensgrav, a Swedish town founded by the twins' ancestors (portrayed by Dylan and Cole Sprouse), only to discover the townsfolk consider the great Martin family as villains. Meanwhile, Marcus and Mr. Moseby want to visit a museum for the Swedish pop group ABBA, but get stuck at a Swedish furniture store, Umaka (a spoof of Ikea) in search of a missing screw for Moseby's Swedish nightstand.

Guest stars: Ed Begley, Jr. as Mayor Ragnar, Katie Gill as Dorta, Mary Kate McGeehan as Helga

35	14	**"Mother of the Groom"**	Rich Correll	Danny Kallis	January 8, 2010	217	3.8[27]

Esteban comes aboard the SS *Tipton* to get married. While the boys have a bachelor party for Esteban, London and Bailey try to help Esteban's mother, who disapproves of the marriage, find something she enjoys aside from taking care of her son, so that she can accept Esteban's marriage and move on with life. **Guest stars**: Charo as Señora Ramirez, Adrian R'Mante as Esteban Ramirez, Marisa Ramirez as Francesca

36	15	**"The Defiant Ones"**	Rich Correll	Dan Signer	January 15, 2010	218	4.0[28]

Cody creates a web of lies when he tries to cover up his failure to do his homework. Meanwhile, Zack and Mr. Moseby are handcuffed together and must learn to get along.

Guest stars: Erin Cardillo as Emma Tutweiller, Michael Hitchcock as Mr. Blanket

37	16	**"Any Given Fantasy"**	Rich Correll	Jeff Hodsden Tim Pollock	January 18, 2010 (Disney XD) January 22, 2010 (Disney Channel)	220	5.2[29]

When Mr. Moseby forbids the students from playing football on the ship, they become interested in playing fantasy football. London talks her way into having a team in the fantasy football league and after impressing the boys with her knowledge of football, London unveils her team's weapon, Kurt Warner. London also promises the winners of the football a golden trophy, as a result, Zack, Marcus, and Woody dress up like mascots to gain London's trophy. Meanwhile, Cody becomes upset by his poor football skills so enlists Kirby as his coach.

Absent: Debby Ryan as Bailey Pickett

Guest stars: Windell D. Middlebrooks as Kirby, Matthew Timmons as Woody Fink, Kurt Warner as himself

38	17	**"Rollin' With the Holmies"**	Mark Cendrowski	Jim Geoghan Dan Signer	January 29, 2010	214	N/A

Cody attempts to solve a mystery surrounding a stolen book that belongs to Queen Elizabeth II. Meanwhile, Mr. Moseby teaches Zack and Marcus how to play croquet so they can compete against London's snobby new crush and his friend in order for Marcus to gain London's affection.

Co-stars: Blaise Embry as Snively, Brad Sergi as Bobby

Guest stars: Charles Shaughnessy as Constable, Jarrett Sleeper as Wicket, Matthew Timmons as Woody Fink

39	18	"Can You Dig It?"	Phill Lewis	Adam Lapidus Jeny Quine	February 12, 2010	223	N/A

When Zack accidentally finds the crown of the ancient Princess Zaria, he takes credit for all the years of research Cody did, making Cody angry. Zaria's spirit possesses Bailey who is now desperate to get her crown back and punishes Zack for taking it. Now, it is up to Cody to save Zack and release the spirit from Bailey.

Absent: Phill Lewis as Mr. Moseby

Guest star: Erin Cardillo as Emma Tutweiller, Alex Cambert as Luis, Lesli Margherita as Isabel

40	19	"London's Apprentice"	Rich Correll	Pamela Eells O'Connell	February 26, 2010	219	3.6[30]

Mr. Tipton wants London to present him with a great new invention, so London offers a one million dollar prize for the person who creates the best new invention. Zack, Cody, Bailey, Marcus, and Mr. Moseby present their ideas to London for her to decide which one is the best. Meanwhile, London gives Kirby the bag containing the one million dollars, but he loses the bag and must retrace his steps to find it.

Co-star: Brandon Ellison as Chefinator

Guest star: Windell D. Middlebrooks as Kirby

41	20	"Once Upon a Suite Life"	Bob Koherr	Jeny Quine Dan Signer	March 5, 2010	225	N/A

Zack, Cody, London, and Bailey fall asleep during class when Ms. Tutweiller is lecturing about fairy tales. They each dream that they are the characters in classic fairy tales such as Snow White, Hansel and Gretel, and Jack and the Beanstalk.

Guest stars: Erin Cardillo as Emma Tutweiller, Matthew Timmons as Woody Fink, Michael Airington as The Mirror

42	21	"Marriage 101"	Rich Correll	Jeny Quine	March 19, 2010	221	N/A

A class assignment requires the students to simulate marriage to learn the challenges that face married couples in everyday life. Cody 'marries' Bailey, Zack 'marries' London, and Woody 'marries' Addison. However, when the "Wheel of Life" gives Cody as injury, he and Bailey begin to fight.

Absent: Phill Lewis as Mr. Moseby

Guest stars: Erin Cardillo as Emma Tutweiller, Matthew Timmons as Woody Fink, Rachael Bell as Addison

Note: London states that her father married eight times, but in "Ala-ka-scram!" she says that Karina, the magician's assistant, is her fourteenth mother, and in the last episode of *The Suite Life of Zack & Cody*, she says her father has had twelve weddings.

43	22	"Model Behavior"	Bob Koherr	Jeff Hodsden Tim Pollock	March 27, 2010	228	N/A

When Mr. Moseby leaves to go to a reunion, Zack and Marcus decide to throw a party on the sky deck with models. Janice and Jessica, from the Boston Tipton, come aboard the ship as models and while Janice tries to draw Zack's attention, Cody believes Bailey is jealous of Jessica. Meanwhile, to distract the modeling agent from discovering the party, Woody pretends to be a male model named Woodlander.

Guest stars: Camilla and Rebecca Rosso as Janice and Jessica, Matthew Timmons as Woody Fink, Cassidy Gifford as Kate

Special guest star: Kathie Lee Gifford as Cindy

44	23	"Rock the Kasbah"	Rich Correll	Adam Lapidus	April 16, 2010	222	N/A

Cody wants to buy earrings for Bailey, but Zack insists he bargain with the cashier for a better price. Meanwhile, London, Bailey, Marcus, and Woody discover a magic lamp that contains a genie willing to grant wishes, causing them to argue over which wishes should be granted.

Guest stars: Amro Salama as Youssef, Matthew Timmons as Woody Fink, Matthew Willig as Genie

45	24	"I Brake for Whales"	Rich Correll	Jeny Quine Adam Lapidus	April 23, 2010	216	N/A

The SS *Tipton* is going straight in the path of endangered blue whales motivating Zack, Cody, Bailey, and Marcus to try their best to change the ship's course. They lock themselves into the engine room hoping the whales will safely pass, however they discover it's not as easy as it seems. Cody begins to faint due to heat exhaustion, Marcus becomes desperate for water, and Zack loses it and tries to break free. Eventually, Kirby and Mr. Moseby break into the engine room to attempt to stop them, but after seeing the whales on Cody's laptop, they decide to go along with plan.

Co-star: Neil Ross as Narrator

Guest star: Windell D. Middlebrooks as Kirby

46	25	"Seven Seas News"	Bob Koherr	Pamela Eells O'Connell	May 7, 2010	224	3.5[31]

The students of Seven Seas High take over the Seven Seas News. Zack and Bailey clash as co-anchors, London is confused by the green screen, and Cody investigates a missing passenger.

Absent: Doc Shaw as Marcus Little and Phill Lewis as Mr. Moseby

Guest stars: Matthew Timmons as Woody Fink, Erin Cardillo as Emma Tutweiller, Windell D. Middlebrooks as Kirby

47	26	**"Starship Tipton"**	Kelly Sandefur	Jeny Quine Dan Signer	May 14, 2010	227	N/A

Many years in the future, Zack's desecendant, Zirk, pulls a prank on a race of alien beings while aboard a starship, which causes destructive retaliation, causing a Moseby robot to be sent back to destroy Zack, prompting Zack, Cody, London, Bailey, Marcus, and Mr. Moseby to travel to the future to stop Zirk from pranking the aliens.

Guest stars: Erin Cardillo as Emma Tutweiller, Joe Green as Robot Moseby, Jonathan Kite as Anterian

Special guest star: George Takei as Rome Tipton

Note: This episode was broadcast in 4:3 letterbox format on Disney Channel's standard-definition feed, instead of the regular 4:3 full-screen pan and scan picture format (the second episode of the series to be aired in this manner, after "Lost at Sea" from earlier in the season).

48	27	**"Mean Chicks"**	Rich Correll	Adam Lapidus	June 11, 2010	226	N/A

Bailey bets London $1 million dollars that she cannot go on one week without insulting her, so London asks Mr. Blanket for help to try not to insult Bailey. When Bailey loses the bet, London insults her one million times. Meanwhile, Cody attempts to avoid the assaults of a seagull after not permitting the seagull to eat fries.

Guest stars: Michael Hitchcock as Mr. Blanket

49	28	**"Breakup in Paris"**	Rich Correll	Pamela Eells O'Connell Adam Lapidus	June 18, 2010	229-230	3.8[32]

Cody and Bailey are planning to celebrate their one year anniversary when the SS *Tipton* docks in Paris. Cody asks London to help him make his date perfect. However, a big misunderstanding begins when Bailey sees Cody with London (who were just practicing the date) and mistakes her as the "hideous French girl". The next day, the day of the anniversary, Cody sees Bailey with another guy, Jean Luc, who was just trying to cheer her up. Bailey and Cody start arguing about the misunderstanding, and decide it would be better if they broke up. Meanwhile, Zack and Woody are pursued by art thieves.

Co-stars: Suzan Brittan as Katarina, Monica Smith as Chloe

Guest stars: Al Benner as Pascal, Nick Roux as Jean Luc, Stelio Savante as Stephane, Matthew Timmons as Woody Fink, Larry Vanburen Jr. as Dante

Note: This is a one hour episode and two versions of the episode exist. The version that aired on June 19, 2010, the night after the episode's original airing, featured a third storyline involving Marcus discovering that a young boy is claiming to be Lil' Little (Marcus' former rap persona), leading him to try to expose the kid as a fraud.

Season 3: 2010

- Doc Shaw is absent for three episodes before leaving the cast as Marcus Little in the episode "Bon Voyage."
- Phill Lewis is absent for five episodes.
- Debby Ryan is absent for three episodes.
- Kim Rhodes reprises her *The Suite Life of Zack & Cody* main role as Carey Martin for one episode.
- Brian Stepanek reprises his *The Suite Life of Zack & Cody* recurring role as Arwin Hawkhauser for one episode.

Overall episode #	Season episode #	Title	Directed by	Written by	Original U.S. air date	Prod. code	Viewers (millions)
50	1	"The Silent Treatment"	Phill Lewis	Dan Signer	July 2, 2010	305	3.4[33]

Cody leaves the ship following his break up with Bailey to join an elite, non-religious, monk-like club which he hopes will help him get over the break up. Zack and Woody are determined to go there and save Cody. Meanwhile, London and Miss Tutweiller try to console Bailey by giving her relationship advice.

Absent: Doc Shaw as Marcus Little and Phill Lewis as Mr. Moseby

Guest stars: Andy Richter as Brother Theodore, Erin Cardillo as Emma Tutweiller, Matthew Timmons as Woody Fink

| 51 | 2 | "Rat Tale" | Joel Zwick | Jeff Hodsden Tim Pollock | July 9, 2010 | 308 | N/A |

No longer a couple, Cody and Bailey must choose who keeps Buck, their pet rat. Kirby investigates both to see who will make the better owner, but Woody is bitten by Buck, creating a super-hero alter-ego "Ratman."

Absent: Doc Shaw as Marcus Little and Phill Lewis as Mr. Moseby

Guest stars: Mackenzie Baker as Sloane, Windell D. Middlebrooks as Kirby, Matthew Timmons as Woody Fink

| 52 | 3 | "So You Think You Can Date?" | Joel Zwick | Mark Amato Sally Lapiduss | July 16, 2010 | 306 | 3.4[34] |

The Seven Seas High dance is coming up. Having broke up, Cody and Bailey lie about having dates to the dance, so they quickly try to find a backup date to backup their lie. Now the pressure is on to see who has the best game. Meanwhile, Woody is tired of Tutweiller and Moseby arguing about who should get the skydeck for the school dance, so he makes them share the skydeck. It is revealed though flashback that Mr. Moseby and Miss Tutweiler's interest in the Middle Ages and 1980s, respectively, comes from the tribulations they endured as outcasts in their youth. Through understanding, Mr. Moseby convinces Emma that they both have become successful adults and have overcome their painful pasts.

Absent: Doc Shaw as Marcus Little

Guest stars: Erin Cardillo as Emma Tutweiller, Rachael Marie as Cissy, Markus Silbiger as Josh, Matthew Timmons as Woody

| 53 | 4 | "My Oh Maya" | Joel Zwick | Jeff Hodsden Tim Pollock | July 23, 2010 | 301 | N/A |

Zack becomes attracted to a girl named Maya, but when he realizes he is actually falling in love with her, he attempts to use the six month plan Cody devised to date Bailey. Meanwhile, Dante, the boy who stole Marcus's identity in Paris, stows away on board to have Marcus produce his next album. In addition, Cody is trying to condition himself to forget about Bailey by flicking a rubber band against his wrist every time he thinks about her while she is visiting her home in Kettlecorn.

Absent: Debby Ryan as Bailey Pickett

Guest stars: Zoey Deutch as Maya, Larry Vanburen, Jr. as Dante, Elle McLemore as Gina

| 54 | 5 | "Das Boots"[35] | Carl Lauten | Pamela Eells O'Connell | July 30, 2010 | 303 | N/A |

Zack, London, Woody, and Maya are all trapped in London's shoe submarine with only enough air for thirty minutes. Meanwhile, Marcus helps Cody prepare to play chess against a beautiful Russian junior champion.

Absent: Debby Ryan as Bailey Pickett

Guest stars: Matthew Timmons as Woody Fink, Erin Cardillo as Emma Tutweiller, Zoey Deutch as Maya, Cody Kennedy as Mischa

| 55 | 6 | "Bon Voyage" | Adam Weissman | Adam Lapidus | August 20, 2010 | 304 | 4.0[36] |

When the new aqua lounge is flooded, Mr. Moseby vows to expel the student responsible for the mess. Although Mr. Moseby assumes Zack is the culprit, Cody, Bailey (who had just returned from Kettlecorn), and Woody all believe they are each responsible for the disaster for different reasons. Meanwhile, Marcus leaves the ship to make a Broadway musical based on his hit song "Retainer Baby."

Guest stars: Matthew Timmons as Woody Fink, Lisa K. Wyatt as Frankie

Note: Doc Shaw leaves the cast as Marcus Little.

| 56 | 7 | "Computer Date" | Joel Zwick | Jeny Quine | August 27, 2010 | 302 | N/A |

Arwin comes on board the SS *Tipton* to improve the ship by adding a robot. However, problems start to occur when it begins to have feelings for Cody. Meanwhile, London and Woody enlist Zack's help to pass a gym class.

Absent: Debby Ryan as Bailey Pickett
Guest stars: Tabitha Morella as Callie, Brian Stepanek as Arwin Hawkhauser, Matthew Timmons as Woody Fink
Notes: Because Disney Channel airs episodes out of production order, Doc Shaw is still listed in the opening credits in this episode. Also, despite her inability to perform in gym class in this particular episode, London was seen tutoring Maddie in P.E. class in an episode of *The Suite Life of Zack & Cody.*

57	8	"Party On!"	Joel Zwick	Jeff Hodsden Tim Pollock	September 10, 2010	309	4.0[37]

Maya's birthday is coming up and Zack decides to do something special for her. When singer Sean Kingston comes on board, he immediately becomes attracted to London. Zack misleads Sean Kingston into throwing a surprise party for London and also making Mr. Moseby believe it is for him, when it is actually a party for Maya. Meanwhile, Cody goes with Bailey to a Belgian chocolate factory on a couple's tour and runs into Woody who mistakenly came instead of attending a hiking trip.

Guest stars: Zoey Deutch as Maya, Napoleon Ryan as Sebastian Nougat, Matthew Timmons as Woody Fink
Special guest star: Sean Kingston as himself

58	9	"Love and War"	Eric Dean Seaton	Jeny Quine	September 24, 2010	311	2.8[38]

Zack and Maya are finally a couple, and Zack is surprising everyone by being a good boyfriend. However, Zack soon faces his first challenge when Maya is chosen to recite a poem at Poetpalooza at the same time as an important guys video game night. Meanwhile, children at a daycare take more of a liking towards London than Bailey, causing Bailey to become increasingly jealous of London.

Guest stars: Zoey Deutch as Maya, Taylor Groothuis as Sally, Matthew Timmons as Woody

59	10	"Trouble in Tokyo"	Eric Dean Seaton	Jeny Quine Dan Signer	September 29, 2010 (Disney XD) October 15, 2010 (Disney Channel)	307	3.4[39]

When the ship docks in Japan, Zack and Cody visit their mom who is doing a new commercial. Meanwhile, London is trying to avoid going to the dentist and Woody challenges a sumo wrestler.

Guest stars: Matthew Timmons as Woody Fink, Americus Abesamis as Mikio, Tom Choi as Mr. Hashimoto
Special guest star: Kim Rhodes as Carey Martin

60	11	"The Ghost and Mr. Martin"	Joel Zwick	Adam Lapidus Jeny Quine	October 8, 2010	310	3.3[40]

While visiting New Orleans, Zack is haunted by the ghost of a captain of a sunken ship. To solve the mystery of the sunken ship, with the help of Cody and Woody, he dives down to retrieve the captain's compass. After examining the compass and doing research, Zack proves history wrong. Meanwhile, London and Bailey try to help Mr. Moseby overcome his fear of playing the piano in front of a crowd.

Guest stars: Matthew Timmons as Woody Fink, Anthony Bonaventura as Captain Entenille
Note: Zack tells Cody that ghosts really exist, because they first saw one while they were living at the Tipton Hotel. He is making a reference to the *The Suite Life of Zack & Cody* episode *The Ghost of Suite 613.*

61	12	"Senior Ditch Day"	Phill Lewis	Mark Amato Sally Lapiduss	October 22, 2010	320	3.5[41]

Zack, London and Woody go to a ritzy beach club for Senior Ditch Day, but when the bouncer won't let Woody in, London and Zack go without him. In an effort to get in, Woody claims himself as royalty and becomes a jerk to London and Zack when they ask to be in a VIP area with him. Meanwhile, in an effort to keep their perfect attendance records, Bailey and Cody show up for class, which annoys Ms. Tutweiller who was looking forward to her day off.

Absent: Phill Lewis as Mr. Moseby
Guest stars: Matthew Timmons as Woody Fink, Erin Cardillo as Emma Tutweiller, Fabio as Captain Hawk, Christiann Castellanos as Valentina, Jack Guzman as Bouncer

62	13	"My Sister's Keeper"	Phill Lewis	Jeny Quine	November 5, 2010	315	3.2[42]

When Woody announces his sister (which both Zack and Cody thought was hideous) will be coming on board, Cody keeps her company, much to the dismay of Woody and Bailey. Meanwhile, London searches for a "twin" to get her to do her dirty work, but things go wrong when her twin falls in love with Zack.

Absent: Phill Lewis as Mr. Moseby **Guest star**: Matthew Timmons as Woody Fink, Linsey Godfrey as Willa Fink, Jane Oshita as London's Double

63	14	"Frozen"	Phill Lewis	Dan Signer	November 27, 2010	312	N/A

Cody visits a remote scientific research station in Antarctica, and Zack and Woody tag along to go snowmobiling. But when the scientist borrows the snowmobile to replenish his supplies, he gets stuck in a snow storm leaving the boys cold, hungry and alone. Meanwhile, London's favorite designer visits the SS *Tipton* to announce his retirement due to lack of inspiration, entitling London and Bailey to inspire him.

Absent: Phill Lewis as Mr. Moseby **Guest star**: Matthew Timmons as Woody Fink, Brian Posehn as Dr. Cork, Todd Sherry as Arturo Vitali

64	15	"A London Carol"	Shelley Jensen	Jeff Hodsden Tim Pollock	December 3, 2010	313	4.1[43]

As Christmas approaches, Cody and Bailey collect toys for needy children. When they both ask passengers for donations, London is too selfish to give anything. On Christmas Eve night, London's mirror takes her back to the past, the present and future to learn her lesson. After discovering that in the distant future, her friends will loathe her and Mr. Moseby will no longer be alive, London learns that it is better to give than to receive, selling her Christmas presents to buy gifts for the needy children, along with Cody, Zack, Mr. Moseby and Bailey. Meanwhile, Zack has trouble waking up on time to go to work, so he and Cody set up an elaborate alarm. **Guest Star**: Michael Airington as The Mirror, Haley Tju as young London.

65	16	"Twister, Part 1"[44]	TBA	TBA	January 14, 2011		
66	17	"Twister, Part 2"[45]	TBA	TBA	January 15, 2011		
67	18	"Twister, Part 3"[46]	TBA	TBA	January 16, 2011		
68	19	"The Play's the Thing"[47]	TBA	TBA	January 17, 2011		
		"Prom Night"[48]	Eric Dean Seaton	TBA	TBA	321	N/A
		"Graduation"[48]	Eric Dean Seaton	TBA	TBA	322	N/A

References

[1] Levin, Gary (September 30, 2008). 30, 2008-nielsens-analysis_N.htm "Nielsens: Presidential debate fights for numbers" (http://www. usatoday.com/life/television/news/September). *Usatoday.Com*. 30, 2008-nielsens-analysis_N.htm. Retrieved July 19, 2010.

[2] "Top 10 Cable TV Rankings: September 22 – 28, 2008" (http://blog.nielsen.com/nielsenwire/media_entertainment/ top-10-cable-tv-rankings-september-22-28-2008/). *Nielsen*. September 30, 2008. . Retrieved September 8, 2009.

[3] "Disney Channel Weekly Ratings" (http://tvbythenumbers.com/2008/10/07/disney-channel-weekly-ratings-highlights-wk-of-929/5853). *TVbynumbers.com*. . Retrieved September 8, 2009.

[4] "Football (though not NFL Network), Jeff Dunham and iCarly lead weekly cable viewing" (http://tvbythenumbers.com/2008/11/18/ football-though-not-nfl-network-jeff-dunham-and-icarly-lead-weekly-cable-viewing/8369). *TVbynumbers.com*. . Retrieved September 8, 2009.

[5] "Updated: Weekly Top Cable Shows" (http://tvbythenumbers.com/2008/11/25/ monday-night-football-wizards-of-waverly-place-and-hannah-montana-lead-weekly-cable-viewing/8775). *TVbynumbers.com*. . Retrieved September 8, 2009.

[6] "Top 10 Cable TV Rankings: December 8–14, 2008" (http://blog.nielsen.com/nielsenwire/media_entertainment/ top-10-cable-tv-rankings-december-8-14-2008/). . Retrieved September 8, 2009.

[7] "Growing by Double-Digit Percentages Week to Week, Disney Channel Extends its Streak as Cable's No. 1 Network in Prime to 193 Weeks in Kids 6-11 and 189 Weeks in Tweens 9-14" (http://tvbythenumbers.com/2008/12/16/ growing-by-double-digit-percentages-week-to-week-disney-channel-extends-its-streak-as-cableâs-no-1-network-in-prime-to-193-weeks-in-kids-6-11-and-189-w 9724). *TVbynumbers.com*. . Retrieved September 8, 2009.

[8] "Updated:WWE RAW, Cinderella, iCarly and Monk lead weekly cable viewing" (http://tvbythenumbers.com/2009/01/21/ wwe-raw-cinderella-icarly-and-monk-lead-weekly-cable-viewing/11185). *TVbynumbers.com*. . Retrieved September 8, 2009.

[9] "Tommy 2 net top television ratings" (http://tommy2.net/content/?p=2270). *tommy2.net.* . Retrieved September 8, 2009.

[10] "WWE RAW, The Closer and Monk lead weekly cable viewing" (http://tvbythenumbers.com/2009/02/24/ wwe-raw-the-closer-and-monk-lead-weekly-cable-viewing/13386). *TVbynumbers.com.* . Retrieved September 8, 2009.

[11] "Disney Channel Shines with "Night of Stars" Programming Event" (http://tvbythenumbers.com/2009/02/17/ disney-channel-shines-with-night-of-stars-programming-event/12981). *TVbynumbers.com.* . Retrieved September 8, 2009.

[12] "iCarly, Burn Notice and WWE RAW top cable charts" (http://tvbythenumbers.com/2009/03/10/ icarly-burn-notice-and-wwe-raw-top-cable-charts/14228). *TVbynumbers.com.* . Retrieved September 8, 2009.; "Tommy 2 Net top television ratings" (http://tommy2.net/content/index.php?paged=4). *tommy2.net.* . Retrieved September 8, 2009.; "WWE RAW, Hannah Montana and Northern Lights lead cable show rankings" (http://tvbythenumbers.com/2009/03/24/ wwe-raw-hannah-montana-and-northern-lights-lead-cable-show-rankings/15073). *TVbythenumbers.com.* . Retrieved September 8, 2009.

[13] "Top 100 Most-Watched Telecasts On Basic Cable For 2009" (http://tvbythenumbers.com/2009/12/29/ espn-domination-top-100-most-watched-telecasts-on-basic-cable-for-2009/37284). . Retrieved 2010-09-21.

[14] "Top Basic Cable Shows For the Week Ending August 9, 2009; iCarly: "iFight Shelby Marx", Burn Notice, The Closer, Next Food Network Star, Royal Pains, Monk, WWE Raw, Jon & Kate Pluse 8, Psych, In Plain Sight, Law & Order: Criminanl Intent, Wizards of Waverly Place, NCIS - TV Ratings" (http://tvbythenumbers.com/2009/08/11/ icarly-burn-notice-the-closer-royal-pains-wwe-raw-and-monk-top-weeks-cable-shows/24562). *Tvbythenumbers.com.* . Retrieved July 19, 2010.

[15] "The Closer, WWE RAW, NASCAR, Royal Pains & Monk Top Week's Cable Shows" (http://tvbythenumbers.com/2009/08/18/ the-closer-wwe-raw-nascar-royal-pains-monk-top-weeks-cable-shows/24957). *TVbynumbers.com.* . Retrieved September 8, 2009.

[16] "Updated: The Closer, WWE RAW, & True Blood Top Week's Cable Shows" (http://tvbythenumbers.com/2009/08/25/ the-closer-wwe-raw-royal-pains-nascar-monk-top-weeks-cable-shows/25330). *TVbynumbers.com.* . Retrieved September 8, 2009.; Joal Ryan. "Did Murder Scandal Kill Your Desire for Megan?" (http://www.eonline.com/uberblog/ b141051_did_murder_scandal_kill_your_desire.html). E! Online. . Retrieved September 8, 2009.

[17] "Cable Ratings For the Week ending September 6, 2009: Monday Night Football, NASCAR Sprint Cup, WWE RAW, Saturday Night College Football BYU vs. Oklahoma, Leverage, Design Star, NCIS, SpongeBob - TV Ratings" (http://tvbythenumbers.com/2009/09/09/ cable-ratings-football-nascar-wwe-raw-lead-weekly-cable-viewing/26551#more-26551). *Tvbythenumbers.com.* . Retrieved July 19, 2010.

[18] Robert Seidman. "Disney Channel is TV's No. 1 Network in Kids 6-11 and Tweens 9-14" (http://tvbythenumbers.com/2009/09/22/ disney-channel-is-tvs-no-1-network-in-kids-6-11-and-tweens-9-14/28046). *TVBythenumbers.com.* . Retrieved September 8, 2009.

[19] "Cable Ratings For the Week ending September 20, 2009: Monday Night Football, , WWE RAW, Hannah Montana, MONK, NCIS, Sons of Anarchy, SpongeBob - TV Ratings" (http://tvbythenumbers.com/2009/09/22/ cable-ratings-monday-night-football-vmas-icarly-and-true-blood-finale/28024). *Tvbythenumbers.com.* . Retrieved July 19, 2010.

[20] "Cable Ratings For the Week ending September 27, 2009: Monday Night Football, , WWE RAW, iCarly, MONK, NCIS, PSYCH SpongeBob - TV Ratings" (http://tvbythenumbers.com/2009/09/29/ cable-ratings-monday-night-football-wwe-raw-monk-top-weekly-cable-chart/28807). *Tvbythenumbers.com.* . Retrieved July 19, 2010.

[21] http://www.multichannel.com/article/356976-ESPN_Scores_Fifth_Straight_Weekly_Primetime_Ratings_Win.php

[22] http://www.eonline.com/uberblog/b147648_david_lettermans_sex_life_real_tune-in.html

[23] "Cable Ratings For the Week ending October 18, 2009: Monday Night Football New York Jets vs. Miami Dolphins ratings, Hannah Montana ratings, NLCS ratings, NCIS ratings, WWE RAW ratings, Monk ratings, Psych ratings, iCarly ratings, Phineas and Ferb Ratings, Wizards of Waverly Place, Suite Life on Deck Ratings - TV Ratings" (http://tvbythenumbers.com/2009/10/20/ cable-ratings-monday-night-football-mlb-playoffs-hannah-montana-and-ncistop-weekly-cable-chart/30972#more-30972). *Tvbythenumbers.com.* . Retrieved July 19, 2010.

[24] "Cable Ratings For the Week ending October 25, 2009: Monday Night Football , Hannah Montana ratings, NLCS ratings, NCIS ratings, White Collar ratings, WWE RAW ratings, Monk ratings, Sons of Anarchy ratings, Psych ratings, iCarly ratings, Phineas and Ferb Ratings, Wizards of Waverly Place, Suite Life on Deck Ratings - TV Ratings" (http://tvbythenumbers.com/2009/10/27/ cable-ratings-football-baseball-monk-white-collar-jeff-dunham-and-sons-of-anarchy-top-weekly-cable-chart/31697). *Tvbythenumbers.com.* . Retrieved July 19, 2010.

[25] "Cable ratings: NFL Football, iCarly and Suite Life on Deck top weekly cable charts - TV Ratings" (http://tvbythenumbers.com/2009/11/ 18/cable-ratings-nfl-football-icarly-and-suite-life-on-deck-top-weekly-cable-charts/33908). *Tvbythenumbers.com.* . Retrieved July 19, 2010.

[26] List of top 15 cable shows in Nielsen ratings (http://www.google.com/hostednews/ap/article/ ALeqM5iXTgVz7rFA0wTYgmKGfWnYo6rL-AD9C3BS580)

[27] Cable ratings: WWE RAW, NCIS, SpongeBob, Secret Life and iCarly Top Weekly Cable Charts (http://tvbythenumbers.com/2010/01/ 12/cable-ratings-wwe-raw-ncis-spongebob-secret-life-and-icarly-top-weekly-cable-charts/38551) Posted on 12 January 2010 by Robert Seidman

[28] Cable ratings: WWE RAW, NCIS, SpongeBob and Sarah Palin Top Weekly Cable Charts (http://tvbythenumbers.com/2010/01/20/ cable-ratings-wwe-raw-ncis-spongebob-and-sarah-palin-top-weekly-cable-charts/39500) Posted on 20 January 2010 by Robert Seidman

[29] Cable ratings: iCarly, Hannity, Big Time Rush and On The Record w/Greta Top Weekly Cable Charts (http://tvbythenumbers.com/2010/ 01/26/cable-ratings-icarly-hannity-big-time-rush-and-on-the-record-wgreta-top-weekly-cable-charts/40196) Posted on 26 January 2010 by Robert Seidman

[30] Cable ratings: WWE RAW, CNN Newsroom, Burn Notice and SpongeBob Top Weekly Cable Viewing (http://tvbythenumbers.com/2010/03/02/cable-ratings-wwe-raw-cnn-newsroom-burn-notice-and-spongebob-top-weekly-cable-viewing/43550) Posted on 02 March 2010 by Robert Seidman

[31] Cable Top 25: NBA Playoffs, WWE RAW, NCIS and Law & Order: SVU Top Weekly Cable Viewing (http://tvbythenumbers.com/2010/05/18/cable-top-25-nba-playoffs-wwe-raw-ncis-and-law-order-svu-top-weekly-cable-viewing/51775) Posted on 18 May 2010 by Robert Seidman

[32] "Cable TV Top 25: Pawn Stars Tops Royal Pains, Burn Notice, RAW, Hot In Cleveland, True Blood - TV Ratings" (http://tvbythenumbers.com/2010/06/22/cable-tv-top-25-pawn-stars-tops-royal-pains-burn-notice-raw-hot-in-cleveland-true-blood/54869). *Tvbythenumbers.com.* . Retrieved July 19, 2010.

[33] "Friday Cable Ratings: Say Yes To The Dress, The Soup, Merlin Finale & More - TV Ratings" (http://tvbythenumbers.com/2010/07/06/friday-cable-ratings-say-yes-to-the-dress-the-soup-merlin-finale-more/56222). *Tvbythenumbers.com.* . Retrieved July 19, 2010.

[34] "Friday Cable: Eureka & Haven Continue to Perform Well for Syfy" (http://tvbythenumbers.com/2010/07/19/friday-cable-eureka-haven-continue-to-perform-well-for-syfy/57624#more-57624). *Tvbythenumbers.com.* . Retrieved July 20, 2010.

[35] Peterson, Heather (June 22, 2010). "Disney/Playhouse Disney July 2010 Highlights" (http://www.disneychannelmedianet.com/DNR/2010/doc/DC_Playhouse_July2010_Highlights.doc) (Microsoft Word document). The Walt Disney Company. p. 23. . Retrieved June 28, 2010.

[36] Cable Top 25: The Closer, Rizzoli & Isles, Pawn Stars, NFL & Jersey Shore Top Week's Cable Viewing (http://tvbythenumbers.com/2010/08/24/cable-top-25-the-closer-rizzoli-isles-pawn-stars-nfl-jersey-shore-top-weekâs-cable-viewing/60881) Posted on 24 August 2010 by Robert Seidman

[37] "Wizards of Waverly Place" and "The Suite Life on Deck" Post Their Best Numbers in Nearly 8 Months Among Key Demos (http://tvbythenumbers.com/2010/09/14/âwizards-of-waverly-placeâ-and-âthe-suite-life-on-deckâ-post-their-best-numbers-in-nearly-8-months-among-key-demos/63281) Posted on 14 September 2010 by Robert Seidman

[38] Friday Cable Ratings: 'Haven' Stable, 'Real Time With Bill Maher,' College Football & More (http://tvbythenumbers.com/2010/09/27/friday-cable-ratings-haven-stable-real-time-with-bill-maher-college-football-more/65406) By Bill Gorman– September 27, 2010

[39] Friday Cable Ratings: Suite Life on Deck, Wizards of Waverly Place, Big Time Rush, Sanctuary, Swamp Loggers & More (http://tvbythenumbers.com/2010/10/18/friday-cable-ratings-suite-life-on-deck-wizards-of-waverly-place-big-time-rush-sanctuary-swamp-loggers-more/68504) By Robert Seidman– October 18, 2010

[40] Friday Cable Ratings: 'Haven' Finale Up; MLB Playoffs, 'Smackdown!" & More! (http://tvbythenumbers.com/2010/10/11/friday-cable-ratings-haven-finale-up-teach-tony-danza-smackdown-more/67570) By Bill Gorman– October 11, 2010

[41] Friday Cable Ratings: Sanctuary Down + Yankees/Rangers, Suite Life on Deck, Pair of Kings, Big Time Rush & Much More (http://tvbythenumbers.com/2010/10/25/friday-cable-ratings-sanctuary-down-yankeesrangers-suite-life-on-deck-pair-of-kings-big-time-rush-much-more/69588) By Robert Seidman– October 25, 2010

[42] Friday Cable Ratings: Sanctuary, WWE Smackdown!, Swamp Loggers, NBA, Tony Danza & More (http://tvbythenumbers.zap2it.com/2010/11/08/friday-cable-ratings-sanctuary-wwe-smackdown-swamp-loggers-nba-tony-danza-more/71190) By Bill Gorman– November 8, 2010

[43] Friday Cable Ratings: NBA Tops; 'Gold Rush: Alaska' Premiere; Plus 'Conspiracy Theory,' 'Sanctuary,' 'Smackdown' & More (http://tvbythenumbers.zap2it.com/2010/12/06/friday-cable-ratings-nba-tops-gold-rush-alaska-premiere-plus-conspiracy-theory-sanctuary-smackdown-more/74368) By Bill Gorman– December 6, 2010

[44] "Twister, Part 1" (http://tv.msn.com/tv/episode.aspx?episode=6b2e15d3-22f0-44ae-8343-d8cb3d37dc2f). *The Suite Life on Deck: Episode Info.* MSN TV. . Retrieved December 12, 2010.

[45] "Twister, Part 2" (http://tv.msn.com/tv/episode.aspx?episode=da70f66d-6c6e-47b8-8bce-af3c97fe0ee1). *The Suite Life on Deck: Episode Info.* MSN TV. . Retrieved December 12, 2010.

[46] "Twister, Part 3" (http://tv.msn.com/tv/episode.aspx?episode=7f636cab-e4f9-477a-bdf0-9397247fc2cd). *The Suite Life on Deck: Episode Info.* MSN TV. . Retrieved December 12, 2010.

[47] "The Play's the Thing" (http://tv.msn.com/tv/episode.aspx?episode=ab03935f-bbe8-4cce-8fb3-7293949d39e9). *The Suite Life on Deck: Episode Info.* MSN TV. . Retrieved December 12, 2010.

[48] "Eric Dean Seaton's Credits" (http://ericdeanseaton.com/credits/). Eric Dean Seaton. . Retrieved October 18, 2010.

General references that apply to most episodes

- "Suite Life on Deck Episodes" (http://www.tvguide.com/tvshows/suite-life-deck/episodes/295379). TV Guide. Retrieved October 18, 2010.
- "The Suite Life on Deck: Episode Guide" (http://tv.msn.com/tv/series-episodes/the-suite-life-on-deck). MSN TV. Retrieved October 18, 2010.

External links

- List of The Suite Life on Deck episodes (http://tvlistings.zap2it.com/tvlistings/ZCProgram.do?t=The+Suite+Life+on+Deck&sId=EP01080240&method=getEpisodesForShow) at Zap2it
- List of The Suite Life on Deck episodes (http://tv.yahoo.com/the-suite-life-on-deck/show/42835/season/68590) at Yahoo! TV
- List of The Suite Life on Deck episodes (http://sharetv.org/shows/the_suite_life_on_deck/guide) at shareTV (http://sharetv.org/)
- List of The Suite Life on Deck episodes (http://www.fancast.com/tv/The-Suite-Life-on-Deck/100569/episodes) at Fancast
- List of The Suite Life on Deck episodes (http://www.pazsaz.com/suitel2a.html) at Paszas Entertainment Network (http://www.pazsaz.com/)

Burnin' Up

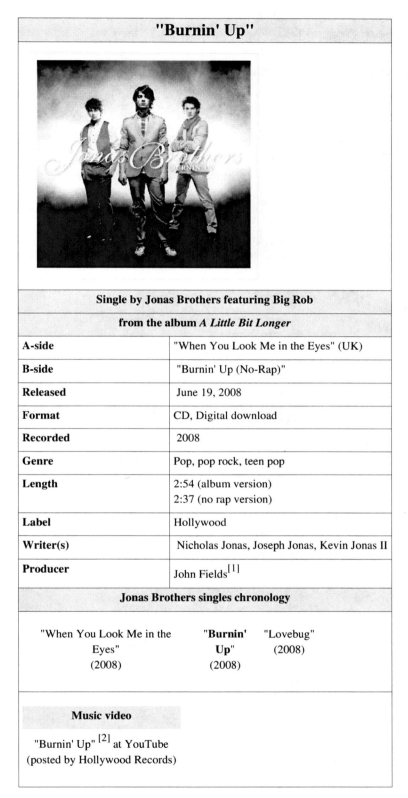

"Burnin' Up"	
Single by Jonas Brothers featuring Big Rob	
from the album *A Little Bit Longer*	
A-side	"When You Look Me in the Eyes" (UK)
B-side	"Burnin' Up (No-Rap)"
Released	June 19, 2008
Format	CD, Digital download
Recorded	2008
Genre	Pop, pop rock, teen pop
Length	2:54 (album version) 2:37 (no rap version)
Label	Hollywood
Writer(s)	Nicholas Jonas, Joseph Jonas, Kevin Jonas II
Producer	John Fields[1]
Jonas Brothers singles chronology	
"When You Look Me in the Eyes" (2008) **"Burnin' Up"** (2008) "Lovebug" (2008)	
Music video	
"Burnin' Up" [2] at YouTube (posted by Hollywood Records)	

"**Burnin' Up**" is the lead single from American pop band the Jonas Brothers' third studio album, *A Little Bit Longer*, and was officially released via Radio Disney on June 19, 2008 as well as other radio stations, and on iTunes on June 20, 2008. In the United Kingdom, it was released as a AA side with "When You Look Me in the Eyes". The single was a hit via digital downloads, and peaked at #5 on the Billboard Hot 100, the group's first top five single in the US and highest charting song to date.

Song information

The band first performed this song on their When You Look Me in the Eyes Tour as well as at the 2008 Disney Channel Games. Their summer tour, titled the Burnin' Up Tour, is named after this song. The song also features a rap from their bodyguard, Robert "Big Rob" Feggans.

The iTunes Store named this single as #1 on their "Best of the Store" Playlist on June 24, 2008, the date of the single's digital release.

Entertainment Weekly stated that the song "was inspired by Jonas Brothers' unlikely appreciation for the work of babe magnet Prince."[3] Nick Jonas also stated that the song is "about this girl — maybe she's at a party — and you feel that immediate connection [and] both know it's there."[3] The song was also included on Grammy Nominees 2009.

Track Listing

US Promo CD

1. Burnin' Up 2:54
2. Burnin' Up (No Rap) 2:37

Europe CD

1. Burnin' Up 2:54

Music video

The music video for "Burnin' Up" premiered after the premiere of the Disney Channel Original Movie *Camp Rock* on Disney Channel as well as ABC on June 21, 2008. In the video, the brothers read over a potential video treatment and imagine how the video would play out, in which they are portrayed as action stars. Nick as James Bond, Joe as a Sonny Crockett parody, and Kevin as a Kung Fu master. Cameos in the video include Selena Gomez, Taylor Swift,Danielle Deleasa, David Carradine, Robert Davi, and Danny Trejo. The video was directed by The Malloys. The video was nominated for Video of the Year and Best Pop Video at the 2008 MTV Video Music Awards, but both lost to Britney Spears and the video for her song "Piece of Me". The video also took notes from Spike Jonze's iconic video for "Sabotage" by the Beastie Boys. This can be most obviously seen in the scenes with Joe Jonas portraying a 70's cop.

Charts

With strong digital sales, "Burnin' Up" debuted at #5 on the US Billboard Hot 100, making it the band's most successful single, with more than 183,000 downloads and sold the single for the first week it went on sale and 2,000,000 copies sold it became their second multi-platinum song behind SOS.[4]

Chart (2008)[5]	Peak position
Australian ARIA Singles Chart	31
Ö3 Austria Top 40	39
Canadian Hot 100	14
European Hot 100 Singles[6]	49
German Singles Chart	39
Indian Singles Chart	2
Irish Singles Chart	21
Italian FIMI Singles Chart [7]	16
Norweigan Singles Chart	12
UK Singles Chart	30
U.S. *Billboard* Hot 100	5
U.S. *Billboard* Pop 100	9

Critical reception

Time critic Josh Tyrangiel named this the fourth best song of 2008.[8]

References

[1] Gardner, Elysa (2008-03-26). "Jonas Brothers' fame is burning hot" (http://www.usatoday.com/life/music/news/2008-03-26-jonas-brothers-main_N.htm). *USA Today*. . Retrieved 2010-08-07.

[2] http://www.youtube.com/watch?v=0z1kSdk7y1A

[3] *Summer Music Preview: Jonas Brothers*. Entertainment Weekly. May 30, 2008.

[4] David Jenison (July 24, 2008). "Jonas Brothers Pushin' the Record Books" (http://www.eonline.com/uberblog/b147740_jonas_brothers_pushin_record_books.html). E! Online. . Retrieved 2008-07-31.

[5] http://acharts.us/song/36537

[6] http://www.billboard.com/charts/hot-100#/artist/jonas-brothers/chart-history/769568?f=349&g=Singles

[7] http://www.italiancharts.com/showitem.asp?interpret=Jonas+Brothers&titel=Burnin'+Up&cat=s

[8] *Time*: 47–48. 2008-12-22.

Selena Gomez & the Scene discography

Selena Gomez & the Scene discography

Selena Gomez & the Scene at a meet & greet in San Francisco.	
Releases	
✗ **Studio albums**	2
✗ **Singles**	4
✗ **Music videos**	4

The discography of Selena Gomez & the Scene, an American band, contains two studio albums, four singles, music videos and other appearances. The band released their debut album, *Kiss & Tell* on September 29, 2009. The album debuted at number nine on the US Billboard 200 and in March the album was certified gold by Recording Industry Association of America (RIAA). The second single from the album, "Naturally", reached the top thirty in the US, and the top twenty in New Zealand, the United Kingdom, Ireland, Canada and Germany. The song has also been certified platinum in Canada.

Their second album, *A Year Without Rain* was released on September 17, 2010.

Studio albums

Year	Album details	Peak chart positions										Certifications
		US [1]	AUS [2]	AUT [3]	CAN [4]	FRA [5]	GER [6]	IRE [7]	NZ [8]	SWI [9]	UK [10]	
2009	*Kiss & Tell* • Released: September 29, 2009 • Label: Hollywood • Formats: CD, digital download	9	—	4	22	24	19	14	21	36	12	• US: Gold [11]
2010	*A Year Without Rain* • Released: September 17, 2010 • Label: Hollywood • Formats: CD, digital download	4[12]	46	19	6[13]	26	22[14]	40	24	37[15]	14	—

Singles

List of singles, with selected chart positions and certifications, showing year released and album name

Title	Year	Peak chart positions										Certifications	Album
		US [16] [17]	AUS [2]	AUT [3]	CAN [18]	GER [19]	IRE [7]	NZ [8]	SWI [20]	UK [10]	SK [21]		
"Falling Down"	2009	81	1	—	9	—	—	—	—	—	—		*Kiss & Tell*
"Naturally"	2010	29	4	3	1	14	7	2	4	1	2	• US: Platinum[11] • CAN: Platinum[22]	
"Round & Round"		24	—	2	1	2	4	—	—	1	3		*A Year Without Rain*
"A Year Without Rain"		35	-	-	-	30	-	-	-	-2	-		
"—" denotes a title that did not chart, or was not released in that territory.													

Music videos

Year	Video	Director	YouTube video
2009	"Falling Down"	Chris Dooley	YouTube Video [23]
	"Naturally/Naturally (Dave Audé Remix)/Naturally (Ralphi Rosario Remix)		Youtube Video [24] Dave Audé Remix [25] Ralphi Rosario Remix [26]
2010	"Round & Round"	Philip Andelman[27]	YouTube video [28]
	"A Year Without Rain/Un Año Sin Ver Llover"	Chris Dooley[29]	YouTube Video [30] Spanish Version Video [31]

Other appearances

Year	Song	Album
2009	"Winter Wonderland"	*All Wrapped Up Vol. 2*
	"Tell Me Something I Don't Know" (Radio Disney version)	*Radio Disney Jams 11*
2010	"Live Like There's No Tomorrow"	*Ramona and Beezus OST*
	"Falling Down"	*Radio Disney Jams 12*

References

[1] "Selena Gomez Album & Song Chart History - Billboard 200" (http://www.billboard.com/search/?keyword=Selena+Gomez#/artist/ selena-gomez/chart-history/1011432?f=305&g=Albums). Billboard. . Retrieved 2010-02-04.

[2] "australian-charts.com - Hung Medien" (http://www.australian-charts.com/showinterpret.asp?interpret=Selena+Gomez). Australian Recording Industry Association. . Retrieved 2010-02-04.

[3] "Discographie Selena Gomez & The Scene" (http://austriancharts.at/showinterpret.asp?interpret=Selena+Gomez) (in German). austriancharts.at. Hung Medien. . Retrieved 2010-10-19.

[4] "Selena Gomez Album Chart History" (http://www.billboard.com/search/?keyword=Selena+Gomez#/artist/selena-gomez/chart-history/ 1011432?f=305&g=Albums). Billboard. . Retrieved 2010-09-27.

[5] "Discographie Selena Gomez & The Scene" (http://lescharts.com/showinterpret.asp?interpret=Selena+Gomez) (in French). lescharts.com. Hung Medien. . Retrieved 2010-09-05.

[6] "Chartverfolgung / Selena Gomez & the Scene / Longplay" (http://musicline.de/de/chartverfolgung_summary/artist/Gomez,Selena+&+ The+Scene/?type=longplay) (in German). musicline.de. Phononet. . Retrieved 2010-09-05.

[7] "Discography Selena Gomez & the Scene" (http://irish-charts.com/showinterpret.asp?interpret=Selena+Gomez). irish-charts.com. Hung Medien. . Retrieved 2010-10-11.

[8] "Discography Selena Gomez & the Scene" (http://charts.org.nz/showitem.asp?interpret=Selena+Gomez+&+The+Scene&titel=Kiss+ &+Tell&cat=s). charts.org.nz. Hung Medien. . Retrieved 2010-10-12.

[9] "Extended Search: Selena Gomez & the Scene albums" (http://swisscharts.com/search.asp?cat=a&artist=selena+gomez& artist_search=starts&title=&title_search=starts) (in German). swisscharts.com. Hung Medien. . Retrieved 2010-09-05.

[10] "Chart Stats - Selena Gomez & The Scene" (http://www.chartstats.com/artistinfo.php?id=12559). The Official Chart Company. . Retrieved 2010-09-05.

[11] Gold & Platinum - Selena Gomez & the Scene (http://www.riaa.com/goldandplatinumdata.php?resultpage=1& table=SEARCH_RESULTS&action=&title=&artist=selena&format=&debutLP=&category=&sex=&releaseDate=&requestNo=& type=&level=&label=hollywood&company=&certificationDate=&awardDescription=&catalogNo=&aSex=&rec_id=&charField=& gold=&platinum=&multiPlat=&level2=&certDate=&album=&id=&after=on&before=on&startMonth=1&endMonth=9& startYear=2000&endYear=2010&sort=Artist&perPage=25) Recording Industry Association of America. Retrieved 2010-09-05.

[12] Up for Discussion Jump to Forums (2009-09-14). "Zac Brown Band Bows At No. 1 on Billboard 200" (http://www.billboard.com/news/ zac-brown-band-bows-at-no-1-on-billboard-1004117424.story?tag=hpfeed#/news/zac-brown-band-bows-at-no-1-on-billboard-1004117424. story?tag=hpfeed). Billboard.com. . Retrieved 2010-11-17.

[13] "Canadian Albums" (http://www.billboard.com/charts/canadian-albums#/charts/canadian-albums). Billboard.com. 2010-11-13. . Retrieved 2010-11-17.

[14] "Album-Charts: Joe Cocker ist die neue Nummer eins - media control" (http://www.media-control.de/ album-charts-joe-cocker-ist-die-neue-nummer-eins.html). Media-control.de. . Retrieved 2010-11-17.

[15] Steffen Hung. "Selena Gomez & The Scene - A Year Without Rain" (http://hitparade.ch/showitem.asp?interpret=Selena+Gomez+&+ The+Scene&titel=A+Year+Without+Rain&cat=a). hitparade.ch. . Retrieved 2010-11-17.

[16] "Selena Gomez Album & Song Chart History - Hot 100" (http://www.billboard.com/search/?keyword=Selena+Gomez#/artist/ selena-gomez/chart-history/1011432?f=379&g=Singles). Billboard. . Retrieved 2010-02-04.

[17] "Selena Gomez & The Scene - Falling Down - Music Charts" (http://acharts.us/song/49198). acharts.us. . Retrieved 2010-02-05.

[18] "Selena Gomez Album & Song Chart History - Canadian Hot 100" (http://www.billboard.com/search/?keyword=Selena+Gomez#/ artist/selena-gomez/chart-history/1011432?f=793&g=Singles). Billboard. . Retrieved 2010-02-04.

[19] "Chartverfolgung / Selena Gomez & the Scene / Single" (http://musicline.de/de/chartverfolgung_summary/title/Gomez,Selena+&+ The+Scene/Naturally+(2-track)/single) (in German). musicline.de. Phononet. . Retrieved 2010-09-05.

[20] "Extended Search: Selena Gomez & the Scene singles" (http://swisscharts.com/search.asp?cat=s&artist=selena+gomez& artist_search=starts&title=&title_search=starts) (in German). swisscharts.com. Hung Medien. . Retrieved 2010-09-05.

[21] ds. "Sns Ifpi" (http://www.ifpicr.cz/hitparadask/index.php?a=interpret&hitparada=18&interpret=42325& sec=08aec74bd51f2677bee8f53c5f6da7cd). Ifpicr.cz. . Retrieved 2010-11-17.

[22] "(CRIA): Gold & Platinum - January 2005" (http://cria.ca/gold/0410_g.php). Canadian Recording Industry Association. . Retrieved 2010-09-05.

[23] http://www.youtube.com/watch?v=RKC3ljpPZPA

[24] http://www.youtube.com/watch?v=a_YR4dKArgo

[25] http://www.youtube.com/watch?v=ItO-ZHNf0Xo

[26] http://www.youtube.com/watch?v=UzF2YofvfEI&feature=BF&list=ULkxtA-9vFXJk

[27] "Music Videos - Philip Andelman" (http://www.partizan.com/partizan/musicvideos/?philip_andelman). Partizan. . Retrieved 2010-11-17.

[28] http://www.youtube.com/watch?v=UfcvO2t8Ntg&feature=BF&list=ULkxtA-9vFXJk

[29] Disney Channel to Present Premiere of Selena Gomez & The Scene's Music Video "A Year Without Rain," Friday, September 3 (http:// tvbythenumbers.com/2010/08/27/ disney-channel-to-present-premiere-of-selena-gomez-the-scenes-music-video-a-year-without-rain-friday-september-3/61274). TV by the

Numbers. August 27, 2010. Retrieved August 27, 2010.

[30] http://www.youtube.com/watch?v=M8uPvX2te0I&feature=BF&list=ULkxtA-9vFXJk

[31] http://www.youtube.com/watch?v=vaoPovB40dQ

Tell Me Something I Don't Know

Another Cinderella Story	
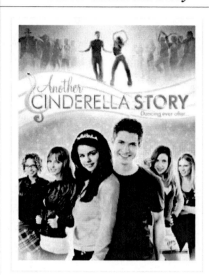	
Directed by	Damon Santostefano
Produced by	Dylan Sellers Damon Santostefano Clifford Werber Neal Dodson Chris Foss Michelle Johnston
Written by	Erik Patterson Jessica Scott
Starring	Selena Gomez Drew Seeley Jane Lynch Katharine Isabelle Emily Perkins Jessica Parker Kennedy Marcus T. Paulk Nicole LaPlaca
Music by	John Paesano Greg Cham Aragorn Wiederhold
Cinematography	Jon Joffin
Editing by	Tony Lombardo
Studio	CS2 Films Dylan Sellers Productions
Distributed by	Warner Bros. Warner Premiere

Release date(s)	September 16, 2008
Running time	88 min.
Country	Canada United States
Language	English
Preceded by	*A Cinderella Story*

Another Cinderella Story is a 2008 romantic comedy directed by Damon Santostefano and starring Selena Gomez and Drew Seeley. The film was released direct-to-DVD by Warner Premiere on September 16, 2008.[1] It was released on DVD in the UK on October 27, 2008.[2] It is a thematic sequel to the 2004 film *A Cinderella Story*, reprising the same themes and situations but not containing any characters from the earlier movie.

The movie was shot in Vancouver, British Columbia, Canada throughout January 2008,[3] and was essentially ignored by critics, but ranked as the number one cable movie in several key demographics when aired on the ABC Family on January 19, 2009. The soundtrack reached number eight on Billboard's soundtrack chart, with one single charting at position 58 on the Billboard Hot 100.

Plot

This movie is a retelling of the Cinderella fairy tale in a modern setting, with Mary Santiago (Selena Gomez), a high school student with ambitions of becoming a dancer, taking the role of Cinderella; Tami (Jessica Parker Kennedy) Mary's best and only friend helps her throughout the movie. Dominique Blatt (Jane Lynch) taking the role of the stepmother; Britt (Emily Perkins) and Bree (Katharine Isabelle) as the two stepsisters; and Joey Parker, (Drew Seeley) now a famous celebrity that has returned to school for his senior year (and also to find a girl to love, which is Mary Santiago), as the prince. A school dance substitutes for the ball, with the role of the glass slippers filled by a Zune.[4]

Cast

Cast	Role	Character Based on
Selena Gomez	Mary Santiago	Cinderella
Drew Seeley	Joey Parker/J.P.	Prince Charming
Jane Lynch	Dominique Blatt	Wicked Stepmother
Katharine Isabelle	Bree Blatt	Evil Stepsister
Emily Perkins	Britt Blatt	Evil Stepsister
Jessica Parker Kennedy	Tami	Fairy Godmother
Marcus T. Paulk	Dustin/The Funk	The Grand Duke
Nicole LaPlaca	Natalia Faroush	Lucifer

Reception

Critics

Amber Wilkinson of *Eye For Film* gave the film four out of five stars, saying that it was better than its predecessor, and praised the musical aspects, saying that "the song and dance numbers are so well-handled and catchy, it's a shame there aren't more of them." However, she also said that the "char[a]cters are so wafer thin they barely cast a shadow."[5] While Wilkinson says that the film is completely different from *A Cinderella Story*, Lacey Walker, reviewing for *Christian Answers*, notes several aspects of the two films that were directly parallel to each other. Walker also gave it three out of five stars, praising the script, saying the writers "peppered this story with a surprising dose of humor and some pleasing plot twists." However, Walker specifically criticized the "glaringly obvious" age difference between the 15 year old Gomez and the 25 year old Seeley.[6]

Ratings

ABC Family presented the television premiere of the film on January 18, 2009.[7] The premiere was watched by 5.3 million viewers. The movie ranked as January 2009's No. 1 cable movie across all key demos: Adults 18-34 (1.0 million, tie), Adults 18-49 (1.9 million) and Viewers 12-34 (2.3 million). In Females 12-34, ABC Family aired January 2009's Top 7 movies on all TV, led by the debut of "Another Cinderella Story" (1.8 million, 1/18/09, 8:00 p.m.) and namesake "A Cinderella Story" (978,000, 1/18/09, 6:00 p.m.). It aired on Disney Channel on July 11.[8] Source: Nielsen Media Research (National Ratings, January 2009: 12/29/08-1/25/09, Most Current: Live + SD, blended with Live + 7, when available).

Soundtrack

The soundtrack was released by Razor & Tie, and reached 116 on the Billboard 200 on Feb 27, 2009. It also reached number eight on Billboard's Soundtrack chart.[9]

Tracklist

No.	Title	Recording artist	Length
1.	"Tell Me Something I Don't Know"	Selena Gomez	3:20
2.	"New Classic (Single Version)"	Drew Seeley, Selena Gomez	3:08
3.	"Hurry Up and Save Me"	Tiffany Giardina	3:50
4.	"Just That Girl"	Drew Seeley	3:17
5.	"Bang a Drum"	Selena Gomez	3:12
6.	"1st Class Girl"	Drew Seeley, Marcus Paulk	3:00
7.	"On Hold 4 You"	Jane Lynch	2:29
8.	"Valentine's Dance Tango"	The Twins	2:12
9.	"No Average Angel"	Tiffany Giardina	2:57
10.	"Don't Be Shy"	Small Change, Lil' JJ, Chani	4:03
11.	"X-Plain it to My Heart"	Drew Seeley	1:15
12.	"New Classic (Live)"	Drew Seeley, Selena Gomez	5:29
13.	"Another Cinderella Story (Score Suite)"	John Paesano	2:39
14.	"New Classic (Acoustic Version)"	Drew Seeley, Selena Gomez	2:41

Tell Me Something I Don't Know

"Tell Me Something I Don't Know"	
Single by Selena Gomez	
from the album *Another Cinderella Story*	
Released	August 5, 2008[10]
Format	Digital download
Recorded	2008
Genre	Pop Teen pop Electropop Dance-pop
Length	3:21 (Album Version) 3:20 (Radio Edit)
Label	Razor & Tie
Writer(s)	Antonina Armato Ralph Churchwell Michael Nielsen
Producer	Armato
Selena Gomez singles chronology	
"Cruella de Vil" (2008) — **"Tell Me Something I Don't Know"** (2008) — "Whoa Oh!" (2009)	

"Tell Me Something I Don't Know" by Selena Gomez was released as a single on August 5, 2008 on iTunes[10] and a Radio Disney version (which removes the Hurricane Katrina reference) was released on September 9, 2008 on iTunes. The song was also featured on the Kidz Bop 15 CD. A new version of the song is featured on Selena Gomez & the Scene's debut album, *Kiss & Tell*.

Music video

The music video starts with scenes reminiscent of (but not from) the film; Gomez cleaning a house and the maid yelling at her. Gomez then leaves the house and does a dance routine with her backup dancers, while the maid watches from the house window. The video also features Gomez in front of a black background with lyrics from the song (such as "I'm ready for it" and "One in a million") flying around her.[11]

Charts

Chart (2008)	Peak position
Australian Hitseekers Singles[12]	13
U.S. *Billboard* Hot 100[13]	58

References

[1] "Andrew Seeley Stars in Another Cinderella Story" (http://www.dvdactive.com/news/releases/another-cinderella-story.html). movieweb.com. .

[2] "Another Cinderella Story" (http://www.dvdactive.com/news/releases/another-cinderella-story2.html). movieweb.com. .

[3] "Drew Seeley Stars in Another Cinderella Story" (http://www.movieweb.com/news/71/25271.php). movieweb.com. .

[4] "Damon Santostefano Brings Us Another Cinderella Story" (http://www.movieweb.com/news/NEF41MHILy5yIO). movieweb.com. .

[5] Eye for Film "Another Cinderella Story Movie Review (2008)" (http://www.eyeforfilm.co.uk/reviews.php?film_id=15319). EyeforFilm.co.uk. Eye for Film.

[6] "Another Cinderella Story Movie Review" (http://www.christiananswers.net/spotlight/movies/2008/anothercinderellastory2008.html). christiananswers.net. .

[7] "ABC Family: Selena Gomez and Drew Seely in Another Cinderella Story" (http://abcfamily.go.com/abcfamily/path/section_Movies+ Another-Cinderella-Story/page_Detail). ABC.com. .

[8] "Battlestar Galactica Flies High, Tween Shows Fly Higher" (http://www.eonline.com/uberblog/ b80120_battlestar_galactica_flies_high_tween.html?utm_source=eonline&utm_medium=rssfeeds&utm_campaign=imdb_topstories). E Online.com. .

[9] Billboard "Another Cinderella Story - Billboard" (http://www.billboard.com/#/album/original-soundtrack/another-cinderella-story/ 1161121). Billboard.com. Billboard.

[10] Tell Me Something I Don't Know - single (http://itunes.apple.com/us/album/tell-me-something-i-dont-know/id286152910)

[11] "*Tell Me Something I Don't Know* Video - Selena Gomez - AOL Music" (http://music.aol.com/video/tell-me-something-i-dont-know/ selena-gomez/2239406). AOL.com. .

[12] "41205 Tell Me Something I Don't Know ARIA Peak Position" (http://pandora.nla.gov.au/pan/23790/20090220-0000/issue988.pdf). pandora.nla.gov.au. .

[13] "Tell Me Something I Don't Know Hot 100 Peak Position" (http://www.billboard.com/bbcom/esearch/chart_display.jsp?cfi=379& cfgn=Singles&cfn=The+Billboard+Hot+100&ci=3106116&cdi=10131142&cid=02/14/2009). billboard.com. .

External links

- Official website (http://http://anothercinderellastory.warnerbros.com)
- *Another Cinderella Story* (http://www.imdb.com/title/tt1071358/) at the Internet Movie Database
- *Another Cinderella Story* (http://www.allmovie.com/work/454235) at Allmovie
- *Another Cinderella Story* (http://www.rottentomatoes.com/m/Another_Cinderella_Story/) at Rotten Tomatoes
- *Another Cinderella Story* (http://tcmdb.com/title/title.jsp?stid=729492) at the TCM Movie Database

Magic (Pilot song)

"Magic"	
Single by Pilot	
from the album _Pilot (From the Album of the Same Name)_	
Released	1974
Genre	Pop rock, soft rock, funk rock
Length	3:06
Label	EMI
Writer(s)	David Paton

"**Magic**" is a popular song from 1974, and is the first commercial success for the Scottish band, Pilot.

It charted most successfully in Canada, where it reached #1, topping the _RPM_ national singles chart on July 19, 1975.[1] It climbed as far as #11 on the UK Singles Chart and reached #5 during the summer of 1975 in the United States on the Billboard Hot 100. The song was included on Pilot's debut album.

Use in fiction

"Magic" is heard twice during _Happy Gilmore_, a 1996 comedy film starring Adam Sandler; the first time being early in the film and the second time playing during the end credits. It is also featured in the 2005 films, _Herbie: Fully Loaded_ and _The Magic Roundabout_, the 2007 movie _Magicians_, All's Faire In Love, a 2009 comedy film starring Christina Ricci (opening credits) and the fourth episode of the television series _Extras_. Additionally, an episode of _Pushing Daisies_ was entitled "Oh Oh Oh... It's Magic", after the song's memorable refrain. In 2009, Selena Gomez sang it for the Disney Channel Original Movie _Wizards of Waverly Place: The Movie_.

Covers

The song was sampled by Girl Talk on his 2006 release _Night Ripper_ on the track "Summer Smoke". The song is also heavily sampled in a song titled "It's Magic" by rap artist J.R. Writer. It was then sampled again by rapper Flo Rida in 2009. The song was also covered by Selena Gomez in the 2009 _Wizards of Waverly Place_ soundtrack, reaching number #61 in the US. The alternative rock band Barenaked Ladies has been known to sometimes close live shows by playing the song as part of a medley. [2]

Use in Advertising

The song featured in a Pillsbury Company commercial in 2007. Pilot's version is heard in a 2010 TV commercial for Chase.

References

[1] http://www.collectionscanada.gc.ca/rpm/028020-119.01-e.php?brws_s=1&file_num=nlc008388.3989a&type=1&interval=24&PHPSESSID=ccntousk30frf6h4jsn237nm12

[2] http://www.youtube.com/watch?v=fcc1Ba5BHMQ

Whoa Oh!

"Whoa Oh! (Me vs. Everyone)"	

Single by Forever the Sickest Kids	
from the album *Underdog Alma Mater*	
Released	April 1, 2008
Format	Digital download
Recorded	2007
Genre	Power pop
Length	3:24
Label	Universal Motown Records Group
Writer(s)	Austin Bello, Caleb Turman, Jonathan Cook
Producer	Geoff Rockwell, Matt Squire
Forever the Sickest Kids singles chronology	
"Whoa Oh! (Me vs. Everyone)" (2008 1st Release)	"She's a Lady" (2008)

"Whoa Oh!"

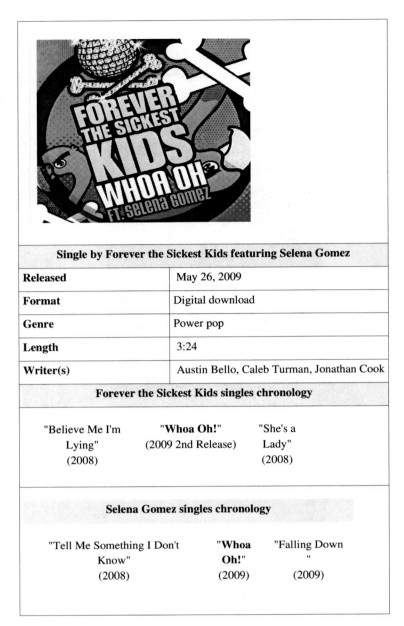

Single by Forever the Sickest Kids featuring Selena Gomez	
Released	May 26, 2009
Format	Digital download
Genre	Power pop
Length	3:24
Writer(s)	Austin Bello, Caleb Turman, Jonathan Cook

Forever the Sickest Kids singles chronology		
"Believe Me I'm Lying" (2008)	**"Whoa Oh!"** (2009 2nd Release)	"She's a Lady" (2008)

Selena Gomez singles chronology		
"Tell Me Something I Don't Know" (2008)	**"Whoa Oh!"** (2009)	"Falling Down" (2009)

"**Whoa Oh! (Me vs. Everyone)**" is the first track and single from Forever the Sickest Kids' debut album *Underdog Alma Mater*. The song was released on April 1, 2008. The video aired on MTV's TRL on June 24. The song has reached #38 on the Top 40 Mainstream, #78 on the Pop 100, and #64 on the Pop 100 Airplay.

Track listing

CD single

1. "Whoa Oh! (Me vs. Everyone)" - 3:24

UK/Ireland single

1. "Whoa Oh! (Me vs. Everyone)" - 3:24
2. "Hurricane Haley" - 3:42

Music video

The music video came out 9 days after the official release of the song on April 10. The video shows the band playing near a race car rally with an airplane in the background. The video goes through showing Jonathan, falling for a race car girl. Jonathan then sneaks into a trailer of a race car driver and gets into uniform. Jonathan gets into a car, precedes to race but crashes. As he exits the race car, the girl rushes to his side to give him a kiss. He then leans in and gives a thumbs up. The video ends with the band walking away into the sunset.

Duet Version

Whoa Oh!, is the duet version bid of the Forever the Sickest Kids and teen star Selena Gomez. It was released on May 26, 2009 on iTunes.[1] [2]

References

[1] "WHOA!!!!! by FTSK/Selena out tomorrow May 26th on iTunes" (http://blogs.myspace.com/index.cfm?fuseaction=blog.view& friendId=302429200&blogId=491031455). Selena Gomez. 2009-05-25. . Retrieved 2009-05-25.
[2] "OKAY ITS OFFICIAL THE SONG HITS ITUNES TOMORROW!" (http://blogs.myspace.com/index.cfm?fuseaction=blog.view& friendID=141529450&blogID=491030644). Forever the Sickest Kids. 2009-05-25. . Retrieved 2009-05-25.

One and the Same

Princess Protection Program	
The DVD cover for the film.	
Directed by	Allison Liddi-Brown
Produced by	Douglas Sloan
Written by	Annie DeYoung David Morgasen (Book)
Starring	Demi Lovato Selena Gomez Jamie Chung Samantha Droke Robert Adamson
Music by	John Van Tongeren
Cinematography	David A. Makin
Country	United States
Language	English
Original channel	Disney Channel Family
Release date	May 20, 2009 (France) June 26, 2009 (United States) (Canada)
Running time	88 minutes

Princess Protection Program is a 2009 Disney Channel Original Movie that premiered on June 26, 2009 in the United States and winner of the Teen Choice Awards 2009 for Choice Summer TV Show.[1] The film is directed by Allison Liddi-Brown, filmed in Puerto Rico[2] written by Annie DeYoung[3] and stars Selena Gomez and Demi Lovato. *Princess Protection Program* was watched by 9.8 million viewers, the third-highest premiere for a Disney Channel Original Movie.[4]

Plot

Princess Rosalinda Maria Montoya Fiore (Demi Lovato) is about to be crowned queen of the small nation of Costa Luna, to take her mother's role in sight of her father, the king's, death. General Kane (Johnny Ray Rodriguez), the dictator of neighboring country Costa Estrella, infiltrates her palace with his agents during her coronation rehearsal, and attempts to stage a coup d'etat against the royal family. Joe Mason (Tom Verica), an agent of the Princess Protection Program, a secret organization funded by royal families that looks after endangered princesses, whisks her away to safety via helicopter. Kane's agents succeed in capturing her mother, Queen Sophia.

The Princess Protection Program hides Rosalinda in Mr. Mason's home in Louisiana, where she is to pretend to be a typical American teenager named Rosie Gonzales. She meets Mr. Mason's daughter, Carter Mason (Selena Gomez), whose mother died and is also an insecure girl who works at the family bait shop and dreams of going to the homecoming dance with her crush, Donny (Robert Adamson). Though Carter is at first openly bitter and hostile towards Rosie, she warms up to her after Rosie explains her situation, and the two become close friends. Carter teaches Rosalinda to act like a normal girl and Rosie shows Carter how to disarm those that scorn them by behaving as a princess. Rosie soon becomes popular at their high school.

In an attempt to trick Rosalinda into exposing her location, General Kane announces plans to forcibly marry Rosalinda's mother. Rosalinda is distraught and tells Carter that she has decided to secretly return home. Knowing Costa Luna is still too dangerous, Carter secretly devises a plan to pose as Rosalinda and then use herself as bait to lure Kane into capture. Mr. Elegante, Rosalinda's royal dress maker, tells Kane that Rosalinda will be attending the homecoming dance and will be wearing a blue dress that he actually sends to Carter. In the meantime, Rosalinda agrees to help Carter behave like a princess by helping a group of girls dress up for the dance; The girls all wear masks, which helps Carter disguise herself as Rosalinda.

According to plan, Kane and his agents mistake Carter for Rosie and lead her to Kane's helicopter the night of the dance. However, Rosalinda narrowly discovers and ruins the plan by exposing herself to Kane, insisting that this is not Carter's fight. Fortunately, agents of the Princess Protection Program, including Mr. Mason, have been waiting inside the helicopter and rescue both girls. The PPP agents quickly apprehend Kane and his henchmen and turn them over to the international authorities.

At the end, Carter realizes what a jerk Donny is and goes to the dance with Ed, her best friend who has had a crush on her for a long time. Rosie is crowned Queen of Costa Luna with Carter, Mr. Mason, Ed, Rosalinda's mother, and Mr. Elegante in attendance.

Cast

- Selena Gomez as Carter Mason
- Demi Lovato as Princess Rosalinda
- Tom Verica as Major Mason
- Sully Diaz as Queen Sophia Fiore
- Johnny Ray Rodriguez as General Kane
- Jamie Chung as Chelsea Barnes
- Nicholas Braun as Edwin Tinka
- Robert Adamson as Donny Wilde
- Samantha Droke as Brooke Angels
- Kevin G. Schmidt as Bull Willilger
- Talia Rothenberg as Margaret Algoode
- Dale Dickey as Helen Digenerstet
- Ricardo Alvarez as Mr. Elegante
- Brian Tester as Principal Bull

Demi Lovato and Selena Gomez at the *Princess Protection Program* premiere

Awards

Year	Ceremony	Award	Result
2009	Teen Choice Awards	Choice Summer TV Movie	Won
		Choice Summer TV Star - Female: Selena Gomez	Won
		Choice Summer TV Star - Female: Demi Lovato	Nominated

Promotion

The film introduced two new songs: a duet recorded by Gomez and Lovato called "One And The Same" and a song recorded by Mitchel Musso called "The Girl Can't Help It." Both songs are featured on the Disney compilation album, *Disney Channel Playlist*, which was released on June 9, 2009.[5] The film also includes Lovato's song "Two Worlds Collide" which was first featured on her debut album *Don't Forget*. Disney Channel promoted the movie's premiere weekend by offering never-before-seen episodes of their original series' *Wizards of Waverly Place* and *Sonny With a Chance* as an online reward if viewers can correctly count the number of times the words "princess," "princesses," and "princesa" are spoken during the movie and enter the correct number, 86, into a section on their website.[6]

The DVD was released on June 30, 2009 in the US.[7] It also features the music video for Gomez & Lovato's duet "One and the Same" and a behind-the-scenes look at the movie. The DVD was released on June 18, 2009 in Germany[8] and four days later in the UK.[9]

Sequel

A sequel for the movie is in development and will be relased fall 2012. The plot of the movie will be "an endangered prince need help from the *Princess Protection Program*, this time Rossie and Carter will be the agents responsible for saving the prince". Is unknow if Selena Gomez or Demi Lovato will be reprise her roles, this is the cause for the sequell will be canceled.

Release

Country	Network(s)	Premiere	Movie Title in Country
France	Disney Channel France	May 20, 2009	Princess Protection Program: Mission Rosalinda
Germany	Disney Channel Germany	May 29, 2009	Prinzessinnen Schutzprogramm
	Pro 7	June 14, 2009	
	Super RTL	November 6, 2009	
Italy	Disney Channel Italy	June 8, 2009	Programma Protezione Principesse
	Italia 1	September 26, 2009	
Spain	Disney Channel Spain	June 13, 2009	Programa de Protección de Princesas
United Kingdom	Disney Channel UK	June 19, 2009	Princess Protection Programme
United States		June 26, 2009	Princess Protection Program
Portugal		June 20, 2009	Programa de Proteção de Princesas
Poland	Disney Channel Poland		Program Ochrony Księżniczek
Middle East	Disney Channel Middle East		Princess Protection Program
Latin America	Disney Channel Latin America	July 26, 2009	Programa de Protección para Princesas
Netherlands		October 03, 2009	Princess Protection Program
Australia		July 25, 2009	
Brazil	Disney Channel Latin America	July 26, 2009	Programa de Proteção para Princesas
Japan	Disney Channel Japan	August 15, 2009	プリンセス・プロテクション・プログラム
Estonia		August 28, 2009	
Norway	Disney Channel Scandinavia	August 28, 2009	Prosjekt Prinsesse
Sweden	Disney Channel Scandinavia	August 28, 2009	Projekt Prinsessa

Brunei	Disney Channel Asia	September 6, 2009	
Cambodia			
Hong Kong			
Indonesia			
Laos			
Malaysia			
Philippines			Princess Protection Program
Singapore			
South Korea			공주님은 내친구/프린세스 구출 대작전
Thailand			
Vietnam			Kế hoạch Bảo vệ Công chúa
Israel	Disney Channel Israel	September 9, 2009	תוכנית תגנהל תנביסת
Taiwan	Disney Channel Taiwan	September 12, 2009	公主保衛戰
Romania	Disney Channel Romania	September 19, 2009	Programul de Protecţie al Prinţeselor
India	Disney Channel India	November 20, 2009	Princess Protection Program
Canada	Family / VRAK.TV	June 26, 2009 / March 1 2010	Princess Protection Program (English) Mission Rosalinda (French)
New Zealand			Princess Protection Program

References

[1] http://www.teenchoiceawards.com/pdf/TC09WINNERSFINALDB.pdf

[2] "*Princess Protection Program* production credits" (http://tv.nytimes.com/show/194599/Princess-Protection-Program/credits). New York Times. . Retrieved 2009-02-23.

[3] "Annie DeYoung" (http://www.imdb.com/name/nm0223395/). .

[4] "Top 100 Most-Watched Telecasts On Basic Cable For 2009" (http://tvbythenumbers.com/2009/12/29/espn-domination-top-100-most-watched-telecasts-on-basic-cable-for-2009/37284). . Retrieved 2010-09-21.

[5] "Disney Channel Playlist by Various Artists" (http://disneymusic.disney.go.com/albums/dcplaylist.html). Walt Disney Records. . Retrieved 2008-05-25.

[6] "Princess Protection Program - Original Movies - Disney Channel" (http://tv.disney.go.com/disneychannel/originalmovies/princessprotectionprogram/premierestunt/index.html). Disney Channel. . Retrieved 2009-06-28.

[7] "Princess Protection Program - On DVD - WD Home Entertainment" (http://disneydvd.disney.go.com/princess-protection-program.html). Walt Disney Studios Home Entertainment. . Retrieved 2009-06-06.

[8] Amazon.de (http://www.amazon.de/Prinzessinnen-Schutzprogramm-Demi-Lovato/dp/B0026L8M6A/ref=sr_1_1?ie=UTF8&s=dvd&qid=1241525486&sr=8-1)

[9] Play.com (http://www.play.com/DVD/DVD/4-/9292109/Princess-Protection-Program/Product.html)

External links

- Official website (http://http://tv.disney.go.com/disneychannel/originalmovies/princessprotectionprogram/)
- *One and the Same* (http://www.imdb.com/title/tt1196339/) at the Internet Movie Database

Send It On (song)

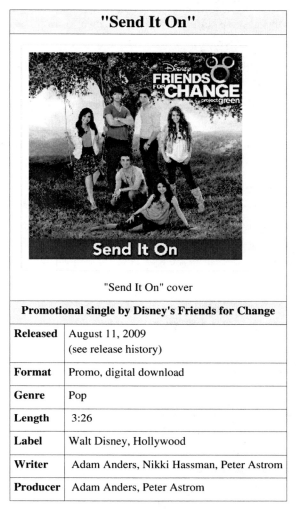

"Send It On"

"Send It On" cover

Promotional single by Disney's Friends for Change	
Released	August 11, 2009 (see release history)
Format	Promo, digital download
Genre	Pop
Length	3:26
Label	Walt Disney, Hollywood
Writer	Adam Anders, Nikki Hassman, Peter Astrom
Producer	Adam Anders, Peter Astrom

"Send It On" is a pop song performed by American recording artists Demi Lovato, the Jonas Brothers, Miley Cyrus, and Selena Gomez. The group, billed as Disney's Friends For Change, stems from Disney's environmental initiative of the same name. "Send It On" was written by Adam Anders, Nikki Hassman, and Peter Astrom and produced by Anders and Astrom. The song was released on August 11, 2009 by Walt Disney and Hollywood Records as a promotional charity single in order to benefit international environmental associations. In regards to the song and the campaign, the six singers noted that it is a good cause and that it is one dear to them. The ballad has predominant power pop characteristics and is lyrically about passing on an environmentalist message.

The song garnered mixed to average reviews from critics, who noted that the lyrics make no mention of the environment. The song received airplay only on Radio Disney and peaked at number twenty on the *Billboard* Hot 100. The corresponding music video has all four acts singing into microphones on top of a brightly lit stage and running across a park setting where many children are following them.

Background

Initially known as "Pass It On", the song was written by Adam Anders and Nikki Hassman in collaboration with Peter Astrom.[1] The four artists went through several recording sessions in early April 2009.[1] Each person shared their opinion in regards to the song and Disney's Friends for Change in an interview with *Access Hollywood*. Joe Jonas said that the song is one with a "great message." He added that the song is about helping the Earth in whichever way possible and that it is mainly about letting "everyone know." Joe Jonas said the song even reminds oneself to be more eco-friendly.[2] Gomez stated,

> "If I could describe the feeling of performing 'Send It On,' it would have to be very empowering. It's more of a power you can't control. It's very sweet and it's got a message behind it. And I think that's what makes it really beautiful, because it's not just about us wearing cute clothes and performing on the stage, it's about us giving this message."[2]

Cyrus mentioned that her favorite part to record was the line "One spark starts a fire." Cyrus said she "loved" the line because it was true for her and that if children send on the message, everyone will know. She also believed that they were "encouraging kids to do it", which she found inspirational.[2] Lovato stated: "It's very important to us to be good to the environment" and that the song is a part of a "big movement" that they are attempting to achieve.[2] Kevin Jonas said it was a "big honor" and that "the vibe [...] is great" because they have "all known each other for years now."[2] Nick Jonas said that the song is just about "taking those tiny steps" that could make the Earth better.[2]

Music, vocal arrangements and lyrics

The song is set in common time with a ballad tempo of 90 beats per minute.[3] It is written in a key of A major.[3] The group's vocals span three octaves, from E_3 to $C\#_6$.[3] The song has the following chord progression, A—F#m—C#m—E5.[3]

The song is sung from a first person viewpoint, allowing an audience to "internalize" the message—which involves everybody—by singing the word "we" together. "Send It On" commences with acoustic guitars and then transitioning to violins. Miley Cyrus and Nick Jonas together sing the first verse, "A word's just a word till you mean what you say." Then the two sing the first chorus together. Demi Lovato and Joe Jonas then sing main lines of the second verse with the other group (Miley Cyrus and Nick Jonas) singing, "If we take the chances to change circumstances." Then, Selena Gomez and Kevin Jonas also join in the second chorus and sing the third verse. For the rest of the song the six of them sing. The overall theme and message of the song is to encourage to pass on the environmental pledge; this can be heavily interpreted from the lines: "Just one spark starts a fire."[4]

Release

Snippets of the song was first heard as the opening theme for commercials that aired on Disney Channel in regards to Disney's Friends for Change.[5][6] "Send It On" later debuted on Radio Disney on August 7, 2009.[5] Later on August 11, the song was released digitally, via iTunes Store.[5][7] Disney will direct 100% of the proceeds from "Send it On" to environmental charities through the Disney Worldwide Conservation Fund (DWCF).[5][7][8] The music video premiered on Disney Channel on August 14 and the day later to Disney.com and ABC.[5] On August 15, a digital extended play was released to the iTunes Store, featuring the song, its music video, two commercials in regards to the project that aired on Disney Channel and a digital booklet.[9]

Reception

Critical reception

"Send It On" received average critical reviews. Bill Lamb of About.com stated: "The song may sound a bit tedious. It's not likely to be much more enduring than the typical *American Idol* winner's finale song. However, the purchase of this song is for a very good cause."[10] Gina Sepre and Whitney English of E! said that the song was Disney's take on "We are the World" by a super-group billed as USA for Africa, a group which included successful acts such as Michael Jackson and Diana Ross.[11] Leo Hickman of *The Guardian* criticized the artists as hypocritical and the song's lyrics as ineffective, noting that "there are no references at all to the environment to be found within the song," as opposed to Cyrus's song "Wake Up America" from her sophomore album which he mentioned was more influential.[12]

Chart performance

The song received mediocre airplay due to it not being released for mainstream radio and only Radio Disney. However, the song debuted at number nine on Hot Digital Songs which led to it making into the *Billboard* Hot 100, issue dated August 29, 2009.[13] "Send It On" debuted and peaked at number twenty in the Hot 100.[14] [15] It then fell to number twenty-one, and stayed on for three more weeks before falling off.[16]

Music video

On June 6, 2009, Lovato confirmed to be on set of the corresponding music video to the song, via her official Twitter account.[17] The music video to "Send It On" was first seen on Disney Channel on August 14, 2009.[5] [18]

Left to right: Joe Jonas, Demi Lovato, Nick Jonas, Miley Cyrus, Selena Gomez, and Kevin Jonas singing into their microphones on top of a stage in the "Send It On" music video.

The music video begins with Miley Cyrus and Nick Jonas sitting on the edge of a dark stage where Nick, also playing the acoustic guitar, and Miley sing the first verse. The video then changes to the two walking onto the brightly lighted stage, singing the chorus, and then being joined by Demi Lovato and Joe Jonas who sing the second verse. The entire group is then shown on the stage as they sing the chorus. Kevin and Joe Jonas then remove a curtain covering the background of stage to reveal a sky-painted backdrop in which Selena Gomez and Kevin Jonas proceed to sing the third verse. The ending of the video follows the entire group running out of a large stage door and through a "park-like" setting while finishing the song. A crowd of minors also begin running behind the group. The video ends with the group jumping onto and sitting on a couch in the middle of the park with the crowd stopping in the background.[18]

Track listings

- **U.S. Digital Download**[7]

1. "Send It On" - 3:26

- **U.S. Digital EP**[9]

1. "Send It On" - 3:26
2. "Send It On" (Music Video) - 3:25
3. "Join Disney's Friends for Change" (Video) - 0:45
4. "Register and Pledge" (Video) - 1:31

Release history

Region	Date	Format
United States	August 7, 2009[5]	Radio Disney
	August 11, 2009[5] [7]	Digital download

References

[1] Kaufman, Gil (April 3, 2009). "Miley Cyrus And Nick Jonas Hook Up For Charity" (http://www.mtv.com/news/articles/1608455/20090403/cyrus__miley.jhtml). *MTV News*. Viacom. . Retrieved November 11, 2009.

[2] "Disney Megastars Come Together For 'Friends For Change: Project Green' Campaign (August 6, 2009)" (http://www.accesshollywood.com/miley-cyrus/disney-megastars-come-together-for-friends-for-change-project-green-campaign-august-6-2009_video_1142708). *Access Hollywood*. NBC Universal Television Distribution. August 6, 2009. . Retrieved August 20, 2009.

[3] "Digital music sheet - Disney's Friends for Change - Send It On" (http://www.musicnotes.com/sheetmusic/mtd.asp?ppn=MN0076762#arrangement). *Music notes.com*. Alfred Publishing. . Retrieved October 30, 2009.

[4] "Digital Booklet - Send It On Digital Booklet" (http://itunes.apple.com/WebObjects/MZStore.woa/wa/viewAlbum?i=325961836&id=325961820&s=143441). *iTunes Store*. Apple Inc. August 15, 2009. . Retrieved August 21, 2009.

[5] Disney Channel (August 6, 2009). ""Send It On," an Anthem by the World's biggest Teen Stars, Miley Cyrus, Jonas Brothers, Selena Gomez and Demi Lovato, for Disney's "Friends for Change: Project Green," Will Debut on Radio Disney, Disney Channel, Disney.com and iTunes" (http://www.disneychannelmedianet.com/DNR/2009/doc/Send_It_On_Disneys_Friends_for_Change_081909.doc) (DOC). Press release. . Retrieved August 20, 2009.

[6] "Help Save the Planet" (http://disney.go.com/videos/#/videos/more/&content=309024). *Disney.com*. The Walt Disney Company. . Retrieved August 30, 2009.

[7] "Send It On (feat. Demi Lovato, Jonas Brothers, Miley Cyrus & Selena Gomez) - Single" (http://itunes.apple.com/WebObjects/MZStore.woa/wa/viewAlbum?id=325770503&s=143441). *iTunes Store*. Apple Inc. August 11, 2009. . Retrieved August 20, 2009.

[8] "Send It On on iTunes" (http://disney.go.com/videos/#/videos/musicvideos/&content=390158). *Disney.com*. The Walt Disney Company. . Retrieved August 20, 2009.

[9] "Send It On (feat. Demi Lovato, Jonas Brothers, Miley Cyrus & Selena Gomez) - EP" (http://itunes.apple.com/WebObjects/MZStore.woa/wa/viewAlbum?id=325961820&s=143441). *iTunes Store*. Apple Inc. August 15, 2009. . Retrieved August 20, 2009.

[10] Lamb, Bill (August 15, 2009). "Disney's "Send It On" Promotes Environmental Responsibility With Miley Cyrus, the Jonas Brothers, Demi Lovato, and Selena Gomez" (http://top40.about.com/b/2009/08/15/disneys-send-it-on-promotes-environmental-responsibly-with-miley-cyrus-the-jonas-brothers-demi-lovato-and-selena-gomez.htm). *About.com*. The New York Times Company. . Retrieved August 20, 2009.

[11] Sepre, Gina; English, Whitney (April 2, 2009). "Miley, JoBros Team Up on "Disney's Version of 'We Are the World'"" (http://www.eonline.com/uberblog/b107432_Miley__JoBros_Team_Up_on__amp_quot_Disney_s_Version_of__We_Are_the_World___amp_quot_.html). *E! Online*. Comcast. . Retrieved August 20, 2009.

[12] Hickman, Leo (August 14, 2009). "Miley Cyrus the Environmentalist? Don't Make Me Weep Tears of Despair" (http://www.guardian.co.uk/environment/ethicallivingblog/2009/aug/14/disney-green-project). *Guardian.co.uk*. Guardian Media Group. . Retrieved August 21, 2009.

[13] "Digital Songs" (http://www.billboard.com/#/charts/digital-songs?chartDate=2009-08-29). *Billboard*. Nielsen Business Media, Inc. August 29, 2009. . Retrieved August 20, 2009.

[14] "Top 100 Music Hits, Top 100 Music Charts, Top 100 Songs & The Top 100" (http://www.billboard.com/#/charts/hot-100?chartDate=2009-08-29&begin=11&order=position). *Billboard*. Nielsen Business Media, Inc. August 29, 2009. . Retrieved August

20, 2009.

[15] "Disney's Friends For Change - Send It On - Music Charts" (http://acharts.us/song/48868). aCharts.us. . Retrieved August 20, 2009.

[16] "Top 100 Music Hits, Top 100 Music Charts, Top 100 Songs & The Top 100" (http://www.billboard.com/#/charts/
      hot-100?chartDate=2009-09-05&begin=21&order=position). *Billboard*. Nielsen Business Media, Inc. . Retrieved August 27, 2009.

[17] Lovato, Demi (June 6, 2009). "Twitter / Demetria Lovato: Videoshoot for send it on..." (http://twitter.com/ddlovato/status/2056540898).
      Twitter. . Retrieved August 20, 2009.

[18] "Send It On Music Video" (http://disney.go.com/videos/#/videos/musicvideos/&content=410333). *Disney.com*. The Walt Disney
      Company. . Retrieved August 20, 2009.

External links

- The official website of Disney's Friends for Change (http://disney.go.com/dxd/index_cds.
  html?channel=260900)
- The official website of Demi Lovato (http://www.demilovato.com)
- The official website of the Jonas Brothers (http://www.jonasbrothers.com)
- The official website of Miley Cyrus (http://www.mileycyrus.com/official)
- The official website of Selena Gomez (http://www.selenagomez.com)
- "Send It On" (http://www.youtube.com/watch?v=jxlr2nKd4Bw&feature=channel) music video on YouTube
  (posted by Hollywood Records)

Cruella De Vil (Selena Gomez Song)

"**Cruella de Vil**," written by Mel Leven, is a song featured in the 1961 Disney-produced animated film *One Hundred and One Dalmatians* and performed by Bill Lee as the singing voice of Roger Radcliffe, a character from the movie. It has been re-recorded by Lalaine, Hayden Panettiere, and Selena Gomez for various releases in the *DisneyMania* album series.

Use in *One Hundred and One Dalmatians*

In the context of the film, it was performed by Roger Radcliffe (singing voice provided by Bill Lee), to describe his wife Anita's schoolmate of the same name. It became Roger's first successful song.

Cover versions

The song has been re-recorded by Lalaine for *DisneyMania 3* in 2005, by Hayden Panettiere for *DisneyMania 5* in 2007, by Selena Gomez in 2008 for *DisneyMania 6*.

The song has also been covered by The Replacements on producer Hal Willner's Disney tribute album, *Stay Awake: Various Interpretations of Music from Vintage Disney Films*, and by Los Lobos on their *Los Lobos Goes Disney* tribute album.

Selena Gomez cover

"Cruella de Vil"	
Single by Selena Gomez	
from the album *DisneyMania 6*	
Released	2008
Format	Promo single
Genre	Pop
Length	3:20
Writer(s)	Mel Leven
Selena Gomez singles chronology	
"Cruella de Vil" (2008)	"Tell Me Something I Don't Know" (2008)

The song was re-recorded in 2008 by Selena Gomez as a promotional single from *DisneyMania 6*. A music video was filmed to promote the 2-Disc Platinum Edition DVD of *One Hundred and One Dalmatians*.

Music video

A music video for Selena Gomez's version of the song aired on the Disney Channel in February 2008. It featured Gomez modeling designs at the House of De Vil fashion house (a reference to the 1996 live-action film), intercut with clips from the movie. The video was included on the *One Hundred and One Dalmatians* Platinum Edition DVD.

References

Magic (Selena Gomez song)

"Magic"	
Single by Pilot	
from the album ***Pilot (From the Album of the Same Name)***	
Released	1974
Genre	Pop rock, soft rock, funk rock
Length	3:06
Label	EMI
Writer(s)	David Paton

"**Magic**" is a popular song from 1974, and is the first commercial success for the Scottish band, Pilot.

It charted most successfully in Canada, where it reached #1, topping the *RPM* national singles chart on July 19, 1975.[1] It climbed as far as #11 on the UK Singles Chart and reached #5 during the summer of 1975 in the United States on the Billboard Hot 100. The song was included on Pilot's debut album.

Use in fiction

"Magic" is heard twice during *Happy Gilmore*, a 1996 comedy film starring Adam Sandler; the first time being early in the film and the second time playing during the end credits. It is also featured in the 2005 films, *Herbie: Fully Loaded* and *The Magic Roundabout*, the 2007 movie *Magicians*, All's Faire In Love, a 2009 comedy film starring Christina Ricci (opening credits) and the fourth episode of the television series *Extras*. Additionally, an episode of *Pushing Daisies* was entitled "Oh Oh Oh... It's Magic", after the song's memorable refrain. In 2009, Selena Gomez sang it for the Disney Channel Original Movie *Wizards of Waverly Place: The Movie*.

Covers

The song was sampled by Girl Talk on his 2006 release *Night Ripper* on the track "Summer Smoke". The song is also heavily sampled in a song titled "It's Magic" by rap artist J.R. Writer. It was then sampled again by rapper Flo Rida in 2009. The song was also covered by Selena Gomez in the 2009 *Wizards of Waverly Place* soundtrack, reaching number #61 in the US. The alternative rock band Barenaked Ladies has been known to sometimes close live shows by playing the song as part of a medley. [2]

Use in Advertising

The song featured in a Pillsbury Company commercial in 2007. Pilot's version is heard in a 2010 TV commercial for Chase.

References

[1] http://www.collectionscanada.gc.ca/rpm/028020-119.01-e.php?brws_s=1&file_num=nlc008388.3989a&type=1&interval=24&
     PHPSESSID=ccntousk30frf6h4jsn237nm12

[2] http://www.youtube.com/watch?v=fcc1Ba5BHMQ

Trust in Me (The Python's Song)

"**Trust in Me (The Python's Song)**" is a song in the widely popular Walt Disney film, *The Jungle Book*, from 1967. The song was sung by Sterling Holloway playing the part of "Kaa, the snake". The song was written by Disney staff songwriters, Robert and Richard Sherman. In the song, Kaa hypnotizes Mowgli, placing him under a trance. As the song concludes, Kaa readies himself to devour the boy, only to be stopped by Shere Khan the tiger in his search for Mowgli.[1]

The Sherman treatment

The Shermans were brought onto the film by Walt Disney due to Disney's feeling that the interpretation was keeping too true to the Rudyard Kipling book. In a deliberate effort to keep the score "light", this song as well as the Sherman Brothers' other contributions generally concern darker subject matter than the accompanying music would suggest. In the case of this song, Kaa speaks and sings with a subtle, lilting lisp giving the song a humorous dimension that it would not otherwise have.[1]

Origins of song

The song started as "**The Land of Sand,** " a song that was written originally for the 1964 musical film, *Mary Poppins*. The song was later discarded when the Sherman Brothers were called upon to write songs for *The Jungle Book*. The lyric for the "Land of Sand" was scrapped and in its place the Shermans wrote the lyric for "Trust in Me", melody intact.

Cover versions

- One of the least traditional uses of a Disney song has been the 1987 Siouxsie and the Banshees cover of "Trust in Me". This cover first appears on the Siouxsie and the Banshees LP, *Through the Looking Glass*, and subsequently on several compilation albums.
- The Holly Cole Trio covered "Trust in Me" on the 1991 release *Blame It on My Youth*.
- Alternative rock group Belly covered "Trust in Me" as a B-side to one of their singles in 1993.
- In Mickey's House of Villains, during the "It's Our House Now" musical number, Minnie is tossed to Kaa, who sings two lines from "Trust in Me" to her.
- Part of the song is on the soundtrack of the *HalloWishes* fireworks show, mixed with AEIOU, song by the Caterpillar of Alice in Wonderland as part of Mickey's Not-So-Scary Halloween Party at the Magic Kingdom in the Walt Disney World resort.
- The Dead Brothers made their version of "Trust in Me" in a very dark, psychedelic and bluesy style. This cover appears on their fourth album *Wunderkammer*.
- Susheela Raman covered "Trust in Me" on her debut album, "Salt Rain" in 2001.
- Selena Gomez covered the song for *DisneyMania 7*.

References

[1] Sherman, Robert B., *Walt's Time: from before to beyond*, Camphor Tree Publishers, Santa Clarita, California, 1998, p 86., ISBN 0-9646059-3-7

Live Like There's No Tomorrow

Ramona and Beezus	
Theatrical release poster	
Directed by	Elizabeth Allen
Produced by	Denise Di Novi Alison Greenspan[1]
Written by	Laurie Craid Nick Pustay Beverly Cleary (novel)[1]
Starring	Joey King Selena Gomez John Corbett Bridget Moynahan Ginnifer Goodwin Josh Duhamel Sandra Oh Hutch Dano
Music by	Mark Mothersbaugh
Cinematography	John Bailey
Editing by	Jane Moran
Studio	Walden Media Di Novi Pictures
Distributed by	Fox 2000 Pictures (USA) Summit Entertainment (International)
Release date(s)	July 23, 2010
Running time	104 minutes (57 minutes of Selena Gomez screen time)
Country	United States
Language	English
Budget	$15 million[2]

Gross revenue	$26,642,435[3]

Ramona and Beezus is a 2010 film adaptation of the book "*Beezus and Ramona*" by Beverly Cleary.[4] [5]

Plot

Young third grader Ramona (Joey King) has a vivid imagination, boundless energy, and accident-prone antics that keeps everyone she meets on their toes, especially her older sister Beezus (Selena Gomez) who is trying to get her cute crush, Henry (Hutch Dano), to go out with her. But her irrepressible sense of fun, adventure and mischief come in handy when she puts her mind to helping save her family's home before its too late.

Cast

- Joey King as Ramona Quimby
- Selena Gomez as Beezus Quimby
- Hutch Dano as Henry Huggins
- Ginnifer Goodwin as Aunt Bea
- John Corbett as Robert Quimby
- Bridget Moynahan as Dorothy Quimby
- Josh Duhamel as Hobart
- Jason Spevack as Howie Kemp
- Sandra Oh as Mrs. Meacham
- Aila and Zanti McCubbing as Roberta Quimby
- Sierra McCormick as Susan Kushner
- Patti Allan as Mrs. Pitt
- Lynda Boyd as Triplet mother

Release

Ramona and Beezus was released in theaters on July 23, 2010, by 20th Century Fox and Walden Media to 2,719 theaters nationwide, and was rated G by MPAA, becoming the studio's fourth film to be rated G since 1997's *Anastasia*.

The trailer was released on March 18, 2010, and was shown in theaters along with *How to Train Your Dragon*, *The Last Song*, *Despicable Me*, *Toy Story 3*, and 20th Century Fox's other films, including *Diary of a Wimpy Kid* and *Marmaduke*. The film premiered in New York on July 20, 2010.

It was released in Irish and British cinemas October 22, 2010.

Critical reception

Ramona and Beezus earned generally positive reviews. Review aggregator Rotten Tomatoes reports that 74% of critics have given the film a positive review based on 68 reviews, for an average rating of 6.3/10.[6] Among Rotten Tomatoes' "Top Critics", consisting of notable critics from the top newspapers and websites,[7] the film holds an overall approval rating of 73%, based on a sample of 26 reviews.[8] The film holds a 56 rating on Metacritic, based on 28 reviews.[9] Eric Snider of Film.com said that "The resulting story is a jumble, and there are too many side characters, but golly if it isn't pretty darned infectious."[10] Jason Anderson of the *Toronto Star* gave *Ramona and Beezus* a good review, saying that "(Ramona and Beezus) is a lively affair, largely thanks to the sweet and snappy screenplay by Laurie Craig and Nick Pustay and to the appealing performances by the cast."[11]

Box office

The film opened at #4 on opening day, grossing under $3 million.[12] It would earn altogether $7.8 million on its opening weekend, earning #6 at the box office. Over its first week, it earned nearly $12.7 million.[13] As of November 20, 2010, its total gross stands at $26,645,939,[3] surpassing its $15 million budget. The film made £84,475 on it's first week-end in the UK (information based on the UK film council).

Home media

The film was released on DVD and Blu-ray combo pack on November 9, 2010.

Soundtrack

Currently, there is only one confirmed track for the film's soundtrack entitled "Live Like There's No Tomorrow", performed by Selena Gomez & the Scene. The song was digitally released as a soundtrack single on July 13, 2010.[14] The song is also part of the band's second album, *A Year Without Rain*. It is unknown whether or not there will be a music video. Other songs in the movie, that may be included on the soundtrack, include "A Place in This World" by Taylor Swift, "Say Hey (I Love You)" by Michael Franti & Spearhead, a song from Peter, Paul, and Mary, "Here It Goes Again" by OK Go, a cover of "Walking on Sunshine by Aly & AJ, Eternal Flame by The Bangles and "(Let's Get Movin') Into Action" by Skye Sweetnam featuring Tim Armstrong.

"Live Like There's No Tomorrow"

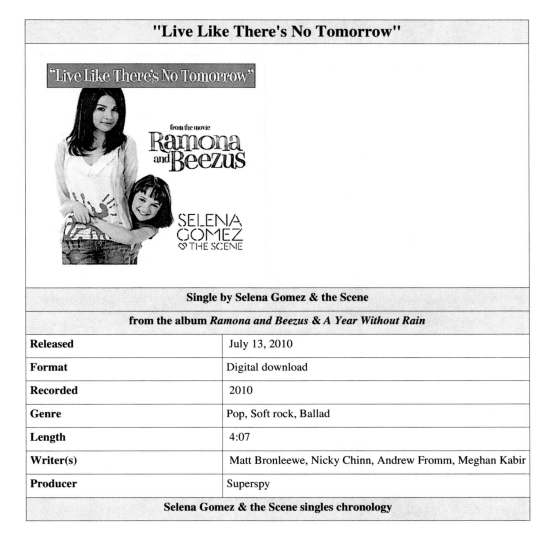

"Live Like There's No Tomorrow"	
Single by Selena Gomez & the Scene	
from the album *Ramona and Beezus* & *A Year Without Rain*	
Released	July 13, 2010
Format	Digital download
Recorded	2010
Genre	Pop, Soft rock, Ballad
Length	4:07
Writer(s)	Matt Bronleewe, Nicky Chinn, Andrew Fromm, Meghan Kabir
Producer	Superspy
Selena Gomez & the Scene singles chronology	

"Round & Round" (2010)	**"Live Like There's No Tomorrow"** (2010)	"A Year Without Rain" (2010)

"Live Like There's No Tomorrow" was released as a single from the upcoming *Ramona and Beezus* soundtrack album on July 13, 2010.[14] This is the one confirmed track of the soundtrack thus far. There is currently no music video for the single. It is performed by Selena Gomez & the Scene and also appears on their *A Year Without Rain* album.

References

[1] "Ramona and Beezus - IMDb Credits" (http://www.imdb.com/title/tt0493949/fullcredits). IMDb.com. . Retrieved 2009-06-22.

[2] Siegel, Tatiana (July 17, 2010). "Female power pushes 'Ramona'" (http://www.variety.com/article/VR1118021858. html?categoryid=2520&cs=1). *Variety.* .

[3] "*Ramona and Beezus* (2010)" (http://boxofficemojo.com/movies/?id=ramona.htm). Box Office Mojo. IMDb. October 31, 2010. . Retrieved Noverber 1, 2010.

[4] Vena, Jocelyn. "Selena Gomez To Star In 'Ramona and Beezus' Movie." (http://www.mtv.com/movies/news/articles/1604489/story. jhtml) MTV.com, 2009-02-06.

[5] Kilday, Gregg. "Young actresses cast for 'Beezus and Ramona.'" (http://www.reuters.com/article/filmNews/idUSTRE51515A20090206) Reuters, 2009-02-05.

[6] "Ramona and Beezus (2010)" (http://www.rottentomatoes.com/m/ramona_and_beezus/). *Rotten Tomatoes.* . Retrieved July 31, 2010.

[7] "Rotten Tomatoes FAQ: What is Cream of the Crop" (http://www.rottentomatoes.com/pages/faq#creamofthecrop). *Rotten Tomatoes.* . Retrieved May 7, 2010.

[8] "Ramona and Beezus (2010)" (http://www.rottentomatoes.com/m/ramona_and_beezus/?critic=creamcrop). *Rotten Tomatoes.* . Retrieved May 27, 2010.

[9] Ramona and Beezus Reviews, Ratings, Credits, and More at Metacritic (http://www.metacritic.com/film/titles/ramonaandbeezus)

[10] Review: Ramona and Beezus Pleases - Film.com (http://www.film.com/features/story/review-ramona-and-beezus-pleases/39369882)

[11] Anderson, Jason (July 23, 2010). "Ramona and Beezus: A family film with a dose of reality" (http://www.thestar.com/entertainment/ movies/article/838995--ramona-and-beezus-a-family-film-with-a-dose-of-reality). *The Star* (Toronto). .

[12] Daily Box Office for Friday, July 23, 2010 - Box Office Mojo (http://boxofficemojo.com/daily/chart/?sortdate=2010-07-23&p=.htm)

[13] Ramona and Beezus (2010) - Weekly Box Office Results - Box Office Mojo (http://boxofficemojo.com/movies/?page=weekly& id=ramona.htm)

[14] Live Like There's No Tomorrow (From "Ramona and Beezus") - Single by Selena Gomez & The Scene - Download Live Like There's No Tomorrow (From "Ramona and Beezus") - Single on i... (http://itunes.apple.com/us/album/live-like-theres-no-tomorrow/id380017649)

External links

- Official website (http://http://www.ramonaandbeezus.com/)
- *Ramona and Beezus* (http://www.imdb.com/title/tt0493949/) at the Internet Movie Database
- *Ramona and Beezus* (http://www.boxofficemojo.com/movies/?id=ramona.htm) at Box Office Mojo
- *Ramona and Beezus* (http://www.rottentomatoes.com/m/Ramona_and_Beezus/) at Rotten Tomatoes

Cruella de Vil

First appearance	*The Hundred and One Dalmatians* (1956)
Created by	Dodie Smith
Portrayed by	Glenn Close (*101 Dalmatians* and *102 Dalmatians*) Rachel York (Broadway musical) Sara Gettelfinger (Musical, after York)
Voiced by	Betty Lou Gerson (*One Hundred and One Dalmatians*) April Winchell (TV Series and *101 Dalmatians: Escape from DeVil Manor*) Susanne Blakeslee (*Disney's House of Mouse, 101 Dalmatians II: Patch's London Adventure* and *102 Dalmatians: Puppies to the Rescue*)
Aliases	Ella (only in *102 Dalmatians* film)

Cruella de Vil is a fictional character and the primary villain in Dodie Smith's 1956 novel *The Hundred and One Dalmatians*, Disney's 1961 animated film adaptation *One Hundred and One Dalmatians*, and Disney's live-action film adaptations *101 Dalmatians* and *102 Dalmatians*. In all her incarnations, Cruella kidnaps dalmatian puppies for their fur. In the live-action version, it is revealed that the reason Cruella chooses to skin puppies is that when short-haired dogs grow older their fur becomes very coarse, which does not sell as well in the fur fashion industry as the fine, soft fur of puppies.

Cruella de Vil ranked 39 on AFI's list "100 Years...100 Heroes and Villains".[1]

Name

Cruella's name is a play on the words *cruel* and *devil*, an allusion which is emphasized by having her country house be nicknamed "Hell Hall". In some translations, Cruella De Vil is known as "Cruella De Mon" to change the play on the word "devil" to one on "demon" because the word "devil" in some languages does not have a clear meaning. An example is Italy, where she is called "Crudelia De Mon" (a pun on "crudele", cruel, and "demone", demon). In the French translation of the Disney's animated movie, she is referred as "Cruella D'Enfer" (Literally, Cruella of Hell or from Hell). In some languages (such as Spanish) where her last name has been left as De Vil, but is not similar to their equivalent of devil, it is taken to be a play on their equivalent of "vile" or "villain". Spelled out as one word; cruelladevil, taken as Cruel Devil.

Appearances

The Hundred and One Dalmatians novel

In the original story, Cruella is a pampered London heiress who knows the owner of the Dalmatian puppies through school. She was a notorious student with black and white plaits. She was later expelled for drinking ink. Now she is the last of her prosperous and notorious family and married to a furrier who supplies her obsession, such as the one piece she is never seen without; a white mink cloak. With this, she wears skin-tight satin gowns and ropes of jewels in contrasting colors, such as an emerald color dress with ropes of rubies. Her chauffeur-driven car is black-and-white striped (Mr. Dearly comments that it looks like "a moving zebra crossing") and has the loudest horn in London, which she insists on displaying to the Dearly family. Such dramatic luxuries were said to be based on Tallulah Bankhead's lavish spending habits, which the producers of the film first read about in a newspaper.[2]

When she has guests for dinner, all of Cruella's food is strange colors and tastes of pepper (alluding to her quick temper). She constantly stokes a roaring fire and complains of being cold despite the elevated temperature. The flat is portrayed as a sort of luxurious version of Hell and sets up Cruella's "devilish" persona for her later crimes. Her guests also meet her abused white Persian cat, which plays a key role in a later part of the story.

When invited to a dinner party held by the Dearly couple, Cruella expresses her sinister interest in the Dalmatians, remarking how she and her henpecked husband have never thought of making clothing from dog pelt before. Yet seeing the spotless skins of the newborn puppies she is revolted and offers to have them drowned at once; her way of getting rid of animals which she views as worthless, including her own cat's kittens. Upon a second visit to the house she picks up the mature puppies and treats them like clothing to be worn.

Cruella also makes a brief appearance, albeit asleep, in Dodie Smith's sequel, *The Starlight Barking*.

Animated films

Cruella De Vil furiously yells at Jasper and Horace, her bumbling henchmen. This image illustrates the exaggerated mannerisms and appearance of De Vil, key to her character's continued success among audiences and critics alike.

Disney's animated version of Cruella first appeared in 1961's *One Hundred and One Dalmatians*, in which she was voiced by Betty Lou Gerson and animated by Marc Davis who together crafted her into an iconic and memorable character. The cool detachment of the original character was replaced by a crazed mania, in which Cruella only barely clung to a sheen of glamour. Anita comments Cruella's above mentioned fur coat is new when Cruella first appears. For unexplained reasons, Cruella's cat and husband were omitted from the Disney version.

The film featured a song, written by the late Mel Leven, using her name as the title, sung by the dalmatians' owner Roger (Bill Lee), who holds the woman in contempt. The lyric begins with: "Cruella De Vil, Cruella De Vil. If she doesn't scare you, no evil thing will..."

Disney considered reusing Cruella as the villain for *The Rescuers*, but decided against it because they did not want to make it a sequel to an otherwise unrelated film. Cruella eventually returned in the 2003 direct-to-video sequel *101 Dalmatians II: Patch's London Adventure*, where she was voiced by Susanne Blakeslee. Blakeslee also voiced Cruella in the 2001 TV series *Disney's House of Mouse*, which featured a running gag in which she inspects dogs from other Disney films with a measuring ruler. Cruella is also one of the Disney Villains Mickey fights in Disney's Hollywood Studios version of *Fantasmic!* Nighttime Show Spectacular in Walt Disney World. In Disney On Ice play 'Celebrations', Cruella De Vil was one of the Villains who appears during the Halloween Party.

From the unsubtle symbolic name to her hideous physical appearance, the evil of Cruella De Vil is overt.[3] In 2002, Forbes ranked Cruella as the thirteenth wealthiest fiction character, citing the single 65-year-old has a net worth of $875 million, obtained through inheritance [4] Cruella was listed as the 39th greatest villain in American cinema in AFI's 100 Years... 100 Heroes and Villains. Also, in Ultimate Disney's Top 30 Disney Villains Countdown, Cruella ranked #6.[5]

Live-action films

In Disney's 1996 live-action remake of the animated film, *101 Dalmatians*, and its 2000 sequel, *102 Dalmatians*, Cruella was played by Glenn Close. The film reinvented Cruella yet again, this time as the magnate of a couture fashion house, "House of De Vil", which specialised in fur couture. The character of Anita (played by Joely Richardson) was a couturière and employee of De Vil. This film increased the physical comedy of the animated film, even veering into toilet humor, such as Cruella falling into a vat of old molasses or having a pig fart in her face. Close's performance was universally well-received, and her sex appeal as the character was also credited.

In Disney's 1996 live-action remake of the animated film, 101 Dalmatians, and its 2000 sequel, 102 Dalmatians, Cruella was played by Glenn Close.

The live-action film was not as critically successful as the animated movie, but Close's performance, as well as her costumes, by Anthony Powell and Rosemary Burrows, received appreciative attention, including a spread in Vanity Fair magazine. Claws were applied to gloves, and necklaces were made from teeth, to add to the idea that Cruella enjoyed wearing parts of dead animals. Nails were also projected from the heels to make them especially vicious in appearance. Close has commented on how demanding the slapstick physicality of the role was while wearing nail-heeled boots and corsets. She was always smoking to give the appearance of a mysterious "villain".

In *102 Dalmatians*, while under effect of Dr. Ivan Petrovich Pavlov's dog conditioning, Cruella wanted to be called "Ella de Vil" because "Cruella sounds so ... cruel". Cruella was completely devoted to saving animals and while experiencing "doraphobia," was scared at the smallest sight of fur fashion, especially since she had all her old fur clothes and the dalmatian coat sketch boarded up. Unfortunately, this new persona does not stay for long, since the effects of Big Ben's bells manage to undo the hypnotherapy, and "Ella" reverts back to Cruella. During the "Ella" stage, Cruella quit her characteristic habits, such as wearing fur, long nails, extravagant hair styles, and of course, smoking. Once the Big Ben jolted her brain waves back into Cruella, her old habits came back. In the end of the movie, she turned into a massive cake and got arrested once again.

Animated series

In the *101 Dalmatians* animated series, Cruella was voiced by April Winchell and was based on Glenn Close's portrayal from the live-action film, but with Betty Lou Gerson's design from the animated film. She appears to be a vegetarian in the show, therefore did not wear clothes made out of animals, nor smoked (although in the episode "Smoke Detectors" she did). Her villainous plot in the show was to steal the Dearlys' farm from them, and using the puppies as a ransom, mainly because the old widow Smedly would not sell it to her and that her mother Malevola demands it. She is an archetypal corporate villain who will seize on any scheme to make money, including drilling oil from the swamp near Dearly farm (thereby polluting it), buying Kanine Krunchies and replacing the nutritious ingredients with sawdust and chalk or sending Jasper and Horace to drive out the owners of Mom and Pop's Grocery Store so she can buy it herself.

In the Christmas episode, "A Cruella Christmas", since she was a child, Cruella wanted a dalmatian puppy but her parents always go on vacations, leaving her with a foreign nanny and clothes for gifts. During her teens was the final straw, which gave her her half white hairline in her fury (earlier she is seen with all black hair and a slight gray-ish streak). Her miserable childhood is what drove her to evil.

The series is also the first time Cruella uses seduction as one of her evil schemes. In the series finale, she uses an inflatable body suit to disguise herself as a sexy blonde bikini surfer to seduce Roger to make Anita think he is cheating her so they will split up and she can get the farm. When Anita goes swimming, she makes her move on him. She asks him to go swimming with her and then tries to kiss him, but her suit is deflated by the puppies' chicken friend, and she turns into a surfboard.

Broadway musical

Cruella also appears as the primary antagonist in the Broadway musical based on the novel. The character was portrayed by Rachel York;[6] however, the actress announced on her blog that she had stepped down from the role of Cruella de Vil to pursue other projects. The role has been taken over by Sara Gettelfinger.[7]

In popular culture

The Queen song "Let Me Entertain You" features the lyrics "I'll Cruella de Vil You!"

The Deadsy song "Cruella" is written about Cruella de Vil.

In 1998's *The Parent Trap*, Hallie & Annie called Meredith "Cruella" when they go camping.

Cruella is indirectly mentioned in the song "Bad Days Ahead" from *The Swan Princess III: The Mystery of the Enchanted Treasure* (1998).

The Spanish singer Alaska made a song called "Cruella de Vil" for the 101 Dalmatians Live-action film.

In The Big Bang Theory episode "The Bat Jar Conjecture", Rajesh suggests that they use an evil laughter as a psychological threat against Sheldon, and Howard points out that his evil laughter is more like a Cruella de Vil's laughter.

Popular video game League of Legends' character Leblanc has an alternate skin based on Cruella de Vil's image.

Parodies

In *The Simpsons* episode, "Two Dozen and One Greyhounds", Mr. Burns plays the role of Cruella De Vil, but unlike her in the movies, where she steals the dalmatian puppies to make them into fur coats, he steals Santa's Little Helper and his girlfriend's greyhound puppies to make them into a tuxedo. And unlike Cruella, who gives in no hesistation to kill the puppies, Burns cannot stand to kill the puppies for himself as they are too cute, so instead, he trains them to be world-class racing dogs.

Coco LaBouche from 2000's *Rugrats in Paris* is a parody of Cruella.

The Dark Eldar, an alien race from the tabletop wargame *Warhammer 40,000*, include a Special Character named "Kruellagh the Vile", whose name is a pun on Cruella de Vil.

Lady GaGa dressed as Cruella De Vil on Halloween in 2010.

References

[1] "100 Heroes and Villains: List Downloads page" (http://connect.afi.com/site/PageServer?pagename=100YearsList). *AFI.com*. .

[2] Disney Archives | Cruella De Vil Villains History (http://disney.go.com/vault/archives/villains/cruella/cruella.html)

[3] Michael A Baldassare (1999). *Can Someone Named "Cruella" Ever Act in Good Faith* (http://students.law.drake.edu/lawReview/?pageID=lrVol48-2). "Cruella de Vil, Hades, and Ursula the Sea-Witch: How Disney Films Teach Our Children the Basics of Contract Law". *Drake Law Review* **48** (2): 351–356. .

[4] "The Forbes Fictional Fifteen" (http://www.forbes.com/2002/09/13/400fictional_14.html). *www.forbes.com*. 2002-09-13. . Retrieved 2007-08-24.

[5] "Ultimate Disney's Top 30 Disney Villains Countdown 10th - 1st Place" (http://www.dvdizzy.com/disneyvillainscountdown/index3.html). *www.ultimatedisney.com*. .

[6] Preston, Rohan (October 14, 2009). "'The 101 Dalmatians': A Canine Caper" (http://www.startribune.com/templates/fdcp?1262504750403). *Star Tribune*. . Retrieved January 3, 2010.

[7] York, Rachel (January 30, 2010). "Parting Is Truly Such Sweet Sorrow" (http://rachelyork.net/blog/?p=135). . Retrieved February 1, 2010.

External links

- Cruella de Vil (http://www.imdb.com/character/ch0010779/) at the Internet Movie Database
- Cruella de Vil (http://www.ultimatedisney.com/countdown4/index3.html) at the UltimateDisney.com Villains Countdown
- Cruella de Vil (http://disney.go.com/vault/archives/villains/cruella/cruella.html) at the Disney Archives

Article Sources and Contributors

Selena Gomez *Source*: http://en.wikipedia.org/w/index.php?oldid=401545113 *Contributors*: 13.M.J.A, 19helena91, 21655, 3193th, 721Tiki, 9993LEO, Abb615, Abelmoreira, Acalamari, Acebloo, Acroterion, Addisonn., Addshore, Admc2006, Agrady8, Aitias, Akcvtt, AkoDanielle, Akrein9, Alan9, Alansohn, Aldo samulo, Alec2011, Alisha208, Alix195, All Hallow's Wraith, Alliepup14, Alphachimp, Altzinn, AlySsa Cyrus, Amalthea, Amchow78, Amer10, Americanidol111, Amprocks, Andonic, Andradetony, Andrew c, Andrewlp1991, Andy19971997, Andybigbro2, Andypp123, Aneesharry, Anen87, AngelaBallard4474, Angelgirlboodyboy, Annapakman, Anonymus232, Antandrus, Antha1313, Antidisestablishmentarianism12804, Antonio Lopez, Arbies92, Ariane Lope, Arlo97, ArrEmmDee, Artistdude64, Artyem95, Ashlawnpb, Ashley401, Asian921, Astral, Astronaut, Atd101, Athn, Auntof6, Avalanchebad, B, BRAINSnfun, BRUTE, Babiian6el, Babiiblooma4eva, Babydollgonewrong, Babyjazspanail, Babywishescute, Bate15, Bazmin, Bebebabiix0, Beeeeeeeeew, Bencey, Bender235, Betacommand, BetoCG, Beverlyhillsx, Bff101, Bibliomaniac15, BigL2066, Bigaireatscheese, Bigdaddy1981, Biggins93, Binabik80, Biodin, Blackguitar316, Blackychan26, Blaineley, BlastingBalloon, Blitz Lutte, Bloodbath 87, Blue37, BlueAg09, Bobo192, Bongwarrior, Bookluvr107, Brackenheim, BragoJJ, BrandonFurtado, Braza258, Brendan4hsm, Brendasong, Briddish, Brittflick 1994, Btilm, Buddy13, C.Fred, C777, CWii, CaRaNt11, Caiaffa, Cait g328, Caitlin202, Calciumwaste, CallidoraBlack, Calliegal, Calvin 1998, CambridgeBayWeather, CamirynAnn, Camw, Can't sleep, clown will eat me, CanadianLinuxUser, Candyo32, CapitalR, CardinalDan, Carl.bunderson, Carlette Quinto, Carlitohm11, Casey1817, Cat333, Cavsdude32, Ccrashh, CeciliaS, CelebrityGossipGirl, Celiesia, Ceres987, Cesium 133, Cest-moi-baybee, Cflat2806, Chantessy, CharCharOverOver11, Charitwo, Charlie White, CharlieFisher, CharmedFreak123, Chasewc91, Chatfecter, Cheesyperson1995, Chelo61, Cheriepoon, Chieframhorn, Chigurgh, Chiharu2shi, Chimchar556, ChocolateRibbons960, Chokolatchp, Chris wong999, Chrissy200714, ChristianGirl2, Churaru, Chzz, Circusstar, Cliff smith, Closedmouth, Cmchannel, Cncxbox, Codywarren08, Coffee, CommonsDelinker, Confession0791, Connormah, Coolgirlnyc123, Coolio348, Corvus cornix, Coventry2423, Cowardly Lion, Cowgod14, Crash Underride, Crystal Clear x3, Crystal101101, CrystalicIsMe, Crythias, Cybercobra, DCEdwards1966, DCFan101, Dancechic123, Daniel, DantODB, Darkspots, Darrenhusted, DasallmächtigeJ, Dasani, David101jam, Debresser, Decodet, DegrassiFreak, Dekan871, Delicious carbuncle, DeltaQuad, Demi1993, Demi2009, Demi2011, Demi818, DemiLovato, DemiLovato15, DerHexer, Destroyer Time, Dha, DianaVickersFan, Diem nguyen, Digitalone, Digomez, Discospinster, DisneyMania, Diving2010, Divya2011, Diwas, Djrash, Doctorkc, Doczilla, Don-dk, Donikanuhiu, Doorsfan2009, Dorella, Dorian200, Dpm12, DrStrangelove64, Dragonmonster8, DramaQueen9118162, DreadfullyDespised, Dreadstar, DreamStar05, Dreamafter, Dumlove, Dvferret, Dylanraymusic, EFMP, ERcheck, Easy12345, Ebyabe, Ecmce, Ed112111, Eddie5000, EdisonLite, Edna23, Eeekster, Either way, El Muñeco Shakes It Up, Baby, Electroide, Elenseel, Elipongo, Emi x3, Emo777, Emoll, Empezardesdecero1718, Ending-start, Enoky, Epbr123, Eronel189, Escape Orbit, Etrigan, Eugh jei, Evb-wiki, Eve27 2009, Evilchild967, Evncollin, Ewigneeo818, Excirial, Exor674, Exuberant, F.morett, Falcon8765, Fanficgurl, Fashungrl04, Fei818, Ff22, Filipão, Fishhead2100, Footballchamp0909, FortyFootEcho, Fourviz, Foxcloud, Fredler Brave, Frehley, Frickeg, Friends007, Fvquebr, GD1223, GMANGRIFFG, Gadeshina33, Gakusha, GateKeeper, Gato101jd, Gboichris, Gdaly7, Gdaly93, Geekboy6, Gellarsgrudge, Gersende, Gertie1999, Gikü, Gilo1969, Gimmetoo, Gimmetrow, Ginab31, GioLib, GiovyGabrielEd, GiovyGabrielEd15, Giovyed, Glane23, GlassCobra, Gman124, Gmangriffg, Gnaturefantasy, Gnowxilef, Gnowydnaxilef, GoPurpleNGold24, GoldFlower, Gongshow, GoodBuy, Gossip--girls-xoxo, Gothica36, Gpratts06, Graceannhill, Greclahah, GreenBayPackersfan09, Greswik, HD325, HJ Mitchell, HalfShadow, Hallen455, Halosecrets0032, Hamad amiri, Hannahcrazy, Hannahhelpz, Happypan21, Happypan26, Harrisju, Harry lp, Harvardstudent, Headstrong neiva, Hekerui, HiLoser, High School Musical909, Hijikilimipiuitiyi, Hipzip 14, Hmains, Hoangquan hientrang, HobbesFriend4321, Hometown Kid, Homezfoo, Honey Bee Real, Horkana, Horse lover 1086, HorseGirl070605, Hoyleslr, Hpmosley, Hughes&kaelin, Huntster, Hwawkk, IGAT, IHateDrama!!101, IW.HG, IamWRENALD, Iangurteen, Ianonavy, Icandy123, Icealien33, Iesorto, Ihrtwiki, Ijnisthepassword, Iknow23, Iloveyoohxx89, Imaginart, Imorthodox23, Intelligentsium, Intelligentsock, Intercom 1, IntoCreativeJan, Ipodnano05, Irishguy, Irrypride, Ivanjim, Ixfd64, J Milburn, J-love-lee, J.delanoy, JASBarney3, JForget, Jack Merridew, Jackgill06, Jackmiami, Jackollie, Jackson 08, Jacksonori47, Jacobsnchz, Jad7753, Jaga185, Jaggers76, Jagunde, JaimeAnnaMoore, JamesAM, Jarjarbinks10, JasonAQuest, Jayce0814, Jeffmeck22, Jeremynxn, Jerome0012, JerryYelton, Jesusmariajalisco, Jimothytrotter, Jj2k8, JoFerg, Jobrogal, Joe59108, JoeJonasMileyCyrus, John Vandenberg, Johncl87, Johnny0929, Jonhmayer-fã, JonoRayner, JosephJames6, Joshbaringer13, Joshua Scott, Jpappas130, Jthemanrock, Juanacho, Juggler821, Juliaisbrittney, Julianster, Jushen, JustSome1, Justicetr, Justin 7758, Justme89, KADcutie44, Kairo davis, Kanonkas, Karaku, Karina-Kaylee, KathyCQ, Kelisi, KelleyCook, Kellylyn93, KeltieMartinFan, Kenny09, Keraunoscopia, Kevin Forsyth, Kevpark, Kielz85, Kiki360, Kikkokalabud, KimMeanu, Kimberly camba, Kimiko20, Kimusa1, King Lopez, King007ofrock, Kitkatleen, Kjramesh, Kkim photo, Kkim photoo, Kmethod, Kmhkmh, Kmstar, Konrad4321, Krisha531, Ktjames, Kudret abi, Kukini, Kurt Shaped Box, Kushal one, Kww, Kya-Sofia, L3eater, LUCY1995, Lady5555501, Lalaliana17, Lancini87, Lane, Laurarobb, Lawl95, Lawrence Cohen, LeaveSleaves, Lexiecreator, Libbreje, LifesWonderful, Lightning41, Lika2672, LilHelpa, Liljabbakid, Limetolime, Linkinaha, Lipesbatista, Liquidkernel, Liquidluck, Lishowronsakura, Lisssii babii, Littlegirlpunk, Live Light, LiveInLove20, LoganTheGeshrat, Logflume12, Logical2u, Looper5920, Lotus Wolf, Lovejbforlife, Lovesongs41, Lpbrunette13, Luckyslimester, Luckyz, Luk, Luna Santin, MBisanz, Mach2moo, Mack2, Mackenziealice, Macoa, Madiiiehh, Magic246, Magioladitis, Maitri.uppaluri, MakeLove91, Maldek2, Mallerd, Malleus Fatuorum, Malpass93, Manuelle Magnus, Marikagirl12, MarkLorica, MarsRover, Martin451, Martin4647, Martinanguiano, Matblinks, Matthewedwards, Maurice16, Mavbab3, Max leon, Mcrfobrockr, Melanie2408, Melikbilge, Meliss402, Mentifisto, Mianghuei, Miiikoooo, Mikha35, Mikokat, Milerz91, Milesbetter, Mileycyrussoulja, Modi mode, Moodgo, Moondyne, MotleySabbathMaiden, Movieguruman, Movingboxes, Mrs.perfect, Mschel, Mu, MusicBoi94, Musicalmelody, Musiclover98765, NIVINCo, Nagy, Nakon, NarutoD444, Neirgb818, Nemesis63, NeoBatfreak, NewInThe2, Nickiwilliams, NigaHigaFan2, Night Fight, Nikiangelz, Nima1024, Ninjawarriordex, Nirinsanity, NrDg, Nv8200p, Nymf, Nyoplaid, OAVJunior, OOODDD, Oda Mari, Odhfan 01, Officialofjennisandtk, Ohmygod1234, Okazakiakane, Okki, Oky103, Olly150, OneWorld91, Onlybyu, Oogadabaga, Ositadinma, Ospinad, Otto4711, Ottre, Oxymoron83, Ozurbanmusic, PMDrive1061, Palmer-Ridge, PancakeMistake, Pandasand, Paola347, Paolina rosa, Patches97l3, Patrickrox11, Paul Erik, Pd THOR, Pedro João, Penguino6, Penn state football, Peregrine Fisher, Pharaoh of the Wizards, PhenomRIP, Philipderby, Pinkgirl1995, Pinkskate8, Pknkly, Plastikspork, Pokerdance, Polly, PowerRanger101, Prepelos, Pretty Girl 101, Prfo, Prodego, PsychoSchuyler, Puertorico1, Purpleshopper210, Qpiango, Qtaha, QuasyBoy, Quell, Quinton100, R8er925, RBBrittain, RORLVR1, Rachel.Lynn, Rafatisd, Rafazero27, Raiandmaya, Raine neiva, Randolph3, Randomjohn, Ratemonth, Razorflame, Rbdfan723, Rebel shadow, Renesemee, RexNL, Rhiannon Taylor, Rickterp, RickyYayo3, RightSideNov, Ripkenfan86, Robert Moore, Rockin56, Rockintheoc, Rodhullandemu, Rogo9878, Romina123456789, RonBatfreak, Rose64bud, Roselily6, Rosemaryamey, Ross92, Rsymone, Runefrost, Ryan-McCulloch, RyanG222, SD5, SamChambers, Samiha rayeda, Sammywand365, Sandwichluver, SbuxPrincess, Scarian, Sceptre, Schinella1, Schmiteye, ScorchOurBodies, ScottMHoward, SelenaFan1089, SelenaRules, Selenaismylife555, Selgomezluvrr, Serbchick93, Seth Bresnett, Sethjohnson95, Setsuna29, Shadzane, Shelfro, ShizukaRose, ShuffleStop, SidCurtis10, Sidonuke, Sierracool92, Silvergoat, Simplebutpowerful, Sinternational, SkyWalker, Slakr, Slatersteven, SlimVirgin, Smijes08, Smileykins, Smithj22, Smithsburg, Snaxbowl, Snowflakerockz, Soccer5525, Soccerguy220, Socutesopretty, Sofia3434, Soophiiaa, Soulyaboy, Spanky1991, Sparks Fly, Sparks13fan, Spears154, SpeedexS-19, Spinneroody, Sprite7868, Stage11, Staka, Stanmar, Star141, Starkluver13, Starrynites, Steam5, Stephanierpicha, Stephe1987, Stephenjamesx, Steven Zhang, Steveo2, Storytellershrink, StrawberryPink, Studerby, Study-Of-The-Stars, SummerPhD, Sunfeet, SuperHamster, Supermanjde1996, Superstar911, Sweet-pea-1981, THAOlula, TKD, TMC1982, Talk2me2day, Talker122, Tarheelz123, Taxman, Taylor Lane, TaylorGurl678, Tbhotch, Tempodivalse, Terrillja, TexasAndroid, ThatRadEmoCass, The Master of disguises, The Thing That Should Not Be, TheBananaRepublic, TheGerm, TheNewPhobia, Theferrariboy, Therealdavo2, Thingg, Tiah12345, Tide rolls, Tiffanyevansfan92, Tinky steph, TinribsAndy, Tinton5, Tiptoety, Toglenn, Tombraiderlegend, Tomcess27, Tommy2010, Tony1, TonyWDA, Torak, Torch1992, Tostadaswithcheese, Toughpigs, Transity, Trom120, Tubesurfer, Tweetsabird, Tykunzelman98, UltimatePyro, Undertaker1965, Undertakerhbk588, Usb10, Usnerd, VJ13A, Varun.mansinghka, Vasocheewm2012, VersaceModella, Vidisha89, Vinsfan368, Vokidas, Volleyballqueen12, VoluntarySlave, Vox Humana 8', WAVY 10 Fan, WadeSimMiser, Waiwaifan, Ward3001, Wayne Slam, Wecry, WelcomeAtlas, Welovelovato, Welsh, Welsh-girl-Lowri, WhatGuy, WibWobble, WikHead, WikiPikiUser, Wikigleek., Wikisergiowiki, Wikiwowwow, Wildhartlivie, Will-Martins, WillSmithsTopFan, Willgustavo, Willthacheerleader18, Woohookitty, Wormow, Wreckedd08, X-xHeadStrongx-x, X2sh0rt4ux, XBree 123X, XESR, Xoxjloveleexox, Xx kidschoice xx, Xxmaddie216, Xxmonikaxx, Y0br4nduhn, Yamla, Yankeesrj12, Yasminerihanna, Yoguy11, YungSilver, ZSoraz, Zach Benjamin, Zaeriuraschi, Zammit123, Zaque 24, Zhou Yu, Ziansh, Zoe, Zrlopez, Zvika, ~Ryan Mckenzie~, Александър, 876 anonymous edits

Alex Russo *Source*: http://en.wikipedia.org/w/index.php?oldid=401980721 *Contributors*: 10metreh, 11snoon, 1tay1011, A, Aden-McKenziee, Affiqcute, Aitias, Ajay44, Allstarecho, Andrew c, Ani4e-95, Animoviera14, Argeboyu155, ArglebarglelV, Atd101, AussieLegend, Avenged Eightfold, Avnjay, Awesome6498, Bender235, Bento00, Beverlyhillsx, Biscuitgirl, Bluerasberry, Bobnorwal, Brawlmantis80, Broadway4life155, Bsadowski1, C.Fred, CBrock055, Calliegal, Cartoonzaq, Chane 815, Chantessy, Cheetahbrian, Cncxbox, ConcernedVancouverite, Confession0791, Cory Malik, Cowmoore7481, Cymru.lass, D, Diem nguyen, Dimitre13, Djarrah, Dthomsen8, E. Ripley, Ecliptor12, EditWikiforLulz, Enigmaman, EoGuy, Epbr123, Erianna, Favonian, Finister2, Frehley, GaryColemanFan, Gertie1999, Girlie99, Girlxgirlx, Hailey C. Shannon, Headstrong neiva, Hmrox, II MusLiM HyBRiD II, Immunize, Imzy, Intothewoods29, Ixfd64, J.delanoy, JabbaWorm, Jairo82798, Jeff G., Junglefury18, KADcutie44, KelleyCook, Kellylyn93, L Kensington, La Pianista, Lancini87, Lannybuoy, Laughtattack, Lawl95, Leafiergreen, Lextex77, Live Light, Lord Opeth, Louieandmaggie, Luk, Lushhhhhhhh, Maddiekate, Magioladitis, Malpass93, MarcowyGnom, Materialscientist, Matt Deres, Mechanical digger, Michal Nebyla, MiniMary12, MithrandirAgain, Mr. College, MultiSaw13, Mystorysforever, Nanami Kamimura, Neorob2, NickW557, Nopmacprime, NrDg, PancakeMistake, Pinar, Poweralex, Qtaha, QuasyBoy, Qwyrxian, Reach Out to the Truth, Reaper Eternal, Rebafan32, Rickthestud, RobertMfromLI, Rodhullandemu, Roguemaster83, Ronhjones, Rsindlin, Ruofan, ScaldingHotSoup, Scarian, SelenaGomez1997, Sellybelly, Sesshomaru, Smijes08, Snowolf, Someguy1221, Spongebobhannah, Staka, Super Bubbles 96, Superjay2001, TexasAndroid, TheMinigolfMaster111, Theda, Thingg, Tpgamble, TreoBoy680, Tsange, Tvtonightokc, Tyw7, Vishnava, VoluntarySlave, Welsh, WhatGuy, Winchelsea, Xp54321, Yoguy11, Yugioh1126, ZSoraz, Zaeriuraschi, Zzhane, 551 anonymous edits

Wizards of Waverly Place *Source*: http://en.wikipedia.org/w/index.php?oldid=401996415 *Contributors*: -), 13.Ikim, 13.M.J.A, 13curseof, 2 Train, 27man27, 3pinkmonkeys1098, 5 albert square, 53180, 6med98, 721Tiki, 9potterfan, A, A little insignificant, A.h. king, A3RO, A8UDI, ABF, AHRtbA==, AJCham, Abbyhayes7, Abc518, Abce2, Abdelrahman Shehata, Achshar, Acidjim, Adyniz, Airplaneman, Aitias, Ajay44, Ajm526, Ajraddatz, Alansohn, Ale jrb, Alec2011, AlexRusso, Alexander.Keays, Alexius08, AlexiusHoratius, Allaboutme2000, AlohaServed, Amberclaw, Amebabame, Americanhero, Andadundi, Ands2, Ani4e-95, Anitrain, Ankur Banerjee, AnonGuy, Anonymi, Antandrus, Antonio Lopez, Aqua37, Arcai, Arielboi15, Arkkkk, Armani1000, Arrieta96, Aruton, Asfooriscool, Ash, Ashneestar, Asmir4567, Aspects, Aspurgeon0091, Astrowob, Atd101, AtheWeatherman, Atif.t2, AtomicAge, AtomicNewWave, AussieLegend, AussieLegender, Avaclon, Awesomeomar, Ayaan03, Ayman9510, Az8free, Aznboy9724873505, Azu Jeuk's back!, B33stm4n, Baileygaz, BaseballChica03, Bassbonerocks, Basti95, Bearcat, Beeblebrox, Bellamy1996, Belovedfreak, Benbe, Berricool01, BexMckinlay18, Bgs022, Biodin, Blackngold29, Blaloupasous, Blanchardb, Bluerasberry, Bobo192, Bongwarrior, Booknotes, Bovineboy2008, Brandizzo, Brandude, Brianhenke, Brodkin, BsaPR1996, Bsman17, Bucephalus, Burningview, Butseriouslyfolks, C.Fred, C45207, CELLrockmusic, CNGLITCHINFO, COlOmBiA gIrL, Califajo, Califajo002, Calliegal, Calor, Can't sleep, clown will eat me, Candy Liz, Candy coated doom, Candyo32, Capricorn42, Captain panda, Carelly, Carl.bunderson, Carlitohm11, Carlosar45, Carrie2002, Chane 815, Chanlyn, Chantessy, Chaoticfluffy, CharmedFreak123, Checker Fred, Cheseball, Chicago god, Chitomcgee, Choppedburgers,

Chost2016, Chris Rocen, Chris oss, Chris the speller, Chrissyboo123, Christian75, Christopher140691, Clerks, Clive386, CloversMallRat, ClutterButter, Cocacolaroxoutloud, Cody574, Codywarren08, Coffee, CollegeMan, Cometstyles, CommonsDelinker, ComputerGuy, Confession0791, Connormah, Conti, CookieMattster, CoolBoy-6789, Cooletster, Coral Bay, Corruptcopper, Cory Malik, Cosmo0, Cosmo16h12, Courcelles, CovertAffairs22, Crash Underride, CrazyKid24, Crythias, Cst17, Cstroka, Ctjf83, Curseof13, Cutie2b, Cxf2015, CyWizard, D, DARTH SIDIOUS 2, DC Fan 5, DCFan101, DJ Clayworth, DMacks, Daboyle250, Dakotagirl1022, DanMS, Danigro89, Danity94, Dannyboybaby1234, Darrik2, Darth Panda, DavidEduardoGarcia, Davidearly46, Davros847, Dayewalker, Debresser, Decco, Deely, DelonDiscountMoore, Deltawarr, Demi2009, Demi818, Demilovatofan1, DentonChrist, Deon, DerHexer, Diem nguyen, Discospinster, DisneyFriends, DisneyNinja, Disneycrules, Divod, Doctorfluffy, Dogbreathx2, Dominic Hardstaff, Don-dk, Don729torossi, Dorian200, Dottiericarox24, Douko, Download, Dr.scholl201, DrakeBellRocksHard, Dreadstar, DreamStar05, Dreamafter, Dude4567898, Dxfan4ever, Dydy23, Dylan6758, DéRahier, E Wing, E2eamon, ERK, EWikist, Easy12345, Ed112111, Edenc1, Edgar181, Editor510, Eeekster, Eeyore7739, Ehwildcats, ElationAviation, Elephant Talk, Eleven even, Elizium23, Ellen Spears, Elsagsd, Emelove-bep, EmmaGomezlovato, Empezardesdecero123, Empezardesdecero1718, Enigmaman, Enviroboy, Epass, Epbr123, Epp, Erebus Morgaine, Erianna, Erica08, Escape Orbit, Everyking, Excirial, Explicit, Extremeguy, FFall1986, Falcon8765, Favonian, Feinoha, Fel7, Felixbelize, Fetchfan88, Ffaadstrbdetete, Fieldday-sunday, Firesoul2x, FjMOVIES, Fladoodle, Flipkid101, Fmyself, For An Angel, Freelover9, Frehley, Friendfriend94, Fruitl00p29, Funnyfarmofdoom, Futurama516, Fuzzyandtoast, GabrielPelareja, Gabrielkat, Gail, Galactic war, Garlic knots, GaryColemanFan, Gdaly7, Geekboy6, Gemingirl, GeneralAtrocity, GeoJoe1000, George2001hi, GeorgeRAS, Gertie1999, Gfoley4, Gh97, Gimme danger, Gimmetoo, Gimmetrow, GinoKolle, Giraffebutterfly, Girlsnightout.com1, Givebackone, Gkm2010, Glacier Wolf, Gnowxilef, GoPurpleNGold24, Gobonobo, Gogo Dodo, Gokufistum, Good Olfactory, Goodvac, GorillaWarfare, Gossip--girls-xoxo, Gprince007, Gracekins, GrantyO, Green21guns, Griffinofwales, Grod102, Gromlakh, Gta Ed, Gurch, Gyrono, HD325, Haha169, Hahaha10253, Hamza aamir, Hannahcrazy, Hannahfanon, Harry972, Hashlimaslah, Hassaan19, Headstrong neiva, Helmoony, Heracles31, HexaChord, Hipzip 14, Hmrox, Hoangquan hientrang, Honey Bee Real, Hoo man, HorseGirl070605, Howlowcanugo1233, Howyoudo, HuckCas1, Hurtme1992, Hut 8.5, Hydrogen Iodide, IEPP158, ILLUCYJTA, IW.HG, IWannaEditWiki, Icealien33, Icy-snowflake, Idol 2006, Ihateuyouhateme123, Iloveseals, Ilovetorres, Iloveyoohxx89, Ilyjoejonas, Imjustbeingme, Immunize, Imnotminkus, ImperatorExercitus, Imzy, Inferno, Lord of Penguins, Insertclevernamehere, Instinct, Intelati, Intelligentsium, Interrobang², Intothewoods29, Ipodnano05, Iridescent, Iroc24, Isamazing, Iwantchikkinnow, J.delanoy, J4lambert, J7y, JCamBoo, JDOG555, JForget, JKos12, JTYS, Jabrona, Jackdyson, Jackiechan646464, JadeGryphon, Jadeellen5233, Jafe, Jaggers76, Jairo82798, Jamielb, Jan eissfeldt, Jashanaas, Jason-209, Jasynnash2, Jaxstephens, Jayce0814, Jeff Boon, Jeff G., Jeffy101yea, Jeremy1354, Jeshan, Jessemckay, Jfarajr, Jhsounds, JimVC3, Jimmy, Jiuju, Jmcd88, Jmishx3, Jo brogirl94, Joes a g, Johnny0929, Johnred32, Jonasseldemiyea, JoshuaZ, Josue100, Jpepperman, Juliancolton, Juncallday1, Jusdafax, JustWong, Justinharrison, KADcutie44, KGasso, Kaiba, Kajal4, KamenKnight, Kanonkas, Karaku, Karuseikaarie, Katalaveno, KathrynLybarger, KathyCQ, Katieh5584, KelleyCook, Kellylyn93, Kevins97, Kgfury, Kid0015, Kido900, King Azu Jeuk, King of Hearts, KingMorpheus, Kingpin13, Kiratmalli, Kittyu, Kkmurray, Kmcxx3, Kmsfvf96, Koolerkat, Koopnut, Krychek, Ktn1, Kubigula, Kuyabribri, L Kensington, LAN9, LAUGH90, LOL, LUCY1995, Ladywood7, Lailat al quadar, Landfish7, Landon1980, Laney151, Languageleon, Lannybuoy, Larssie1993, Laughtattack, Lazulilasher, Lazy Bunny Forever, LazyOaf, Leagreen, Lear's Fool, LeaveSleaves, Lee3319, Legoman64, Level6 BM204 DeLaSalleLipa, Lightning41, Lilcarlitoisnow14, Lilcoolgirl5656, Limetolime, Limideen, LinkToddMcLovinMontana, Liquidluck, Little Mountain 5, LittleDuude8, Live Light, Livetc77, Lizziegirl96, Logical Fuzz, Lokioak, Lolalol1234567899, Lolboy52, Lord Opeth, Lorenaherrera5, Lorin Schonfeld, Lucariohumper123, Luns1118, Luvatomi, Lyon Kiborg, M4bwav, MC RIDE, MER-C, MJLRGS, Madchester, MaggieRockz, Mahnoor moon, Malevious, Malpass93, Mandy443, Mankar Camoran, Maquirri91, Marek69, Martin451, Mason172, Materialscientist, Matthew Yeager, McSly, Mcmillin24, Meap77777, Meepo1118, Megakoolkid, Megara, Megaroo3florida, Melanie2408, Meme3389, Memphis670, Mentifisto, Merbabu, Mezowi, Mgliotta, Micione, Mickeymouseclubhouse, MidwesternDiva, Mifter, Mikani, Mikeyc4023, MilaSveta13, Mileylover33, Mjquinn id, Mkilki, Moanna, Mokoniki, Momanso, Mouseinthehouse, Mr. College, Mr. Comedian, Mr.west 1984, MrJaywod1, MrRadioGuy, MrStalker, Mrschimpf, Mrusso18, Mspraveen, Muriloofbrazil, Mynameinc, Mysdaao, Myzou, N5iln, NMChico24, Natasha Wilson, Nathan92295, Naunumanzor, Navy Blue, Ncmvocalist, Ndrwatthedisco, Ned Scott, Neirgb818, NellieBly, Nemo24, Neptune5000, Nick Levine, Nickmilton, NielsenGW, Night Fight, Nikiangelz, Nonexistent me, Norsehorse89, Np2535, NrDg, NuclearWarfare, ObsessiveJoBroDisorder, Omdgf22, Onala94, OneWeirdDude, Onevalefan, Oobug, Ophois, Orry Verducci, Ositadinma, OverlordQ, OwenX, Oxymoron83, Ozcrash, PPVMonstaNetwork, Pabulus, Pairadox, PancakeMistake, PaperMarioFan684, Paste, PaterMcFly, Pax85, Paxsimius, Pcs3075, Pdcook, Pedromiguel1982, Pewwer42, Pharaoh of the Wizards, PhenomRIP, Phil Boswell, Philip Trueman, Philipmanil, Piano non troppo, Piblup, Pilif12p, Pinkiee15, Pizzalc11, Pleasetalktome, Possum, Postcards123, Propaniac, Pseudomonas, PsychoSchuyler, Purplemonkey8899, Pyfan, QuasyBoy, Quercus basaseachicensis, Quinsareth, Quintez, R'n'B, R13n13, RCGSpectre, RJFJR, RJaguar3, Rachelfan2, Raiku Samiyaza, Raine neiva, Rallybrendan2006, Randersontt, Randolph3, Randompeoplesunited, Rapjul, Rbdfan723, Reaper Eternal, Redl@nds597198, Reiner rubin, Renesemee, Repoed2, Rettetast, Rfsilveira, RightSideNov, Rising*From*Ashes, Rissalicious, Rivemont, Rjwilmsi, RkOrton, RobertMfromLI, Robishot, RockMFR, Rockermert hsm, Rockin56, Ronark, Ronhjones, Rosario lopez, Royerdelisle, Rrburke, Rror, Rsindlin, Rsrikanth05, RyanCross, Rzryr, S3000, Salvio giuliano, Salz360, Samaira yaseen, Samgibbs, Samiam18, Sammywand365, Samuel Blanning, Sarwicked, Saturn star, Saylaveer, SchfiftyThree, Schroeder74, Scoops, Scoutjd, Secretchamberman, Selaromar, Selenafan815, Selgomezfan496, Serienfan2010, Sesshomaru, Setsuna29, Sexysimba, Sgdljb, Sgs101, ShadowRanger, Shahab, Shayanshaukat, Shenshenly, Shiningstar11, Shirulashem, Shootmaster 44, Shortride, ShuffleStop, SidP, Sidney159, Sidonuke, SigKauffman, Signalhead, Sik403471, Silvonen, Sk8rdude623, Slips, Smijes08, Snoborder93, Snubbiesluver15, SoCalSuperEagle, SoWhy, Soldat Bigfield, Someguy1221, Sonew24, Sonicforest, SonyWonderFan, Sophie, Sparks13fan, Spazure, Spears154, Specs112, Spellmaster, Spencer, SpikeJones, Spongebobhannah, SpookyTown98, Sposato, Staka, StaticGull, Steam5, Stephenjamesx, Stephwade, Stifle, Stoogeyp, Strikers5, Strongy820, Suiteman, SummerPhD, SuperHamster, SuperWiki8, Supershow97, Superstargirl98, Susan Capetinga, Susfele, Sweetchocolatecutie, SwirlBoy39, Swizzletwizzle, T.V. Watcher 98, TH43, THUYNGA, TPIRFanSteve, TRLIJC18, Tabercil, Tabletop, Taonelly12, TaylorAV, Tbhotch, Tcatron565, Tcspriggs, Tedder, TerriersFan, Terve2, TexasAndroid, Thatguyflint, The Cool Kat, The Master of disguises, The Thing That Should Not Be, The Utahraptor, The hegemon, The suite life, TheMinigolfMaster111, TheRealFennShysa, TheSuave, TheTruthiness, TherealJHONNY, Therealmileycyrus, Theresa knott, Thezachatttack96, Thingg, Thorn12, Tide rolls, Tilla, Timtom4444, Tinkerbell9383, Tiriter, Tkynerd, Toinfinitie, Tombraiderlegend, Tommy2010, TonyTexas254, Toughpigs, Towerrumble, TracyLinkEdnaVelmaPenny, Treh03, TreoBoy680, Tricksterson, Troy 07, Trusilver, Tubesurfer, TutterMouse, Tvtonightokc, Tweetsabird, Twilightsaga129, Tyleredwards9908, Tyrah343, Ukexpat, Ulric1313, Ultimate Ranger, Ummangsb, Ummit, Uncle Dick, Unpilot15, Unscented, Uucp, Uyer, VJ13A, VX, ValiantRed600, Vanessa winder maker, Vanessahudgens22, Vanessarks, Vanis314, Vanished User 1004, Varael, Venny85, Versus22, Vhtimetraveler8, Vicenarian, Victorianicole99, Vinnyvinny2, ViperSnake151, Voyagerfan5761, Vyshnavi11, WAVY 10 Fan, WDFUNK, WOWP Anti-Vandals, WadeSimMiser, Wakawakadis, Wambochimambo, Ward3001, Warregubbi, Washburnmav, Watchmenwatch, Waterproof00, Werewolfzoo, Wes sam brown, West.andrew.g, WhatGuy, Whitemist101, WikHead, Wiki Raja, WikiEditor44, WikiMaster500, WikiSpector, Wilburthepig, WildMIKE123, WildcatMaster3000, Willking1979, Willy555666, Wirelessxyz, Wisebubi, Wixer398, WizMagno, Wizard113, Wknight94, Woogee, Woohookitty, Wowaconia, Wreckedd08, Wrexham25, Wuhwuzdat, X!, Xp54321, XxXFabul0usXxX, Xxshaggy9xx, YOYO134, Yamakiri, Yaniskir Aroht, Yankeesrj12, Ycbaby619, Yngvarr, Yoguy11, Yort-8-dean, Yugiduelslikeanamateur, Yugioh1126, ZSoraz, Zachary115, Zachlipton, Zacsmiledtridely, ZanessaYay, Zarahussain, Zhou Yu, Zhouf12, Zoeadorable1778, ZooFari, Zordon123456789mlw7, Zt93, Zulrock, Zyalover, Île flottante, Žiedas, 5133 anonymous edits

Another Cinderella Story *Source*: http://en.wikipedia.org/w/index.php?oldid=401755142 *Contributors*: A3RO, ABF, Abby 94, Acather96, Ageton, Alansohn, Altarep, Anythingspossibleforapossible, Arnell2010, Aspects, Babyjazspanail, Bart133, Billy4kate, Blahbalhcookies, Blahblahblahcookies, BloodDoll, BlueSquadronRaven, Bobo192, Brittflick 1994, Bucephalus, C.Fred, Calle, Calliegal, Carrie2002, Chamal N, CharmaineLim, Classicjazzbari, Cliffordlw, Cliffordlw1, Coozbi, DantODB, Dbunkley6, Dennissell, DerHexer, Discospinster, Djbj16, Don-Don, Download, Drbreznjev, DreamStar05, Drmies, Duncan, ESMIMMAS, Eeekster, Eric444, Erik, Excirial, FDJoshua22, FF2010, Fishhook, Flewis, Frehley, Furuba9, Fæ, GLaDOS, Gdaly7, Geekboy6, Gersende, Gfoley4, Gnowxilef, GoPurpleNGold24, Gogo Dodo, Granpuff, Haein45, Happysailor, Harley doggie 1, Haseo9999, Headstrong neiva, Heisenbergthechemist, High School Musical909, Holiday56, Iknow23, Iloveyoohxx89, Imnotminkus, Ipodnano05, Iridescent, J.delanoy, JaimeAnnaMoore, Jake Wartenberg, Jason.cinema, JavierMC, Jayce0814, Jezreelver, Jobella21, JodyB, Johnny0929, Justinbieberonetime, Jwein, Khunglongcon, Kikkokalabud, Kimijonas, Kww, Kylexy93, LAUGH90, La Pianista, LeaveSleaves, Legoman64, Life=Randomness, Limetolime, Lolalol1234567899, Longhair, Loveandberry411, Luisj07, Luna Santin, Lyveluvlyfe, Malcolmxl5, Maldek2, Maludancer4, Materialscientist, Mbmbmb123456789, Mzbartlett, Nagy, Nathan, Nathanial1987, Nathanvd, Ndenison, NeoBatfreak, Neurolysis, Nickmd, Nikiangelz, NorthernThunder, NuclearWarfare, Oddharmonic, Oky103, OlEnglish, PC78, Pau4me, Philip Trueman, Piano non troppo, Pinethicket, Pinkadelica, Plastikspork, Poct, Pokerdance, Pop princess 1, QuasyBoy, Randolph3, ReginaRing12, Reiner rubin, Rich Farmbrough, RickyYayo3, Rrburke, S h i v a (Visnu), Secvan henshall, Setsuna29, ShadowRanger, Shadzane, ShazzaBabyxo, Soccerdud, Southsloper, Spellcast, Sprite7868, Steam5, Sugar1996, SummerPhD, Supertalies, TDC99, TPIRFanSteve, Tabletop, The Thing That Should Not Be, TheMovieBuff, Thingg, Tigressoflndia, TracyLinkEdnaVelmaPenny, Treasure12347890, TreoBoy680, Triwbe, Underworldon345, Versus22, Weeliljimmy, WikiPikiUser, Woohookitty, Xtinadbest, Zhou Yu, ZooFari, 621 anonymous edits

Princess Protection Program *Source*: http://en.wikipedia.org/w/index.php?oldid=402008673 *Contributors*: Acebloo, Adrian Parratt, Adyniz, Agash C, Alec2011, Alexa 4949, Alfred Lau, AlohaServed, Americanhero, Ammubhave, Angel OF Kool, Aspects, Ayush J, BD2412, BabyFacee914, BaldMonkey, Benscripps, Biodin, Blaloupasous, Bleelow, Bobo192, Bovineboy2008, Brat1234567890, Brianga, Britneyistoxic, BsaPR1996, Carlitohm11, Chane 815, Chaoticfluffy, CharlesCasiraghi, Chunghoto, Cncxbox, Colleen8463, Couturegalx3, Cssiitcic, DaBomb619, DaniDF1995, DanielAguilar, DantODB, Debresser, Deepthi d, Disneygalxx123+abc, DrDoog, Dydy23, Easy12345, Edna23, Edtatem, Emilyfromnz, Es.ntp, FFall1986, Falkonry, Fixer23, Flowerpotman, Flying thoughts, FrankTobia, Frehley, Gabrebenque, Gdaly7, Geekboy6, Glane23, GoPurpleNGold24, Gracelouisad, Gracie1008, Grafen, GroovySandwich, Hannahcrazy, Hoomanator, Hqb, Huntster, Info002, Ipodnano05, J.delanoy, JDHWIKI, Jalma04, JamieS93, Jannah 09, Jayce0814, Jemily4ever, Johnny0929, Kelly maddie, Kingpin13, Krisallenno1fanindaworld, Kww, LalalandxDemi, Lazytv8, LeaveSleaves, Leonardo Andres Sánchez, Liquidluck, Little Mountain 5, Littletung, LiveInLove20, Loborocky, Logical Fuzz, Lotje, Lovesongs41, MBisanz, MacGyverMagic, Madhero88, MadiieLovegood285, Magioladitis, Mahnoor moon, Man of I-Mages, Maxgab, McSly, Mianghuei, MichaelQSchmidt, Mild Bill Hiccup, Mrschimpf, Msmyth, NarSakSasLee, NarutoD444, Natexpress13, NawlinWiki, Nikiangelz, Nikofeelan, Ninjawarriordex, NrDg, OffiMcSpin, OliverOken123, PeterSymonds, PhilKnight, Pigby, Pinoiboi23, Pokerdance, Proofreader77, Puppies dressed as cats, Qpally, QuasyBoy, Quique217, RBD22, Randolph3, Ratemonth, Rockin56, Roy1944, Rysiu18, S h i v a (Visnu), Schank1234, ScottMHoward, Selaromar, Seldemlovgom, Selenagomezfan12345, Ser Amantio di Nicolao, Setsuna29, Shego123, Sky Captain, Smijes08, Smileygirl14, Spears154, Staka, Steam5, Stunna Shades, Suffusion of Yellow, SummerPhD, SweetPinkCandy, THUYNGA, Techman224, The Thing That Should Not Be, ThomasAnime, Trusilver, Tsluecke, TunnelSnakesRule, Tweetsabird, Twistedspikers, Tyw7, USN1977, Ulric1313, Vitbjorn, WikipedianMarlith, Wikisergiowiki, WinterChocolatt, WizMagno, Writergirlrocks, Yankeesrj12, Éovart Caçeir, 740 anonymous edits

Beezus Quimby *Source*: http://en.wikipedia.org/w/index.php?oldid=401513346 *Contributors*: AlbertGray, All Hallow's Wraith, Amchow78, Bearcat, CommonsDelinker, Confession0791, David Gerard, Demihannahselenamiley1234, Dogman15, Gertie1999, Gyrofrog, Hugo999, Iowamutt, Levk1, LucyNarnia101, Malcolma, Milerz91, Miss Dark, Peregrine Fisher, PreciousStar26, RHaworth, Rich Farmbrough, Sassbucket, Seraphimblade, ShelfSkewed, Skulligan, TheMovieBuff, 46 anonymous edits

Ramona and Beezus *Source*: http://en.wikipedia.org/w/index.php?oldid=401070263 *Contributors*: 1Matt20, AbsoluteGleek92, After Midnight, Agiseb, Airplaneman, Alexjonathan, All Hallow's Wraith, Alliance Entertainment, Awiseman, Axxonnfire, Bencey, BenjyBoy2000, Bigjehart2009, Bovineboy2008, C.Fred, Charlola99, Cooliogal212, Cventura25, Dbunkley6,

Ddlovatofan, DemiRox, Diem nguyen, Download, E2eamon, Esprqii, Filmested, Flomen, Formula 86, Freshh, Frostandchill, Funandtrvl, GD 6041, GabrielEdnuelle15, Gertie1999, GiovyGabrielEd, Gnowxilef, Honey Bee Real, Iknow23, ItsTheClimb17, Jayce0814, JohnDorianyeah, Johnny0929, Jweiss11, Kidinstreet, Klasky-Csupo, Kww, L-l-CLK-l-l, Lena Cops, Maddog11111, Mandy443, Mannafredo, Matty-chan, Mccabe86, Melfurd, MikeAllen, Mistersims31, MithrandirAgain, My76Strat, Mzfly23, Nathan and the Gang, Nathan92295, NeoBatfreak, OrangeDog, PMDrive1061, Pernelldh, Prolog, Propaniac, Pwt898, Quasihuman, QuasyBoy, RaNsOmGiiiirl, RamonaBeezus, Randolph3, Reach Out to the Truth, Reconsider the static, Regancy42, RickyYayo3, Riverstepstonegirl, Rmosler2100, Robert Moore, Rockin56, Roelsu, Roselily6, Rrburke, Salamurai, SelGKT, Setsuna29, ShuffleStop, Spears154, Supersmashbrawl, Teknocrat123, TennageDesire, TheMovieBuff, TheValentineBros, Tide rolls, Tocool678, Tweetsabird, Usb10, Vickers830, WikHead, Wikipelli, Woohookitty, XenonX3, Xoxjloveleexox, Z57N, 340 anonymous edits

Selena Gomez & the Scene *Source*: http://en.wikipedia.org/w/index.php?oldid=402004805 *Contributors*: 2006griffin, 4twenty42o, Ablebreak, Agusx12, Aka042, Alansohn, Aldeeanehh, Alexshunn, Alvinlala, Amunoz928, AndrewN, Andy Munoz, Autoerrant, Avicennasis, BD2412, Babyjazspanail, Backtable, Beverlyhillsx, Bigjehart2009, Binko711, Bongwarrior, Boomshadow, Briannaisbeast123, C.Fred, CambridgeBayWeather, Candyo32, Caru2, CharmedFreak123, CheMechanical, Cheriepoon, Churaru, Circusstar, ClamDip, CloversMallRat, Compact97, Courcelles, Dannychatterjee, DantODB, Ddlovatofan, Deaneconomos, Decodet, Diem nguyen, Easy12345, Edgar181, Either way, Elizium23, EnDaLeCoMpLeX, Ending-start, EoGuy, Erikhansson1, Expomarker11, Falcon8765, Famemonster123, Fetchcomms, Firsfron, Funnysox24, GabrielEdnuelle15, Gene93k, Geoffica Swanson, Gimmetrow, GiovyGabrielEd, GiovyGabrielEd15, Giovyed, GoingBatty, Goodvac, Greatpham, Harry McGuire, Hashlimaslah1, Heenotheducky, Iknow23, Imaginart, Imperial Monarch, Intelligentsium, Iridescent, JForget, JNW, Jeff G., Jerove, JohnFromPinckney, Jonhmayer-fã, Joseph (Bowen) Ferri, Jrs1200, Julia mate, Jusdafax, Kww, L Kensington, Laurinemall, Leiijonas, Lesleyofficialp, LilHelpa, Lim0010, Lotus Wolf, Manuelle Magnus, Masqblood, Merynancy, Mikayladee44, Musicalsuperstar, Mzfly23, Natevd95, Ncmvocalist, NichlausRN, Nymf, Nyttend, Orthoepy, Panterabecoming, Pedro João, PixieLottFan, Plastikspork, Pointer1, Pvae, QuasyBoy, R'n'B, Rafatisd, Renesemee, Robert Moore, Rokata96, Ronhjones, Roselily6, ScottMHoward, Seasky123456, SelGKT, SelGomez354, SelenaGomez111, Selenagomezhater, Selenaismylife555, Sethjohnson95, Silvergoat, Sirius85, Skier Dude, Slon02, Smithj22, Snowolf, Soccergirl788, Starsking, Taylorselenataylor, Tbhotch, Theburning25, Tide rolls, Tinton5, Tommy2010, Turian, TylerBarlow, Vickyswiki, Vitorvicentevalente, Waterfox, Welsh, WikHead, Wompwompafonso, Woohookitty, Xxheymickeyxx, Xxomgitsmimizxx, Zacharee, Zacman9, 577 anonymous edits

Barney & Friends *Source*: http://en.wikipedia.org/w/index.php?oldid=401857628 *Contributors*: (jarbarf), -=Mega Man=-, 23skidoo, 334455gmail, A cimino, A gx7, Aaron Schulz, Aaronkavo, Abby 94, Abby 96, Adam Scott 89, Adashiel, Adik2ha, Ae jeans, Airplaneman, Alai, Alakey2010, Alansohn, Albegood, Alex B. Goode, Alex0274, Algebra, Alias Flood, Alphachimp, Alshaheen15, Aluisios, Alynna Kasmira, Amoscare, Andrewpmk, Andy Bugay, AngelMeiru, AngelOfSadness, Anger22, Angie Y., Angrygurl2007, Animoviera14, Anonymous Dissident, Another-anomaly, Anthopos, Antidonnie, Antipode, Antonio cruzazul, Apple1013, Aranherunar, Arashamedani, Arthur Ellis, AuburnPilot, Aude, Autobahnz, AxG, Ayrton Prost, AzaToth, Azumanga1, BNLfan53, BQZip01, Babygoweewee, Bachrach44, Bantosh, BarkerJr, Barnyard JHod, Barrettmagic, Bart133, Bayyoc, Bdelisle, Bearcat, Beeblebrox, Beemer69, Belinrahs, Beto, Bettedewitez, Bevers93, Biederman, BigH-11, Bill37212, Billiken, BinaryTed, Birdym2003, Biseup, Bjelleklang, Blankfaze, Blargman24, Blue Danube, BlueMario1016, Bluebr5555, Bmarty11, Bmicomp, Bobisbob, Bobo192, Boogyman1, Booksworm, Bovineboy2008, Brajamine, Bratsche, Brian Crawford, BruceGrubb, Bryanwillett, Buchanan-Hermit, Bucketsofg, BulsaraAndDeacon, Burner0718, Burrito84, Butros, Butters0422, Buxarentor, CT Cooper, Caladria Napea, Call me Bubba, Caller-X, CambridgeBayWeather, Can't sleep, clown will eat me, CanadianCaesar, Canderson7, CardinalDan, Carl.bunderson, Casey J. Morris, Caster23, Catrix12, Ccosta, Ch'marr, Chanting Fox, Chase me ladies, I'm the Cavalry, Chazza125, Cheese831, Chick Bowen, Chimpchunk1, ChipmunkRaccoon, Chirpy123abc, Chris the speller, Chriscool334, Christopher Parham, Citicat, Citizen Premier, CobraWiki, Codyfinke6, Coolboy818, Cooler2445, CountPenguin, Cpastern, Crash Underride, Crazed666, CrazyInSane, CrazyLegsKC, CreamOfTheCrop, Crocitto49, CryptoDerk, Csari, Curps, Cyan, DJ BatWave, DJ Zephora, DVD R W, Da Pwnzer, DaMo, DaProx, Daa89563, Damian Yerrick, Dan East, Dan100, Dan390, Dan729, Danaman5, Daniel, Daniel Case, Danieljuravsky, Danteorange2012, David Schaich, Dawn Bard, Dcelano, Dcljr, Ddb4070, Dduvjfa9, Deadcorpse, Deathawk, Decade03, Deflagro, Delirium, Deltabeignet, Demidivinity, Dentsai, Deprifry, Derktar, Dillio917294791234, Dina, Discospinster, Dl2000, Dlohcierekim's sock, Dockevin, DoctorWho42, Dogg1243, Dontgotnoname, Donut dog, Doody 09, Downwards, Doyledude547, Dp462090, DragonBlazer57, Dreadstar, Drew Pickles 45, Drew Pickles Is Cool!, Drewpicklesfan98, Drknexus, Druidhills, Dustpelt96, Dwanyewest, Dwp49423, DylanGeck123, Dysepsion, Dysprosia, EEMIV, ESkog, Eddywasonofcumberland, Edenc1, Edited by you, Eik Corell, Eje211, ElKevbo, Elakhna, Elmo12456, Emersoni, EmoMan13, Emurphy42, EngineerScotty, Enkauston, Enviroboy, Epbr123, Equanimity, Erebus555, Erik.sg, Essjay, EstebanF, Etron81, Evaulator, Evercat, Everyking, Evilwill2, FF2010, Fair Deal, Falconleaf, Famspear, Fan-1967, Fanzachstic, Fastrerb, FatM1ke, Fearmeforiamdeath, Feitclub, Feliciaisscinas, Filceolaire, Finkefamily, Finngall, FirefoxRocks, Fireplace, Firsfron, Fisher 81, FisherQueen, Flummery, Foregone conclusion, Fosnez, Francs2000, Freakofnurture, Frecklefoot, Freddydsfgg, Fredrik, FreeKresge, Freeleet, Friday, Frosty0814snowman, Frungi, Fualkner Asiniti, Fun guy 3, Furrykef, GD1223, GHe, Gabriel mark, Garion96, Gary King, Gatorosa, Gazman567, GeorgeMoney VandalProof, Georgia guy, Gettingtoit, Giant Blue Anteater, Gilliam, Gladys j cortez, Glaxanax, Glen, GoPurpleNGold24, Gods10rules, Gogo Dodo, Golbez, Goldlw1, Goramona, Goteboat, GraemeL, Grandmasterka, Grandpafootsoldier, Green1234, Greendaynator, Greeves, Ground Zero, Gurch, Gwernol, Gzuckier, HJ Mitchell, Hackah, Hadal, Hagerman, Hailey C. Shannon, HalJor, HalfShadow, Handface, HappyCamper, Harej, Hatmatbbat10, Haukurth, Haxxor1888, Heartagrammatic, HeatherSM, Heimstern, Hellothere21, Hermeneus, Hinotori, Hisworldizxtreme, Hmr, Hnsampat, Hondasaregood, Howcheng, Hq3473, Husond, Hydraton31, Ian Pitchford, Iapetus, Icairns, IceManNJD, Icecube505, Igotsomeapples, Iluvteletubbies, Insanity Incarnate, InvisibleK, Iridescent, Irishguy, IronChris, Isotope23, J Di, J Milburn, J04n, JASBarney3, JCarriker, JForget, JRHorse, JSpung, JYOuyang, Jacob97321, JahMarley & The Boys, James Weeks, Jammingothicfreak, Jayjg, Jedi Master Dil, Jersey Devil, JesseGarrett, Jetfire85, Jetpower45, Jfitts, Jhinman, Jihad man, Jmlk17, JoeyDawgJAC, John Reid, Johnleemk, JohnsonMahogany, Jonghyunchung, JordanSamuels, Josborne2382, Jose philapino, Josh Parris, Joshua H-Star-R, JoshuaZ, Joyous!, JpRimeXg3, Jstemperature, Jtkiefer, Juggaleaux, Junekoman, Just2day, Jwissick, K1Bond007, KJS77, KRW, KVE, KWoolley, Kaffryn, Kagome 77, Kagome 85, Kagome2008, Kal-El 2000, Karazachi, Kbthompson, Kcordina, Keegan, Kel-nage, Kelly Martin, Kencaesi, Kesac, Kesh, Khaosworks, Khoikhoi, Kidlittle, Kimal, KinseyLOL, Kirsten5400, Kitch, KnowledgeOfSelf, KojieroSaske, Kona27, Koolboi141, Kosebamse, Krich, KrunchyKrunchKrunch, KsprayDad, Kubigula, Kungfuadam, KurtRaschke, Kuru, LaLaJoey, Lady yuna, Lahs08, Lalala95, Lalalo9888, Larkspur23, Larry laptop, Laughingcat945, Lectonar, Lh80127, Lightdarkness, Lightspeedchick, Lightsup55, Linmaru, Linnell, Lionkingpwns, Live or die, LizzieBabes419, Llort, Loansince, Logoboy95returns, Longhair, Longhornsg, Lpkids2006, Lpython, Lucky 6.9, Luisedgarf, Luna Santin, Lunellaysunni, MBisanz, MER-C, MLRoach, MZMcBride, Madchester, Magicmage, Magister Mathematicae, Magog the Ogre 2, Mailer diablo, Majorclanger, Majorly, MakeRocketGoNow, Malo, Mangojuice, Marineman400, MarjorieCook, Markendust, Martin Hinks, Marychelle, Marysunshine, Master Jay, Mattcraft, Mattderojas, Maxamegalon2000, Maxis ftw, Mayme08, Mbenzdabest, Me myself & er, Measure, Megafonico, Megaman en m, MegastarLV, Megathon7, Megatronacepticon, Melesse, Mercinary, Meteordes, Metzby, Meweight, Mewtwowimmer, Michael B. Trausch, Michael Voytinsky, Michaelbusch, Mike (usurped), Mike Rosoft, Mikebuer, Mikethecoolloser, Mikhailov Kusserow, Millahnna, Milliken, Millionsandbillions, Mimihitam, Mindspillage, Mirv, Mithent, Mjen52, Mjpieters, Mjrmtg, Mms, Modulatum, Moe Epsilon, Moguera, Monkeydoodle122, Monkeydoodle123, Monkeyman, Monkeys rule 99, Moocowsrule, Mooman72v2, Mophoplz, MosheA, MovieMan123, Mr Adequate, Mr Stephen, Mr Tan, Mr.Z-man, Mrschimpf, Mrtgrady, Mufka, Mynameiscliff, Nakon, NapVan, Narutard10, Narutochaos, Nate Speed, NawlinWiki, Nbagigafreak, Neander7hal, Neelix, NeilN, Nerd05, Neurolysis, Neverquick, NickBush24, Nickptar, Nikabelar, Nintendo Maximus, Nishkid64, No Guru, Noeminewton, Nol888, Norm mit, NorseOdin, Ntropolis, Nughty54245452, Nwwaew, OOODDD, Ollie the Magic Skater, Omega user, Omicronpersei8, Omphaloscope, Omtay38, OrangeDog, Otto4711, OwenX, PDH, Pais, Patinthehat1, Paul August, Paul mccartney, PaulGS, Pbandj, Pearle, Penguinpc, Persian Poet Gal, Peruvianllama, Peter Fleet, Pgk, Philippe, Philipsutherland, Piggywiggy2446, Pigslookfunny, Pikawil, Pilotguy, Pimpinclown24, Pinkgothic, Plainnym, Plau, Poorleno, Porqin, Powergate92, PrimeCupEevee, Princess kitty, ProhibitOnions, Proteus, Protozoic Waste, ProveIt, PseudoSudo, Psy guy, Pumpinplatta, Punkrokgrl, PurpleRain, Quaque, QuasyBoy, Queen kitten, Quickbeam, Quicksandish, Qwerty Binary, R.E. Freak, RAWRMAN, RJWiki27, RJaguar3, Rabbit 20, Rachel Cakes, RainR, Ram-Man, RandomOrca2, Rb26dett, Rebochan, Reconsider the static, Redvers, Redwolf24, ResonantOne, Retired username, RexNL, Rgrizza, Rhobite, Riana, Rich Farmbrough, Richhoncho, RickK, Ripkenfan86, Riverhead, Rizzleboffin, Rjm656s, Road Village, Road Wizard, Robchurch, Robert Merkel, RobertG, Rockstrock, Rod14, Roman Bay, Rory096, RoyBoy, Royalguard11, Rray, Rukia-chan, Runewiki777, Ryan Holloway, S-mchurls05, SEJohnston, SMP0328., Sadfgsdfg, Sailorknightwing, Salexb, Sango123, Saturn 44, Savo187, Scarian, Sceptre, Scientizzle, Sciocco123, Scohoust, Scottmsg, Scoty6776, Sean345, Seattlenow, Secfan, Semperf, Sephy26946, Sgeureka, ShadeofTime09, Shadow ken 42, Shadow rocks101, ShadowKittyKat, Shadowmario64fan, ShadowyCaballero, Shadzar2, Shalomdom, Shang912345, SharkEmpress01, ShaunES, Sheepo39, Shreshth91, Sillstaw, Simfake, SimonP, Simulation12, SinkingDiamond, Sir Vicious, Siroxo, Skeet954, Skier Dude, Skoosh, Smably, Smalljim, Smurffart, Snackypcrackers, SodiumHydroxide, Sokir4, Solipsist, SonicHOG, Sopranosmob781, Soundwave106, SpectrumDT, Spiderpigpagano, Splat, Split, Spobmur, Srborlongan, Srleffler, Srushe, Stacerific, Stalkerman, StaticGull, Steel, Steelersfan2, Stefani, Stefano KALB, Stormie, Stubblyhead, Sunshine rocks101, SuperDude115, Supertyper, Survlv4l1st, Swimm212, Sycthos, Symmetry, T66T, TNTfan101, TTN, TVfanatic2K, Tabercil, Tangotango, Tanthalas39, Tapir Terrific, Tassedethe, Tavix, Tawniz, TedE, Tedius Zanarukando, Terence, Terraguy, Tesi1700, TgreatALL, Thanatosimii, Thatdog, The Anome, The Arachnid, The Dark, The Kirby, The Powerful, The Rogue Penguin, TheAllSeeingEye, TheCustomOfLife, TheKMan, TheMovieBuff, TheiGuard, Themasterofwiki, Therealmikelvee, Theunicyclegirl, Thiswontgowell, Tide rolls, Tigerbreath13, Timothy Chavis, Tinlion09, Tmopkisn, Tom, Tom harrison, TomGesq, Tomballguy, Tomber, Tony1, Trainfan01, Trav256536, Tree Biting Conspiracy, Tregoweth, Trevor MacInnis, Trixen, TtothelMMYY, Ttwaring, Two Bananas, U.S.A.U.S.A.U.S.A., UberScienceNerd, Ugur Basak, Upholder, UsahName, UtherSRG, Uyanga, Valhallia, Veinor, ViolinGirl, Viraljuice, VonRojohnRubio, Wafulz, Waggers, WayKurat, Weatherman87, Websurfer246, Wellsdebater, Wenli, WereSpielChequers, Wertdunk999, Wexquif, Weyes, WhisperToMe, Whitetiger01, Whomp, Wi-king, Wiki alf, Wikibofh, Wikipedian64, Wikipediarules2221, Wildthing61476, Wilemon23, Will-Martins, Will122194, Wiwaxia, Wizardman, Wknight94, Woohookitty, WpZurp, Wrinehart, Xerto757, Xizer, Xubelox, Xxatreyuxx, Xzillerationer, Y0u, YUL89YYZ, Yepieelya, Yfighter2, Yo-Yo Man, YohemJar630, Yomangani, Yossarian, Yugiduelslikeanamateur, Zalgo, Zanimum, Zephyr103, Ziva David, Zordrac, Zsinj, Zzyzx11, Шизомби, 1441 anonymous edits

Tinker Bell (film) *Source*: http://en.wikipedia.org/w/index.php?oldid=398166440 *Contributors*: 3DFan101, Angie Y., AnmaFinotera, Ardavu, AshTFrankFurter2, Atama, AtomicAge, Benzy19, BigBoy8701, Bisbis, Bluejay berry, Bobistall, Bovineboy2008, Bronks, Calor, Can't sleep, clown will eat me, Casbboy, Celtic fiddler, Chris1219, Chriswolvie, Colonies Chris, Darkness2005, Dewelar, Dgoldwas, DisneyMania, Disneymaniac18, Dmcman, Doomstink, DuaneThomas, DutchDevil, Dycedarg, Eagle eyes, Eddie Cruise, Erianna, Esn, FigmentJedi, Finister2, FriscoKnight, Gabrielkat, Garion96, Geniac, Giant Ken's Glowball, Gr8person, Grey Matter, Headstrong neiva, Honkerpeck, Insanity Incarnate, Ioeth, Jacobsnchz, Jamesbanesmith, JasonAQuest, Jasonbres, Jock Boy, Johnlongbond, JuJube, Jvsett, Kagome 77, Kasper2006, Kbdank71, Kww, Lampbane, Li'l Shooter, Libcub, Libro0, Lighthope, Lord Opeth, Macslost, MakeLove91, Malcolmxl5, MarkBanks92, Maverick9711, Mikani, Milerz91, Movingimage, NMS Bill, Nemeses9, NoseNuggets, Purgatory Fubar, QuasyBoy, Quidam65, RLipstock, RainbowWerewolf, Rayhana, Really21, Rich Farmbrough, Roaring Siren, RobJ1981, SMG055, Scam Guy, SchuminWeb, Shadzane, Shniken1, SidP, Sinsia, Sionus, Sirius85, Spyderchan, Squids and Chips, Steam5, StephenBuxton, Subcelestial, TMC1982, Tabletop, Tanthalas39, Tenchichan, Test3, TheMovieBuff, TimBentley, Touchpath, Tregoweth, VML, Versmilitude, WIKI-GUY-16, Wowaconia, Xario, Yamh91, Ziva David, 157 anonymous edits

Spy Kids 3-D: Game Over *Source*: http://en.wikipedia.org/w/index.php?oldid=401942564 *Contributors*: 152.163.xx.xx, AB, AdultSwim, Albmont, Alison22, Andrzejbanas, Arrowsparrow, Asml8d, Aspects, Avillalvazo6475, Bardiak, Bencey, Benjaminso, Blu-Gruff, Bobo192, Bovineboy2008, BsaPR1996, Calebaldwinjun9, Can't sleep, clown will eat me, Casper's Glowball, Ceauntay38, CharlieRCD, Cheddarjack, Chris1219, Ckatz, Closedmouth, Codyfinke6, Cometstyles, ContiAWB, Dctrdr, Deavenger, DellTG5, Demi818, Digata200, Dihiddy, Don9-dk, Donald McKinney, DoomGeek, Doshindude, E.M., EoGuy, Erik, Evilgidgit, Falphin, Fan of u, Fortdj33, Frankenpuppy, Freshh, Gaius Cornelius, Gdaly93, Gmaspoiledbrat, Granpuff, Green Kirby, Groovenstein, Guanaco, Hallpriest9, Harry Blue5, Hephaestos, Hmains, Hornean, Hoverfish, Hybrid Guy, Hydrogen Iodide, Hyperion777, Insanity Incarnate, Inspector 34, Intelligentsium, ItsTheClimb17, J Greb, J.delanoy, JNW, Jacrio, Jadentheman, Janadore, Jay-r101, Jnelson09, Joe Sewell, Joeinpz, Jthm53, Juan Cruz, Keraunoscopia, KiasuKiasiMan, Kintetsubuffalo, Knowledgesmith, Kuralyov, LilHelpa, Lily122, Liquidluck, Littledanno, Lmvp990766271, Lord Crayak, Lord Seth, Macrophone Guy, Mandarax, Martin451, MartinHarper, Mattymoo16., Mboverload, Metal Sonic PL, Michael, Misterkillboy, Mojo15, MonoAV, Mr. Hi-Hi de Lo-Lo, Mw66, NativeForeigner, NawlinWiki, Nezickson, NrDg, OG Loc 246, Owayda, Plastikspork, Pokerdance, Possum, Postcardsaremine, Prepelos, Pzmrz, RainbowWerewolf, Rmosler2100, Rtkat3, Rubixmike14, Rumble Guy, Rypcord, Ryulong, SMC, Sam Korn, Sbamkmfdmdfmk, ScribbleKid, Sexy Back 16, Shadowjams, Sipi1230, Skier Dude, Smurfy, Sprite7868, Stemonitis, Super Rad!, TKD, Taylor Karras, TexasAndroid, The.super.guy123, Thedarxide, Themeparkgc, Tide rolls, TigerK 69, TracyLinkEdnaVelmaPenny, Tregoweth, TreoBoy680, Trusilver, Vader200591, Vegetable man38, VerasGunn, Violetriga, WereSpielChequers, Wisekwai, X0ilov3him14x0, Yinyang1195, Yos233, Zer0431, 440 anonymous edits

Horton Hears a Who! (film) *Source*: http://en.wikipedia.org/w/index.php?oldid=401922560 *Contributors*: AKR619, AWeenieMan, Abce2, Abefoulkes, Abrech, Acebloo, Advanced, Aitias, Alansohn, AlbertSM, Alex2631, Alexf, Allen4names, Allsaints23, Andromedabluesphere440, Andromine, Andrzejbanas, Andycjp, Angel caboodle, AniMate, Anticipation of a New Lover's Arrival, The, Aomd, Apple1013, ArchonMagnus, Arkyopterix, Art1991, AshTFrankFurter2, Asifsys23, Aswomekid122, Atlan, Avelinforl32, Avoided, Babyboy808, Badonkadonkhr, Bat12, Batman Fan, Bdve, Beach drifter, Bella Swan, Bender235, Benzy19, Betterthanbond, Beve, Bewareofdog, BigBang616, Bigkeyshawn, Bill bo, BirgitteSB, Blueliteway, Bobo192, Bostongal247, BoulderDrop, Bovineboy2008, Boygenius97, Braza258, Brclmu, Brianhenke, Brookie, CBFan, CWY2190, Caet, Cahk, Caloscalante1518, Calvin 1998, Cartoon Boy, Cat's Tuxedo, Catcher Block, Catgut, Cheddarjack, Christian Swenson, Christianster45, Clarince63, Closedmouth, Cnota, Conny, Coralmizu, CraigFoye80, D6, Dacman6688, DaffyDuck619, DanMat6288, Danielfolsom, Danski14, Dark Prime, Dav93Lov, DavidDCM, Davie400, Dcfreak114, DeadlyTaco, Deanb, DerHexer, Derrty2033, Discospinster, DisneyLover41, Dlwr300, Dmane1, Dmurawski, DocNox, Dougmcarthur0, Dr.Quentin X. Mathews, DrBat, Drewdy, Dycedarg, Dynesclan, Edward cookie cutter, Eeeppp, Elendil's Heir, Elephant Talk, Empezardesdecero1718, EoGuy, EoinMahon, Errorlines, Esn, Eternal Pink, Eumolpo, EwanMclean2005, Fbv65edel, Frekeeehobo, Frightwolf, FriscoKnight, Frymaster, FuriousFreddy, Gabrielkat, Gail, Gary King, Genedecanter, Gnowxilef, Goa103, Gobonobo, Gogo Dodo, GoingBatty, Gojira09, GrahamHardy, Gran2, Grandpafootsoldier, Granpuff, Green Sheet, Green caterpillar, Gregfitzy, Gtr57, Guy1423, Haon 2.0, Headstrong neiva, Hectorferjr2, Hyrulian93, Immblueversion, Iridescent, Irishguy, Irk, J.delanoy, J4musicals, JCO, JPG-GR, JacksonMiller, Jacob valliere, Jake Wartenberg, JamesBWatson, Jarrod Baniqued, Jasonbres, JayKeaton, Jayce0814, Jayron32, Jaz246, JeanColumbia, Jeremiah2man, Joshschr, JudgeSpear, Jusdafax, JustSomeRandomGuy32, Kakofonous, Kanonkas, Karl-a-mon, Katalaveno, Kchishol1970, King0fpenguins, Kintetsubuffalo, Kollision, Krismorel, Kubrick, Kww, LDEJRuff, Leonidas23, LilHelpa, Limetolime, Limonns, LinkToddMcLovinMontana, Lipton sale, LiteraryMaven, Madmardigan53, Magicboy666, Magioladitis, Malinaccier, Markyopp, Mathew5000, Meegs, Mice never shop, MilborneOne, Milonica, MissSox, Mlaffs, MonkeeJuice, Morpose, Mouse's Ear, MovieRatIan, Movieguru2006, Movingimage, Mr. Absurd, Mr.Knox, MrBumpFan, Muerte, Mwpich, Myscrnnm, N. Harmonik, NJZombie, Nargis 2008, NawlinWiki, Ndboy, Nedloyd1970, Nehrams2020, Neorge, Nikofeelan, Nips, Noclevername, Norcaldaydreamer, NoriMori, NotNina, NrDg, Nshady16, ObsessiveJoBroDisorder, Oerjan, Oofpoot, Ortizurzaiz, Ottovonguericke, Pascal.Tesson, Patrick, Paulley, Pb12, Pegship, Philip Trueman, Phoenix1304, Phydend, Pixelface, Pizzadinosaur, Polarbear97, Powerofjuju, Psychonaut3000, Pyrrhus16, RJaguar3, RMikes, Rabidanimals, Re non verbis, Renaissancee, Reptoid333, RevWaldo, Rgoodermote, Rhindle The Red, Rockysmile11, Roth 300, Rtkat3, Ryan Holloway, Ryan the Game Master, SAkora1, Salamurai, Salvio301, Sandcastle84, SausageSandwich, Scarian, Schmiteye, SchnitzelMannGreek, Schultmc, Sesshomaru, Seussfan, Shadowagent 0, Shawisland, Shorespirit, SiameseSoul, SidP, SideshowBob99, Silent Tom, Silvlasdfj, Sjones23, SkyWalker, Smalljim, Snowman Guy, Soccerdud, Soetermans, Sorabond007, Spellmaster, SpikeJones, Spmonahan, Springnuts, SquidSK, Ste1n, Stealth500, Steven Zhang, Stfu Roy, Stwalkerster, Sugarlandfanatic, SummaBritt, Sunil060902, Swiftink, TMC1982, Tabletop, Tacrolimuses, TaerkastUA, Tango, Tb4000, Tech408, The Arachnid, The Evil Spartan, The Obfuscator, The Rogue Penguin, The Swagga, TheGoldStandard, TheRealFennShysa, TheValentineBros, TheXenocide, Thecomedian, Thewikipopo, Thingg, Tiddly Tom, Tide rolls, Tkynerd, Tnxman307, Toddst1, Tommyt, Tony Webster, Toughpigs, TracyLinkEdnaVelmaPenny, Tregoweth, TreyMarsh20, Twaz, Tylers2009, UK Liberal, Ub3rn008, UberMan5000, UnfriendlyFire, UrsaLinguaBWD, Uytku, Vchimpanzee, Versus22, Vidgmchtr, Viewdrix, Vuerqex, Wack'd, Websurfer246, WhisperToMe, WikHead, Wikibarista, Wikiboy243, Wikieditboy, Wile e2005, Winterheart, Wtooher, X3ni, Xflipypet3x, Xoxpeacexox, 1763 anonymous edits

Arthur and the Vengeance of Maltazard *Source*: http://en.wikipedia.org/w/index.php?oldid=335983988 *Contributors*: All Hallow's Wraith, Angie Y., Bencey, Blackgaia02, Boredblake, Bovineboy2008, Bw101, C.Fred, Chris the speller, Europacorpnewmedia, Everard Proudfoot, Freiheit 89, Iamtotallyawesome, JasonAQuest, Jevansen, JohnInDC, Kaboomboys123, Ksmplusfive, MWAK, Ndboy, NeilN, Panterabecoming, Patrick, Pedro João, Princeajb 007, Secret Saturdays, SilentGuy, SkyWalker, The White Duke, Varlaam, Wool Mintons, Zordon, 133 anonymous edits

Monte Carlo (2011 film) *Source*: http://en.wikipedia.org/w/index.php?oldid=402014387 *Contributors*: Bovineboy2008, Briddish, Churaru, Crystal Clear x3, Dekan871, Drewbieee, EoGuy, Forever awesome, GoingBatty, GroovyandPears, InfamousPrince, Jayce0814, Jerome0012, Juju 2402, Ketonali, L Kensington, Liquidluck, Mohdessam123456, Mzfly23, Oregongirl0407, Ottre, QuasyBoy, RemedyLonesome2, Ser Amantio di Nicolao, Shannon Tucker, Skier Dude, Tide rolls, Wool Mintons, Zombie433, 167 anonymous edits

Wizards of Waverly Place: The Movie *Source*: http://en.wikipedia.org/w/index.php?oldid=401974563 *Contributors*: 13.Ikim, 13.M.J.A, 190fordhouse, 1989 Rosie, 24 biggest fan, 2help, 721Tiki, A.h. king, Abdelrahman Shehata, Abdullah788, Abyss123, ActivExpression, Akcvtt, Aktsu, Alan Isherwood, Alansohn, AlbertHerring, Allmightyduck, Anakinskywalker450, Andadundi, Andrewrp, Anik Ghosh, Bakilas, Ben-Bopper, Bigaireatscheese, Biodin, Bleelow, Booczakos, Bovineboy2008, BsaPR1996, Btilm, Buraimi, C.Fred, CaRaNt11, Calmer Waters, Carlitohm11, CarlosLovers, Ceauntay59, Chane 815, CharanRANDOM, Checker Fred, Christian75, Cleavon B., Cocytus, Codywarren08, Cpl Syx, Crash Underride, D6, Daman1992, DaniDF1995, DantODB, DePiep, Debbie rocks, Debresser, DeltaQuad, Deon, DisneyChannelRussia, DisneyFriends, Dlohcierekim, Dogoan200, Donnaxlb, Download, Dramaqueenzm-s, DreamStar05, Dreambend5, Dxfan4ever, Easy12345, Eduardow10, Elio97, EoGuy, Erik9, Evncollin, FFall1986, Fakhoury2nv, Falcon8765, Felixbelize, Fetchfan88, Fireman8347193018, Futurama516, Galactic war, Gbondy, Geekboy6, Gilliam, Gimmetrow, Goku1st, Gokufistum, Good Olfactory, Gossip--girls-xoxo, GreenBayPackersfan09, HD325, Hannahcrazy, Happygogirl, Hassaan19, Hello, I'm a Wikipedian!, HexaChord, HighSchoolMusical, Hoangquan hientrang, Hurtme1992, IWannaEditWiki, Imorthodox23, Ionutzmovie, Irbisgreif, ItsTheClimb17, Itstimeformileycyrus, J.delanoy, Jake Wartenberg, JamesBWatson, Javert, Jeff G., JeffHardy1998, Jeremy1354, Joe Chill, JoeJonasMileyCyrus, Joes a g, Kah ogawa, KathyCQ, Katy85, Khut, Kingdomhearts123, Kollision, Krilleh, Kww, L Kensington, LAUGH90, LUCY1995, Leonardo Andres Sánchez, LilHelpa, Live Light, Llspiro, Lonniestabler, MakeLove91, Mariusz4477, Mark Sheridan, Mason172, Mifter, Mnbvcxz9000, Mrschimpf, Munlax, Muriloofbrazil, MylesCoulter, Mzbartlett, NMJK01060516, Nascar1996, Ncmvocalist, Nmj321, Nqs2011, NrDg, Ojay123, OliverOken123, OneWeirdDude, P Carn, PMDrive1061, Pedro João, Pedro thy master, Philip Trueman, Pikiwyn, Piper987, Pleasetalktome, Professor Fiendish, QuasyBoy, QueenCake, RIPMichaelJackson, RadioFan, Randolph3, Rankora, Reach Out to the Truth, Rockin56, Roguemaster83, RohanMalik1999, Rrburke, Rsrikanth05, Rugratsmaster, Rysiu18, SamHall01, Sarrus, SchnitzelMannGreek, Sciurinæ, Selenafan123, Shawnhath, Shego123, Shekickedmydog, Shiverting101, ShuffleStop, SiMpLyStAr975, SidCurtis10, SignoPack, Silvergoat, Smijes08, Snowflakerockz, Sophisol1, Sp604, Spears154, SpongeBobfanforlife1, Sportygirl96, Study-Of-The-Stars, SummerPhD, Sunshineisles2, SuperSecret, Swaggd Outt32, THUYNGA, Tennispro45, The Cool Kat, TheRealFennShysa, Thesuitelifeofzackandcody, Tide rolls, Tombraiderlegend, Treati, Tvdude103, Tweetsabird, Undertakerhbk588, Vader200591, Versus22, Waiwai933, Wayne Slam, WhatGuy, WizMagno, Woohookitty, Wtmitchell, Zubia14, ZydrateSupporter, 梅酒, 1161 anonymous edits

List of *The Suite Life of Zack & Cody* episodes *Source*: http://en.wikipedia.org/w/index.php?oldid=401558156 *Contributors*: 07mattrhys, 08ellisd, 0dd1, 13nov95, 1989 Rosie, 21655, 9999bryan, A, A1016neo, Abhay26, Abodas1234, Acalamari, Adambiswanger1, Adityamanutd, Aewak, AgentPeppermint, Ahmetyal, AldoNadi, Ale jrb, Alec2011, Alex.muller, Alexfusco5, Ali-Luvs-Zac, Alix195, Allied45, Amdrag568, Amie326, Andre-nico, AndrewHowse, Andrewpmk, Anhjimmy16, Anish5490, Anonymi, Anonymous Dissident, Antandrus, Anthony Appleyard, Anturiaethwr, Apparitive, Applejaxs, ArielGold, AshTFrankFurter2, Ashleyfan172, Asphatasawhale, Atg3000-thekraken, AussieLegend, Barts1a, Batman tas, Bbb2007, Bearcat, Belovedfreak, Ben-spam, Bigaireatscheese, Billysuite, BlackRanger, Blakebs, Blanchardb, BlazeFirey, Blehfu, BlitzerNatu, BlueAg09, Bluedolphin359, Bobo192, Bondiabondia, BoogerD, Bossman 08, Bovineboy2008, Brianyau323, Broadway boy 85, Buddyrod, Burg44, Burnsky55, C.Fred, COlOmBiA gIrL, CaRaNt11, Calebaldwinjun9, Calvindixon, Camile123, Candy Cridol, Candygarret, Candyo32, Cannachan, CaramelQueen, Carrie2002, Cesar1992, Cggirlpower, Cgkimpson, Chanlyn, Chase me ladies, I'm the Cavalry, Checker Fred, Chibi-mickee, Chirchona, Chircona, ChocolateCheese, Chriistiian06, Chris the speller, Christianb5, Ckimpson, Clerks, Clintonleefitz, Cloverboy19, CloversMallRat, Cmoney8, Coffee, Colee41, CollegeMan, CoolBoy-6789, Cooliogal212, Corbinb8, Cornpuppy, Cortez94, Cory Malik, Cperea1994, CrazyChemGuy, Cristan, Crocketmeow, Crogcrog, Ctjf83, Cutie546, DCFan101, Dadude3320, Daiquiri6, Dakotacoons, Dallasfan37, DanJ, DanTD, Daniagarcia, Daniel Case, Danigro89, Dannebrog Spy, DarksoulXZ22, Darth Faber, Davehi1, Dccnnn9, Dcoolmagic, DeLaSalleLipaBM204, Debuskjt, Dee1213, Deoxys911, DerHexer, Dgpink89, Diem nguyen, Digiron, Discospinster, Dismas, DisneyChannelFan015, Djandjoel, Dmdrox!, DocSigma, Doggieal1000, Doggy467, Don-Don, Don729torossi, Donagon, Dondfan998, Dragonfire EX, Drakebell xx lover, DramaQueen9118162, Dreadstar, Dsantesteban, Dthdc4, Dxdunk, Dylan Damien, Ean5533, EastHighWildcats101, Eatcacti, EdBever, Edenc1, Edokter, Eduardow10, Edward321, Elected, Eleos, Elitegirl94, Elockid, Emp395, Empezardesdecero1718, Enviroboy, Epbr123, Erased Paper, Eusebeus, Everyking, Extra Mark, Fabrictramp, Falcon8765, Fancynancy4314, FayssalF, Felipesousa, FergieFan101, Fieldday-sunday, Fighting for Justice, FinalRapture, Fish 800, Flewis, Flippytoon123, Fllmtlchcb, Flyby1300, Frankenpuppy, Friends1994, Fullmetal Ink, Furuba9, Gdo01, Gesoyrn, Ghostriderrb, Gimmetrow, Ging dong21698, Gino26, Gobonobo, Gprince007, Grafen, Granf, Grey Matter, Gunmuny, H6056, HD324, HFRS, Haemo, Hairy106, Hannahcody71197, Hannahcrazy, Hasek is the best, Hawksfan101, Hayz07, Headstrong neiva, Heatface, Hede2000, Hello32020, Hidude123, High School Musical909, Hill03, Hipzip 14, Hithere2008, Hjkgk, HorseGirl070605, HoworHow, Hsmstar14, Huntster, Husond, Huss11, I love zack and cody, Icealien33, Iciclethe828, Idol 2006, Ihrtwiki, Iloveboyds, Insertclevernamehere, Interfear2, Ionutzmovie, Iridescent, Irulagain, Ishamikey, Ixfd64, J.S.thehedgehog, JLKTENNIS43, Jaardon, Jac16888, Jack Merridew, Jackol, Jackollie, Jacob Pea, Jaga185, James327, JamesOludareFadoju, Janbirth93, Jarrett krissa, JasonXL-V2, Jasontsao1234, Jazzy910, Jedi94, Jeff Jack Hardy, JeffHardy5555, JeffW, JetLover, Jfarajr, Jimmysal, Jj137, Jmlk17, Jobe 87, John Kenneth Fisher, JollyMooly, JonasBrother1, Jorgef1, Juanacho, Juliancolton, JustAGal, KPH2293, Kablammo, Kalathalan, Katanin, Kball65, Kdkatpir2, Khfan93, Kid0015, Kieranjguy, KikiBeatz, Kikkid851, Killereditors, Kimchi.sg, KingPancake, Kinkadjou, KnowledgeOfSelf, Kodster, Koolo, Kuru, Kylexy289, LAUGH90, LAX, Langa0808, Leagreen, Legofilms2345, Level6 BM204 DeLaSalleLipa, Lightdarkness, Lightrealm, LilHelpa, Little Mountain 5, LittleDuude8, Lizziegirl96, Lkk, LlwynogCymru, Loelle24, Logical2u, Loveaozora, Lozzbub, LpSamuelm, Lucas&Ashley, Lucy53, Luigeach, MCcoupe7, MER-C, MJisnotmylover, MaddieGa, Magioladitis, Majorclanger, Malevious, Mansteel, Maquirri91, Mastertayo, Matt Hilton, Matt3327, Matthew, Mattschreiber, Mayamussa, McSly, Mcgovern01, Meaghan, Megakoolkid, Mel Etitis, Memmem, Mervn, MiguelL0pz, Mikey3497, Mikokat,

Miranda, Mitsuki3, Mjmoves, Mlf134679, Moanna, Moanster, Mohammedaqeel9, Mohsin12345, MoneyMonth, Mono, MooMoox0x12, Mproxla, Mr. College, Mr. Prez, Mspraveen, Mstatedawgs23, Muse6, Mushro0mHobo, Mynameisorange, Mysdaao, NFS Rave, Ned Scott, Need08, Neon.heart, Nicic, Nickiwilliams, Nickptar, Nicorocks9, Nihonjin Akuma, Nishkid64, Nn123645, Noahheels, Nordale36, NrDg, Nsaa, Nuggetman08, Obaidz96, ObfuscatePenguin, Ohconfucius, Ohmygodeven, OneWeirdDude, Oohoui1123, Otto4711, Ouzo, OwenX, PMDrive1061, Pa55wor6, PacBird, Pbrinco, Penguino6, Peregrine Fisher, Phanaj, Phydend, Piblup, Pikakandy, Pinkadelica, Pinkypud, Plasticup, Pokecrazy99, Ppntori, Princessseashell, Purplemonkey8899, Qsung, QuasyBoy, Rahaeli, Raine neiva, Randolph3, Raymondwinn, Raysa1, Redford500, Redmy, Reigel553, Res2216firestar, Rhindle The Red, Rhys Is The Word, Rich Farmbrough, Richardhuff, RightSideNov, Riverstepstonegirl, Rks117, Robert 47, Robth, Rodby88, Rowndin2389, Rror, Rtieu, Rtkat3, Runewiki777, Rysiu18, Ryulong, SJP, SLJCOAAATR 1, SMC, SSTwinrova, Saber girl08, Sagittarius95, Samykitty, Sanvir, Scarian, Sceptre, Schmiteye, Sd31415, Seb az86556, Sexysimba, Shanes, Shego123, ShelfSkewed, Shelfro, SideshowBob99, Signalhead, SillieStacie, SilverStar, Singer1996, SirGrant, Skateboard123, Snoborder93, Snowy Summer, Someguy1221, Sonictrey, Soronow, Spidernee, Spirals4ever, Spkonner, Spongebeb, Spongefan, Stage11, Staka, Startennis24, Static Universe, Steelcity95, Stephenjh, Steven Zhang, StewieK, Strikers5, Suduser85, Sunshine4921, Sunshineisles2, Superstar18, Switchfo0t813, Syrthiss, TG193, TJ Reyes, TSLcrazier, TTN, Tabletop, Tajtheman, Tarheelz123, Tazz765, Tcatron565, Teeple12, Temmy277, TempeBrennan, Tfkalk, The Rogue Penguin, The suite life, TheDJ, TheMinigolfMaster111, TheNewPhobia, TheOllieTrolley, TheWatchDude, Thieu Nguyen, Thorpe, Tim1357, Tiptoety, Tisdale4life, Toe202, TracyLinkEdnaVelmaPenny, Trainra, Triping, Trusilver, Txomin, USN1977, UltimatePyro, Ultra JG (es), Ultraexactzz, Ultraviolet scissor flame, UnDeRsCoRe, United Force, VI, Vangjako, Vanna51, Varlaam, Victorhariki, Vinnyvinny2, Viridae, Voyagerfan5761, Vyshy101, WAVY 10 Fan, WOSlinker, Wateverman, WeeklyJumpman, Wenli, WereSpielChequers, Wesselbindt, WhatGuy, Whatdoidoforauser, Whenoby, Wikialexdx, Wikiboy num 1, Wikilover00, Wikipe-tan, Wikireader72, Wizard113, Woohookitty, Wwefan980, Xcv47x, Xcvista, Xxgsecretagentxx, Yamla, Yankeesrj12, Yoguy11, Yoshi032192, YvetteMike, ZSoraz, Zachary115, Zackry93, Zalgo, ZanessaYay, Zelmerszoetrop, Zoom Boy 101, Zshortman, 曹孟德, 3495 anonymous edits

List of *Hannah Montana* episodes *Source*: http://en.wikipedia.org/w/index.php?oldid=401863465 *Contributors*: -Jonatinhas-, 10metreh, 117Avenue, 13.Ikim, 2D, 3jz01bcs, 5 albert square, 5xmdc7jt, A, A More Perfect Onion, AOL Alex, Aaia5, Abbyn10, Abce2, Abcw12, Abdul Islamic Enpowerment, Acather96, Accdude92, Ace of Spades, Acebulf, Acoustic Electric, Adriel001, Adryoanna, AgentPeppermint, Airhunger, Aka042, Akshayverma19, Alansohn, Albmont, Alec2011, Alessgrimal, AlexHale, Alexrules43, Ali-Luvs-Zac, Alikm, Alison, Allied45, Altarep, AlwaysUnderTheInfluence, Amalie9213, Anakinjmt, Andadundi, Andrewcmcardle, Andrewrp, Andrezilla, Android Mouse, Anish587, Anna Lincoln, Anonymous anonymous, Antandrus, Antodav2007, Aquateensown, Aremith, ArglebargleIV, Art LaPella, Art1991, AshJenny, AshTFrankFurter2, Ashleyleggat404, Asilver97ny, Astute Learner, Auntof6, AussieLegend, Avenged Eightfold, AzaToth, BPL43, BRG, Bacchus87, Bart 2110, Basti95, Bastian95, Bayerischermann, Bearcat, Beardo, Ben-spam, Bert-Healy, Best picture, Bibliomaniac15, Bigaireatscheese, Billyparkes, Biodin, Black-Velvet, Blackflyingbats, Blanchardb, BlastOButter42, Bobdisme, Bobo192, Boing! said Zebedee, Boomshadow, Bpeps, Brandon, Brandon J. Marcellus, Brandon Marcellus, Brandonrc, Bratzwq, Brian809, Brittanymouse, Brocee2000, Bsadowski1, Btilm, BubbleGumGrrl86, Bubbletea03, Bubbloe2, Burner0718, C.Fred, CBM, CP1994, Caiaffa, Caine501, Calliegal, Caltas, Calvin 1998, Camillalx, Can't sleep, clown will eat me, Canthusus, Capricorn42, Carlitohm11, Carlitohm3, Carlosar45, CastAStone, Catgut, Cavalier2392, Ceranthor, Chander Jagtiani, Chane 815, Chanlyn, Chantessy, CharlotteWebb, Charmer216, Cheesyperson1995, Chickyfuzz14, Chirchona, Chircona, Chocolate349, Christianb5, ChristinaMJ, ClamDip, Click23, Closedmouth, Cobe2001, Codster9, ColCad4144, Coldwave680, Colonies Chris, Cometstyles, Comicist, ConCompS, Cooper101, Coral Bay, Corvus cornix, Cory Malik, Courcelles, Craw-daddy, Crazy Boris with a red beard, Crazy Chick13, Criccraze, Crystal4935, Ctjf83, Czar Brodie, DC Fan 5, DCFan101, Dabomb87, Dachshundboy25, Damicatz, DanTD, Dancer204, Dannebrog Spy, Darkfight, Darkman882005, DarksoulXZ22, Darrik2, Darth Panda, Daryljustinbalagtas, Davidcmagic, Ddbeni16, Ddouglasinc, Deathlive2, Debresser, Deconstructhis, Demi11lovato11, Demi818, DerHexer, Derild4921, Deshaun14, Diablo1123, Didem ece11, Dis Enemua, Discospinster, Disney Producer, Disney500, Disney768User, DisneyChannelFan015, DisneyFriends, DisneyLover41, Disneydex, Disneymaniac101, Divod, Dj-kid, Dmdrox!, Dnvrfantj, Docsteel92, Doggieal1000, Doggy467, Dogposter, Don-dk, Don729torossi, Dondfan998, DonelleDer, Donkie737, Donmccullen, Doublestressfull, DougsTech, Download, DragonRush44, DramaQueen9118162, DreadfullyDespised, Dshibshm, Dspradau, Dthdc4, Dumlove, Dylan Damien, Dylan620, Earlypsychosis, Eboy2021, Ed, Ed112111, EdisonLite, Edokter, Eevmoney, Elephantboy, Elockid, Emily Bourne, EmmaRen, Empezardesdecero123, Epbr123, Eric444, Erik9, Esseeman, Eternal Pink, Euryalus, Evergreengirl, Everyking, Excirial, ExtraordinaryAnn, F141998, Falconer3, Fedex456, FelisLeo, FergieFan101, Fgurakid, Firetrap9254, Flewis, Flyby1300, FlyingOtter, Fofitf, For An Angel, Frankee vergara, Frehley, Freshstart, Friends1994, Frizzyr, Fugi4rk, Funny96, Furuba9, Fuzzyandtoast, Gary King, Gdo01, Gdoggie, Geekyboy87, Geni, GeorgeMoney, Giarc37, Giftedgrrl, Gilliam, Gimmetrow, Gingerbread101, Gmv45, Gobbleswoggler, Goku1st, GoldFlower, Goodforlife, GotchaFool90, Gprince007, Graciebeebee, Grafen, Grande13, Gryllida, Guccigirl303, Gunmuny, Gurch, Gwinva, HD123, HD325, HFRS, HJ Mitchell, Haha169, Hairy106, HaleybobIII, Halosecrets0032, Halwa, Hannahcrazy, Hannahfanon, Happy5214, Haseo9999, Hawthornelover, Haza-w, Hbent, Headstrong neiva, Hectorthebat, Hehehedoughnuts, Hellevision123, Hesaidshesaid, HexaChord, High School Musical909, Hill03, Hmrox, Hmsarahdhm, Hoangquan hientrang, Hotdoglane, Hugemileyfan, Hwood96, Hydrogen Iodide, II MusLiM HyBRiD II, IRP, Icairns, Icarlyfan01, Icealien33, Iluv2write, Imnotminkus, Imzy, Insanity Incarnate, Intelligentsium, Into The Fray, Io Katai, Ionutzmovie, Ipodnano05, Irishguy, IronGargoyle, Irrypride, Irulagain, J.delanoy, JForget, JFreeman, Jack Merridew, JackSchmidt, Jackol, Jagged, Jaggers76, Jairo82798, Jake Wartenberg, JamesOludareFadoju, JamieS93, Jammylmd, Jared9, Jashan Pashu, Jashanaas, JasonXL-V2, Jasonbres, Jedi94, Jediliz, Jeff G., Jeff Jack Hardy, Jenna the whale, Jeremy1354, Jeremyb, JeyDoesntCare, Jfarajr, Jfaster, Jiraffe, Jj137, Jjoonnaasslloovvee, Jman125, JoFerg, Joekellyiii, John of Reading, John254, Johnanth, Johncage1000, Johnny0929, Johnven, JollyMooly, Jordan pruitt22, Jordylee, Joseph Ferri, Joshwim8, Jovitoaa2005, Jso1995, JuJube, Juar, Jukeboxhero515, Juliancolton, Justi521, Jôntanas, Kachubbsnubb, Kanonkas, Keilana, Keller29072, Kellylyn93, Kencokamo, Kerotan, Kesac, Keyang tay, Khut, Kid0015, Kiepleloi, Kiki360, Kingpin13, Kings bibby win, Kitten12341, Kiwidude, Kkailas, Koalnut, Koavf, Kooliod, Kristen Eriksen, Kumfart, Kwlkielan, Kww, Kyle1278, Kylu, Kyriakos, L Kensington, LWYMI, La Grande Reverteur, La Pianista, La bella muerte17, La la land la, Lacila, Lady5555501, Laithf97, Lakers, Latka1, Laubbaum, Laughxoutxloud, Laxgrl22493, Leagreen, LeaveSleaves, LedgendGamer, Lifeoftheparty90, Lights, Lilcarlitoisnow14, Lilgraps, Lilmo1996, LinkToddMcLovinMontana, Lipe rbd rbd, Liquidluck, Lisafaceasdf, Lizziegirl96, LizzyBuzy, Logan, Lonestar662p3, Lovelaughlive97, Lovelypet, Ludde23, Luigeach, Luk, LukeBlueFive, MER-C, Maciek1102, MacottoEditor, MaddieGa, Mahewa, Maia78, Malevious, Malpass93, Mand1314, Manda 518 2007, Manplush, Maquirri91, Mario9996, Marisa2012, Marshall167, Martha Runs The Store, Martinsizon, Mattschreiber, Maxim, McSly, Mcandgdrox, Mcollins909, Mcyrusfan, Mdxxx, MeLiSsA, Meaty85203, MegX, Meka11218, Meldiva48, Meme00123, Mentifisto, Mhiji, Michael Devore, MichaelMcShae, Mickeedee, Mickeymouseclubhouse, Micsam77, Midnyterain, MiguelL0pz, Mike Rosoft, Mike126beatles, Miles16, Mileycyrus16, Mileycyrusc, Mileysaysgoodbye123, Miztahrogers, Mmathe3257, Mmxx, Mnkybusiness25, Moanna, Moanster, Mohsin12345, Momanso, MonoAV, Moolie23, Moudy4, Mouseinthehouse, Mr. College, MrStalker, Mslaffalot, Msw1002, MuZemike, Murphlecreator, Musicalmelody, Mw93, Mynameisorange, Myzou, Mzperfection42, N5iln, NJ Rock, Nahallac Silverwinds, Nalren, NaminesPetals, Nascar1996, Nauticashades, NawlinWiki, Ndenison, Ned Scott, Neirgb818, Neon.heart, Neon48, NexopiaLive, Nicky Nouse, Nicorocks9, Night Fight, Nn123645, NrDg, Nsaa, NuclearWarfare, Nuggetman08, Nyxaus, Ocexpo, Omicronpersei8, OneWeirdDude, Onebrothertoomany, Oreos, Original-julz, Orry Verducci, Outriggr, Pan41, PaperMarioFan684, Patar knight, Pedrito930, Pedro1997100, Penguino6, Pennywisdom2099, PepitoTKT, Peregrine Fisher, PerfectStorm, Peripitus, Perisheroftheuntruth, Peti817172M, Pharaoh of the Wizards, Phil Boswell, Philip Trueman, Philipy333333, Phydend, Piano non troppo, Piblup, Pillowpc2001, Pink saturn, Plot101, Princess olivia, Puccafan920, Pumpkin Pie, Punk-Lova, PunkNerd5, Purplemonkey8899, Purplewowies, Purplicious13, Pyrospirit, Quantpole, QuasyBoy, R'n'B, R8er925, RPlunk2853, RY23, Rabbit 20, Race t, Rachael Lampa Fan, Rahin1195, Rainbow sprinkle, RainbowOfLight, Raine neiva, Randolph3, Randomaustralian, Rangermups, Ravens Gate, Rawkinaly937, Razorflame, Rcharmz, Realpath, Redford500, Redmy, Renanx3, Res2216firestar, Retiono Virginian, Rhys Is The Word, Richard0612, RicoSurfShop, Road Wizard, Robert 47, Robors, Rochchick26, Rockin56, Rodby88, Rohanrns, Roleplayer, Ronhjones, Royalguard11, Rsrikanth05, Ruby.red.roses, Rubyrox1907, Rulep1996, Ryanmo97, S77u8, SJP, ST47, Saddleclub4444, Saidada, Sambobuk, Sammywand365, Sandman138, Sanvir, Sarah123456789, Sceptre, Schneckcl3, Schwnj, ScottAHudson, Scottymileyfan, Sd31415, Sean Whitton, SeanB102, Selenalovato3, Seresin, Serienfan2010, Shadow1, ShadowRanger, Shakeitcecerocky, Shakeitcecezendaya, Shanabug, Shanes, Shannernanner, Shara25, Shaznfaru, ShelfSkewed, Shelfro, Sherlock Boy, Shimmera, Shirulashem, SideshowBob99, Sigma 7, Signalhead, Simsimtigger, Sirideroo, Sirsai, Skarebo, Skarl the Drummer, Skeral, SkittlzAnKomboz, Slon02, Slumbergirls101, Smatei7502, Smileyface 12 91, Smileymileyrule, Smokizzy, Snubbiesluver15, SoWhy, SoapTalker, SofaKing381222, Someguy1221, Sonnywithachance2, Sopranosmob781, SpaceFlight89, Spears154, SpecialReserve, Spinningspark, Spongebobhannah, Spongemaster0, Spyguy41, Squibbles0, Ss112, Static Universe, Stayawayplz, Stevenwazhere, Stickee, Storkk, Strawbrylovr, Strikers5, Stroppolo, Study-Of-The-Stars, Stylishdiva, SunAquarius129, Sunshineisles2, SuperDMChan, SuperHamster, SuperJumbo, Sushiflinger, Swilkins13, Synella, THEN WHO WAS PHONE?, TSLcrazier, TTN, Tabletop, Tamajared, Tassedethe, Taytaytaylorswift, Tbrueggeman, Tcatron565, Techman224, Tempodivalse, Tennisballs1234, Tennisgir5, That Guy, From That Show!, The Bomb, The Cool Kat, The Hybrid, The System 3000, The Thing That Should Not Be, The undertow, TheGerm, TheOllieTrolley, Thedemonhog, Thefreakshow, Thefroggiechick, Thelb4, Therefore, Thesaur, Thingg, Thissén, Thryth, Tiah12345, Tide rolls, Tjtaz, Tohd8BohaithuGh1, Tommy0987, Tommy2010, Tommy920998768, Totaldramaman, TracyLinkEdnaVelmaPenny, Trevor MacInnis, Tslocum, Tstephent, Tubesurfer, Tuspm, Tykunzelman, TylerG518, Ukexpat, Ultimate Ranger, Unschool, Useight, Ussamah, Valnetinoyipee, Vanished 6551232, VasilievVV, Versus22, Vfddinamarkvfd, Victorhariki, Vipinhari, Vyshnavi11, Vyshy101, WAVY 10 Fan, Wamke4, Ward3001, Warwickavenuestation, Washburnmav, Waterpolofreak3, Wayne Slam, WeeklyJumpman, Welsh, Wenli, WhatGuy, Whisky drinker, WhisperToMe, Whitepelt, Who then was a gentleman?, WikHead, Wiki Raja, WikiDickiPickiHiki, WikiMaster500, Wikialexdx, Wikipelli, Wikiviewer, WildcatFever, WildcatMaster3000, Will-Martins, Willking1979, Wingsofhalo, Winhunter, Wizardman, Wjfkljdsbjudf, Wjmummert, Wknight94, WorstNinja, Writergirl123, Wtmitchell, X LadySweetness x, Xelusive memoriesx, XenonX3, Xtremedude2317, Yankeesrj12, Yinyang1195, Yoguy11, Yohan775, Yohan77550, Ysabel 1022, Yuri Dutra, YvetteMike, ZSoraz, ZacTroyLinkJoeShane, Zachary115, Zalgo, Zanessa001, ZanessaYay, Zhou Yu, Zntrip, Zshortman, Zulrock, 4210 anonymous edits

List of *Sonny with a Chance* episodes *Source*: http://en.wikipedia.org/w/index.php?oldid=384259272 *Contributors*: -Jonatinhas-, 100sbo10, 1234r00t, 13.Ikim, 13.M.J.A, 13curseof, 1989 Rosie, 4everdemilovato, 5 albert square, 7, Abce2, AcinerbSkai, ActivExpression, Addihockey10, Adryoanna, Adyniz, Aferz3, Ajraddatz, Alansohn, Alec2011, AlexiusHoratius, Alfred Lau, Alice.haugen, Aliceson M, Amebabame, Andy Munoz, Angela6251, Angelkinns, Ani4e-95, Anitascorzo, Apple30933, Ashleyleggat404, AubreyEllenShomo, AussieLegend, Austin512, Austinkg543, Awesomejb, Babiiita xd 1996, Babyblue12, Babygirl57, Baileygaz, Barras, Bearcat, Beeeeeeeeew, Bettertthanf, Bhavya34, Blaloupasous, Blaxthos, Blaze Roxton, BloginFan101, Blurpeace, Boomshadow, Brandon J. Marcellus, Brandon8552, Bretts23, BridgitMendlerFan41, Brookedevicallie, Bubbles62681, Bulbakuki, C.Fred, CaRaNt11, Caeden Lovato, CalvinDavidson, Camwhitey, Candypopgirl101325, Carlosar45, CarolinahurricanesEr, Causa sui, Ceauntay59, Ceeboyz3, Chad Dylan Copper, Chander Jagtiani, Chane 815, Chanii3220, Channayy, Channy Marie101, Channy4ever, Charmer216, Checker Fred, Chocolatechipwhipcreampie, Chunghoto, Ciphers, Cirt, Clerks, Clinity Kane, ClutterButter, Colatastic, Commit charge, Connormah, Cool3, Coral Bay, Cory Malik, CraigFoye80, Crystalfire786, Curseof13, Cxz111, D 4 I S Y, DD2K, Daboyle250, Damonluemaxwell97, DanTD, DanielDeibler, Dawynn, DayHT, Debresser, DegrassiFreak, Denali567, Disney Channel Celeb Showdown, Disney avatar, DisneyDemi, DisneyLover41, Disneygalxx123+abc, Divod, Dlatimer, Doniago, Dorkull06, Dorkull789, Download, DramaQueen9118162, DuchessofSutherland, Dylan620, Easy12345, Ecmce, Edna23, Ehwildcats, EmmaBerry, Ericorbit, Exeunt, Fabulous Dandelion, Fastily, Fernie2010, Fraggle81, FredTheBread, Frehley, Freikorp, Funny003, Funny96, Furuba9, Gabrebenque, Gdaly7, Ged UK, Geekboy6, Gesoyrn, Gilliam, Gimmetrow, Gio717, Glamgirljaspreet101, Glane23, Gnaturefantasy, Gnowxilef, Gossip--girls-xoxo, Greylion11, Grooviemania, HAJFan, Hadger, Haha169, Hahachuckles, HairyPerry, Hannahcrazy, Harold2010, HeinzDoofenshmirtz, Hellevision123, HexaChord, Hickz08, Howlingwolf570, Hoyleslr, Hugzandhearts, II MusLiM HyBRiD II, Icarlyfan01, ImperatorExercitus, Ionutzmovie, Ipatrol, Ipodgeek, Irrypride, Islandgurl 96, ItsTheClimb17, J.delanoy, J04n, JForget, Jacksonmerritt, Jairo27, Jaksmata, Jamesofur, Jasonbres, Jasz45, JeanitaChiquita, Jedi94, Jediliz, Jeff G., JeffCena3, Jeremy1354, Jfarajr, Jknwilson,

Jmundo, JoeJonasMileyCyrus, Joes a g, Johnello, Johnny0929, Josh1ten, Joshu2010, Joycedseok, Judicatus, Katieh5584, Kehrbykid, Kelly10526, KennaBeth717, Kenriolover789, Ketsue Khut, Kiki99736, Kingpin13, Kitty catcat123, Konrad4321, Kourtnye, Kwtr, Kww, LAAFan, Lacila, Laurabeedliote2, Leahclake, Leonardo Andres Sánchez, Leuko, Lifeispinislife, Lifeispinkislife, LilHelpa, Lilsissy2, Limideen, Lipesbatista, Livnic, Logical Fuzz, Lolmaniac808, Lucyette, MC10, Machine Patience, Mafaw10, Maquirri91, Mario96, Marmoset Emergency, Martin 7937, Martin451, Marx01, Math Champion, McLar eng, Mcjohnv, Meaghan, Meme00123, Memoryfoam, Mentifisto, Mia673, Michal Nebyla, Mild Bill Hiccup, Milerz91, Miles16, MileyJBNileyFan, MillyFleur14, Miniview, Miquonranger03, Momos555, Morbeen4444, Mr. College, MrStalker, Mrsdemicorbisiere92, Mupplan, Musicgirl123, Mysdaao, Nari25, Nari50, NawlinWiki, Nazanin29, Neetfreak, Nerfari, NickelodeonFan, Night Fight, Nikiangelz, Noctibus, Nonexistent me, NrDg, NuclearWarfare, Od Mishehu, Odie5533, Oon23, Osarius, PMDrive1061, PancakeMistake, Peace! rockon!, Perfectanonimous, PeterAKer, PhilKnight, Pokemon656, Porchcrop, Pparazorback, Prerna Dodeja, PurpleSunflower, QuasyBoy, Queen Rhana, RL0919, Rabbit 20, Rafatisd, Rapjul, RaseaC, Ratemonth, Reach Out to the Truth, Reason says, RebeccaTaylor, Recognizance, Reeses125, Renatabls, Rida1996, Ringostar27, Rita.Rockz, RobertFan, Rockin56, Roxy33333, RoyBoy, Rrburke, Rsrikanth05, Rysiu18, Saebjorn, SailorScoutX, Sammywand365, Samohad, Sceptre, Scfansite, Scoutjd, Selena 92, Selenafan815, Senkris, Serienfan2010, Setsuna29, Shego123, Shenshenly, Shhhsecret1234321, ShuffleStop, SiMpLyStAr975, Signalhead, Simplebutpowerful, Skier Dude, SkyTraveler, Smijes08, Smith2298, Smooth Criminal 2, Someguy1221, SonnyWithAChance1, Sonnywithachance11, SopOquis, Sorandom97, Spears154, Spera5, Spitfire, Staka, StarbucksMusic37, Study-Of-The-Stars, Sty3459, Sweetaspie09, SweetoHolic104, Tabletop, Tangent747, TaytaymileyxD, Taytaytaylorswift, Tbhotch, TeddyBear124, The Cool Kat, The Thing That Should Not Be, Theepowerful, Thissén, Tide rolls, Tiggerjay, Tohd8BohaithuGh1, Tomtom0624, Tomtom0697, Toonlinkmasterfood, Touch Of Light, Tsange, TutterMouse, Tvshow man, Tvtonightokc, Tweetsabird, TyDwiki, Tyallda, Utility Monster, VJ13A, Versus22, Vicenarian, ViperSnake151, Vlany57, Volleyballqueen12, Vyshy101, Wamke4, WarFox, Wayne Slam, Welsh, WereSpielChequers, WhatGuy, Whitegrb, WikHead, Wiki Helper3, WikiChicken81112, WikiLaurent, WikiMaster500, WikiPikiUser, Wilderbiz, WillH, WizMagno, Wolfer68, Woohookitty, Wormow, Wrseclen, Wtmitchell, XotheREALemilyntolentinoXo, Xoxoangel3333, XxDisneyRoxX, Xxelementz, YUL89YYZ, Young V.I.P, ZacEfronFan123, Zarayasminshah, Zeen08, Zhou Yu, Zobzy, Zyalover, 3128 anonymous edits

List of *The Suite Life on Deck* episodes *Source*: http://en.wikipedia.org/w/index.php?oldid=401887348 *Contributors*: -Jonatinhas-, 1001Triwizard, 13.Ikim, 13.M.J.A, 1989 Rosie, 21312crown12321, 24 biggest fan, 27christian11, 3jz01bcs, 721Tiki, 82ironman14, ABF, AWESOMESMILEYFACE.99, Abhay26, Acroterion, Adyniz, Aeonx, Aktopps, Alan4753, Alansohn, Alec2011, Aliceson M, Ally555, Alyson93, Amdrag568, Andadundi, Andyross, Angela6251, Ani4e-95, Annierox613hf, Aoi, Aquadrago24, Asmafayaz, Astatine-210, Atd101, AussieLegend, Austingray123, Austinkg543, Avnjay, BRG 12, Bakerychaz, Barts1a, BastianGT, Bean1223, Bearcat, Bento00, Bidgee, Bigaireatscheese, Billysuite, Birchington, Blahs22, Blaloupasous, Bluemargay, Blurpeace, Bobo192, Boing! said Zebedee, Books12, Bovineboy2008, Braceout, Brandon J. Marcellus, Bretts23, Bso98, Bulbakuki, Burg44, Burmiester, Buzzer25, C.Fred, C.m1994, CL, CaRaNt11, CalvinDavidson, Camoline, CanadianLinuxUser, Caribbean H.Q., CarlosLovers, Carlosar45, CarolinahurricanesEr, Carrie2002, Ceeboyz3, Chander Jagtiani, Chane 815, Checker Fred, Cheeseprincess, ChiBear1993, Chilimypop, Christianb5, Christianity922, Christopher Tsakonas, ChrstphrChvz, Cit helper, Clinity Kane, Codykennedy5, Coltsrock4ever, Confession0791, Conti, CoolPikachu!, Cooliogal212, Coolioride, Coral Bay, Coreyrock66, Cory Malik, Cperea1994, CrazyKid24, Crazywikihero999, Crystal4935, Curseof13, Cyberbakugan, DC Fan 5, DCFan101, Daboyle250, Dachampz, Dakotacoons, Damonluemaxwell97, Darkmaster2004, Darth Panda, Davepusey, Davidmoen2009, Demilovatorocks, Dexter555, Dferg, DisMupp, Discospinster, Disney avatar, DisneyChannelFan015, DisneyFriends, DisneyLover41, Disnoman, Divod, Doryupq, Dougweller, Doulos Christos, Download, Drago18, Dragonfly730, Drickzone, Drills, Drmargi, DuchessofSutherland, Dude13131616, Dundy222, Earlypsychosis, EdJohnston, Eeekster, Eevmoney, Elockid, ElviaJonas, Epass, Epbr123, ErMiEvJa, Erikrainiercabling, Excirial, Extremeguy, Falcon8765, Falconer3, Falkinboy19, Fangtiming, Favonian, FearFactorPhony, Ferdinand h2, Fernie2010, Ffaadstrbdetete, Fireburn95, Flippytoon123, Francisco97, Frankenpuppy, Frantzedward.cha, Funny96, Furuba9, Gadeshina44, Gamer24, Gdaly7, Ged UK, Ghm92, Giarc37, Gilgilgilgilad, Gimelthedog, Gimmetrow, Glane23, Goku1st, Gordan3194, Gossip--girls-xoxo, Goth67, Gotttambeme, GrantyO, Gökhan, HD 19033, HJ Mitchell, Hadger, Hallpriest9, Hannahcrazy, Harold2010, Harry-hill101, Hassaan19, Hawksfan101, Hborockz, Headsdown1010, Hellevision123, Hickz08, High School Musical909, Highzac96, Horsegirl047, Hughcharlesparker, Icealien33, Iheartwiki4ever, IzzahA 1804, J.delanoy, JILTSL, JLKTENNIS43, JNW, Jabed111, Jack goold 347, Jairo27, Jake Noble, Jalfredl, Jbrookdale, Jedi94, Jeff G., Jellyfish101, JeremyWJ, Jfarajr, Jhjackson97, Jimmy, Jknwilson, Jman1017, Jmuppeton, JoFerg, Joao20p, JoeJonasMileyCyrus, Joes a g, Johnny0929, Jojhutton, Jon23812, JonnyBJon, Joshu2010, Joshua Scott, Joycedseok, Juliancolton, Junglefury18, Jweng888, Jôntanas, Kalkaski, Kassjab, KennaBeth717, Kf93, KimchiNoodle, KingPancake, Kingpin13, Kiore, Kjghjhg, Kmmontandon, Koalnut, Kololok94, Kralizec!, Kww, KylieTexas, L Kensington, LRobbo88, LUCY1995, Lame-ofan55, Lampsite27, Lankiveil, Lanzel, Liberalgenius, Lightrealm, LilHelpa, Liljabbakid, Lincofire, LindeVeen, Lipesbatista, LittleDuude8, Littlealy, Lmp883, Longdeademperor, Lorin Schonfeld, LpSamuelm, Luckytobyx, Luigi-San, Luke Bundrum, LukeTheSpook, Lunchscale, MC10, MJF2000, MJisnotmylover, Magnius, Makro, Maquirri91, MarkRobbins, Mason172, Max Russo, Meaty85203, Meme00123, Mervn, Message From Xenu, Metor, Michal Nebyla, Milan95, Milerz91, Minotaurspore, Minuteman53, Miquonranger03, MissyMusic13, Mizzcp, Mmathe3257, Moanna, Mohsin12345, Mr. College, Mr. Comedian, MrRohanM, Mrteddylupin, Mupplan, Muppmaster, MusicBoi94, Musicalmelody, Mykalman02, N5iln, NarutoD444, Nazanin29, Ndthuy112, Neurolysis, Nica0987, Night Fight, Nihiltres, Nonexistent me, NrDg, Nsaa, NuclearWarfare, OkayDock, Oldag07, OllieFury, OneWeirdDude, Onecatowner, PerfectAngelKK, Pharaoh of the Wizards, PhilKnight, Phoumyvong, Pianoajd, PoohBearAndVideoGames, Possum, Purplemonkey8899, QuasyBoy, Qwert123disney, R'n'B, R13n13, RA0808, RY23, Rabbit 20, Raiku Samiyaza, Randolph3, Rapjul, Rcharmz, Rebyiscool, Redruby451, Retro 2010, Rich Farmbrough, Riomet, Roasher, Robert Skyhawk, Rockin56, Rollopets, Roory24, Rowndin2448, RoxJack, Rsrikanth05, Ruofan, Ryguy412, Rysiu18, Rzhm, Sagittarius95, Sailorscoutx, Sceptre, Schank1234, Seddon, Serienfan2010, ShabnamSahebi, Shego123, Shelfro, Shenshenly, Shoesquashfan5000, ShuffleStop, Skulcouncilor08, SoWhy, Sonnywithachance2, Sorandom97, Sparks13fan, Spears154, SpiderTre, Spore live in moore, Squidster6, Staka, StewieK, StoneCold89, Student XIIE, Study-Of-The-Stars, StupidJaguar, Suitelifeondecklover, Sunshineisles2, Superdeoxys, Superjay2001, Superspyguy, Swaggd Outt32, Swearengin, Sweetaspie09, TFOWR, TMC1982, TV Boy, Tbhotch, Tca achintya, Te4threebush, Techman224, Teendisney27, The Cool Kat, The Thing That Should Not Be, The suite life, TheRealFennShysa, ThinkBlue, Thorn12, Tide rolls, Tim1357, Timotheus Canens, Tommy2010, Tommystar, Tony1, Toontown59153, Torry13YuT, Total Drama Act, Totaldramaman, Trentisland, Tristinarocks, Tubesurfer, Tvguy347, Tvtonightokc, Tyrah343, USN1977, Unreal7, Urbanatoller, VOFFA, VP44444, Valik90210, Vanessarks, Vik255, ViperSnake151, Vlad4, Volleyballqueen12, Voyagerfan5761, Vyshy101, Waiwai933, Wakawakadis, Wallyiscoo, Wayne Slam, Weatherandmp5, WhatGuy, Whenaxis, Whitemist101, WikHead, WikiFreakster, WikiSpector, Wikialexdx, Wikimalta, William Avery, WizMagno, Wjmummert, Wolfer68, Wormow, Writergirl7, Wsim12, Wwehurricane1, XalD, Xhaoz, Xobellaswan, XuryaX, XxCrimsonXAngelxX, Yankeesrj12, Yoguy11, Yonatan. A, Yunzei5ds, Zacbaxter1, Zany zacky, Zobzy, Zulrock, Zxcvboy97, 2088 anonymous edits

Burnin' Up *Source*: http://en.wikipedia.org/w/index.php?oldid=401510341 *Contributors*: 2D, 4twenty42o, AEMoreira042281, AUG, Abcmeg123x3, All-american-soda, Amer10, Andyandsamy, Anshuk, ArCgon, ArglebargleIV, Arjoccolenty, Artcutie93, Ashishvats23, Aspects, AtheWeatherman, Bensin, Biggaa, Binary TSO, Blanchardb, BlastMaster209, Bmitchelf, Bobo192, Bobtastic13, Bovineboy2008, BsaPR1996, Btg0907, Btup627, COMPFUNK2, Calliegal, Camo111, CanadianLinuxUser, Capricorn42, Chamal N, Chris wong999, Codenameriley, ConCompS, Conidancerdude, Cst17, Cue the Strings, Cyfal, DAJS, DCEdwards1966, DCFan101, Danielle122, Dennissell, Dicklover4lyfe, Diego145, DignityWithLove, Dirtyterdy, Discospinster, DoubleBlue, DreamStar05, Efe, Ericorbit, Everyking, Extransit, Felipe1219859, FelixtheCatHM, Flewis, Frankenpuppy, Freakmighty, Frehley, Gamaliel, Gnowxilef, Gogo Dodo, Gokus Girl, Goodnightmush, Headstrong neiva, Hell6awaits6you, Hellgaroo, High School Musical909, Holiday56, Hometown Kid, Hydrogen Iodide, Ilovejonasbrothersmore, ImperatorExercitus, Iridescent, Itsbecca512, J-love-lee, J.delanoy, J7y, JForget, JaGa, JamieS93, January, Jarajet89, Jclemens, Jdrewitt, Jeffrey Mall, JhanCRUSH, Jimmy tisdale, JoFerg, Jomi4Life, Jonas101, Jrugordon, Juanacho, Jube93, Kamoisia, Karin127, Katalaveno, Kaylerrobert, KeNiJoe, Kiepleloi, Kikkokalabud, King of Hearts, King007ofrock, Ksy92003, Kuriboi2k6, Kww, Landon1980, Lewis7a, Luigi-ish, Luisrios94, MBisanz, Marek69, Martin4647, McSly, Mcbird13, Mfowler11, Mkjgd, MuZemike, Musicupdated, Myweeneeisharderthanyours, NawlinWiki, Nevermore27, Nguyên Lê, Nikiangelz, Nopmacprime, NrDg, NuclearWarfare, On the sixth day God created MANchester, Onopearls, Pedrito930, Pharaoh of the Wizards, PhilKnight, Poco a poco, Pokerdance, PsychoSchuyler, QuadrivialMind, RaptorJesus2, Real-Me23, Realist2, Rebornaudioslave, Res2216firestar, Rmsome, Rockin56, Rror, SJP, SKS2K6, SaraLovesJonas, SaturdayNightMorons, SchfiftyThree, Sharkdude95, Sheilab0002, Snaxbowl, Snigbrook, Soulyaboy, Ss112, Stephanierpicha, Stifle, Strongy820, TFunk, Takeover22, Tanthalas39, Tbhotch, Tedhole, Terneris, That1indnkid, The Arbiter, TheSimpsonsRocks, Thingg, Thoseguiltyeyes, Triping, UOFan44, Vininn, WAVY 10 Fan, WikiCheckee, Wild Matt12, William Avery, Winchelsea, Wolfer68, Woohookitty, XThe Dark Thunderx, XXpaulineCzkaXx, Xtinadbest, Yanra36, Youyoho, Yuoiuysdh, Zntrip, 573 anonymous edits

Selena Gomez & the Scene discography *Source*: http://en.wikipedia.org/w/index.php?oldid=401832762 *Contributors*: 101cantbetamed101, 69babypixie, Aaron north, Access Denied, Akcvtt, Akerans, Andrewlp1991, Auntof6, Bbbnbbb, Biodin, Brendan4hsm, Candyo32, Cece7o, Cesaravila, CharmedFreak123, ChrisHardy, Churaru, Circusstar, CloversMallRat, Cocky93, Danjo5588, Datafolk, Decodet, Dt128, Ecmce, EnDaLeCoMpLeX, Ending-start, Ericorbit, GD1223, Gabe19, GabrielEdnuelle15, GiovyGabrielEd, Giovyed, Groupemptuy89, Helpalot, Hometown Kid, Ihrtwiki, Iknow23, Jackgill06, JamesBWatson, JoFerg, Juanacho, Keepie838, Keke69, Krispy1995, Kww, Luigi-ish, MC10, MazurJacek, Merynancy, Minimac, Mister sparky, Nima1024, Nyttend, OAVJunior, Pepepe2009, QuasyBoy, Rforb001, Ronhjones, Roselily6, RyanG222, Satlena69, SelGKT, Selenaismylife555, Sethjohnson95, Sgs101, Sheljd21, SilkTork, Sllewellyn7, Ss112, Tassedethe, TheHQHDmusic, Tide rolls, Tinton5, WeedDJ, Woohookitty, XX morettino Xx, Zac Perera, Zacharee, Zurak26, ~Ryan Mckenzie~, 260 anonymous edits

Tell Me Something I Don't Know *Source*: http://en.wikipedia.org/w/index.php?oldid=391974232 *Contributors*: A3RO, ABF, Abby 94, Acather96, Ageton, Alansohn, Altarep, Anythingspossibleforapossible, Arnell2010, Aspects, Babyjazspanail, Bart133, Billy4kate, Blahbalhcookies, Blahblahblahcookies, BloodDoll, BlueSquadronRaven, Bobo192, Brittflick 1994, Bucephalus, C.Fred, Calle, Calliegal, Carrie2002, Chamal N, CharmaineLim, Classicjazzbari, Cliffordlw, Cliffordlw1, Coozbi, DantODB, Dbunkley6, Dennissell, DerHexer, Discospinster, Djbj16, Don-Don, Download, Drbreznjev, DreamStar05, Drmies, Duncan, ESMIMMAS, Eeekster, Eric444, Erik, Excirial, FDJoshua22, FF2010, Fishhook, Flewis, Frehley, Furuba9, Fæ, GLaDOS, Gdaly7, Geekboy6, Gersende, Gfoley4, Gnowxilef, GoPurpleNGold24, Gogo Dodo, Granpuff, Haein45, Happysailor, Harley doggie 1, Haseo9999, Headstrong neiva, Heisenbergthechemist, High School Musical909, Holiday56, Iknow23, Iloveyoohxx89, Imnotminkus, Ipodnano05, Iridescent, J.delanoy, JaimeAnnaMoore, Jake Wartenberg, Jason.cinema, JavierMC, Jayce0814, Jezreelver, Jobella21, JodyB, Johnny0929, Justinbieberonetime, Jwein, Khunglongcon, Kikkokalabud, Kimijonas, Kww, Kylexy93, LAUGH90, La Pianista, LeaveSleaves, Legoman64, Life=Randomness, Limetolime, Lolalol1234567899, Longhair, Loveandberry411, Luisj07, Luna Santin, Lyveluvlyfe, Malcolmxl5, Maldek2, Maludancer4, Materialscientist, Mbmbmb123456789, Mzbartlett, Nagy, Nathan, Nathanial1987, Nathanvd, Ndenison, NeoBatfreak, Neurolysis, Nickmd, Nikiangelz, NorthernThunder, NuclearWarfare, Oddharmonic, Oky103, OlEnglish, PC78, Pau4me, Philip Trueman, Piano non troppo, Pinethicket, Pinkadelica, Plastikspork, Poct, Pokerdance, Pop princess 1, QuasyBoy, Randolph3, ReginaRing12, Reiner rubin, Rich Farmbrough, RickyYayo3, Rrburke, S h i v a (Visnu), Secvan henshall, Setsuna29, ShadowRanger, Shadzane, ShazzaBabyxo, Soccerdud, Southsloper, Spellcast, Sprite7868, Steam5, Sugar1996, SummerPhD, Supertalies, TDC99, TPIRFanSteve, Tabletop, The Thing That Should Not Be, TheMovieBuff, Thingg, TigressofIndia, TracyLinkEdnaVelmaPenny, Treasure12347890, TreoBoy680, Triwbe, Underworldon345, Versus22, Weeliljimmy, WikiPikiUser, Woohookitty, Xtinadbest, Zhou Yu, ZooFari, 621 anonymous edits i.wikipedia.org/w/index.php?oldid=398161402 *Contributors*: Aerotheque, Aia94, Andy Johnston, AnonMoos, Art1991, Ary29, Brianhenke, alvinNelson4, Cesaravila, CommonsDelinker, Cortomaltais, Crusty4545, DFS, Danielsmith, DantODB, Dbunkley6, Dennissell, Derek R Bullamore, Dl2000, ., Efyoo, Enscalado, Fanficgurl, Feudonym, Feydey, Foreverprovence, GD1223, Gareth E Kegg, Gfoley4, Giovyed, Grstain, Hiddenstranger, ano05, Itstimeformileycyrus, JGabbard, Jenna12381, Joe59108, Kaiser Taylor, Kidlittle, Kurt Shaped Box, LtPowers, Luka89, Lunarc, MartinSFSA, World91, Piniricc65, Pokerdance, Qwerty Binary, Randolph3, Reconsider the static, Rihanna Knowles, Rockin56, Rockysmile11, Schroeder74, Sethjohnson95, 'ennessee Wood, The Utahraptor, Thebeatlestoday, Thumperward, Tim Long, Tinton5, Tomer M, Vitorvicentevalente, Wolfer68, 122 anonymous edits

pedia.org/w/index.php?oldid=292518482 *Contributors*: Alansohn, CiWWAFx, Dirtysk88, Fanficgurl, Fantasydragon, Gnfnrf, Icelandic Hurricane, Iknow23, izman, Jr, Naomiap, Optimous, Plastikspork, Randolph3, RickyYayo3, Rjwilmsi, Socoxo, Twsx, Vitorvicentevalente, 35 anonymous edits

//en.wikipedia.org/w/index.php?oldid=334101773 *Contributors*: Acebloo, Adrian Parratt, Adyniz, Agash C, Alec2011, Alexa 4949, Alfred Lau, AlohaServed, Americanhero, Ammun......, gel OF Kool, Aspects, Ayush J, BD2412, BabyFacee914, BaldMonkey, Benscripps, Biodin, Blaloupasous, Bleelow, Bobo192, Bovineboy2008, Brat1234567890, Brianga, Britneyistoxic, BsaPR1996, Carlitohm11, Chane 815, Chaoticfluffy, CharlesCasiraghi, Chunghoto, Cncxbox, Colleen8463, Couturegalx3, Cssiitcic, DaBomb619, DaniDF1995, DanielAguilar, DantODB, Debresser, Deepthi d, Disneygalxx123+abc, DrDoog, Dydy23, Easy12345, Edna23, Edtatem, Emilyfromnz, Es.ntp, FFall1986, Falkonry, Fixer23, Flowerpotman, Flying thoughts, FrankTobia, Frehley, Gabrebenque, Gdaly7, Geekboy6, Glane23, GoPurpleNGold24, Gracelouisad, Gracie1008, Grafen, GroovySandwich, Hannahcrazy, Hoomanator, Hqb, Huntster, Info002, Ipodnano05, J.delanoy, JDHWIKI, Jalma04, JamieS93, Jannah 09, Jayce0814, Jemily4ever, Johnny0929, Kelly maddie, Kingpin13, Krisallenno1fanindaworld, Kww, LalalandxDemi, Lazytv8, LeaveSleaves, Leonardo Andres Sánchez, Liquidluck, Little Mountain 5, Littletung, LiveInLove20, Loborocky, Logical Fuzz, Lotje, Lovesongs41, MBisanz, MacGyverMagic, Madhero88, MadiieLovegood285, Magioladitis, Mahnoor moon, Man of I-Mages, Maxgab, McSly, Mianghuei, MichaelQSchmidt, Mild Bill Hiccup, Mrschimpf, Msmyth, NarSakSasLee, NarutoD444, Natexpress13, NawlinWiki, Nikiangelz, Nikofeelan, Ninjawarriordex, NrDg, OffiMcSpin, OliverOken123, PeterSymonds, PhilKnight, Pigby, Pinoiboi23, Pokerdance, Proofreader77, Puppies dressed as cats, Qpally, QuasyBoy, Quique217, RBD22, Randolph3, Ratemonth, Rockin56, Roy1944, Rysiu18, S h i v a (Visnu), Schank1234, ScottMHoward, Selaromar, Seldemlovgom, Selenagomezfan12345, Ser Amantio di Nicolao, Setsuna29, Shego123, Sky Captain, Smijes08, Smileygirl14, Spears154, Staka, Steam5, Stunna Shades, Suffusion of Yellow, SummerPhD, SweetPinkCandy, THUYNGA, Techman224, The Thing That Should Not Be, ThomasAnime, Trusilver, Tsluecke, TunnelSnakesRule, Tweetsabird, Twistedspikers, Tyw7, USN1977, Ulric1313, Vitbjorn, WikipedianMarlith, Wikisergiowiki, WinterChocolatt, WizMagno, Writergirlrocks, Yankeesrj12, Éovart Caçeir, 740 anonymous edits

Send It On (song) *Source*: http://en.wikipedia.org/w/index.php?oldid=401704871 *Contributors*: Akcvtt, Ary29, Bigaireatscheese, Candyo32, ChrstphrChvz, DantODB, Dbunkley6, Dennissell, Edward, Falcon8765, Gabbyrockinlol, Ghostrider, Iknow23, Impala2009, Ipodnano05, Joseph (Bowen) Ferri, Legolas2186, Liquidluck, LyokoWarrior5139, Materialscientist, Mileyizthebest, NickelodeonFan, Nikiangelz, Nverhoeven, OAVJunior, Plastikspork, Renesemee, Rjwilmsi, Rockin56, Saulornelas, Setsuna29, ShuffleStop, Solotwilight, Spears154, Szymon7210, TehRandomPerson, The Thing That Should Not Be, Vitorvicentevalente, WikHead, Wiki libs, Wikiuser9207, Woohookitty, Xmusicloverx127x, 108 anonymous edits

Cruella De Vil (Selena Gomez Song) *Source*: http://en.wikipedia.org/w/index.php?oldid=306668543 *Contributors*: Badger151, Candyo32, FluffyWhiteCat, Gfoley4, Gnowxilef, HeySoulSister, Ipodnano05, Johnny0929, Jomidi, Kww, Lord Opeth, Mclay1, Plastikspork, Pokerdance, RickyYayo3, Sammyday, ShelfSkewed, SummerPhD, The Thing That Should Not Be, TheNoOneBoy03, 12 anonymous edits

Magic (Selena Gomez song) *Source*: http://en.wikipedia.org/w/index.php?oldid=308420302 *Contributors*: Aerotheque, Aia94, Andy Johnston, AnonMoos, Art1991, Ary29, Brianhenke, Brutananadilewski, CactusWriter, CalvinNelson4, Cesaravila, CommonsDelinker, Cortomaltais, Crusty4545, DFS, Danielsmith, DantODB, Dbunkley6, Dennissell, Derek R Bullamore, Dl2000, Doug2dj, Duncan, Durova, Eeekster, Efyoo, Enscalado, Fanficgurl, Feudonym, Feydey, Foreverprovence, GD1223, Gareth E Kegg, Gfoley4, Giovyed, Grstain, Hiddenstranger, InnocuousPseudonym, Intgr, Ipodnano05, Itstimeformileycyrus, JGabbard, Jenna12381, Joe59108, Kaiser Taylor, Kidlittle, Kurt Shaped Box, LtPowers, Luka89, Lunarc, MartinSFSA, Merynancy, Musicalsuperstar, OneWorld91, Piniricc65, Pokerdance, Qwerty Binary, Randolph3, Reconsider the static, Rihanna Knowles, Rockin56, Rockysmile11, Schroeder74, Sethjohnson95, ShuffleStop, Steven J. Anderson, Tennessee Wood, The Utahraptor, Thebeatlestoday, Thumperward, Tim Long, Tinton5, Tomer M, Vitorvicentevalente, Wolfer68, 122 anonymous edits

Trust in Me (The Python's Song) *Source*: http://en.wikipedia.org/w/index.php?oldid=391806211 *Contributors*: BRG, Ccacsmss, Edward321, Ericorbit, Granpuff, Howard352, Hypno Psychic, II MusLiM HyBRiD II, Jasonbres, Leszek Jańczuk, Lilypads, Lord Opeth, Milerz91, NoseNuggets, Parmesan, Paul A, Richhoncho, Rocket000, Smoodaloo, Wknight94, Wolfer68, Xiii33, ~Ryan Mckenzie~, 30 anonymous edits

Live Like There's No Tomorrow *Source*: http://en.wikipedia.org/w/index.php?oldid=391934807 *Contributors*: 1Matt20, AbsoluteGleek92, After Midnight, Agiseb, Airplaneman, Alexjonathan, All Hallow's Wraith, Alliance Entertainment, Awiseman, Axxonnfire, Bencey, BenjyBoy2000, Bigjehart2009, Bovineboy2008, C.Fred, Charlola99, Cooliogal212, Cventura25, Dbunkley6, Ddlovatofan, DemiRox, Diem nguyen, Download, E2eamon, Esprqii, Filmested, Flomen, Formula 86, Freshh, Frostandchill, Funandtrvl, GD 6041, GabrielEdnuelle15, Gertie1999, GiovyGabrielEd, Gnowxilef, Honey Bee Real, Iknow23, ItsTheClimb17, Jayce0814, JohnDorianyeah, Johnny0929, Jweiss11, Kidinstreet, Klasky-Csupo, Kww, L-l-CLK-l-l, Lena Cops, Maddog11111, Mandy443, Mannafredo, Matty-chan, Mccabe86, Melfurd, MikeAllen, Mistersims31, MithrandirAgain, My76Strat, Mzfly23, Nathan and the Gang, Nathan92295, NeoBatfreak, OrangeDog, PMDrive1061, Pernelldh, Prolog, Propaniac, Pwt898, Quasihuman, QuasyBoy, RaNsOmGiiiirl, RamonaBeezus, Randolph3, Reach Out to the Truth, Reconsider the static, Regancy42, RickyYayo3, Riverstepstonegirl, Rmosler2100, Robert Moore, Rockin56, Roelsu, Roselily6, Rrburke, Salamurai, SelGKT, Setsuna29, ShuffleStop, Spears154, Supersmashbrawl, Teknocrat123, TennageDesire, TheMovieBuff, TheValentineBros, Tide rolls, Tocool678, Tweetsabird, Usb10, Vickers830, WikHead, Wikipelli, Woohookitty, XenonX3, Xoxjloveleexox, Z57N, 340 anonymous edits

Cruella de Vil *Source*: http://en.wikipedia.org/w/index.php?oldid=400985986 *Contributors*: 97198, AEMoreira042281, Abby 94, Agustinaldo, Alansohn, Alexf, Andrews Palop, Anilro, AnmaFinotera, Apostrophe, Arny, Asarelah, Auric, BD2412, Bedwyr, Beeblebrox, Bigbluefish, Bnosnhoj, Bobo192, Boduke343, Bonadea, Bongwarrior, Boothferry, Bunchofgrapes, Businessman332211, Cactusjump, CanadianCaesar, Captainjacksparrow, Carmichael95, Chris1219, Chrislk02, Clerks, Colonel Warden, Colt Smith 6892, DarthSidious, Dayle14, Deskana, DisneyVillain, Docboat, DrBat, Drakehellman, Drpryr, DuanePhelps6790, Duke100, Dustin Pearson, Elmo6633, Emkaer, Fact check, Fancykid101, Fishnet37222, GB fan, GDonato, GSheen, Galactic war, Garrepi, Gdgourou, Georgia guy, Gilliam, GirasoleDE, Grutness, Grvsmth, Gubblebubbleyehman, Hailey C. Shannon, Hatruthnoble, HeinzDoofenshmirtz, Hektor, Hilanin, Hpyossikilz, Hydrogen Iodide, IT'S A LION!, IllaZilla, Imladros, Immblueversion, Iridescent, IronGargoyle, J.R., J.delanoy, JMyrleFuller, Jamesooders, Jayron32, JazzD, Jeff Muscato, Jienum, Joey12345345, John of Reading, Johnny Arrombador 01, Johnny0929, Jojhutton, Juan Cruz, Jwy, Kbdank71, Kchishol1970, Keilana, Killerman2, Kimchi.sg, KingFanel, Klassykittychick, Kooky, L Kensington, La Pianista, Lacie101, Lancini87, Lappado, Lord Opeth, Luciphine, Luiz48, Magioladitis, Marckie12345, Markwiki, Matteh, Matthew Cantrell, Mayamussa, Mia ken, Michal Nebyla, Microwave09, Mike Selinker, Mike Teavee, Musha, Mysekurity, N5iln, NawlinWiki, Nemeses9, Nick Number, Nintendo Maximus, NoseNuggets, Notmicro, NrDg, Nv8200p, Oldiesmann, PMDrive1061, Paul A, Pazuzu413, PeruAlonso, Photobeast, Phydend, Pnkrockr, Popageorgio, Portillo, QuasyBoy, R'n'B, RJFJR, Rammings, Recognizance, RedKiteUK, Redmess, Reinyday, Rjwilmsi, Rsgranne, Ryanmalik01, Ryanmer, SFH, Schneelocke, Scj2315, Sephiroth1311, Shanes, Signalhead, Silentaria, Small5th, Snowolf, Sophysduckling, SpikeJones, Starionwolf, Stephenb, Supermorff, TMC1982, Tabletop, Tassedethe, Technobabble1, Teknocrat123, TexasAndroid, The Man in Question, The wub, Themeparkfanatic, UltimatePyro, Ultimatehooly, Vanished User 1004, Vortex Dragon, Walloon, Walter Breitzke, Wargameruk, Wellesradio, Wikivis2342, WildMIKE123, WordyGirl90, X!, Zadduel86, Zone46, Zrebbesh, Zundark, 360 anonymous edits

Image Sources, Licenses and Contributors

File:Flag of Haiti.svg *Source*: http://en.wikipedia.org/w/index.php?title=File:Flag_of_Haiti.svg *License*: unknown *Contributors*: User:Chanheigeorge, User:Denelson83, User:Lokal_Profil, User:Madden, User:Nightstallion, User:Vzb83, User:Zscout370

File:Flag of Mexico.svg *Source*: http://en.wikipedia.org/w/index.php?title=File:Flag_of_Mexico.svg *License*: Public Domain *Contributors*: User:AlexCovarrubias, User:Zscout370

File:Flag of Panama.svg *Source*: http://en.wikipedia.org/w/index.php?title=File:Flag_of_Panama.svg *License*: Public Domain *Contributors*: -xfi-, Addicted04, Duduziq, Fadi the philologer, Fry1989, Klemen Kocjancic, Liftarn, Mattes, Nightstallion, Ninane, Pumbaa80, Reisio, Rfc1394, Thomas81, ThomasPusch, Zscout370, Фёдор Гусляров, 17 anonymous edits

File:Flag of Peru.svg *Source*: http://en.wikipedia.org/w/index.php?title=File:Flag_of_Peru.svg *License*: Public Domain *Contributors*: User:Dbenbenn

File:Flag of Paraguay.svg *Source*: http://en.wikipedia.org/w/index.php?title=File:Flag_of_Paraguay.svg *License*: Public Domain *Contributors*: Republica del Paraguay

File:Flag of Uruguay.svg *Source*: http://en.wikipedia.org/w/index.php?title=File:Flag_of_Uruguay.svg *License*: Public Domain *Contributors*: CommonsDelinker, Fry1989, Homo lupus, Huhsunqu, Kineto007, Klemen Kocjancic, Kookaburra, Lorakesz, Mattes, Neq00, Pumbaa80, Reisio, ThomasPusch, Zscout370, 6 anonymous edits

File:Flag of Venezuela.svg *Source*: http://en.wikipedia.org/w/index.php?title=File:Flag_of_Venezuela.svg *License*: Public Domain *Contributors*: Bastique, Denelson83, DerFussi, George McFinnigan, Herbythyme, Homo lupus, Huhsunqu, Infrogmation, Klemen Kocjancic, Ludger1961, Neq00, Nightstallion, Reisio, ThomasPusch, Vzb83, Wikisole, Zscout370, 12 anonymous edits

File:Flag of the Republic of China.svg *Source*: http://en.wikipedia.org/w/index.php?title=File:Flag_of_the_Republic_of_China.svg *License*: Public Domain *Contributors*: 555, Bestalex, Bigmorr, Denelson83, Ed veg, Gzdavidwong, Herbythyme, Isletakee, Kakoui, Kallerna, Kibinsky, Mattes, Mizunoryu, Neq00, Nickpo, Nightstallion, Odder, Pymouss, R.O.C, Reisio, Reuvenk, Rkt2312, Rocket000, Runningfridgesrule, Samwingkit, Sasha Krotov, Shizhao, Tabasco, Vzb83, Wrightbus, Zscout370, 72 anonymous edits

File:Flag of Japan.svg *Source*: http://en.wikipedia.org/w/index.php?title=File:Flag_of_Japan.svg *License*: Public Domain *Contributors*: Various

File:Flag of Albania.svg *Source*: http://en.wikipedia.org/w/index.php?title=File:Flag_of_Albania.svg *License*: Public Domain *Contributors*: User:Dbenbenn

File:Flag of Chile.svg *Source*: http://en.wikipedia.org/w/index.php?title=File:Flag_of_Chile.svg *License*: Public Domain *Contributors*: User:SKopp

File:Flag of Romania.svg *Source*: http://en.wikipedia.org/w/index.php?title=File:Flag_of_Romania.svg *License*: Public Domain *Contributors*: User:AdiJapan

File:Flag of the Czech Republic.svg *Source*: http://en.wikipedia.org/w/index.php?title=File:Flag_of_the_Czech_Republic.svg *License*: Public Domain *Contributors*: special commission (of code): SVG version by cs:-xfi-. Colors according to Appendix No. 3 of czech legal Act 3/1993. cs:Zirland.

File:Flag of Slovakia.svg *Source*: http://en.wikipedia.org/w/index.php?title=File:Flag_of_Slovakia.svg *License*: Public Domain *Contributors*: User:SKopp

File:Flag of Hungary.svg *Source*: http://en.wikipedia.org/w/index.php?title=File:Flag_of_Hungary.svg *License*: Public Domain *Contributors*: User:SKopp

File:Flag of Russia.svg *Source*: http://en.wikipedia.org/w/index.php?title=File:Flag_of_Russia.svg *License*: Public Domain *Contributors*: Zscout370

File:Flag of Serbia.svg *Source*: http://en.wikipedia.org/w/index.php?title=File:Flag_of_Serbia.svg *License*: Public Domain *Contributors*: ABF, Avala, B1mbo, Denelson83, EDUCA33E, Herbythyme, Imbris, Mormegil, Nightstallion, Nikola Smolenski, Nuno Gabriel Cabral, R-41, Rainman, Rokerismoravee, Sasa Stefanovic, Siebrand, ThomasPusch, Túrelio, Zscout370, 7 anonymous edits

File:Flag of Slovenia.svg *Source*: http://en.wikipedia.org/w/index.php?title=File:Flag_of_Slovenia.svg *License*: Public Domain *Contributors*: User:SKopp, User:Vzb83, User:Zscout370

File:AAnotherCinderellaStory.jpg *Source*: http://en.wikipedia.org/w/index.php?title=File:AAnotherCinderellaStory.jpg *License*: unknown *Contributors*: Melesse, QuasyBoy, Sdrtirs, Skier Dude, Thingg, 3 anonymous edits

File:Tell Me Something I Don't Know.jpg *Source*: http://en.wikipedia.org/w/index.php?title=File:Tell_Me_Something_I_Don't_Know.jpg *License*: unknown *Contributors*: Arlonuelle, Good Olfactory, Jrs1200

File:PrincessProtectionProgramDVD.jpg *Source*: http://en.wikipedia.org/w/index.php?title=File:PrincessProtectionProgramDVD.jpg *License*: unknown *Contributors*: QuasyBoy

File:Demi lovato y su mejor amiga selena gomez en la premiere de programa de protedcion a princesas.jpg *Source*: http://en.wikipedia.org/w/index.php?title=File:Demi_lovato_y_su_mejor_amiga_selena_gomez_en_la_premiere_de_programa_de_protedcion_a_princesas.jpg *License*: unknown *Contributors*: yo

File:Flag of Estonia.svg *Source*: http://en.wikipedia.org/w/index.php?title=File:Flag_of_Estonia.svg *License*: Public Domain *Contributors*: User:PeepP, User:SKopp

File:Flag of Brunei.svg *Source*: http://en.wikipedia.org/w/index.php?title=File:Flag_of_Brunei.svg *License*: Public Domain *Contributors*: User:Nightstallion

File:Flag of Cambodia.svg *Source*: http://en.wikipedia.org/w/index.php?title=File:Flag_of_Cambodia.svg *License*: Public Domain *Contributors*: User:Nightstallion

File:Flag of Laos.svg *Source*: http://en.wikipedia.org/w/index.php?title=File:Flag_of_Laos.svg *License*: Public Domain *Contributors*: User:SKopp

File:Ramona and Beezus Poster.jpg *Source*: http://en.wikipedia.org/w/index.php?title=File:Ramona_and_Beezus_Poster.jpg *License*: unknown *Contributors*: Diem nguyen, Fastily, Quentin X, Salavat

File:Liveliketheresnotomorrowsingle.jpg *Source*: http://en.wikipedia.org/w/index.php?title=File:Liveliketheresnotomorrowsingle.jpg *License*: unknown *Contributors*: Melesse, SelGKT

File:Selena_and_the_scene_concert_meet_and_greet.jpg *Source*: http://en.wikipedia.org/w/index.php?title=File:Selena_and_the_scene_concert_meet_and_greet.jpg *License*: Public Domain *Contributors*: User:Selenaismylife555

File:Barneylogo.png *Source*: http://en.wikipedia.org/w/index.php?title=File:Barneylogo.png *License*: unknown *Contributors*: Bovineboy2008

Image:Barney & Friends season 1 title card.JPG *Source*: http://en.wikipedia.org/w/index.php?title=File:Barney_&_Friends_season_1_title_card.JPG *License*: unknown *Contributors*: Fastily, J Milburn, Jj98, Rodhullandemu, Tomballguy

File:Tinker Bell DVD.jpg *Source*: http://en.wikipedia.org/w/index.php?title=File:Tinker_Bell_DVD.jpg *License*: unknown *Contributors*: BigBoy8701, 2 anonymous edits

File:Spy Kids 3-D movie poster.jpg *Source*: http://en.wikipedia.org/w/index.php?title=File:Spy_Kids_3-D_movie_poster.jpg *License*: unknown *Contributors*: Capricorn42, Casper's Glowball, Quentin X, Skier Dude, Wisekwai, 2 anonymous edits

File:Star full.svg *Source*: http://en.wikipedia.org/w/index.php?title=File:Star_full.svg *License*: Public Domain *Contributors*: User:Conti, User:RedHotHeat

File:Star half.svg *Source*: http://en.wikipedia.org/w/index.php?title=File:Star_half.svg *License*: Creative Commons Attribution-Sharealike 2.5 *Contributors*: User:Conti

File:Star empty.svg *Source*: http://en.wikipedia.org/w/index.php?title=File:Star_empty.svg *License*: Creative Commons Attribution-Sharealike 2.5 *Contributors*: User:Conti, User:RedHotHeat

File:Horton a who.jpg *Source*: http://en.wikipedia.org/w/index.php?title=File:Horton_a_who.jpg *License*: Attribution *Contributors*: 20th Century Fox

File:Arthur_and_the_vengeance_of_maltazard_ver4.jpg *Source*: http://en.wikipedia.org/w/index.php?title=File:Arthur_and_the_vengeance_of_maltazard_ver4.jpg *License*: unknown *Contributors*: Pedro João

File:Wizards Of Waverly Place The Movie Cover.jpg *Source*: http://en.wikipedia.org/w/index.php?title=File:Wizards_Of_Waverly_Place_The_Movie_Cover.jpg *License*: unknown *Contributors*: Hoangquan hientrang

File:Flag of Puerto Rico.svg *Source*: http://en.wikipedia.org/w/index.php?title=File:Flag_of_Puerto_Rico.svg *License*: Public Domain *Contributors*: User:Madden

File:Flag of Quebec.svg *Source*: http://en.wikipedia.org/w/index.php?title=File:Flag_of_Quebec.svg *License*: Public Domain *Contributors*: User:DarkEvil

File:Flag of Cyprus.svg *Source*: http://en.wikipedia.org/w/index.php?title=File:Flag_of_Cyprus.svg *License*: Public Domain *Contributors*: AnonMoos, Bukk, Consta, Dbenbenn, Denelson83, Duduziq, Er Komandante, Homo lupus, Klemen Kocjancic, Krinkle, Mattes, NeoCy, Neq00, Nightstallion, Oleh Kernytskyi, Pumbaa80, Reisio, Telim tor, ThomasPusch, Vzb83, 15 anonymous edits

File:Flag of the Turkish Republic of Northern Cyprus.svg *Source*: http://en.wikipedia.org/w/index.php?title=File:Flag_of_the_Turkish_Republic_of_Northern_Cyprus.svg *License*: unknown *Contributors*: Absar, Anime Addict AA, Artem Karimov, Bjs, Carnildo, Dbenbenn, Fry1989, Himasaram, Homo lupus, Juiced lemon, Mattes, Multichill, Neq00, Ninane, Nokka, Pumbaa80, Reuvenk, Slomox, Wutsje, 10 anonymous edits

File:Burnin' Up Single Cover.JPG *Source*: http://en.wikipedia.org/w/index.php?title=File:Burnin'_Up_Single_Cover.JPG *License*: unknown *Contributors*: Calliegal, Geniac, Rettetast, Skier Dude, 1 anonymous edits

File:Selena and the scene concert meet and greet.jpg *Source*: http://en.wikipedia.org/w/index.php?title=File:Selena_and_the_scene_concert_meet_and_greet.jpg *License*: Public Domain *Contributors*: User:Selenaismylife555

File:FTSKWhoa-Oh!.jpg *Source*: http://en.wikipedia.org/w/index.php?title=File:FTSKWhoa-Oh!.jpg *License*: unknown *Contributors*: Optimous

File:Whoa-Oh!FTSK_Sel.jpg *Source*: http://en.wikipedia.org/w/index.php?title=File:Whoa-Oh!FTSK_Sel.jpg *License*: unknown *Contributors*: Johnny0929

File:Send It On.png *Source*: http://en.wikipedia.org/w/index.php?title=File:Send_It_On.png *License*: unknown *Contributors*: Ipodnano05, Ryoji.kun, Skier Dude, 1 anonymous edits

Image:Senditonmusicvideo.jpg *Source*: http://en.wikipedia.org/w/index.php?title=File:Senditonmusicvideo.jpg *License*: unknown *Contributors*: Ipodnano05, Rockin56, TheDJ

File:Selena_Cruella.jpg *Source*: http://en.wikipedia.org/w/index.php?title=File:Selena_Cruella.jpg *License*: unknown *Contributors*: Johnny0929

File:Movies cruella.jpg *Source*: http://en.wikipedia.org/w/index.php?title=File:Movies_cruella.jpg *License*: unknown *Contributors*: Anilro, EagleOne, Jonghyunchung, LordBleen, Melesse, Paul A, Zanimum

License

CPSIA information can be obtained at www.ICGtesting.com
Printed in the USA
LVOW121944300911

248623LV00001B/3/P